Stafford Library
Columbia College
1001 Rogers Street
Columbia, Missouri 65216

INTELLECTUALS INCORPORATED

POLITICS AND CULTURE
IN MODERN AMERICA

Series Editors:
Glenda Gilmore, Michael Kazin, and Thomas J. Sugrue

Volumes in the series narrate and analyze political and social change in the broadest dimensions from 1865 to the present, including ideas about the ways people have sought and wielded power in the public sphere and the language and institutions of politics at all levels—local, national, and transnational. The series is motivated by a desire to reverse the fragmentation of modern U.S. history and to encourage synthetic perspectives on social movements and the state, on gender, race, and labor, and on intellectual history and popular culture.

INTELLECTUALS INCORPORATED

Politics, Art, and Ideas
Inside Henry Luce's Media Empire

ROBERT VANDERLAN

UNIVERSITY OF PENNSYLVANIA PRESS

PHILADELPHIA · OXFORD

Copyright © 2010 University of Pennsylvania Press

All rights reserved. Except for brief quotations used
for purposes of review or scholarly citation, none of this
book may be reproduced in any form by any means without
written permission from the publisher.

Published by
University of Pennsylvania Press
Philadelphia, Pennsylvania 19104-4112

Printed in the United States of America
on acid-free paper
10 9 8 7 6 5 4 3 2 1

Library of Congress Cataloging-in-Publication Data

Vanderlan, Robert.
  Intellectuals incorporated : politics, art, and ideas inside Henry
Luce's media empire / Robert Vanderlan.
    p. cm. — (Politics and culture in modern America)
  ISBN: 978-0-8122-4271-3 (acid-free paper)
  Includes bibliographical references and index.
  1. Luce, Henry Robinson, 1898–1967—Political and social
views. 2. Time, inc.—History. 3. Periodicals—Publishing—
United States—History—20th century. 4. Mass media—United
States—History—20th century. 5. United States—Intellectual
life—20th century. I. Title.
Z473.T54 V36   2010
070.5092—dc22   2010005566

For my family:
Audrey
Benjamin
William

CONTENTS

Introduction: Intellectuals in Mass Culture America ... 1

Chapter One: On the Road to Time Inc. ... 25

Chapter Two: Giving the People the Truth the Time Inc. Way ... 61

Chapter Three: The Search for a "Radical Capitalism"
at *Fortune* Magazine ... 91

Chapter Four: Intellectuals Visible and Invisible ... 124

Chapter Five: The Intellectual as Insider at Time Inc. ... 167

Chapter Six: Journalism and Politics at *Time* Magazine ... 209

Chapter Seven: Interstitial Intellectuals and the Liberal Consensus ... 258

Epilogue: Intellectuals in Their American Century and in Ours ... 302

Archival Sources and Abbreviations ... 307

Notes ... 309

Index ... 363

Acknowledgments ... 369

INTRODUCTION

Intellectuals in Mass Culture America

As the big clock ticks on and on, the trap closes slowly but steadily around George Stroud. A highly paid editor for a popular magazine, Stroud is in trouble. He has been picked to head his company's search for a man spotted leaving the scene of a murder. Stroud knows that the organization's explanation for why the man needs to be found—something about involvement in an international conspiracy—is a ruse. The real reason? Only this mysterious stranger can connect the company's head, press baron Earl Janoth, to the murder of Janoth's girlfriend. Stroud knows the organization will kill the man when they locate him. Stroud knows all these things because he is the man he is assigned to find.

Pursued by Janoth and his assistant, Stroud walks a tightrope, appearing to run a thoroughly efficient manhunt while continually trying to deflect the organization's attention away from its quarry. As he works privately to prove that Janoth committed the murder, his official investigation begins to uncover the leads and bring in the witnesses that will reveal his own identity. He feels the noose steadily tightening, until he finds himself trapped inside the company's office building, as a room-by-room search begins that will reveal his identity.

This is the premise of Kenneth Fearing's 1946 novel, *The Big Clock*, one of a host of novels appearing after the Second World War that focused on the struggle of the individual for autonomy inside journalism organizations such as Time Inc.[1] All these novels centered on idealistic young men and women who found themselves writing for mass-market magazines and who struggled to make their work meaningful. Each featured press magnates based on Henry Luce, owner and publisher of *Time*, *Fortune*, and *Life* magazines and the *March of Time* newsreels. These Luce figures controlled magazine empires of extensive reach and power, and they were willing to distort journalism for political ends. In all these novels the writers' attempts fail, as they discover they cannot reconcile their own principles to Luce's brand of journalism. Most of these novels are told as realistic moral and ethical struggles. Fearing, however, takes the figurative struggle for autonomy and makes it a literal struggle for life. Janoth, his Luce figure, is not a spiritual murderer but a man who has bludgeoned his girlfriend to death with a brandy decanter.

Janoth's foil, George Stroud, is an odd mixture of noir hero and intellectual. He is quick with bantering patter ("Me? Dangerous?" he tells Janoth's girlfriend, "Kittens a month old get belligerent when they see me coming") and hard-boiled observations ("Hagen was a hard, dark little man whose soul had been hit by lightening, which he'd liked"). He also self-consciously sets himself apart from the people with whom he works. They are unimaginative journalists; he is an intellectual who works for the magazine on his own terms. The plot hinges on his ability to recognize and appreciate art. On the day of the murder he purchased a painting by an important, if little-known, artist. That painting, and therefore his own connection to the world of avant-garde art, places him in the greatest danger. As the searchers track down his movements, the painting hangs above his office door for anyone to identify. But of course nobody else on the magazine can recognize the painting; it is a scarlet letter viewed by colorblind journalists. The painting also proves to be the key to his rescue. When the artist is called in to identify him, she realizes that he alone of the journalists appreciates her work, and she declines to give him up.

Both as noir hero and as intellectual, Stroud is separated from the other journalists working for Janoth. Stroud believes he can live a double identity, committed both to his job and to his own values. He distinguishes himself from the other journalists who have sacrificed their independence and autonomy to the organization, men whom Stroud dismisses as "gelded birds in gilded cages." But the stance Stroud seeks to maintain is not tenable. He knows "the big clock," Fearing's mechanical metaphor for the absence of human agency, inexplicably missed him this time, but, he concludes, "I had no doubt it would get around to me again. Inevitably. Soon."[2] The organization could not make room for the individual; it was no place for an intellectual.

Fearing's novel dramatizes how postwar intellectuals viewed the threat posed by mass culture in general, and Henry Luce in particular. Large corporate culture producers such as Time Inc. were death to the intellectual. The organization of contemporary society required the intellectual to retain independence. Attempting to work within corporate institutions was by definition a form of selling out. It could result in nothing but frustration, or worse, corruption.

This is a familiar way of thinking about working for large corporations, or for large institutions more generally. Intellectual integrity, it is supposed, requires a stance of principled independence. Institutional employment requires the sorts of compromises that corrode intellectual endeavor. Yet Fearing's fear, born of his own experience as a journalist for *Time*, was relatively novel when he gave it dramatic weight in 1946. The work of Fearing and others was part of a redefinition of intellectual life, a reaction to and an attack on the "cultural front" of the 1930s that had seen countless intellectuals go to work for mass culture producers. Even while Fearing wrote, many intellectuals were writing for Henry Luce's magazines. Fully aware of the threats Fearing sketched, they nonetheless found sustenance in producing journalism for a mass market audience. The successful redefinition of intellectual life undertaken by Fearing and others has meant the trivialization of their experiences ever since.

From the 1920s through the 1950s, serious writers struggled to work as intellectuals for *Time*, *Fortune*, and *Life*, the nation's most popular and influential mass circulation magazines, the harbingers of a newly corporate media. These writers were intellectually and politically ambitious, committed to values built upon artistically apprehending and representing the world and (frequently) to the democratic political aspirations of the New Deal and the left. Writing for Luce's magazines, these writers sought to reach a larger audience than was available to them in any other form, working to alter, shape, and even control the editorial content of *Time* and *Fortune*. In so doing, they made important contributions—including shaping the political culture of the New Deal and developing a distinctive form of literary journalism—at a key moment in the emergence of American corporate liberalism. The struggles that working for Time Inc. entailed also drove them to develop perspectives, ideas, arguments, and criticisms unavailable to intellectuals working from outside this corporate environment.

Scholars have generally dismissed the significance of a band of radicals and poets producing *Fortune* or editing *Time*. They accept the assumptions that structure virtually all understandings of the role of the intellectual in American society: that the proper stance for the "true" intellectual is independence, that employment within corporate media producers is necessarily a form of selling out, that the only way to retain intellectual, artistic, or political commitments is to treat working for Henry Luce as little more than a financial necessity. This ideal of intellectual independence took root in the years following World

War II, precisely at the time Fearing was writing *The Big Clock*. Independence was a defensive reaction to the growth of mass culture (and "the Lucepress" specifically), the threat of totalitarianism (abroad and at home), and the deradicalization of the 1950s. The insistence on independence delegitimized the attempts intellectuals at Time Inc. had made, and were still making, to adhere to their intellectual commitments while employed by Henry Luce.

Contrary to this insistence on independence, these writers might better be characterized as "interstitial intellectuals," working from locations within institutions, thickly embedded in the corporate culture industries. Their experiences working within Time Inc. are complicated and compelling. They repay attention because they redraw the map of intellectual life in the middle of the twentieth century and because they challenge our understanding of intellectual responsibility today. This book tells the story of the serious writers who pursued intellectual commitments while working for mass culture corporations. It also tells the story of how those commitments became increasingly difficult to sustain as intellectuals embraced independence and scorned institutions in the years following World War II.

By the late 1940s, many intellectuals viewed Luce and his magazine empire with unremitting hostility. Seeing *Time*, *Life*, and *Fortune* as purveying political simplification, business valorization, and cultural vulgarization to middle class readers, critics took the "Lucepress" as emblematic of the threat of mass culture. Intellectual hostility toward mass culture—a term signifying the music, books, magazines, movies, radio, and television produced largely by entertainment "factories" for consumption by a broad audience—reached its pinnacle in the 1950s. The rise of fascism had convinced intellectuals of the populace's susceptibility to manipulation, while the vast popularity of cultural producers such as Hollywood and the Lucepapers threatened the intellectual's status as cultural arbiter. The result was an outpouring of vitriol directed at mass culture.

Dwight Macdonald penned the most influential of these critiques in a series of articles appearing in *Partisan Review* and his own magazine, *Politics*. Macdonald argued that mass culture served up diluted, predigested culture that appealed to the least discriminating of palates. Offering neither "emotional catharsis" nor "aesthetic experience," it anaesthetized its audience by prepackaging reactions. It sought less to entertain than to distract. In its middlebrow variant, which particularly disturbed Macdonald, it stripped high culture of its complexity, allowing middle-class readers to acquire culture much as they bought cars. As Macdonald claimed, middlebrow culture had all the essential elements of mass culture, "the formula, the built-in reaction, the lack of any standard except popularity—but it decently covers them with a cultural figleaf."[3] Time Inc. publications, with their pithy summaries of difficult ideas, reproductions of the great masters, and avowed goal of providing readers with everything they needed to know about the world in a format that could be read in an hour every week, exemplified this middlebrow threat.

Macdonald and his compatriots at *Partisan Review* were engaged in what might be seen as the central modernist project: the attempt to separate high culture from the corrupting embrace of mass culture.[4] By the 1950s, these critics worried that mass culture posed a threat not just to high art but, more fearfully, to artists and intellectuals themselves. How intellectuals should respond to this threat became a preoccupation of the decade. The 1952 *Partisan Review* symposium on the changing place of the intellectual in American society, "Our Country and Our Culture," asked the question directly: "Must the American intellectual and writer adapt himself to mass culture?" Or would this lead to a "mass culture that will overrun intellectual and aesthetic values?"[5] For many of the respondents, mass culture posed exactly this danger and employment in the culture industry meant an inevitable abandonment of the intellectual vocation. As Irving Howe wrote in "This Age of Conformity," his follow-up essay on the symposium, when intellectuals "became absorbed into the accredited institutions of society they not only lose their traditional rebelliousness but to one extent or another *they cease to function as intellectuals*."[6] Instead they became, in the words of C. Wright Mills, "the hired men of the information industries."[7]

Again Time Inc. was the proximate threat, seducing intellectuals by overpaying for their services. Norman Mailer lambasted those "writers, intellectuals, critics . . . who have moved their economic luggage from the WPA to the Luce chain."[8] Critics noted how Luce had brought Fordism to journalism, inventing an anonymous "group journalism" built on the assembly line production of prose. In a typical formulation, Gertrude Himmelfarb described writing for Time Inc. this way: "the organization is all: it is the brain, it is the pen, the conscience of every employee; everyone is a tool, dispensable and interchangeable, a pawn to be shuffled about at will."[9] Macdonald sought to police a divide between intellectuals and Luce's journalists. He advised young writers concerned about what it might mean to "sell out" to Luce and his ilk: "sell out if you can, since if you can you don't have anything of value and you might as well cash in on it."[10] Writing for Luce, therefore, meant automatic dismissal by serious writers. These sentiments reached their hyperbolic apogee in Wallace Makefield's description of the "gas chambers of... Luceland," and Murray Kempton's characterization of the fate awaiting ambitious young writers working for Luce: "As a slaughterhouse of moral integrity, *Time* is a Verdun for the young."[11]

In response to the mass culture threat of institutional incorporation, critics such as Howe, Macdonald, Mailer, and Mills stressed the necessity of intellectual independence. Independence had been a long-time goal of American intellectuals disdainful of the academy and solicitous of control over their writing, but in the 1950s independence was transformed from a personal goal to a vocational imperative.[12] Reacting to the extinguished radical hopes of the 1930s and the renewed popular legitimacy of corporate leadership, critics argued that honest intellectual engagement required independence from institutional constraints. Macdonald celebrated avantgarde intellectuals who "by an act of will dictated by necessity (the necessity of surviving as a creator, rather than a technician)" worked from outside and against society.[13] Irving Howe, seeing all life as a conspiracy against the ideal of independence, despaired that "the whole idea of the intellectual vocation—the idea of a life devoted to values that cannot possibly be realized by a commercial civilization—had lost its appeal."[14] Howe raised again the banner of independence as the only standard under which intellectuals could march. C. Wright Mills claimed the intellectual technician, selling his brains as a commodity, had gradually eclipsed the free intellectual. A renewed independence provided the only escape from the "essential facts of defeat and powerlessness" in American intellectual life.[15] "The independent artist and intellectual," argued Mills, were "among the few remaining personalities equipped to resist and to fight the stereotyping and consequent death of genuinely living things."[16] Fearful of being co-opted by the "wrong kind of success," critics were seeking to fortify the boundaries between the inauthentic mass culture they despised and the authentic art they cherished.[17] In lamenting the disappearance of the independent intellectual, critics such as Macdonald, Howe, and Mills were in fact creating the ideal of independence.

Both ideas—intellectual independence as an ideal and the distrust of the corrupting embrace of the market—had existed for decades, but both became increasingly pervasive after the war. And both have remained enormously important, continuing to influence contemporary understandings of the relationship between intellectuals and the market. The success of postwar writers in framing the proper stance of the intellectual as that of outside critic and judge has effectively obscured the more complex history of relations between intellectuals and mass culture purveyors such as Henry Luce and Time Inc.

Political radical Dwight Macdonald, main architect of the mass culture criticism edifice and especially the wing devoted to attacking middlebrow pretensions to high culture, spent the Depression years, a high-water mark for the American left, writing for *Fortune* magazine. He later wrote an essay titled "Selling Out," in which he attempted to explain away his years writing for Luce. Macdonald quipped, "I kept falling asleep in the very act of prostitution."[18] This mea culpa is typical both of Macdonald's pungent prose and of the increasingly prevalent idea that intellectual seriousness could not be reconciled with work at Time Inc. or anywhere else in the culture industries. According to Macdonald, his *Fortune* work was both boring and corrupt. In making this claim, he was seeking to bolster the growing barrier dividing artists and intellectuals on one side from middle class magazines and their audience on the other. The only trouble with Macdonald's explanation is that it was just not true. Macdonald left *Fortune* in 1936 driven not by boredom or by concerns he had sold out. In fact, his aspirations for his *Fortune* journalism had grown increasingly bold in 1935 and 1936. He left because he lost a political battle over how far the magazine would let him pursue his strenuous exposé of the U.S. Steel Corporation.

This retrospective tendency to distort the experience of working for Luce was hardly Macdonald's alone. The poet Archibald MacLeish, whom Macdonald was fond of dismissing as the epitome of middlebrow culture, worked alongside Macdonald at *Fortune*. MacLeish also felt the need to alter the circumstances of his employment by Luce. MacLeish had been Luce's star writer during *Fortune*'s first eight years, a time MacLeish described as his "essential education." Yet in later reminiscences MacLeish made his decision to write for Luce seem driven by the Depression, conveniently forgetting that he joined the staff before the stock market crash. He also preferred to remember the magazine only in its most critical guise, ignoring the celebratory content of the early years.[19] By the late 1950s, the desires and aspirations that drove young intellectuals such as Macdonald, MacLeish, and others to work for Luce had become difficult to remember and impossible to credit.

Contrary to the impressions created and accepted years later, the relationship between intellectuals and mass culture producers such as Time Inc. had not been wholly antagonistic before World War II. Indeed, a surprising number of intellectuals sought to work *as* intellectuals for Time Inc. They sought the large audience Luce's magazines provided and they hoped to exercise editorial control over the contents. They sometimes succeeded, in different magazines for particular periods of time. They were able to publish their own ideas and views in the pages of the widest circulating magazines in the country. And the perspectives they developed as journalists, far from sounding the death knell to their intellectual life, frequently enriched their work in important ways. In short, in the middle of the twentieth century, these intellectuals found mass-market journalism to be both viable and vital.

From the beginning, Luce recruited novelists and poets to write for his magazines. These aspiring young writers provided most of the copy for *Time*'s early years. MacLeish and Macdonald, joined by James Agee and others, developed *Fortune*'s distinctive investigative and imaginative journalism in the 1930s, and established the magazine's peculiar identity as simultaneous business celebrant and critic. In the 1940s T. S. Matthews, an aspiring novelist and ambitious intellectual, led a drive with Luce's support to make *Time* more intellectually serious and respectable. Matthews worked with Agee, Robert Cantwell, Whittaker Chambers, Robert Fitzgerald, John Hersey, Irving Howe, Louis Kronenberger, and Theodore White at *Time*. He succeeded to the extent that Cyril Connelly saw fit to compare the cultural departments of *Time* favorably with the more respected English literary press. Even into the 1950s, when the intellectual disparagement of Time Inc. was at its peak, William H. Whyte's criticisms of corporate conformity and Walker Evans's portfolios of post-industrial landscapes were regular features in *Fortune*. Irving Howe was a staff reviewer for *Time*. Daniel Bell, Russell Davenport, Peter Drucker, John Kenneth Galbraith, and Alfred Kazin also wrote for Luce's magazines. Even literary critic Edmund Wilson was said to have asked for a job on *Time*.[20] Adding to this list were countless other Time Inc. writers who published now obscure novels or poetry and wrote reviews and essays for other publications. They were employed as journalists, but they considered themselves intellectuals. Some of these writers stayed briefly, others stayed longer than they ever expected. For some, working for Time Inc. spurred their intellectual development. For others, it marked a dead end. For intellectuals minor or major, Time Inc. provided an institutional home, welcoming or not, temporary or not so temporary, where they tried to balance their own interests with the requirements of the job.

For these writers, Time Inc. offered a financially secure base from which they could pursue their own literary, aesthetic, or political interests. More than that, Time Inc. offered a large readership and possibilities for wielding power within the organization, which appealed to intellectuals confident in their abilities but often ambivalent about the impotence of a life devoted solely to ideas. For Time Inc., intellectuals improved the quality of the magazines and bolstered their credibility and prestige. For Luce, the trick was to recruit and retain intellectuals while seeking to control their work. For intellectuals, the trick was to retain prominent placement in the magazines while maintaining control over what they created. The conflict between these competing interests formed the core of the history of intellectuals at Time Inc.

For many of the writers and artists involved, the struggle to further their intellectual commitments in the face of the imperatives of corporate journalism drove them to develop ideas and perspectives impossible to form elsewhere. Time and again their most fruitful ideas emerged from the crucible of their journalism. Archibald MacLeish developed a conception of himself as a public intellectual with crucial responsibilities in the development of a democratic culture. James Agee used his position as a journalist to attack journalism's inescapable falsifications while insisting on its equally inescapable necessity. Daniel Bell strenuously sought to balance engagement and alienation, and found a model for doing so while writing for *Fortune*. John Hersey turned his war reporting into attempts to write "novels of contemporary events," seeking to develop a new form bridging literature and journalism. William Whyte asserted from the pages of *Fortune* that resistance to organizational America must arise from within corporations. Walker Evans visually documented the price of progress, adapting his aesthetic to develop a counternarrative to corporate triumph. All of these ideas and innovations owed their origins to their author's experiences at Time Inc.

In sociological terms, of course, all journalists at Time Inc. could be considered intellectuals. C. Wright Mills offered a typical definition, claiming intellectuals were "people who specialize in symbols . . . [who] produce, distribute, and preserve distinct forms of consciousness."[21] Treating all journalists as intellectuals, however, leaves little room for the necessary—and to the writers in question, obvious—distinctions between different sorts of writers. There were professional journalists at Time Inc. who aspired to be nothing more. There were also intellectuals, who held the same jobs, but considered their primary allegiance to be to the world of ideas rather than professional norms. Though the distinction between the two might not be rigid, both the journalists and the intellectuals who worked for Henry Luce recognized it.

If sociological definitions are too sweeping, the definitions offered by many of the participants in the debate over the fate of the intellectual were too narrow. When Mills reached beyond the definition quoted above, he borrowed from the German theorist Max Weber, claiming that intellectuals "are people who live *for* and not *off* ideas."[22] American sociologist Lewis Coser's influential book, *Men of Ideas*, adopted the same line.[23] Unfortunately, Mills and Coser built their argument—that intellectuals are and must be separate from those who manipulate symbols as part of their job—into their definition. In this formulation, intellectuals must choose between living for ideas or off ideas. They cannot do both. But, of course, intellectuals need to eat the same as everyone else. As the bohemian critic Randolph Bourne once asked, "What then is a literary man to do if he has to make his living by his pen?"[24] The intellectuals who worked at Time Inc. chose to write for Henry Luce as one means of answering Bourne's question. They were engaged in an effort to live simultaneously off and for ideas. After leaving his own job at *Time*, Irving Howe claimed such an attempt was ridiculous. He railed against editors at *Time* who "were sufficiently self-intoxicated to think they had 'intellectual obligations.'"[25] Rather than accepting Howe's condemnation at face value, it is worth considering what writers at Time Inc. meant by their intellectual obligations and how they went about discharging them. It is also worth asking why Howe felt it necessary to undermine their claims to obligations greater than those of the organization that signed their checks.

The term "intellectual" is used here with a calculated imprecision. Rather than attempting to imprison the men and women who worked for Luce, and those that did not, in conceptual straightjackets, a loose usage allows greater fidelity to the complexity of the intellectual's experiences in particular historical and cultural contexts. The intellectuals here cannot always or easily be separated from journalists, nor from artists, nor even at times from left liberals. The term intellectual bleeds across many boundaries. Such is life. By adopting a biographical approach, the diverse ways in which the writers discussed here defined themselves emerges, and some of the essential characteristics and qualities of intellectual life stand in bolder relief. Equally important, close attention to the idiosyncrasies of each writer's intellectual journey contributes to a richer, more complete map of the field of cultural production in the middle years of the twentieth century.[26]

Intellectuals went to work for Henry Luce for myriad reasons. Money was certainly the most common. Supporting a family as a freelance writer was difficult and Luce paid well. Most writers hoped to earn enough money at Time Inc. to support their independent work. As Irving Howe put it, "I was giving the devil a part of myself in order to gain freedom for the other part."[27] This instrumental reason dominated retrospective accounts, often (as MacLeish's example suggests), out of all proportion to its actual importance.[28] Dwight Macdonald's reminiscences, for example, ignored his youthful fascination with business leaders and his disdain for intellectuals who he perceived as powerless. Though financial worries were real, the first generation of intellectuals to work at Time Inc. were also pushed by ambivalence about the value of living an intellectual life divorced from practical concerns and pulled by the audience Luce's magazines promised.

Their experiences once they arrived varied enormously. Pursuing the life of the mind in the pages of *Time*, *Fortune*, or *Life* was hardly idyllic. The conditions were difficult and the magazines produced were far from exemplary. As countless critics have pointed out, *Time* could be crude, vulgar, and politically unreliable. Its journalistic technique, emphasizing simplicity over complexity and certainty over uncertainty, assuaged reader anxieties with a false sense of security and was easily manipulated for political ends. *Fortune* pandered to business leaders' sense of their own importance, creating an image of an enlightened, cultured business aristocracy that bore little relation to reality. *Life* alternated the serious with the frivolous so relentlessly it became difficult to maintain distinctions between the two (In Macdonald's famous example: "Just think, nine pages of Renoirs! But that roller-skating horse comes along and the final impression is that both Renoir and the horse were talented."[29]) Yet dismissing the magazines because of their failings means ignoring the aspirations that drove intellectuals to write for them.

By the middle of the 1950s, more than a quarter of the adult population was reading *Time*, *Fortune*, or *Life*. *Life* was far and away the most popular magazine in America; *Time* dominated the other newsmagazines and was third (behind *Life* and the *Saturday Evening Post*) in total advertising dollars; *Fortune* was the most widely read business publication in the country. This audience was heavily skewed toward the comfortably middle class, with more than half of *Time*'s audience consisting of professionals or proprietors.[30] Luce's magazines effectively reached a significant proportion of middle-class readers every week.

The writers at Time Inc. were engaged in an effort to use this mass medium to reach a broad public with their ideas. Henry Luce was originally drawn to journalism because of the possibilities it afforded for educating his fellow citizens. He saw the press as capable of creating a better-informed public. In his typical capital-letter prose, Luce claimed that "The hope of Democracy is Intelligence and the food of Intelligence is Information."[31] These conventionally Progressive sentiments, uttered in 1922, found resonance with many of the intellectuals attracted to Luce and his magazines in the late 1920s and early 1930s. T. S. Matthews and Robert Cantwell, who shared book reviewing responsibilities at *Time* in the middle 1930s, disparaged the magazine in their correspondence, but also hatched plans to improve it, fully aware of the opportunity *Time*'s audience presented. Matthews believed that journalism and poetry should unite to the betterment of both, an idea he pursued at *Time* for more than a decade. James Agee and Walker Evans continued to make ambitious plans for Luce's magazines, even after *Fortune* refused to run the text that became *Let Us Now Praise Famous Men*. They found possibilities at Time Inc. for a journalism simultaneously critical and popular. Alfred Kazin spent hours arguing with Luce about the "American proposition," American literature, and whatever else Luce felt like arguing about.[32] Even Irving Howe, who likened writing for *Time* to giving in to the lure of "Satan's gold," admitted he had been "foolish enough to try and write something serious" for Luce.[33] In short, there was more common ground between Luce's ambitions for his magazines and those harbored by the intellectuals he hired than has been generally realized.

There was also a great deal at stake. In the 1920s American intellectuals, frustrated by the conservative and anti-intellectual atmosphere of the decade, turned their back on their homeland. But the Depression brought a revitalized American politics, and intellectuals once again sought a more direct involvement in the nation's cultural and political life. The New Deal, the resurgence of the left, the rise of fascism, the Popular Front, and the darkening war clouds all raised the political stakes and propelled most intellectuals toward political engagement. Debates about the proper political role of the intellectual intensified throughout the 1930s, as intellectuals struggled to define their relationship with their nation.[34]

These debates mirrored larger questions about America's changing role in the world. *Time* had shared the general American skepticism toward involvement in European politics during the 1930s, but by the end of the decade Luce—pushed by writers such as MacLeish— hoped to prepare the American people to embrace both involvement in the war and a larger international role for the United States. In 1941 he published his famous essay "The American Century" in *Life* magazine, exhorting Americans to recognize both that they were already involved in the war, and that the war itself provided a great opportunity for the expansion of American political power and economic might. Luce's essay—and especially its title—became a key shorthand for America's expansive postwar role.

In short, the mid-century decades were crucial years in the emergence of America as the preeminent world power and in the restructuring of American capitalism. Responding to the Depression, the rise of fascism, the Second World War, and the postwar conflict with the Soviet Union, Luce's magazines played an important role in formulating and articulating the key components of American international activism and domestic corporate liberalism. The mid-century decades, from the Popular Front to the Cold War consensus, were also key years in determining the relationship between intellectuals and mass cultural providers on the one hand and between intellectuals and the American public on the other. Archibald MacLeish, Dwight Macdonald, John Hersey, Whittaker Chambers, Irving Howe, William H. Whyte and others were key participants in these struggles both behind the scenes at Time Inc. and in the larger society.

Intellectual work at Time Inc. was impossible for some, difficult for many, easy for no one. There were those whose work suffered from the attempt. Robert Cantwell's writing after joining Time Inc. never measured up to the promise of his early proletarian novel *The Land of Plenty*. Others, Dwight Macdonald among them, found it necessary to leave before their talent flourished. Nevertheless, for those of the right temperament, important work was possible. Historian Michael Denning justly observes that Archibald MacLeish's "*Fortune* essays, though never collected, are as much classics of depression reportage as Edmund Wilson's *American Jitters*."[35] While working for *Fortune* he simultaneously produced four books of poetry, three plays, a ballet, a word-and-picture book on Depression America, and more than thirty essays for other publications. Many of these, such as *Frescoes for Mr. Rockefeller's City*, bore the direct traces of his *Fortune* experience. Agee and Evans conceived and produced the core of *Let Us Now Praise Famous Men* on assignment for *Fortune*. The movie reviews Agee wrote for *Time* and the film essays he penned for *Life* have become classics of film criticism. John Hersey's first three books grew out of his writing for *Time* and *Life*, including his Pulitzer Prize-winning novel *A Bell for Adano*. Daniel Bell wrote *The End of Ideology* during his stint as labor editor for *Fortune*. William H. Whyte's *Organization Man* originally appeared in *Fortune*. The largest single body of Walker Evans's photographs—and some of his best, if least known pictures—were those he took for *Fortune* between 1945 and 1965.

Intellectuals at Time Inc. were by definition sacrificing independence. But taken together their experiences suggest an alternative model of intellectual life. Rather than independent intellectuals, the writers at Time Inc. became interstitial intellectuals, pursuing intellectual interests from the spaces available within institutions.[36] The text James Agee wrote for *Let Us Now Praise Famous Men* is as idiosyncratic, individual, and odd a piece of work as can be found in American literature. The demands of moral inquiry, intellectual honesty, and plain stamina it places on the reader were totally antithetical to the mass culture emphasis on programmed reactions and easily digested ideas. Yet *Famous Men* grew out of a *Fortune* assignment. More than that, the ideas it pursued, its great strength as individual moral testimony, grew from its implicit opposition to the journalism it purported to be. The techniques Agee employed—the long lyrical evocations of place, the listing of the particular and the ordinary, the repeated stops and starts seeking the proper angle, the attempt to write objectively as a camera records yet simultaneously subjectively as the mind engages, the distrust for the capacity of facts to speak for themselves while using them as bricks in the edifice he was building—were all developed and refined in his previous work at *Fortune*. Even after their failure to see their original text in *Fortune*, Agee and Evans continued to work for Luce and continued to experiment with ways to marry their intellectual interests with the mass market demands of Luce's magazines.

Agee is perhaps the most striking example of the interstitial intellectual, but others occupied a similar position, including Evans, MacLeish, Hersey, Chambers, Bell, and Whyte. Working in the hothouse atmosphere of Time Inc., constrained by the medium for which they wrote, the editors they had to satisfy, and ultimately by the audience they sought to reach, interstitial intellectuals nevertheless developed perspectives unavailable elsewhere. They produced significant work both in the pages of *Time*, *Fortune*, and *Life* and in their independent work written simultaneously. They wrote for audiences unavailable to outside writers. They altered the development of Time Inc. itself. More significantly still, they played an important role in helping shift public opinion, legitimating the social values that underscored the New Deal years and undermining the corporate values that threatened its achievement. From within the heart of corporate liberalism they developed and articulated perspectives beholden to their own intellectual inquiry, not to corporate values.

Historians have offered compelling accounts of the corporate and managerial pressures that shaped American society from the late nineteenth through the mid-twentieth centuries. The rapid expansion of American business in the late nineteenth century knit together a national market served by massive new corporations. The need for access to this market drove the development of mass culture outlets that could carry the advertising necessary for continued capitalist expansion. The restructuring of American capitalism on a large scale, corporate model altered the nation's politics, refashioned its laws, and thoroughly penetrated its culture. A new middle class arose, governed by professional and managerial elites in white-collar corporations, universities, government agencies, professional associations, and media outlets. The old culture of production, with its attendant individualism rooted in the Protestant work ethic, gave way to a culture of consumption selling hedonistic release even as it demanded disciplined management of behavior. Corporate advertising and public relations managed desire and shaped public perceptions of the corporate world, gradually replacing fears of corporate bigness with comforting images of personal and paternalistic corporate rule.[37]

In some respects, the growth of Time Inc. fits easily into this larger narrative of corporate liberal triumph. Henry Luce was a prototypical liberal businessman, whose views easily moved from New Era associationalism in the 1920s, to the search for business-led alternatives to the New Deal in the 1930s and 1940s, to an embrace of the corporate liberal consensus of the 1950s. His magazines succeeded because of their ability to reach new audiences produced by the expansion of the middle class and the growth of white-collar managers. *Time* sought to equip middle-class readers with the political and cultural news that served as a vital form of social capital. Historians have viewed *Fortune* as a key voice in articulating different variants of corporate liberalism, even going so far as calling it "the house journal of the new corporatism."[38] *Life* actively constructed a mythical American nation of white middle-class homogeneity.[39] All told, Henry Luce's magazines can be seen as a product of the corporate transformation of American society. Further, their content helped perpetuate and legitimate managerial and corporate control in mid-twentieth century America.

Likewise, it might be possible to view the intellectuals who wrote for Luce as part and parcel of this process. In this telling, mid-century intellectuals were seeking their own professional identity, one not altogether different from the managerial identity championed by *Fortune* and other corporate liberals. The insistence among intellectuals that the development and perpetuation of art necessitated the separation of high culture from middlebrow and folk cultures helped intellectuals set themselves up as artistic arbiters. Just as corporate managers were styling themselves as responsible for the effective functioning of the American economy, intellectuals were positioning themselves as the guardians of art and culture. Over time, both intellectuals within the mass media and their opponents outside migrated to the universities. There intellectuals established the professional base for their limited but secure status.[40]

There is something to be said for these arguments, but it is not the interpretation offered here. Such an account exaggerates the strength and cohesiveness of twentieth-century corporate liberalism. It poorly reflects what intellectuals thought was at stake at the time. The intellectuals at Time Inc. were involved in larger social transformations, but these transformations were never seamless or smooth. Intellectuals working at Time Inc. were subjected to commercial and professional pressures, but they struggled against them as well. It is important not to lose sight of the larger historical forces shaping the environment intellectuals encountered, but the emphasis here is on understanding these figures on their own terms.[41] To see the world through the eyes of the intellectuals struggling to shape public opinion is to see again the possibilities they saw. To inhabit the world they inhabited is a step toward a more expansive and more connected conception of the responsibilities and possibilities of intellectual life.

Henry Luce ran his company as a commercial enterprise, but as a commercial enterprise with cultural and eventually political aspirations. Commercial pressures were ever present, but were confronted by competing impulses. Luce was driven by a missionary sense of idealism, a deep commitment to public service, a Progressive-era faith in the power of facts, a conviction that his country was or could be an instrument of providence, and an overwhelming personal ambition. This complicated amalgam drove him in building his magazine empire, an empire that succeeded partially due to Luce's conviction that his magazines had a vital role to play in the creation of an educated middle class and an enlightened business leadership. Luce's convictions and his ability to convince others of the importance of these projects were crucial in attracting and retaining intellectuals. Luce had a serious respect for intellectuals and for literature, and was much influenced by the intellectuals with whom he surrounded himself. In the 1930s, writers such as Archibald MacLeish sharpened Luce's criticism of business and increased his receptiveness to the New Deal. In the early 1940s, Russell Davenport pushed him to better articulate his business liberalism. By the middle 1940s, Whittaker Chambers and William Schlamm were urging him to oppose communism more forcefully, and were fighting with John Hersey, Theodore White and others over how Luce and his magazines would cover relations with the Soviet Union and over how much room would remain at Time Inc. for intellectuals. All of these writers came to Time Inc. with different personal and political agendas. Nothing they produced at Time Inc. can be reduced to simple market determinism.[42]

If commercial pressure did not dictate content at Time Inc., neither did a second key influence on twentieth-century journalism, professionalism. The professionalization of journalism as an occupational field was a key development of the first half of the twentieth century. This professionalism however, was little in evidence at Time Inc., especially in the early years. *Time* fought many of the professional conventions in place when it began publication in 1923. In its desire to make its prose readable and memorable, *Time* dispensed with the deadly dull tone of "objective" journalism. Abandoning the inverted pyramid style employed by the newspapers, *Time* used a narrative structure to turn every article into a story. It never claimed objectivity as a goal, arguing from the very beginning that it would have a distinct point of view and never hesitate to instruct its readers on which side in a political dispute had the better argument.

The source of much criticism, *Time*'s antiprofessional ideology also functioned paradoxically to make it more serious and respectable. T. S. Matthews, the dominant shaper of *Time* magazine during the 1940s, was actively hostile to the profession of journalism. He sought to balance the "professional" journalists on the staff with amateur intellectuals, believing that "the trouble with journalism was that you didn't have enough poets in it." He fought the growing number of newspapermen at *Time*, because "I considered their professional standards too low and [thought] that a few gifted amateurs could make them look pretty sick."[43] Thus, rather than a simple story of the market corrupting journalism and professionalism rationalizing content, Time Inc. was a battleground. Market pressure toward sensation and simplification, and political pressure toward manipulation were countered by struggles to make Time Inc. more serious, respectable, responsible, and important. These countering impulses may have served to make Time Inc. more legitimate and, therefore, more profitable, but they were not themselves market-driven. The character and function of the organs of journalism was not the result of their nature as a commercial medium but instead were the result of competing pressures and ideologies.

Commercialization and professionalization did help structure the practice of twentieth-century journalism. But they did not dictate content. There were spaces available within these larger discourses, and ideas that might be mobilized to mitigate their effect. The educating mission, aristocratic notions of service, democratic ideas of an educated populace, an enduring progressive faith in the power of facts, artistic experiments in representation, and the insistence of intellectuals that they understand and represent the world on their own terms, were mobilized in defense of different journalistic practices. It is the creation and development of these discourses from within spaces created and defended at Time Inc., spaces explored and exploited by a coterie of intellectuals, that makes up the story of Time Inc. and the intellectuals.

Existing biographies of the intellectuals who worked at Time Inc. have typically given short shrift to their journalism. Biographers have implicitly accepted the assumptions that underscore our understanding of the role of the intellectual in American society. Assuming that the proper stance for the "true" intellectual is independence, that employment by corporate media producers is dangerously close to selling out, and that the only way to preserve their subject's intellectual or artistic seriousness is to treat working for Henry Luce as little more than a financial necessity, they accept their subject's later dismissals at face value and ignore troubling evidence. Laurence Bergreen's biography of James Agee, for instance, regularly repeats an anecdote where Agee fantasizes about shooting Luce. Bergreen assumes this fantasy sufficiently explains Agee's feelings for his work, but leaves unexplained why Agee continued to work so hard as a journalist for all those years.[44] Michael Wreszin's collection of the letters of Dwight Macdonald, to cite just one more instance, omits all the letters in which Macdonald expresses his aspirations for his *Fortune* work, but retains each letter in which he gives voice to his doubts about his work.[45]

In the face of this, the approach here is necessarily biographical. Recovering the aspirations men such as Macdonald and Agee held for their journalism requires situating these aspirations within the contours of each man's life. It involves reinterpreting their lives, paying attention to the ways in which family background, educational experience, social class pressures, developing intellectual interests, and personal psychological needs all combined to make mass market journalism both a professional possibility, but also a profession with possibilities. The result, one hopes, is a richly contextualized account of each person, that sees each as simultaneously conditioned by their environment and an active agent in their attempts to exploit the possibilities and transcend the limits of mass market journalism.

The fierce debates over the proper place for the intellectual in American society that dominated intellectual discourse during the 1950s—and helped solidify the separation of mass and intellectual culture—were eclipsed by the breakdown of the relative political quietude of the 1950s and the return of radical politics in the 1960s.[46] They have reemerged, however, in the last two decades, another period marked by an impotent left and a reigning political orthodoxy. Russell Jacoby's 1987 book *The Last Intellectuals* revives the 1950s conception of the independent intellectual in launching a new debate over the fate of the intellectual in American life.[47] Jacoby rechristens the independent writers of the 1950s "public intellectuals," only to announce their lamentable disappearance.

For Jacoby, the threat to the intellectual, which for 1950s critics such as Mills and Macdonald had been the risk posed by mass culture, has shifted. Like Mills, Jacoby traces the decline of the independent intellectual to "the increasing substitution of corporate employment for independent businessmen, workers and craftsmen," but the real culprit is the academy. The public intellectuals of the past have been replaced by "high-tech intellectual consultants and professors—anonymous souls, who may be competent, and more than competent, but who do not enrich public life. Younger intellectuals, whose lives have enfolded almost entirely on campuses, direct themselves to professional colleagues but are inaccessible and unknown to others." Calling for intellectuals to abandon the security of the academy, Jacoby presents the intellectuals of the past as a model: a public intellectual must be "an incorrigibly independent soul answering to no one. Yet this does not suffice; the definition must include a commitment not simply to professional or private domain but to a public world—and a public language, the vernacular."[48] Intellectuals must abandon the cloistered halls of the university and reengage a broad public.

This ideal of the public intellectual—with a lineage running from Julien Benda through the New York intellectuals, to Jacoby and, more recently, Edward Said—has itself come under attack in the last decades.[49] These attacks follow efforts by Michel Foucault to replace the ideal of the independent intellectual with what he called the "specific intellectual." For Foucault, the specific intellectual works not with "the 'universal,' the 'exemplary,' the 'just-and-true-for-all,' but within specific sectors, at the precise points where their own conditions of life or work situate them."[50] Taking up this idea, Andrew Ross, Bruce Robbins, John Michael, Hugh Wilford, and others criticize the ideal of independence as a blind for the protection of intellectuals' cultural power.[51] According to Robbins, speaking both of the intellectuals of the past and of their contemporary champions, Jacoby among them, "in the name of the public, this line of argument has been an attempt to restrict and thereby control the public sphere."[52] Rejecting independence, critics such as Robbins instead have sought to take the institutional position of the intellectual as a given. Instead of lamenting the lost public intellectual, they are engaged, in Wilford's words, in "constructing an oppositional identity for institutionally grounded intellectuals."[53] The institutional homes they consider, however, are essentially limited to the academy. Their account has the virtue of seeing institutionalization as a beginning, not an end point, but they join with those they criticize for championing the public intellectual in their neglect for institutional locations outside the academy. Just as they reverse the valence on independent intellectuals, they also reverse field on mass culture. Ross captures both changes nicely in an attack on 1950s intellectuals who "saw popular culture as a filthy contaminant of democratic life and to left thought alike, rather than an opportunity for intellectuals pumped up on high moral seriousness to learn something about the messy world of popular pleasures, popular resentments, and popular prejudices."[54] Gone are the denunciations of mass culture, now renamed popular culture. A fascination with the content of popular culture, however, is not accompanied by an awareness that intellectuals might have been involved in its creation.

The argument put forward by 1950s critics such as Howe and Mills, that intellectual work was impossible from within the maws of mass culture, has been accepted on all sides. Lewis Coser rated "The chances for intellectuals in the mass-culture industries" as low. He claimed employment by organizations such as Time Inc. could only lead to "systematic alienation and frustration."[55] Jacoby echoes Coser, seeing journalism as the inevitable dilution of intellectual work and the corporation as an inevitable threat to independence. Joseph Epstein's recent examination of the revived interest in public intellectuals restates the common view, claiming writers in the 1950s were "always in danger of selling out to the devil, with the devil usually envisioned as Henry Luce and hell as Time Inc."⁵⁶ Even those critical of this view have yet to suggest serious intellectual work was possible within mass culture industries, being more interested in the consumption of popular culture than in its production.

A more modest and fruitful approach has been suggested by Michael Walzer. Renouncing the transcendent standpoint sought by those valorizing independence, yet avoiding the academic cul-de-sac Ross and his followers find themselves patrolling, Walzer seeks what he calls the "connected critic." As he puts it, "the everyday world is a moral world, and we would do better to study its internal rules, maxims, conventions, and ideals, rather than to detach ourselves from it in search of a universal and transcendent standpoint." In illuminating this claim, Walzer looks at the careers of model social critics, people such as Randolph Bourne, George Orwell, Albert Camus, and Simone de Beauvoir. The stance Walzer values—the maintenance of an "antagonistic connection" to society rather than a cultivated alienation from society—might also be glimpsed in the careers of intellectuals at Time Inc. who grappled with moral questions mixed with the messy realities of putting together mass-market magazines.⁵⁷

I offer this depiction of the interstitial intellectual not as an ideal type, but as an apt description of certain intellectuals at Time Inc. between 1930 and 1960. The spaces available for such intellectuals were not constant. They changed magazine to magazine, department to department, year to year. The nature of the editors, the composition of the staff, and the qualities of the individual writers all influenced the prospects for intellectual endeavor. Looking beyond these ephemeral fluctuations, however, a larger trajectory of change emerges. Simply put, opportunities for intellectuals emerged first at *Fortune*, growing to a peak between 1935 and 1937. While *Fortune* retained a sizable contingent of intellectuals thereafter, their aims were more modest. In the middle 1940s *Time* emerged as the preferred location for serious writers, until it too declined in the late 1940s. By the 1950s, intellectuals at Time Inc. were few. Those that remained were isolated and solitary, mostly on *Fortune*.

This pattern of change mirrored changes taking place in the larger culture, as the expansive visions of the 1930s were replaced by the Cold War consensus of the 1950s. The struggles within Time Inc.—fights over the magazines' political coverage and battles over the writers' intellectual obligations alike— and the politics of the wider culture is a theme of this study. Again and again the story within Time Inc. is intertwined with conflicts in the broader culture, as the participants were ensnared by the reigning cultural assumptions.

Contrary to the mythology of the independent intellectual, it is useful to be reminded that intellectuals, too, swim in the same cultural currents as their fellow citizens. Or as Cynthia Ozick reminds us, "the responsibility of intellectuals includes also the realization that we cannot live above or apart from our own time and what it imposes on us; that willy-nilly we breathe inside the cage of our generation and we must perform within it."[58]

There were also more proximate causes for the gradual erosion of space available for intellectual endeavor at Time Inc. Henry Luce's changing politics was the most important, as Luce tacked sharply right from a mild business liberalism to a strident Cold War conservatism. The changing climate at Time Inc. exacerbated this change, as the small, youthful corporation of the 1930s grew to a large international conglomerate, insulating Luce from his writers with layers of middle-aged business managers. Competition from other magazines, and eventually from television, also played a role. As Time Inc. publications lost their dominance, market pressure curtailed the experimental edge, rationalizing editorial content. Finally, intellectuals themselves bore some responsibility for the shrinking of the spaces available to them. Intellectuals had been most successful at Time Inc. when they were present in great enough numbers to influence the character of a given magazine or section of a magazine. Whether at *Fortune* in the 1930s or at *Time* in the 1940s, intellectuals had been most effective when they competed for the ear of Luce with arguments gauged to sway him. For such arguments to succeed they had to be made by important figures and backed by forceful factions. By the middle 1950s this was impossible. There were no longer sufficient numbers of intellectuals, nor were they backed with prominent sympathetic editors, to compete with the often anti-intellectual corporate journalists that increasingly surrounded Luce. The hostility that intellectuals directed at Luce and his magazines effectively burned the last bridges spanning the chasm between intellectuals and Time Inc.

In the end, of course, intellectuals at Time Inc. ran into unavoidable facts of power. Henry Luce and his management ultimately controlled the direction and content of his magazines. Intellectuals could challenge him from within Time Inc. and they could take advantage of the platform his magazines provided. But Luce was the final arbiter, and no interstitial work by intellectuals could fully finesse this uncomfortable fact. Certainly the interstitial intellectual is a pale figure when measured by the "utopian imagination" Russell Jacoby calls on us to rediscover.[59] Yet, as John Updike once observed, "Surely a culture is enhanced, rather than disgraced, when men of talent and passion undertake anonymous and secondary tasks. Excellence in great things is built on excellence in small."[60] Irving Howe's ideal of the intellectual vocation—"the idea of a life dedicated to values that cannot possibly be realized by a commercial civilization"—is as vital as ever. What has become clearer in the years since Howe wrote is that the search for such values can only take place from within commercial civilization.

CHAPTER ONE

On the Road to Time Inc.

> Hell, why don't I say it's the money? That's what everybody says,
> and it's a good answer because it's simple and it cuts off any reply.
> The trouble is it's never quite the whole truth.
> —John Brooks, *The Big Wheel*

In 1923 Archibald MacLeish abandoned a successful law career to devote himself to poetry full-time. The decision was sudden. Coming home from work one night, MacLeish balked at the smell of the subway. Walking the length of Massachusetts Avenue in the moonlight instead, he ruminated on his unhappiness. Realizing "I would either get out of law then, or I never would," MacLeish decided to quit the law, pack up his family, move to Paris, and devote himself to the private pursuit of poetry.[1] As MacLeish later remembered, on the very day the prestigious Boston firm of Choate, Hall, and Stewart offered him a partnership, he told them he was quitting. He, his wife, and their two young children would travel to France, joining the exodus of American writers who abandoned their homeland for the intellectual culture and cheap living of postwar Paris. Though MacLeish had published his first book of poems in 1917, his writing had always taken a back seat to the necessities of making a living. He had tried writing poetry while supporting his family by teaching, journalism, and practicing law, but his poetry always seemed to be pushed aside by the exigencies of each job. At the age of thirty-one, fed up with the sacrifices required by work, and worried that if he failed to make a clean break now the suffocating pressures of success would prove inescapable, MacLeish dedicated himself to intellectual life.[2]

MacLeish stayed in France for most of the rest of the decade, living the expatriate literary life, developing close friendships with writers such as

Hemingway and Fitzgerald, and establishing himself as a poet. His Paris years were formidably productive. MacLeish published five volumes of poetry, including many of his best (and still anthologized) poems. His work attracted growing notice, so much so that by the end of the decade he was invariably included in estimations of the most promising young American poets.[3]

Yet, in 1929 MacLeish accepted a full-time job writing for *Fortune*, Henry Luce's new magazine designed to celebrate and capitalize on American business culture. He spent the next seven years as the most prolific writer on the fledgling magazine. Unlike his earlier flight to Europe, this time MacLeish composed no lyrical explanation for his decision. No moonlit walk, no agonized decision, no feeling of liberation. In later years he claimed he was driven to the job by the Depression, but that explanation fudged both the timing and his motivation. Why MacLeish gave up on his devotion to art for art's sake and undertook a career in journalism remains very much an open question. And his journey from intellectual inspiration to journalistic perspiration was hardly unique.

Countless other young men and women in the early 1920s shared MacLeish's dream of living a life dedicated to art. They held to a common understanding that such a life was impossible within the framework of established convention. They were a class in the making, repudiating their middle-class roots and defining themselves as intellectuals. MacLeish made this separation physical, putting an ocean between himself and his parents. Younger writers found other means of walling themselves off from the dominant values and mores of their class. At Exeter, a precocious Dwight Macdonald and two friends fashioned themselves into an exclusive club, the Hedonists, whose motto, "Pour épater les bourgeois," accurately captured this self-conscious rupture. At Princeton, T. S. Matthews formed small clubs devoted to socialist politics and poetry. These small societies were characteristic expressions of a generation Malcolm Cowley described as "adhering to a theory of art which held that the creative artist is absolutely independent of all localities, nations or classes."[4]

MacLeish, Macdonald, and Matthews were among the many aspiring young writers and artists repudiating the middle-class world of their parents and, in the process, beginning to form a distinctive intellectual class. MacLeish's romantic account of his moonlit walk from legal briefs to poetry stanzas captures the self-conscious rupture such writers felt as they left the world of their fathers. Abandoning the conventional career tracks that stretched before them, they cleared their own paths, paths now worn bare by the many historians who have followed them.[5]

Young intellectuals such as MacLeish, Matthews and Macdonald adhered to a theory of art and life that tried to separate art from the workaday world. Malcolm Cowley claimed this as a credo for young intellectuals in the early 1920s: "Art is separate from life; the artist is independent of the world and superior to the lifelings."[6] This divide preoccupied MacLeish. During the 1920s his greatest fear "was being caught in a regular day-in, day-out job."[7] The separation of art from the world of work easily elided into the denigration of less exalted vocations. The young T. S. Matthews was typical, if blunt: "I felt only pity or contempt for the majority who were content to drift into 'a job.' I intended to be a writer."[8]

When aspiring young writers faced the threat of work they often had a particular job in mind. The career that most young writers were best qualified for, and that held the most appeal, was journalism. As such, paradoxically, journalists came in for rough treatment. "Wary of any impediments to full freedom of expression, this generation approached journalism suspiciously," Steven Biel notes.[9] Matthews recorded in his diary about a schoolboy friend, "'I am very much afraid Rummy Marvin is going to be nothing but a journalist.'"[10] This disdain for journalism was widely shared. As a college student Dwight Macdonald saw the workers for magazines such as *Time* and the *New Yorker* as "technicians, who know how to write it or paint it or design it or compose it, but who have nothing particular to write, paint, design, or compose." He had little interest in "grinding out stuff" for such magazines, identifying himself instead as a "creator" whose writing would reveal his genius.[11]

To would-be writers such as Matthews and Macdonald journalism represented a multifaceted threat. It was part and parcel of the burgeoning culture industries that made culture into a product to be packaged, sold, and consumed like "motor cars, Ivory soap and ready-to-wear clothes."[12] Commercial journalism meant writing on assigned topics following dictated rules on style and content. The whole process was controlled by editors who doubled as business managers, tailoring content to keep advertiser dollars flowing. But the attack on journalism also took hold with aspiring young writers because it represented a likely fate for many. The magazines and newspapers of New York were replete with aspiring young writers who imagined journalism as a stepping stone and bitter older journalists who had failed to make the step.[13] Seen in this light, their attacks on journalism articulated the fear that they might prove no better writers than the hacks who wrote for pay to prescribed formulas. The fear expressed by Dwight Macdonald of sinking into the mass of cultural technicians appears repeatedly in the accounts of young writers. If they were not good enough to express their genius in writing, or if they lacked the necessary dedication, the strength to stand aside while many of their peers prospered, journalism might be their ultimate fate. So spurning the career paths chosen by their peers and the expectations of their families, men such as MacLeish, Matthews, Macdonald, and countless others devoted themselves to the task of becoming writers.

MacLeish went to Paris and discovered the muse that had heretofore escaped him. T. S. Matthews also spent the early 1920s writing. His college poetry was included in a volume published by his literary society, the Tuesday Evening Club. After two years at Oxford, he spent the remainder of the decade writing book reviews and essays for the *New Republic* while making "the first steps in beginning to learn how to write."[14] Macdonald, younger than the others, spent his college years writing for campus publications and planning his future as a great writer.

Yet in 1928 MacLeish moved back to the states, and in 1929 he took the job writing for *Fortune*. He anchored *Fortune*'s editorial lineup until 1938 as one of the most prolific and certainly the most important writer during the magazine's first decade. He simultaneously produced a wide range of poetry, plays, and essays for other publications. T. S. Matthews joined *Time* in 1929, reviewing books, editing the cultural "back of the book," and eventually becoming editor of the entire magazine before leaving in 1953. He also published essays, reviews, and two novels during the 1930s. Dwight Macdonald also began at *Time* in 1929, before shifting to *Fortune*, where he stayed from the magazine's founding until 1936. While at *Fortune*, he edited and wrote for a small literary bimonthly, the *Miscellany*. Together MacLeish, Matthews, and Macdonald formed the core of the first generation of intellectuals to work for Time Inc. As this generation grew in the 1930s, it included James Agee, Robert Cantwell, Russell Davenport, and many others now forgotten.

What explains this drastic turnaround? Why did these three writers and others like them put aside their vision of a life devoted to art and literature, swallow their distaste for journalism, and go to work for Time Inc., an organization even then recognized as a journalism factory? The most obvious answer is the most prosaic: they needed the money. MacLeish lived in Paris on an allowance provided by his father. By the late 1920s he had returned to the States, had children to educate, and received less from his family. A steady job provided a solid income and a needed measure of security. Financial stability loomed even larger in the thinking of young writers once the Depression settled in. This argument of necessity is the answer provided by the writers themselves when later asked about their stints with Time Inc. Dwight Macdonald explained his *Fortune* years this way: "Excuses swarm: I was young; the articles weren't signed; hard times; and I needed the dough to support my aging mother, and myself."[15] In later years this first generation of intellectuals at Time Inc. agreed that necessity forced them to work as journalists. All hoped to preserve some time for their own work, creating a wall between writing as vocation and as avocation.

Certainly there is some truth to these claims, but the argument of necessity falls apart under careful scrutiny. In each case, this line of justification was created in later years and poorly reflected their thinking at the time. MacLeish, Matthews, and Macdonald's ideas about intellectual life rested on assumptions about art and its proper relation to life, the nature of success, and their own relationship with the cultural values of their families and class. Despite their avowed determination to become great writers, what is most striking about the young Matthews, Macdonald, and even MacLeish is the ambivalence of their commitment to intellectual life. For each, intellectual pursuits were partially motivated by the need for recognition of their talents. While they clearly felt compelled to stand apart from a society to which they felt superior, they also craved the recognition and acceptance of this society. They were dedicated to intellectual endeavor, yet feared it marginalized them socially and cut them off from other avenues of power and prestige. Though these ideas manifested themselves in different ways for each writer, together they embodied attitudes widely shared by intellectuals.

But the ambivalence MacLeish, Matthews, and Macdonald felt toward intellectual life cannot fully explain their simultaneous arrival at Time Inc. The ideas they shared, after all, were basically formed by the time they were in college; many dated from their childhood. That is to say, the same ideas that underpinned and legitimized their exceptional devotion to art were also at the root of their switch to journalism. A fuller explanation, therefore, depends on an understanding of the changing context in which these ideas operated. The year 1923—when MacLeish left for Paris, Matthews joined the staff of the *New Republic*, and Macdonald was emulating H. L. Mencken—was a very different cultural moment from the year 1929, when each joined up at

Time Inc. Historians frequently note how the tendency to break history down into component decades exercises a pervasive tyranny over the historical imagination. This point is usually invoked to draw attention to how ideas and strains of thinking leak from one decade into the next. Rarely noted are the marked differences that occur within decades. The 1920s are particularly susceptible to this trap. Beginning with the end of the war and the eclipse of progressivism and ending with the stock market crash, the 1920s appear as one long run of Republican normalcy and business dominance. This compartmentalization blinds us to important changes during the course of the decade. The cultural world that encouraged and enabled the intellectual ambitions of the early 1920s had altered by 1929, placing different pressures on MacLeish, Matthews, and Macdonald.

Intellectuals receive no special dispensation to resist the power of the surrounding culture, a fact the young Macdonald recognized when he noted in a journal entry about Walter Lippmann, "no one can detach himself from life, can avoid being caught up in the tangled web of his environment."[16] Business and business values became increasingly dominant as the decade wore on, spinning a dense web of entanglement for bright young men graduating from elite colleges and looking to make their mark on the world. Even established intellectuals could feel the tug of these webs. As Edmund Wilson perceptively remarked, the best writing from the decade was the product of "attempts on the part of more thoughtful Americans to reconcile themselves to a world dominated by salesmen and stockbrokers."[17] Wilson's characterization hardly fits the early years of the decade—was Sinclair Lewis reconciling himself to the world of George Babbitt?—but it takes on greater force as the decade progresses. Indeed, Wilson may have been subconsciously speaking of his own novel, *I Thought of Daisy* (1929). Published just before the stock market crash, the novel charts the protagonist's trajectory from cultivating Greenwich Village bohemians to developing an appreciation for the virtues of America's hard-working business class.[18] If America's business culture influenced Edmund Wilson, long viewed as the epitome of autonomy by those lamenting the loss of the independent intellectual, how much more might it have affected young writers less established?[19] MacLeish, Macdonald, Matthews, and many others of the intellectual generation just setting out in the 1920s, came from cultural and economic backgrounds that reinforced this deepening tension between art and success.

The self-conscious rejection of the world of business and conventional success on the part of intellectuals such as MacLeish, Matthews, and

Macdonald obscured their connections to this business class. Intellectuals often came from the same families, attended the same schools, and depended on the same sources of income as those against whom they were defining themselves.[20] All three writers, and most of the others who joined them at Time Inc., were members of the upper-middle-class elite, raised in comfort, educated at private preparatory schools and prestigious universities, and at ease assuming leadership roles in American society. The social and familial connections with the business elite gave them a clear view of what they were rejecting, but they also exerted a persistent pull. Christopher Lasch observed that members of the incipient intellectual class were "*predisposed* to rebellion as the result of an early estrangement from the culture of their own class; as the result, in particular, of the impossibility of pursuing within the framework of established convention the careers they were bent on pursuing."[21] This is certainly true for the cohort of writers who went to work for Time Inc. Yet this predisposition to rebel could exist hand in hand with the pressure to conform. While in Paris, MacLeish was peppered with letters from an aunt urging him to put an end to this foolishness and return to his aborted legal career.[22] Tom Matthews's pursuit of writing left him a constant disappointment to his father.[23] Dwight Macdonald's mother importuned him with letters pleading that he not jeopardize the important social opportunities his Yale education afforded.[24]

Defining themselves as intellectuals meant a rupture with their own class, with the hopes of their families, the expectations of many of their teachers, the lives of many of their peers. For MacLeish, Matthews, and Macdonald, this rupture was only partially effected. For them and others, Time Inc. served as a sort of halfway house, affording a double identity as both creative writers and well-paid professionals. It allowed them to effect a reintegration into their parent's world of success without turning their backs on their intellectual aspirations. Time Inc. provided the environment where they could work through their internal struggles over intellectual identity, where they could sort out their relationship to their family, class, and society, where they could reassess their identity as intellectuals. The attempt to fashion themselves as intellectuals—as part of a class that could stand self-consciously apart from the middle class yet achieve a measure of cultural influence—was only partially successful. They were not the *Intellectuals on the Road to Class Power* that sociologists György Konrád and Iván Szelényi described years ago.[25] Their sense of themselves ambivalent, their destination unclear, they were intellectuals on the road to Time Inc.

The Muse Goes to Work

Young Archie MacLeish grew up in a household dominated by a distant and formidable father, a model of the successful American businessman, and a devoted and caring mother who inculcated her profound belief in service. Largely educated by his mother, MacLeish struggled constantly to gain the notice and approval of his father. Partially in consequence, MacLeish seemed to excel at everything. He was a star football player, won friends easily, and was always at the top of his class in school. First at his Connecticut preparatory school Hotchkiss, and later at Yale, however, he never remembered being happy in school. He was constantly pulled between competing impulses, especially between his devotion to the essentially private pursuit of poetry and the promise of practical influence his success augured and his father respected.

At a very young age MacLeish was already trying to sort out his conflicting feelings about the relationship between art and the rest of the world. During his time at Hotchkiss, he wrote an essay on John Milton. The great poet had been called away from his art to serve the cause of Cromwell, a decision MacLeish depicted in these terms: "His pen, which once had traced the sweetest poetry, was turned to work any scribbler could have done." Yet MacLeish maintained Milton had been correct in his choice, for his active engagement with the world prepared him for the greater poems to follow. "Now there gathered in his brain the threads of the great realities of life and death," he concluded, and it was this that enabled him to write *Paradise Lost*.[26] Negotiating the line between art and a broader engagement with the world became and remained the animating question of his intellectual life.

While compiling a sterling academic, social, and athletic record MacLeish still worried over how to balance his competing interests. At Yale, he found it hard to sustain the optimism contained in his earlier Milton essay. He felt it to be an inopportune place to write poetry. His athletic achievements were celebrated, his classroom success venerated, but his poetry (or maybe it was his odd combination of poet/athlete) fell somehow outside the narrowly prescribed bounds of Yale identity.

Despite a small literary renaissance in the late teens, Yale in the 1920s still bore strong resemblance to the school depicted in the popular schoolboy novel *Stover at Yale*.[27] Written by Owen Johnson, a member of the class of 1900 (a class whose "interest in scholarly things," Yale's historian notes, reached "its lowest point in the history of the college"), *Stover at Yale* served simultaneously as the story of a hero, a criticism of Yale's conformity, and a sort of orientation manual for entering students.[28] Picking up on how Yale had trimmed its sails to the increasingly materialist winds, Johnson emphasized the degree to which undergraduate life revolved almost entirely around athletics and social clubs. As the religious focus of the university had steadily receded in importance, the gap was filled not by scholarship but by social competition.[29] Johnson criticized Yale, and other colleges, for functioning merely as training grounds for businessmen. He singled out athletics as instilling business values such as competition and organization, all deployed toward achieving success. He made the same point about the competition to edit the Yale papers: "the struggle for existence outside in the business world is not one whit more intense than the struggle to win out in the News or Lit competition."[30]

The anti-intellectual trend Johnson described was somewhat arrested in the teens, as Yale produced a corps of important writers, including Sinclair Lewis, Stephen Vincent Benét, Thorton Wilder and, of course, Archibald MacLeish. But the presence of ambitious and talented writers did little to alter the school's pervasive orientation toward business and social success.[31] MacLeish, certainly, felt Yale provided little support for his poetry and resented the poverty of his education. Academically, MacLeish recalled, "Yale was really pretty close to the bottom."[32] Despite a minority intellectual culture, Yale continued to drift along comfortably within the currents of business civilization.

This success ethic did not dampen MacLeish's literary enthusiasm (he edited the *Literary Review*, joined the Elizabethan Club and a smaller literary band, the Pundits, and wrote the class poem), but it did seem to color his view of the esteem accorded literary endeavor at Yale. Seeking to characterize the *Lit*, he invoked Matthew Arnold's description of the poet Shelley, describing the magazine as "a beautiful ineffectual angel."[33] The rest of the passage, unquoted by MacLeish, ran "beating in the void his luminous wings in vain."[34]

MacLeish continued to ruminate about the relationship between art and society through discussions with his most influential professor, Larry Mason. Mason was a committed philosophical idealist who believed and taught that the life of the mind was all, and art the only suitable subject for the mind. MacLeish swallowed a great deal of Mason's idealist draught, but could not always keep it down. He found it difficult to accept a life lived for art alone. Challenging Mason on one exam, he wrote "If all our thoughts are thoughts and there is no red fruit of action, shall we throw gay flags to the autumn winds and add joyousness to the 'eddies of purposeless dust'?" Mason scribbled his reply in the margin: "But is the life of 'action' really so dust-proof, so fruitful?"[35] MacLeish's first book of poems, *Tower of Ivory* (1917), owed its title to Mason, who also wrote the introduction, claiming MacLeish's poems as support for his idealist beliefs. Despite Mason, this positioning of art and life in opposition continued to worry MacLeish.

Upon graduating from Yale the question posed itself with particular force. His literary successes at Yale whet his appetite for writing poetry, but he knew that making poetry into a career was impractical. He wanted desperately to marry his longtime love Ada Taylor Hitchcock, a plan his father would not approve unless he embarked on a career. For a while he considered going into academics, but he disliked the picture of academic life presented by his professors. Fearing the trap of being "caught in a regular day-in, day-out job," he eventually settled on the law, believing that as a lawyer he would have the best opportunity for finding time—"summers, Sunday mornings, an evening now and then"—to write.[36]

MacLeish found law school to be surprisingly satisfying, with far more intellectual appeal than he expected. As always, he excelled in the classroom and soon established himself near the top of his class. But he found little time to write, being "constantly aware of the basic incompatibility of the two masters he was serving." Things did not improve after law school, when he accepted a job with the Boston law firm of Choate, Hall, and Stewart. There he found the actual practice of law exhilarating, but complained that lawyers might just as easily be replaced by professional duelists. No matter who won or lost any case, "the effect on the human race or the welfare of society or the development of the individual [was] just exactly and precisely zero."[37] Despite his skepticism of the law and the suspicion that only material considerations kept him practicing, he kept at it for two years. He wrote almost no poetry.

This was his position when he quit the law, packed up his family, and headed to France. Despite his literary success abroad, MacLeish faced continual family pressure, primarily from a meddlesome aunt, to reconsider his decision. He forcefully resisted these intrusions, proclaiming his determination to stick to poetry. Summarizing one such argument, he wrote to his mother: "I replied as frankly that I would never give up the profession of letters while I could afford to stick at it, that I didn't believe in her world of active affairs, & that poetry is an art & not a means of purveying bread of any variety."[38] Here he gave full voice to his determination to live for art and art alone. As he wrote in the famous last lines of "Ars poetica," "A poem should not mean, but be."³⁹ Forsaking the example of Milton, MacLeish had joined Mason and the idealists.

His aunt's facile conflation of prestige and quality, and her total lack of appreciation for poetry (she only came to accept MacLeish as a poet once her literary friends assured her that he was "one of the outstanding figures meriting the closest attention in his school of poetry") made her an easy foil.⁴⁰ But in 1927 her insistence that he play a role in "active affairs" soon received support from an unlikely but more formidable quarter. In that year literary critic Edmund Wilson wrote an article titled "The Muses Out of Work," where he took the most promising young poets, MacLeish included, to task for their excessive devotion to their art. Wilson wondered whether greater interaction with the larger world might deepen their perspective and enrich their poetry. As he put it, "What is wrong with the younger American poets is that they have no real stake in society. One does not want them to succumb to society; but one *would* like to see them, at least, have some sort of relation to it." He invoked Milton as the proper model. The review brought Wilson a hailstorm of protest, as poets such as Hart Crane and John Crowe Ransom criticized the idea that poetry need be more closely connected to the mundane world.⁴¹ MacLeish also resisted Wilson's conclusions. The article, which included Wilson's judgment that MacLeish's poetic idiom was largely a pose, helped spur him to compose a scurrilous piece of doggerel about Wilson, which he mailed to Ezra Pound (the only thing MacLeish ever wrote that Pound liked).⁴² Wilson's unwanted advice likely deepened MacLeish's insistence on separating his art from the rest of the world.

In other moods, however, he was less certain. He sometimes felt his commitment to the "economically unsound practice of cutting sentences up into lines" while he had a family to support was irresponsible.⁴³ By 1928 he seemed to be searching for some middle ground, between the worlds of modernist art and his aunt's world of "active affairs." In January his father died, and MacLeish's inheritance brought a new measure of financial security. It also freed him from his difficult relationship with his father. MacLeish had continually tried to get his father to appreciate his accomplishments. He recalled enlisting the president of Yale in an effort to convince Andrew MacLeish of his son's success and promise, that he was "a lad of parts." MacLeish continually feared his father did not properly understand or value his success. Yet he also abandoned one field Andrew MacLeish did understand, the law, and plainly refused to consider having anything to do with his own father's most comfortable milieu, the world of business. Andrew MacLeish had entertained hopes his son might join him in business, but Archie's resolve to write poetry had effectively quashed any such plans.[44]

Shortly after his father's death MacLeish bought a farmhouse in Conway, Massachusetts, and he and his wife left France and settled in the States for good. In a suggestive letter written at the same time, he implied he might be backing away from his extreme devotion to art for art's sake. Writing to an old college friend, he argued, "I agree with you about the avant-garde view of the universe. It is almost as false and nearly half as silly as the American Business Man's (and I don't mean you) professional optimism. The first is due to a festering introspection & the latter to the absence of thought, feeling & sense, inner & outer."[45] What is remarkable about this passage is its equation of the position of the avant-garde artist with that of the businessman as equally false. It may be that MacLeish was having second thoughts about the poem he had just completed, *The Hamlet of A. MacLeish*, certainly a work of "festering introspection."

MacLeish's *Hamlet*, published in late 1928, was his most personal and self-critical work to date. The poem drew on a distinction he observed between his time and Elizabethan England: "Your modern is Hamlet—but Hamlet without the ghost, without even the dead father, with nothing but the soliloquies—which are not overheard."[46] His *Hamlet*, then, would be his attempt to confront and overcome his own ghosts, including the recent death of his father. His poem would be a merciless exercise in self-criticism. He especially had in mind his own extreme dependence on the opinions of others, his deep need for praise, and his inability to face criticism. The search for such praise led him to exploit his feelings, his relationships, and his personal tragedies in the making of his poems. In the finished poem these feelings were manifested as self-loathing:

> Why must I speak of it? Why must I always
> Stoop from this decent silence to this phrase
> That makes a posture of my hurt? Why must I
> Say I suffer? . . . or write out these words
> For eyes to stare at that shall soon as mine
> Or little after me go thick and lose
> The light too, or for solemn lettered fools
> To judge if I said neatly what I said?—
> Make verses! . . . ease myself at the soiled stool
> That's common to so swollen many! . . . shout

> For hearing in the world's thick dirty ear! ...
> Expose my scabs! ... crowd forward among those
> That beg for fame, that for so little praise
> As pays a god off will go stiff and tell
> Their loss, lust, sorrow, anguish! ... match
> My grief with theirs! ... compel the public prize
> For deepest feeling and put on the bays! ...
> O shame, for shame to suffer it, to make
> A skill of harm, a business of despair,
> And like a barking ape betray us all
> For itch of notice[47]

MacLeish followed this up by laying out the precise nature of his despair. The result was a powerful poem. It simultaneously conveyed his need to write poetry while it indicted that need. He convicted himself of exploiting his own (and his family's) grief to meet his personal insecurities. MacLeish reestablished the artist's connection to the world. In his most personal poem he explored the intimate relation between the poet as artist and the poet as a man, a man in relationships with and with responsibilities to other people. The entire poem works as an attack on his own independence, on the idea that art can be separate from life.

In this poem, MacLeish laid himself bare for the critics, and baited them besides, a dangerous act for a man whose self-image was tightly bound by their opinions. The critics rose to the bait. His previous works, despite a few determined detractors such as Edmund Wilson, had won critical acclaim and his reputation had grown rapidly throughout the 1920s. His 1926 volume *Streets in the Moon* garnered warm praise from Malcolm Cowley, Alan Tate, Louis Untermeyer, and Conrad Aiken. *The Hamlet of A. MacLeish*, on the other hand, was greeted with, in MacLeish's summation, "perfunctory notices and tepid hostility" except where it was "violently attacked."[48] *Hound and Horn*'s reviewer, R. P. Blackmur, published a savage attack, an assault not just on the poem but on MacLeish's integrity as a poet. Blackmur concluded, "as a poet Mr. MacLeish has no life of his own."[49] Conrad Aiken, a friend of MacLeish's, called his *Hamlet* counterfeit and false, a judgment MacLeish felt deeply ("a stroke at the heart and the knife goes in").[50] Aiken's opinion was echoed in the *New Republic*.[51] This reaction stung MacLeish. As he wrote to his friend Louis Untermeyer, who had written a review notable more for its warm feelings for the author than for an acute perception of the poem's intent: "I counted on you to hear the voice. If you didn't it was as much my fault as yours. And if I still believe in the poem it is because I know I shan't do better."[52]

With his confidence shaken, MacLeish altered the direction of his poetry. He began to concern himself with reaching beyond the small world of poets and critics in an attempt to address a broader audience. He again entertained ideas about how he might reenter the mainstream, if not of American life, then of his educated class. It was at this time that Henry Luce called with an offer to come to work for his new business magazine.

The proximity of *Fortune*'s creation to the Depression made it easier for MacLeish to perpetuate the view that he took the job because of financial pressure and to further cloud the picture of his thinking at the time. Responding to a 1976 article by Brooks Atkinson, who wondered why MacLeish could have gone to work for "the enemy," MacLeish claimed "He was thinking about *Fortune* as it is now. *Fortune* as it was then was a wholly different thing. Because of the fact that it opened for business in the middle of the Depression, it was not at all a business magazine."[53] But *Fortune* did not open for business in the middle of the Depression. Conceived when the boom was in full swing, the magazine appeared in the immediate wake of the crash, in February 1930, long before there was a real understanding of the severity of the Depression. Despite his later recollections, Archibald MacLeish signed on to work for *Fortune* during flush times.[54] He was one of the founding editors of a magazine devoted to celebrating the beauty and grandeur of America's business civilization, at a time when that grandeur still seemed real.

MacLeish's decision to take a job as a journalist was just as sudden as his abandonment of the law had been six years earlier. Given the timing, his friends found it difficult to understand. Hemingway, who always considered MacLeish wealthy, wrote friends wondering what MacLeish could possibly be thinking. Granted that MacLeish's later pleading poverty does not explain his decision, what does? It is not possible to know for sure, but a number of factors likely weighed in the decision. Luce's generosity may have played a role. MacLeish claimed the publisher agreed to let him work half time, working six months a year while being paid for twelve. The unusual offer promised a good living and half of his year for poetry (though there is no contemporary record of its existence, and it was years before he took his first six-month leave). Belying the evasive answer he gave Atkinson, MacLeish held no strong hostility toward business. He had frequent contact with businessmen as a lawyer, never voicing strong objections to them as a class (it is suggestive that he reestablished a connection with the business world soon after his father's death). MacLeish also had a great deal in common with Henry Luce. They had been educated at the same schools, had similar records of achievement (Luce had grown up trying to match MacLeish's earlier record), and a similar sense of the social responsibilities that went with their station in life.

The most important factor leading MacLeish to *Fortune*, however, was his changing attitude toward his poetry and the proper relationship between art and society. MacLeish was questioning his single-minded devotion to poetry. He had been stung by the critics and frustrated by his isolation. The letters he wrote at this time to his editor at Houghton Mifflin, Robert Linscott, continually detailed MacLeish's attempts to have his poetry packaged, priced, and marketed for a wider audience. Burned by the critical reception of his most personal work, MacLeish turned to writing an epic of the Spanish conquest of America, which would have greater mainstream appeal (as it did, winning him his first Pulitzer Prize in 1933). His move to Conway cut him off from the avant-garde world he had mingled with in Paris. Clearly, MacLeish's commitment to following the poetic muse, independent of the demands of the rest of society, was wavering. Stripped bare of retrospective assumptions, MacLeish's desire to balance his poetry with a wider engagement with society explains his decision. Journalism might not satisfy the full run of his ambitions, but for the present it was convenient, lucrative, and, with Henry Luce's ambitions, it might prove to be important. It was the same conclusion other young intellectuals were arriving at in the last year of the 1920s.

Working for What You Despise

While the conflict between inviolate art and social engagement drove MacLeish, Thomas Stanley Matthews was motivated by darker psychological demons. Like MacLeish, Matthews developed an early interest in literature and aspired to be a writer. His thinking also stressed the divide between intellect and action, and he, too, felt the tug of both. For years he wanted to be either a great writer or a revolutionary. Unlike MacLeish, who spent the decade pursuing art and neglecting the world of active affairs, Matthews was attracted to people who combined intellect and action. Whether revolutionaries such as Trotsky, his first hero, or fellow students such as his best friend Schuyler Jackson, they served as models stressing the separation of the artist/revolutionary from ordinary people. This satisfied Matthews's desire to break with the social world in which he grew up and it nourished his own sense of his superiority. These complex and often contradictory notions—a commitment to being a writer, an attraction to the dynamism and power of the revolutionary, a need to set himself apart from and above ordinary people—guided him on the road to Time Inc.

The son of a minister father and an heiress mother, Tom Matthews spent his early years in Cincinnati. His father, the Rev. Paul Matthews, was a prominent Episcopal clergyman who eventually rose to the position of bishop of New Jersey. His mother, Elsie, was a daughter of the eminent Procter family, of Procter and Gamble. The Matthewses, wealthy in their own right, had been an established fixture in Cincinnati politics and upper-class society. Stanley Matthews, Paul's father, had been elected to the U.S. Senate and served on the U.S. Supreme Court. The Procters' standing in Cincinnati was of a more recent vintage, but their great wealth gained them immediate prestige and influence. As the only son of a marriage that unified two of Cincinnati's most powerful families, Tom grew up in the rarefied environment of the upper class, under the expectations and scrutiny that came with his position.

Paul Matthews's work compelled the family to live in downtown Cincinnati during Tom's youth, but Tom had little contact with the outside world. Educated by a series of governesses, prevented from playing with neighborhood boys, seeing the outside world refracted through the lens of his parents' class prejudice, he developed a deep sense of his separation from, and superiority to, the rest of the world. These attitudes became inextricably connected with his developing intellectual interests. His desire to live "a dedicated life," to become either a great writer or a great revolutionary, stemmed from his need to keep himself apart from society, but also to compel its notice.[55]

By the time Tom was seven, the Matthewses had moved from their urban home to the suburb of Glendale, a small, sheltered "village inhabited and dominated by the Procters and Matthewses." In Glendale, Tom was removed from even the visual reminder of other classes of children. Without other boys to play with, he spent most of his time playing with his sisters and reading. His first original story was a long tale detailing the exploits of a Spanish gentleman-brigand, told in the floweriest language he could muster. This provided his first experience as a writer, and it made a deep impression: "I felt hungrily that there was some better relationship with words, if I could achieve it, than I could ever find with any person I knew." His early heroes extended beyond pirates and swordsmen, however, as an essay on Socrates written about the same time showed. In it, Matthews recounted Socrates' trial and death, emphasizing his goodness and superior wisdom, and the jealousy and prejudice of the Athenians who killed him. Matthews already felt the appeal of living a life devoted to high ideals in opposition to the mob, and of being martyred for the effort. He was all of nine years old.[56]

At the age of fourteen he was sent to prep school at St. Paul's in New Hampshire, the school his father had attended. Forced to begin school midterm due to a registration foul up, and possessing no athletic ability, young Tom found it hard going. Unable to trade in the acceptable currency of athletic achievement, Matthews instead secretly wrote poetry and stoked a growing desire to show his classmates that they had misjudged him. He determined to become "a hero of revolutionary politics or a great writer." Wanting to be a writer followed naturally from his facility with words and the satisfaction he found in writing. Aspirations of revolutionary heroism were doubtless inspired by the Russian Revolution, then less than a year old, and by a radical teacher who exerted a strong pull on the imagination of a number of young students. Such fantasies of a life as an outsider, but one the rest of the world could not ignore, helped him maintain a separation from his fellow students, a conventional lot of future "Philadelphia lawyers, Long Island stockbrokers, and Boston merchants."[57]

After St. Paul's Matthews moved on to Princeton, also his father's alma mater. His family had recently settled in Princeton, after his father's ascension to the bishopric of New Jersey. As at St. Paul's, he found at Princeton an environment where athletic and social skill mattered more than intellectual attainment. It was in 1920, when Matthews was a sophomore, that F. Scott Fitzgerald memorably characterized Princeton as "the pleasantest country club in America."[58] Matthews might not have agreed with the adjective, but he certainly would have seconded Fitzgerald's depiction of Princeton as an elite institution centered on social pursuits. Even more than at Yale, intellectual pursuits were taken lightly, politics shunned. Fitzgerald's classmate Edmund Wilson noted, "At Princeton, too great seriousness tends to be considered bad form or merely unnecessary."[59]

It galled Matthews that at a school with such a modest intellectual life, he was still not properly appreciated. As he wrote, "My position in college vaguely dissatisfied me; I felt that I was not being recognized as I should be." He again responded by cultivating his status as an outsider at an institution where nonconformists were "exceptional and unwelcome," and again pursuing his dual dreams of revolutionary politics and writing. He founded two school clubs where he could take a leading role while pursuing these dreams.[60]

The first was a short-lived attempt to bring radical politics to the Princeton campus. Matthews organized a small group calling itself the Socialist Society. A dozen or so young men showed up for the organizational meeting, and after a struggle for control Matthews emerged as its president. The school administration promptly forced him to rename it the Society for the Study of Socialism. In his capacity as the group's leader, Matthews served as Princeton's delegate to meetings of the Intercollegiate Socialist Society, where he met John Dos Passos. The group attracted a small but committed membership, and Matthews organized a lecture series. Interest in the club peaked with a campus appearance by Norman Thomas, the later Socialist candidate for president and a Princeton alum, though one no longer welcome at his old school. The event provoked a storm of controversy and led one professor to try to get Matthews expelled. Despite (or because of) this notoriety, the group's membership dwindled, and a lack of funds eventually killed it.[61]

His brief career as a radical organizer over, Matthews concentrated his energies on a literary club. Calling themselves the Tuesday Evening Club, Matthews and a dozen or so friends met weekly to read their poems and discuss life and literature. Together they pursued the intellectual interests for which they found little support at Princeton. The club flourished under the leadership of Matthews and his best friend, the talented poet Schuyler Jackson. It eventually published a small volume of the member's poetry.[62] The success of the club furthered Matthews's intellectual ambitions. More important, in Schuyler Jackson he had found a real life model to emulate. As a self-conscious outsider, but one widely recognized and admired for his brilliance, Jackson combined elements of Matthews's two goals: he was both a man of words and a man of action.[63]

Matthews first met Jackson at the end of a bayonet. As did most freshmen at Princeton in the fall of 1918, Matthews joined the Student Army Training Corps soon after arriving on campus. Jackson, "grim-lipped and stripped to the waist," muscular and athletic, was his opposite number for bayonet practice. Though Jackson made an impression on Matthews that lingered, they did not become friends until Jackson joined the Tuesday Evening Club two years later. Jackson was filled with grand literary ambitions, certain he was to be an important poet. His extreme devotion to art and his spurning of convention attracted Matthews, as did his flattering insistence that Matthews's poetry deserved to be taken seriously. Jackson encouraged Matthews in his "growing determination to prove that I was somebody, to make the successful people I envied and despised admit that I was as good as they were. As good? Better!"[64]

One of those "successful people" was another of Jackson's coterie of admirers, Johnny Martin, who resembled Jackson in his dynamism and drive. Martin, who later became managing editor of *Time* magazine and brought Matthews to *Time*, was chairman of the *Daily Princetonian*. Despite the loss of an arm in a shooting accident, he was a first rate golfer and soccer player. (Indeed, according to Time Inc. legend, his golf prowess proved a serious setback to the attempt to raise capital for *Time* magazine, then being organized by Martin's cousin Briton Hadden and his partner Henry Luce. On a swing through the nation's country clubs in search of old Yale men to hit up for funding, Martin refused to be beaten on the links. Being beaten by a one-armed golfer did little to put potential investors in a generous mood.[65]) Matthews was flattered by Martin's faith in his literary talent and saw Martin as a model of someone to whom, despite his disability, success came easily. His dynamic personality and easy charm were exactly what Matthews felt himself lacking.

After graduating in 1922, Matthews remained unsure of what to do next. As he later described his thinking, "I intended to be a writer, though I knew I wasn't ready yet; the one thing I was sure I wouldn't do was to take a job, sit at a desk in an office. Meanwhile I would go to Oxford and get another degree."[66] He spent two years at Oxford as a Rhodes Scholar, and then one unhappy year at a fund-raising job, before landing a job with the *New Republic*. He started in with proofreading and make-up, then slowly placed a few columns and reviews. Attracting notice for his prose (describing the writing of a phony tough guy of the time, Matthews quipped, "Jim Tully is so goddam hard-boiled his spit bounces"), by November 1927 he was appearing on the masthead as the associate editor.[67] He regularly reviewed books, wrote unsigned editorials and parodies, and occasionally contributed larger pieces.

By going to work at the *New Republic*, Matthews had become a journalist, despite his earlier disdain for the profession. But he did not consider the *New Republic* to be journalism of the sort he had previously dismissed, and he was not the only one to feel this way. As he wryly admitted, after four years working for the journal "no newspaper man would have said I was a journalist at all."[68] For his part, Matthews remembered that he "personally looked very much down on newspapermen" because their writing lacked the depth, style, and intelligence of what appeared in the *New Republic*.[69] Instead of viewing himself as a journalist, Matthews saw his experience at the *New Republic* as an apprenticeship, where he began the long and hard work of becoming a writer. Moreover, he thought he had found a place where he could combine his desire to be a writer and his remaining interest in leftist politics. Though no longer an active socialist, Matthews's politics fit well with the left liberalism of the *New Republic*. (It helped that his taking the job infuriated his father.) Working for a journal that took both literature and politics seriously, Matthews could balance his interests in the two.

The *New Republic* in the 1920s struggled for an identity. Two thirds of its founding troika were gone, with Walter Weyl passing away in 1919 and Walter Lippmann moving on to a career as a newspaper editor and syndicated columnist soon thereafter. Herbert Croly continued to lead the magazine, but the debacle of the war and the eclipse of progressivism left him dispirited. He turned increasingly to religious mysticism. The magazine still attracted good writers, and its quality remained high, but its content took on the defensiveness typical of a progressive magazine in an era hostile to reform. It was not until the onset of the Depression, well after Croly's death, that the magazine regained some of its vitality, again operating in the mainstream of the reform movement.[70]

Despite his awe for the writers and a strong affection for Croly, Matthews did not find the *New Republic* to be the intellectual home he had envisioned. Although he had been warned by his family to expect long-haired radicals, he instead found most of the writers to be "grizzled and gray-haired." He compared the magazine's influence at the time to that of "a voice crying in the wilderness."[71] The sense of editorial drift and the aging of the writers discouraged young Matthews, as did the heavy and serious atmosphere. Though he viewed the writers as "objects of veneration," he felt suffocated breathing such rarefied air.[72] These writers little resembled Schuyler Jackson, who remained his ideal of a writer, making as he did devotion to literature seem dynamic and heroic. The writers at the *New Republic*, writing intelligently on art and politics, melded Tom's two main interests, but nobody would call them heroic. Matthews's description of the office lunches, when the staff gathered to entertain an influential guest, suggested his disappointment. Matthews found the hushed and intense conversation, frequently with a visiting economist, often impenetrable and usually boring. Urged by Edmund Wilson to liven things up, Matthews called on his Princeton friend Johnny Martin. On a day when no economists were coming, Matthews invited Martin, a writer for the fledgling *Time*, as the guest of honor. In Matthews's account, Martin "was not the least impressed with the company, was perfectly natural, talked a lot, smoked a pipe, and dominated the whole table. It was a great success." Matthews's vivid account of Martin's performance revealed his doubts about intellectual life and his complaints about the *New Republic*. He contrasted Martin's naturalness with the artificial nature of the usual intellectual conversation, and was clearly attracted by Martin's ability to dominate the table full of intellectuals. He was coming to prefer Martin's dynamism, ease, and self-confidence to the erudite but ineffective world of Croly and his colleagues.[73]

Matthews found more congenial company, and a more fulfilling model of intellectual life, among the followers of religious mystic A. R. Orage. He shared this involvement with Croly, who was searching for greater meaning outside political journalism for reasons of his own. Though their relationship began awkwardly, over an interview conducted in "a frenzy of tongue-tied silence," Croly and Matthews slowly warmed to each other.[74] In the middle 1920s they both came under the influence of Orage. The former editor of the respected English journal *The New Age*, Orage had quit to become a disciple of the Russian mystic G. I. Gurdjieff.[75] Orage had been sent to America to spread Gurdjieff's message. A brilliant man and a spellbinding orator, he quickly picked up a strong following among various literary intellectuals in New York. Among those who began attending his classes were Margaret Anderson, Kenneth Burke, Hart Crane, Waldo Frank, Mabel Dodge Luhan, and Jean Toomer, in addition to Matthews and Croly. Circles of Orage followers grew up around various magazines, including the *Little Review*, *Seven Arts*, and *New Republic*.

Through rigorous physical and psychological self-discipline, Gurdjieff and Orage taught, individuals could break through the stale routine of life and achieve a higher consciousness. Though in principle "the Method" was available to anybody who undertook the necessary discipline and training, in practice it played into the belief of many intellectuals that they were capable of achieving a level of consciousness not available to ordinary people. As Croly's wife Dorothy put it in a letter to a friend, "It's really delivering both of us from some of the handicaps all human beings have in one form or another."[76] Gurdjieff manipulated this sense of being special to increase the attractiveness of his group. On his first trip to America, he staged demonstrations of his peculiar music and dance regimens. Standing outside the theater, Gurdjieff walked among the waiting crowd, looking people in the eye to decide if they were worthy of being allowed inside.[77] This means of separating oneself from the rest of the world must have held a powerful appeal for Matthews, serving as tangible evidence of his own superiority.

In his memoir *Name and Address*, Matthews wrote little about his experience with the Gurdjieff cult. He treated his involvement with Orage and Gurdjieff lightly, as if it was a dabbling interest.[78] He did the same with his early attraction to socialism. This affectation of bemused skepticism toward his former beliefs obscured his intense identification with the movement. Like other followers, he attended three-hour study sessions twice a week, plowed through the master's long and obscure writings, and engaged in the strenuous physical training that was supposed to bring mastery over the physical world. None of these were the activities of a skeptical observer. Croly eventually backed away from Orage in 1927 or 1928, but Matthews remained loyal to Orage even when he broke with Gurdjieff and returned to London to begin again as a journalist.[79] The combination of intellectual and physical dominance and the goal of transcending the limitations of the existing world met important needs in Matthews's psyche. It would not be the last time he got involved with a fringe group intoxicated with its own self-importance.

Matthews left the *New Republic* about the same time he broke with the Gurdjieff cult. In 1929 he left the magazine for a job writing for *Time* magazine and his friend John Martin. Matthews described his move this way: "When Johnny Martin telephoned to offer me a job on *Time*, I didn't have to think it over very long; it was almost as if I was expecting the call. I felt that I was taking a step down just the same."[80] He may not have been expecting the call, but he was certainly prepared for it.

Matthews later gave a couple of reasons for his switch to *Time*. First, Croly's stroke in 1928 had made his status at the *New Republic* uncertain. Matthews had been something of Croly's protégé, and his relationship was not close with the other members of the inner circle. This perhaps explains his need to leave the *New Republic*, but leaves unexplained why he moved to *Time*, a very different kind of magazine practicing a very different kind of journalism. The typical explanation for moving to Time Inc., a need for more money, did not apply either, at least in this simple form. The job for *Time* paid no more than he had made for the *New Republic*. In either case, the money would not have supported Matthews and his young family. His parents supplemented his income throughout these years, and bought him a house in Princeton.

Matthews offered a second explanation in his autobiography. He claimed to have been increasingly uncomfortable with the fact that the *New Republic* failed to pay its own way (a pair of "angels," Willard Straight and his wife, had long subsidized it). As Matthews described the situation: "In different degrees and ways we all, I think, sometimes felt like kept men and babies that don't trust the nurse not to drop them; and nobody likes that."[81] This concern with the subsidized status of the *New Republic* did not seem to have bothered him until his disaffection with the magazine was well established. It did reflect a growing interest in success (Martin and his magazine were clearly succeeding, the *New Republic* was not) as well as some curious ideas about independence. If he was concerned with the effects of subsidies on the content of magazine, if he feared its ability to exist independent of outside influence, the move to *Time* was a strange one. Though *Time* supported itself, its journalism operated under a much more severe editorial discipline than the *New Republic*. It is more likely that Matthews's concern over the subsidized nature of the *New Republic* represented fears of his own dependency on the money of his parents. He was willing to sacrifice independence in his work to gain a greater independence in his life. Even if *Time* paid the same now, his connection with Martin gave him a good entry into a small but ambitious and growing company. Matthews was restless living under the discipline of his parent's financial support; in exchange, he accepted the discipline of *Time*'s strict formula and editorial control.

Other factors played a role in his decision. Writing for *Time* brought with it a larger audience, an idea that appealed to Matthews. The possibility of eventually running a magazine with a circulation already ten times that of the *New Republic* likely stoked his ambition and rekindled his political interests. Matthews's tendency to downplay his early politics makes it difficult to gauge how important they might have been. The evidence is clear, however, that he had not abandoned his earlier radicalism. He voted for the Socialist Party in both the 1928 and 1932 elections. *Time*'s politics had yet to solidify into solid Republicanism. The idea that as a writer and later an editor he could use *Time* as a political instrument would have held deep appeal. In the late 1930s it played a key role in his decision to pursue power within Time Inc.

Also pushing Matthews in the direction of *Time* was his long-held belief in his abilities and his need to earn recognition from those he regarded as his inferiors. Describing his feelings about the magazine, Matthews wrote, "I wanted to show *Time* . . . that it was entertaining an angel unawares."[82] This was a favorite formulation of Matthews's. It comes from Hebrews 13.2, "be not forgetful to entertain strangers: for thereby some have entertained angels unawares." He later used the phrase *Angels Unawares* for the title of his last book, a collection of reminiscences of great people he had encountered in mundane surroundings.[83] The image appeared in his Princeton poetry and in his letters from the 1930s.[84] The idea that *Time* had an "angel unaware" in

Matthews justified his job by separating him from those who did the same work. Not only did he cultivate this view of himself, as an angel among the fallen, but he also may have actually sought to put himself in a position where this self-perception was sustainable. Belief in his own exceptional talents was difficult to maintain among the writers of the *New Republic*, so Matthews lapsed into habits of thinking that minimized their influence. Working at *Time*, however, placed him again among undereducated young men such as those he had known at Princeton. He described the contrast between the two magazines as "between scholarly, distinguished men and smart, ignorant boys." In fact, he repeatedly overemphasized the uneducated nature of the "ill-read crew" at *Time*, and especially of the founders, Hadden and Luce. Paradoxically, Matthews seemed more at home as the house intellectual among the philistines than as a minor writer among the eminencies of his profession. He could once again feel the obscure pleasure of the outsider, unappreciated by his ignorant colleagues, taking comfort in his own separation from their devotion to this "cheap, brash, ignorant little paper."[85]

"The Power Is All in Business"

Though much younger than either MacLeish or Matthews, Dwight Macdonald, like Matthews, liked to think of himself as an intellectual set against the rest of society. But the intellectual values he admired—power, technique, creative innovation—proved easily adaptable to fields outside of literature. By the late 1920s, these values seemed to Macdonald to be better reflected in the world of business than they did in literature. This realization made Macdonald susceptible to the lure of business, though his actual contact with the world of retailing made him miserable. *Fortune* magazine presented itself as a workable bridge between Macdonald's self-identification as a writer and his attraction to wealth, power, and prestige.

Macdonald described growing up in a "lower-middle class, shabby-genteel" family from Binghamton, New York.[86] His conception of his family was probably colored by the economic backgrounds of the children with whom he attended school, for there is little in his youth suggesting lower-middle-class life. Macdonald's father, Timothy Dwight Macdonald, was a lawyer, though not a very successful one. He was descended from a prominent family, however, a relation of the Dwight family that included two past presidents of Yale. His mother, Alice Hedges, was the daughter of a wealthy Brooklyn merchant. The importance of family ties for the Macdonalds is suggested by the naming of their children, Dwight for his parents' most illustrious ancestors, and his brother Hedges for his mother's family.

Unlike MacLeish or Matthews, the young Dwight Macdonald had a warm and close relationship with his father. He admired his father's "open, imaginative, emotional, and impractical" nature, though he also believed that these traits were what kept him from being truly successful in business.[87] Timothy Macdonald had attended Phillips Exeter Academy and Yale and then worked his way through law school by tutoring the children of the rich. As a lawyer he gravitated to the film industry. His most successful years were spent as chief legal counsel to the Triangle Film Co. In 1919 he parlayed his knowledge of the movie business into a position lecturing at Yale on the history and development of the industry. Overall it was not a bad career, but it was not very lucrative. The Macdonald's standard of living never measured up to that of most of Dwight's friends and classmates, and was far below that of the other Hedges.

Alice Hedges certainly had higher aspirations for her husband. Dwight likely shared in these expectations, for he always identified his father as a failure in business. Yet he loved him all the more for this failure. He reflected on their relationship in a number of letters written soon after his father's 1926 death. In what was to become a typical intellectual habit, Dwight divided the world in half, between cold, hard, efficient people on the one hand and soft, warm, ineffectual people on the other. "The latter are generally despised and overreached by the former," he concluded. His father had been the latter, "too ready to run after rainbows, to plan great things that never came off." This had been his great appeal but also his downfall. As he wrote, "His life was a great tragedy—the tragedy of a man who realizes that he has failed. His love for his family must have been at the same time a torment—for he could not give them all he wanted to." He blamed the "hard ones," and business generally, for this tragedy, concluding one letter "God how I hate BUSINESS!"[88]

Macdonald grew up on the Upper West Side of Manhattan, attending a series of private schools and summer camps before being sent to Exeter at age fourteen. There he discovered an environment that satisfied his hunger for intellectual sustenance. He encountered a faculty who encouraged his literary aspirations and buoyed his confidence with intellectual conversation over afternoon teas. He found ample outlet for his writing, publishing stories, poems, essays, and criticism in the *Phillips Exeter Monthly* and parody and satire in an independent magazine. Perhaps most surprisingly, he found his literary interests did not place him with the school misfits. In the eyes of more popular classmates, he and his band of teenage intellectuals were tolerated as "licensed lunatics."[89]

Among the small circle of seriously bookish young men, Macdonald and two of his friends joined together to form their own club, the Hedonists. Outfitted in monocles, batik ties, and walking canes, the trio of teenagers modeled themselves after their heroes, H. L. Mencken, George Jean Nathan, Charles Baudelaire, and Oscar Wilde. Along with their motto "*Pour epater les bourgeois*," they inscribed their notepaper with a list of their most cherished values: "Cynicism, Estheticism, Criticism, Pessimism." The Hedonists were the first example of a persistent practice in Macdonald's life. He regularly banded together with like-minded friends in opposition to the larger society. In this case, Macdonald and his friends clearly felt themselves to be, as biographer Michael Wreszin notes, "superior to the majority in matters of culture, sensitivity, breeding."[90] Their club functioned as a noticeable (in those costumes, extremely noticeable) signal of their detachment and superiority. This separation did not, however, imply a rejection of the world of wealth and social status. Instead, he and his friends were fashioning themselves as intellectual aristocrats.

After Exeter, Macdonald followed in his father's footsteps by attending Yale in the fall of 1924. He found it a startling contrast to his prep school experience. Yale had been swept up in the rising tide of new college admissions. Its undergraduate population increased rapidly in the 1920s. The changes this brought to Yale were similar to changes effecting American colleges and universities generally. The expanding white-collar middle class looked at education to ensure their upward mobility and their increasing numbers helped alter the face of the university.[91] Instruction in the classics declined while courses in more "practical" matters increased.[92]

A growing emphasis on the utilitarian and instrumental value of higher education reached the highest levels of American education. Business schools sprang up during the decade, and business courses worked their way into an increasing number of undergraduate curriculums. Even at schools such as Yale and Princeton, among the few schools where the explicit integration of business courses was resisted, the general tenor of the age influenced the school. The *Daily Princetonian*, in an editorial likely written by Tom Matthews's friend Johnny Martin, applauded the Harvard Business School for its "legitimization of business on par with the other professions."[93] The rapid increase in admissions in the late 1920s at Yale "tended to weaken hard won-standards and deteriorate the norms of instruction. It shifted the basis of attendance to considerations of social gain and material profit."[94] At Yale, these trends further skewed the undergraduate experience toward the tangible benefits a Yale education provided and away from serious intellectual endeavor. As Macdonald saw it, "About 4/5ths of the undergraduates aspire to be Yale Men. The remaining are either the Peoria High School mental incompetent types, or 'cranks.'"[95] Presumably, he numbered himself among the cranks.

Macdonald's reaction to Yale revealed his already well-developed talent for invective. Writing to his best friend Dinsmore Wheeler, who had gone to Harvard, he declaimed, "This is a hell of a college . . . . All the intellectuals here are either 'nice boys' with a gentlemanly inclination toward the better known works of Keats and Arnold, or embryo pedants and bores. To be intellectual, say intelligent, reserved, individual, and sensitive, is to be solitary."[96] Nevertheless, he wrote prolifically and pursued intellectual camaraderie as he had in prep school. He contributed to the *Yale Lit* his freshman year, and was accepted into the prestigious Elizabethan and Lantern literary societies as a sophomore. Eventually he edited the *Lit* and a campus humor magazine, and contributed a regular column to the *Yale Daily News*.

It did not take long for him to find sympathetic friends. As at Exeter, he quickly discovered a small group of like-minded serious young writers. These included Wilder Hobson, cousin to Thornton Wilder and a serious admirer of jazz, G. L. K. Morris, a painter and later financial supporter of *Partisan Review*, and Fred Dupee, who became an English professor at Columbia. With them, he cultivated an attitude scornful of the majority of their classmates. These budding intellectuals used their devotion to literature to beat back the pressure of Yale's emphasis on success. As Matthews had, Macdonald enjoyed this psychic separation from those around him. It helped reinforce his own sense of himself while removing him from direct competition with his classmates.

For his first year at Yale, however, Macdonald kept his criticism of Yale mostly to himself, sharing his ambivalence with a few friends. His letters to Wheeler were harshly critical of Yale and its students. Yet he remained enamored of the prestige that came with good breeding. He wrote letters to his mother reassuring her that he was cultivating friendships with boys from families of wealth and distinction. He remained aristocratic in outlook, and part of his hostility toward many of his classmates might be interpreted as resentment of their competition for social favor.

Beginning in his sophomore year Macdonald began to work out his complicated feelings about Yale in public. His attacks on the faculty, which had previously been confined to his private notebooks or letters to friends, now appeared in letters to the university president and then the *Yale Daily News*. His criticism of the English department as a collection of entertainers and popularizers (already a dirty word for him), culminated in an attack on William Lyon "Billie" Phelps that was so insolent that the *News* refused to publish it. When Macdonald tried to get it printed as a handbill he was called before the dean (not his first such call onto the carpet) and forced to desist at the risk of expulsion.

Macdonald turned his attention to his fellow students and the social system that propelled Yale life. He devoted his regular *Daily News* column to an examination of college social life and its emphasis on external social emulation over internal intellectual direction. Calling his piece "Success! A little brochure on Getting Ahead at Yale," he wrote, "The one great rule for success here in New Haven was to make getting ahead your primary, secondary, and tertiary interest in college life." He claimed that "you must devotedly follow the star of success," even if it meant "trampling books, conversation, friends, and pleasures under foot" and dropping friends who were not sufficiently important. Following these rules carefully from the beginning of freshman year until Tap Day would usher you into a senior society, where you would emerge, he bitterly guaranteed, "with your social position assured, the golden aureole of success illuminating your head."[97]

Macdonald's criticism of Yale social life was essentially the same as that voiced by Owen Johnson in 1912. In Johnson's novel, Dink Stover came to realize that the success he so dearly wanted at Yale could only come at the expense of his interests and friends. Stover jeopardized his class position by developing friendships of his own with students placed outside the accepted social system because of their family, or their studiousness, or their unorthodox opinions (precisely "the grinds, the wet smacks, the lame ducks, the eccentrics" that Macdonald urged those who craved success to avoid in his column).[98] Stover's reaction was also Macdonald's, if more theatrically staged. Pressured by the members of his society, Stover ripped his fraternity pin off his chest, stomped on it and turned his back on the whole system in anger. He persevered, overcoming the ensuing social isolation, standing on principle, and still being triumphantly tapped last for Skull and Bones.[99] Johnson took comfort in the belief that it was possible to both resist the system and still enjoy its recognition.

This was naïve, but the young Macdonald seems to have shared Johnson's hopefulness. Despite his scathing attack on the entire social system, he still felt its attraction. Social success was his mother's dearest wish for her son. He expected to be selected for a senior society, though he and his coeditor of the *Lit*, Wilder Hobson, talked of refusing the honor in protest. He wanted social success, but he wanted it on his own terms, envying it while holding those who had it in contempt. Unfortunately for him, his revolt was less successful than Stover's. On Tap Day, he was left standing in the yard, an almost unprecedented slight for someone with his illustrious record. His articles had almost certainly kept him from election.

In the month's leading up to Tap Day, Macdonald's behavior had horrified his mother. She warned him to express himself more temperately after a particularly harsh review he published of a book by an English professor. He responded by making it into an issue of integrity, writing "if you mean that one should keep silent in the face of cant and lies and silliness and stupidity and injustice in order to save one's own hide, I do not." But his mother pursued her point, and when his harsh attacks on the school got him into trouble she interpreted this as vindication of her position. She accused him of deliberately sabotaging his chances of making his Yale career a success. She could not understand why he persisted in his "ridiculous pose of free-thinking radicalism," "ruthlessly disregarding" the sacrifice she and his father had made to give him this opportunity. She involved her brother George, who had been supporting the family ever since Timothy Macdonald had died. Uncle George threatened to cut off his funds (again threatening his ability to return to Yale) and tried to force him to work in a bank during the summer, in a futile attempt to make him more pliable and practical. Macdonald managed to appear contrite enough to convince the administration and his family to allow him to return for the last year of his Yale education. He split the summer between Uncle George's bank job and the Wheeler's family farm, returning to Yale for his final year in September of 1927.[100]

In his senior year, Macdonald's interests underwent a subtle shift. Up until this point all evidence pointed to his firm commitment to be a writer. His primary interest had always been literature; his heroes had been writers. For years he had modeled himself on his vision of what a writer should be: he dressed like a writer, kept a notebook because "all great writers do," and associated with those who shared his literary aspirations.[101] By his senior year, however, he was taking more history classes than English classes, and was busily adapting his ideas about what made for a great writer to the worlds of business and politics. Historian Robert Cummings notes that his critical writings of the time were increasingly infused with a vocabulary "drawn from the world of business." Where in previous years he had disdained classmates for holding to ambitions that extended no further than the world of business, now he began to favorably compare the world of business to the university. He wrote essays analyzing Henry Ford's creative genius, employing a set of criteria he had developed to measure genius in writers.[102]

It is unclear what drove this change, but contributing factors are not difficult to locate. Macdonald faced graduation and with it the necessity of finding a job. His uncle had supported the family since his father's death, but now he would be expected to contribute. His family clearly expected him to get a job and hoped he would abandon his impractical writing. Under these pressures, he may have been turning a necessity into a virtue in his discovery of positive elements in business. He was also likely influenced by the surrounding culture. His crucial college years were spent "living in a culture that valued business success and denied intellectual endeavors the laurels granted the creative geniuses of the Chamber of Commerce," as cultural historian Paula Fass vividly characterized the decade.[103] America's obsession with the stock market and its lionization of American business leaders grew apace during these years. Such values had thoroughly penetrated Yale.

Whatever the cause of the change, it is clear that the values Macdonald cherished in literature translated easily to the world of business. In essays he wrote for English classes he had tried to formulate a theory to determine what made a writer a genius. He settled on "creative power," a never very carefully defined term that often meant merely the absence of mediocrity. For him it connoted the technical mastery and vital energy that he cherished in writing. During his senior year he began to make the connection between literary greatness and "men of genius" generally. "The distinguishing mark of great men," he wrote, "is creative power." He elaborated: "the big men prove their greatness by what they do; it is not a matter for debate or nice analysis. You have their products and you can take them or leave them, but you cannot deny their existence."[104] This understanding of genius is problematic when applied to writers, since debate and nice analysis is precisely what critics do in assessing a writer's quality. Worse, the world at large certainly could and did ignore literature. When applied to business and political leaders, however, it took on greater resonance. Woodrow Wilson and Henry Ford had taken action. They had imposed themselves on the world and forced the world to take note. In a notebook collage he made of "Leaders in American Industry" Macdonald confessed his awe and terror in the face of such men. "Can an artist survive in a society dominated by such titans?" he wondered, "Will he not be, as it were, browbeaten and abashed? In the presence of such towering, bleak, massive cliffs what timid flower of art can bloom, *dare* bloom?"[105]

With these thoughts preying on his mind, Macdonald spent the latter half of his senior year looking for a job. His uncle arranged some interviews while he checked out advertising agencies. Eventually he settled on a job with Macy's, working in their executive training program. As graduation approached, and with it his entry into the world of business, his enthusiasm increased apace. In an extraordinary letter to Wheeler, he set down his feelings after a day interviewing with Macy's managers. Macdonald saw this interview as crystallizing a significant change. "My whole aim in life is, or seems to be right now, changed," he confessed. "Up to this time, as you know, literature was my be-all and end-all and my greatest ambition was to some day create it. Well, right now I honestly don't care very much whether I ever set pen to paper again." Macdonald went on to describe the new power he had encountered:

> These men were so cold, so keen, so absolutely sure of themselves, and so utterly wrapt up in business that I felt like a child before them. They were so sure of their values that I began to doubt mine. Then my courage began to return, and it occurred to me that the sort of power those men had was the dominant power in America today and that it was what I wanted for myself . . . . I tell you, Dinsmore, that American art, letters, music, culture is done. There are hundreds of business men, thousands of them that are better in their line than the best poet or painter we have today. The power is all in business: these men I saw were all of them keener, more efficient, more sure of their power than any college prof I knew.[106]

This letter reads almost as a prospectus for the magazine for which he would soon work. Macdonald immediately drew back from the extremity of this position, appending a capitalized qualification: "THIS IS ALL TOO EXAGGERATED." He reassured his friend that he had not given up on literature, but that he was eager to get into business and see what it was about.

Macdonald's heroic depiction of business could hardly stand up to the mundane reality of retail, and it did not take long at Macy's for his disillusionment to set in. He hated the work, was contemptuous of the customers, and resented the waste of his time. Worse, he was not a very good junior executive. He lacked practical sense, found it difficult to pay attention to detail, and was uncomfortable exercising authority. Within three months he knew he had made a mistake. In five months time he quit, to the relief of all parties concerned.

Macdonald landed on his feet, for his friend Hobson found him a job at *Time*. He started by writing for the business department and was soon drafted for the staff of *Fortune*, the new business magazine. "Business seems to stalk my footsteps," he wrote to a friend.[107] When Macdonald later claimed to have worked for *Fortune* solely to support himself and his mother and to subsidize his literary writing, he misrepresented his thinking at the time. Clearly he did face family pressure to find a job and contribute to the family income. But he approached his work at *Fortune* with a level of enthusiasm he later chose to forget. Though Macdonald was often unhappy at *Fortune*, the job proved a far more congenial environment than he found at Macy's or was likely to find elsewhere in the business world. He was well paid, and still found time for his own outside writing. He had found an acceptable middle ground: living by his pen, but also living well, and in closer proximity to the power and influence that simultaneously attracted and repelled him.

"Summoning a Generation to its Service"

Archibald MacLeish, T. S. Matthews, and Dwight Macdonald all walked their own particular paths to Time Inc. For MacLeish, the desire to better support his family, a growing frustration with the insular world of poetry, and a rekindled need to take a more active role in things prepared him for Henry Luce's phone call. Tom Matthews's conviction that intellectuals were ineffectual, his attraction to a life of action, and his need to set himself apart from his colleagues all made his seemingly inexplicable decision to leave the *New Republic* appear inevitable. Dwight Macdonald's adherence to a theory of literature that worshipped the creative genius for his ability to impose his will on his environment bled easily into an interest in becoming himself a great man in the world of business.

Despite these differences, the paths they were walking were parallel. Though they were separated in age by more than a decade, they each began the decade committed to pursuing intellectual life and disdainful of the economic realities that might threaten that dream, and ended the decade by backing away from their absolutist vision of intellectual life while settling into jobs as salaried journalists. In the conflict between what Van Wyck Brooks termed the creative instinct and the acquisitive instinct, they each moved toward the latter as the decade progressed.[108] The need to support his family was not enough to keep MacLeish in the law in 1923, but the desire to increase their already comfortable standard of living played a role in his decision to join *Fortune* in 1929. The *New Republic*'s troubled finances were of no concern to Matthews in 1925. By 1929 they worried him a great deal. In the early 1920s Dwight Macdonald's pantheon of heroes was reserved for writers. By 1928 Henry Ford presented himself as a plausible model worth emulating.

They were not the only ones who followed the same rough path. Manfred Gottfried was the first writer hired at *Time*, coming to the magazine straight away after graduating from Yale. He left in early 1926 to go to Paris and write a novel. Explaining his decision, he said, "for me, journalism was not a romance, but a marriage of convenience; my romance was with fiction."[109] While abroad he wrote his novel, which appeared in 1928 to strong reviews.[110] In early 1929, however, he gave up fiction to return to *Time*, where he eventually succeeded Martin as managing editor. Wilder Hobson, Macdonald's college roommate and coeditor of the Yale *Lit*, went to *Time* immediately upon graduation. Parker Lloyd Smith, an ambitious classicist and poet from Princeton, gave up his poetry to write the business department for *Time* before becoming the first managing editor at *Fortune*. He was soon joined by Russell Davenport, another literary young man who joined Luce's staff. Ralph Ingersoll had published his first book in 1924, and worked as a writer and managing editor for Harold Ross's *New Yorker* while he worked on a novel, before joining *Fortune* in 1931.

These similarities suggest the conditioning influence of the surrounding culture. In the early 1920s these writers found greater sustenance for their belief that it was possible and desirable to live a life devoted to art and disdainful of conventional careers. The prevailing intellectual discourse, with its criticism of middle-class economic and social ambitions, and its celebration of modernist art walled off from popular culture, enabled these beliefs. Intellectual aspiration depended on the insistence that financial matters were inconsequential. In the early 1920s countless writers placed art above money, at least for a while, even to the point of embracing poverty. When Edmund Wilson returned from Europe in 1919, he abandoned all hope of earning "an honest living," instead deciding he would "spend a life of simplicity, more or less poverty, and relentless application to the service of Apollo."[111]

This prevailing discourse altered as the 1920s wore on. Most of the attacks on middle-class conformity and business civilization came early in the decade. Sinclair Lewis published *Main Street* in 1920, *Babbitt* in 1922. The heyday of the little magazines was the early 1920s. By 1926 the *Little Review* had been reduced to a quarterly, before folding in 1929. *Broom* had been swept away by the censorship of the Postal Service. The *Dial*'s great influence as modernist champion had passed by mid decade and it too failed at decade's end. Its editor, Gilbert Seldes, had abandoned the world of the little magazines for the better paycheck of the *Saturday Evening Post*, writing articles "debunking" the intellectual poseurs of the decade.[112] Harold Stearns's collection of essays lambasting America for its lack of civilization came in 1923, whereupon many of the contributors, following Stearns's lead, up and left for France.[113] By the late 1920s many of these expatriates, Archibald MacLeish among them, were trickling back and looking for jobs. Many of them settled in New York City, or joined in the "great exodus toward Connecticut, the Catskills, northern New Jersey and Bucks County, Pennsylvania," all within working distance of the city.[114]

Despite a great deal of scholarship stressing the complexity of the 1920s, historians seem loathe to give up the Jazz Age depiction of New York City in the 1920s. For one "giddy and glorious" decade, literary historian Ann Douglas gushes, "New York held out to its new inhabitants an extraordinary promise of freedom and self-expression." In this telling, New York City during the 1920s represented an acme of cultural possibility, an endlessly renewable canvas for personal expression. As home to the remnants of bohemia, center of the emerging mass culture industries, not to mention Wall Street and Madison Avenue, New York attracted a generation of young people on the make, both culturally and economically. Douglas depicts New York in the 1920s as "cornering, expanding, and reinventing the nation's cultural market," and, she notes, "it summoned a far-flung generation to its service."[115] Her view echoes an editorial in the *Nation* near the end of the decade, "All over the country the ambitious and the eager, the want-to-be-wealthy and the would-be smart, have their eyes on Manhattan Island."[116] All of this recycles Malcolm Cowley's depiction of a New York filling up with remnants of his generation, who settled in New York, took jobs in advertising agencies or public relations firms, but continued to write poems and plan magazines. It ignores the implications of a generation of writers "serving" anything but their own creative muse. Historians have recovered the polyglot influences acting on intellectuals, yet overlooked the impact the decade's worship of business and success might have had on young writers.

The young intellectuals who came to New York did not find a city ripe for remaking. They found a city whose position at the heart of the emerging consumer culture disciplined more than it liberated. The 1920s saw an explosion of the culture industries—the advertising agencies, the public relations firms, the new magazines, the radio stations—all based in New York City. As Malcolm Cowley noted, as "American business entered the boom era, it needed more and more . . . public relations counselors . . . advertising artists and copywriters, it needed romancers to fill the pages of the magazines."[117] Few intellectuals relished the opportunity to function as "romancers," yet many felt the lure of success. The pull became stronger as the stock market went up and up, creating massive paper wealth and increasing the size of the ancillary managerial work force of bankers, accountants, brokers, and traders. The stock market bubble became central to the culture, even if only a small percentage of Americans held stocks (stories of chauffeurs hitting it big notwithstanding).[118] By and large, the people making money were from the same class, often from the same families, as the intellectuals. Contrary to the prevailing assumption that intellectuals and artists exist entirely separate from America's business civilization, except when they stoop to criticize it, the reality was messier. The lure of wealth and success exercised a tenacious hold on intellectuals.

Exceptions existed, of course, and many writers resisted the pressures to jump on as the bandwagon of prosperity picked up speed. But intellectuals such as MacLeish, Matthews, and Macdonald proved especially susceptible. They were all ambivalent about the worth of intellectual endeavor, fearing that as intellectuals they would be ineffective and inconsequential. Each felt the pressure to succeed and believed in his own exceptional ability. In the early decade this self-confidence manifested itself as scorn for conventional success, but as the valorization of business success intensified it found another outlet. Intellectuals could achieve success without coming to resemble the Babbitry. They could succeed while maintaining their identity as intellectuals.

Carrying this baggage, MacLeish, Matthews, Macdonald and others arrived at Time Inc. Almost immediately, the Depression dealt a severe blow to their hopes and expectations, to the ideas of success they had come to accept. Nor was the job what any of them expected. But the Depression increased the economic pressure to stay, even as it lessened the appeal. Intellectuals at Time Inc. faced two new questions. Could writing on salary for Time Inc. provide any sort of meaning or satisfaction? The answer to that question depended a great deal on the nature of Henry Luce, Time Inc., and the magazines *Time* and *Fortune*. More important, could they maintain their own writing and thus sustain a commitment to intellectual life while toiling on a journalism assembly line? Could they be journalists and intellectuals at the same time? MacLeish, Matthews, and Macdonald would find different answers to these questions in the years ahead.

CHAPTER TWO

Giving the People the Truth the Time Inc. Way

> I would like to be Alexander if I were not Socrates
> —Henry Luce, age twelve (1910)

On 3 March 1923, some 9,000 people received the first issue of a twenty-eight-page publication called *Time, The Weekly Newsmagazine*. Nobody knows how many people saw the first issue, since some subscribers were mailed two or three copies while others received none. The magazine, summarizing the week's news in twenty-two departments, was meant to package the news for easier consumption. Aimed at "every man and woman in America who has the slightest interest in the world and its affairs," *Time* would provide a summary of everything they needed to know about the world, in a format that could be read in an hour.[1] The magazine itself was rather unprepossessing for such aspirations, with a pen and ink drawing of Joe Cannon, Speaker of the House of Representatives, adorning the first cover, and pictures that looked, in Robert Benchley's description, "as if they had been engraved on pieces of bread."[2] The new venture was the brainchild of two recent Yale graduates, Briton Hadden and Henry Luce. Its debut met with, in Hadden's description, "a burst of total apathy on the part of the American public."[3]

From those meager beginnings emerged Henry Luce's media empire. *Time* overcame early struggles to become the dominant newsmagazine (a term it invented) of the century. Following *Time*, and the untimely death of Hadden in 1929, Luce published *Fortune* in 1930, a gargantuan magazine devoted to celebrating and chronicling the world of business. In 1931 the radio program and newsreel "March of Time" debuted, and Westbrook Van

Voorhis's booming voice intoned "Time Marches On!" to more than fifteen million Americans every month. And in 1936 Luce introduced *Life*, the first photo magazine in America, which soon eclipsed the venerable *Saturday Evening Post* as the nation's most popular magazine. By the late 1940s, Luce's publications reached one in five mostly middle-class Americans every week.

In an apt summary of Henry Luce's career, historian James Baughman wrote, "Had Luce died in 1940 he would have been remembered for his inventions. Instead, he lived another thirty-seven years and came to be hated . . . for his prejudices."[4] Baughman's judgment highlights a change that occurred around 1940. Until that date, Luce had been primarily interested in building his media empire. Beginning with the 1940 Wendell Willkie presidential campaign, however, he set out to use the power he had acquired. Luce's 1941 article, "The American Century," exemplified both his new desire to influence the course of American development, and the worldview he would consistently push in the coming years. Luce spent the remainder of his years working on behalf of, in his words, "God, the Republican Party, and free enterprise."[5] In pushing his views, his magazines helped shape the contours of the American foreign policy debate, mold America's midcentury self-conception as a white, middle-class nation destined to remake the world in its image, and sketch the contours of postwar corporate liberalism. In so doing, Luce developed a formidable array of enemies, especially among intellectuals.

For a long time the animosity between Luce and his critics made it difficult to view him or his magazines clearly. At the height of his influence during the 1950s and 1960s, widely inflated views of his power were commonplace. In the first book length account of the Luce empire, John Kobler wrote, "few private citizens ever wielded greater power" than Henry Luce, a man who "controlled access to millions of minds." Robert Hutchins, a friend of Luce's, agreed, "Mr. Luce and his magazines have more effect on the American character than the whole education system put together."[6] Joseph Epstein's summary of his career sounded like the newsreel summary of Charles Foster Kane's life in the movie *Citizen Kane*, which was based on Luce's "March of Time." Epstein described Luce in impressive sounding, yet ultimately meaningless terms, calling him a man of "indisputable magnitude," and proclaiming Luce's power as "obviously great," "probably unmeasurable."[7] Intellectuals were not inoculated against such hyperbole, as Gertrude Himmelfarb, Garry Wills, and Murray Kempton all published worried assessments of Time Inc.'s great power.[8]

W. A. Swanberg's 1972 biography, *Luce and His Empire* echoed this assessment, penning a highly tendentious interpretation of Luce as a power-craving, anticommunist ideologue whose personal prejudices had caused great harm to America.[9] Critics such as Swanberg overestimated the power of mass media, depending on the assumption that ideas could be injected directly into readers' minds. The power to manipulate the public had fascinated and scared intellectuals ever since the Creel Commission's great success whipping up support for the First World War.[10] Theories of public opinion emphasized the passivity of the mass audience and the ability of propaganda to direct public opinion.[11] Early criticism of mass culture depended on a passively receptive public, an assumption that Swanberg and similar critics accepted implicitly.[12]

Luce's critics also tended to overestimate the centrality of his magazines to American culture. Ironically, *Time*, *Life*, and *Fortune* had been so successful in fostering a picture of America as a middle-class society that critics came to believe in its accuracy. Time Inc. publications reached only a minority of the American public. The difficulty the press had in influencing readers was clear to see in the failed quadrennial campaigns against Roosevelt. Despite this, critics took on faith Luce's ability to influence American politics through his manipulation of the news.

These hyperbolic assessments have gradually led to more accurate, if modest, assessments of Luce's importance. As the decades have passed, so has the mythologizing of Luce's power. Now that the elections he sought to influence have faded, the Cold War he championed has ended, and the preeminence of his magazines has disappeared, he and his magazine empire begin to emerge with greater clarity.[13] Nevertheless, the earlier assessments are a striking testament to how large Luce loomed over the cultural life of the nation during the decades he described as "the American Century." They also help account for the otherwise inexplicable attraction Luce's magazines held for intellectuals such as Archibald MacLeish and T. S. Matthews.

From the start Henry Luce viewed his magazines as instruments of persuasion, as part of an educating mission. Named for what he presciently identified as the century's scarcest resource, *Time* was designed to keep busy Americans better informed. By organizing and summarizing the week's news, *Time* made its consumption more efficient. Less explicitly, Luce viewed the magazine as an antidote to the disease most perilous to American democracy, the lack of an informed and educated citizenry. *Time* magazine would provide middle-class Americans with the information they needed to govern themselves. It would educate them to their responsibilities. Luce believed an intelligent citizenry was democracy's best protection, and "the food of Intelligence is Information."[14] His magazine was designed to keep Americans well nourished with information. This pedagogical function was even more pronounced in Luce's business magazine, *Fortune*, through which Luce sought to create a new liberal business leadership.[15] Despite the vast differences between the two magazines, they were part of a shared project of instruction. Luce and his magazines set themselves up as the teacher, in some ways as the creator, of the sort of middle-class citizenry and business leadership that he felt the country needed to counteract the dangers he perceived in mass society.

This project appealed to young intellectuals who shared Luce's educational and class background, who were imbued with similar beliefs in their responsibility to exercise cultural and political leadership, and who chafed at the isolation of literary circles. Writers were driven to work at Time Inc. partially due to their ambivalence about intellectual life. Similar anxieties concerning the relationship between the place of ideas in the world of power beset Henry Luce. Intellectual life infatuated Luce even as he remained constantly aware of the divide between ideas and practical politics. Ideas attracted Luce, but he consistently refashioned a complex world into a simple worldview. Luce's own simplification and domestication of ideas became the basis of his success, as this process became one of *Time* magazine's most important innovations. Building his contradictory attitude toward intellectuals into the heart of his magazines, Luce both provided intellectuals with opportunities and circumscribed the extent of their influence.

The Missionary's Son

Born in 1898 in Tengchow, China, the son of Presbyterian missionaries, Henry Luce grew up at once part of a privileged class and cut off from the cultural elite in his own country. A curious, serious, and religious child, who composed his own sermons at age six and produced his own hand-written newspaper soon thereafter, Luce spent his youth in a walled-in missionary compound. From his father, Henry Winters Luce, a devout man driven by the desire to succeed, Luce imbibed a peculiarly strong mixture of mission and ambition. Luce's Protestantism laid heavy emphasis on the obligation to serve God through hard work and self-sacrifice. It impressed upon young Luce a deep sense of social responsibility. If Max Weber had been searching for a contemporary illustration of his Protestant work ethic, he could have done worse than the Luce family. Though Luce's religious faith carried through his life, he ultimately put his missionary impulses to work in secular fields.[16]

Except for a year when he was seven, young Luce lived outside the States until he attended Hotchkiss at age fourteen, arriving a few years after MacLeish graduated. Although Hotchkiss embodied the ideals and the prejudices of the white, Republican, Protestant upper middle class, ideas he had absorbed from afar, Luce still felt himself an outsider. He enrolled as one of a small number of scholarship boys who had to work for his keep. Arriving ill dressed in clothes a Chinese tailor had patterned on old American magazine illustrations, ignorant of American slang (the crucial currency of youth), shy and taciturn by nature, and affected by a crippling stammer, Luce faced formidable obstacles at Hotchkiss. There, and afterward at Yale, Luce overcame these impediments through hard work, excelling in the classroom through application and determination. He put together an outstanding record in both schools, edited literary magazines and school newspapers, and was tapped for membership in Yale's most prestigious secret society, Skull and Bones.

Luce capped his Yale career by winning the cherished DeForest Prize for his 1920 oration "When We Say 'America.'" This essay announced many of Luce's core beliefs about American power and mission. He catalogued America's growing strength and forecast increased international influence in the years ahead. Yet he decried the lack of purpose accompanying this growing power. "But is our greatness after all merely for the sake of greatness?" Luce questioned, "Are we big to no purpose?" In answer, Luce insisted American power must be linked to a social mission worthy of its growing international prominence. "When we say America," Luce concluded, it should mean to the world "that American interests shall be respected, . . . [that the] American business ideal [shall be] recognized" but also "that America may be counted on to do her share in every international difficulty, that she will be the great friend of the lame, the halt, and the blind among nations, the comrade of all nations that struggle to rise to higher planes of social and political organization, and withal the implacable and immediate foe of whatever nation shall offer to disturb the peace of the world."[17] This address, heavily imbued with the Wilsonian idealism of the time, was also a précis for his famous 1941 essay, "The American Century." Equally, it was a personal exhortation. Like America, Henry Luce saw himself as destined for greatness, and he was determined that his power too would serve humanity. Building on the belief that good works provided evidence of election, Luce felt that dedication to service would demonstrate that both he and his country were providentially endowed instruments of God's will.

The hubris in this view was of a piece with Luce's personality. He was simultaneously shy and arrogant. His range of social niceties was extremely limited, always sacrificed to his prodigious curiosity and his fear of wasting valuable time in pointless pursuits. He was an omnivorous conversationalist, ever eager to learn new things from people who had something to teach him, but brusque and rude to those who he believed had little to offer him.[18] Though he later became famous for his prejudices, as a young man he could be talked out of positions, convinced to rethink his ideas. He voted Democrat in 1928, wrote an article that year for the *Saturday Review of Literature* proposing the Constitution be retired as obsolete, ridiculed the idea of supply and demand as a "natural law," and concluded that conservative thinkers had failed to come up with a single compelling idea in more than one hundred years.[19] It was only with age and power that his thinking calcified and ideology consistently trumped curiosity.[20]

In the 1920s Henry Luce was a man beset by missionary ambition, full of confidence and do-gooder zeal, in active pursuit of power but with vague and fluctuating ideas of what to do with power once gained. That is not to say his views were stated tentatively—they never were—but rather that his firm political convictions were few. What convictions he had were typical of the more progressive variant of New Era thinking: he distrusted the unregulated market and the chaotic competition it encouraged; he feared democracy in the hands of an uneducated public; he believed in the ability of elites such as himself and his class to manage political institutions and administer the economy. Luce felt, as he put it, "a confidence which arises from a positive ambition and a positive determination to bring about, by conscious planning and conscious management, an ordered society."[21] To accomplish this, America needed better leadership, greater organization, renewed reliance on the expertise of its best men. Luce had no compunction about listing himself among this elite.

By the time Luce graduated from Yale in 1920, he had settled on a career in journalism as the quickest path to influence. As he wrote in a letter to his parents, "I believe that I can be of greatest service in journalistic work and can by that way come nearest to the heart of the world." Journalism served Luce's missionary impulse, with the newspaper serving as a modern pulpit. It satisfied the service ethic cultivated by his class and grown particularly strong in Luce. More important, perhaps, journalism offered a field for his growing ambition and his outsider's attraction to power and prestige.[22] Luce began discussions with Briton Hadden, a rival at both Hotchkiss and Yale, about launching a new magazine.

Like Luce, Briton Hadden was an extremely bright young man and an editorial prodigy. He dictated stories to his mother as soon as he could talk, spent a year composing a poem longer than Coleridge's *Rime of the Ancient Mariner* just to show he could do it, and published his own newspaper as a young schoolboy. Unlike Luce, he grew up in the bosom of the American upper class. The son of a stockbroker, who was in turn the son of the president of the Brooklyn Savings Bank, Hadden had illustrious connections on both sides of his family. He grew up in prosperous ease and was educated at the usual assortment of private schools.[23]

Both were hard working and determined to succeed, but while Luce still fought a stutter and tended toward a dour seriousness, Hadden was amusing, brash, and frivolous. The contrast is illustrated by Hadden's reputed quip to a passing Luce, head down as he hurried across campus, "Careful Henry, you'll drop the college."[24] All their lives Hadden and Luce seemed to arrive on common ground from opposite paths. From a mission in China and a banker's family in New York they attended Hotchkiss and Yale. From stuttering self-consciousness and brash self-confidence, they edited the *Hotchkiss Record* and *Yale Daily News*. These differences, stemming from their varied backgrounds and personalities, played a key role in shaping their magazine and the early culture of Time Inc.

Hadden, the most popular man on campus, made friends with athletes and campus politicians, "the men of action" in Time Inc. historian Robert Elson's phrase, "and he affected scorn for those whom he called 'contemplators.'" Yet Hadden was elected to the Elizabethan Club, the heart of literary Yale, and bragged of the literature he read in letters home. Though he enjoyed the recognition brought by literary attainment, he remained deeply skeptical of the "smarty high brows." Hadden shared the prevalent belief that intellectuals were cut off from American life. Intellectual, to him, was synonymous with ineffective. His distancing of himself from intellectuals identified him as a man of action, placing him at the center of Yale undergraduate life in a way no "mere intellectual" could ever emulate. By simultaneously demonstrating himself to be literary but not effete, Hadden sought the benefits of intellectual attainment without the stigma.[25]

Luce, on the other hand, devoted much of his energy to literature. Though always interested in politics and world affairs, and an adept business administrator and salesman for the campus papers, his primary writing interest was poetry. While Hadden specialized in composing editorials, Luce spent more time editing literary journals and publishing his poems. As school friend Culbreth Sudler remembered, Luce's favorite poet was Milton, probably for the same reasons he appealed to the young Archibald MacLeish. Luce "said he wanted to be a poet," Sudler recalled, "He would have liked to be as good as Milton."[26] His pursuit of poetry seems to have subsided only after he took Henry Seidel Canby's advanced writing course. The class included Stephen Vincent Benét and Thornton Wilder and was often visited by recent alumni, among them MacLeish, John Farrar, and Philip Barry. Struggling to measure up to such competition, Luce perhaps concluded that his gifts lay elsewhere. He retained an attraction to intellectual life, however, writing in a later editorial in the *News*, "those who are entrusted with the guardianship of things of the spirit should . . . see to it that intellectual activity becomes increasingly and notably characteristic of this place."[27]

More than limited talent turned Luce away from literature. His ambition led him to seek bigger fields to conquer, in arenas closer to political and social power. As he wrote to his parents from Oxford in 1920, where he spent a year, "My desire is to go into public life and whatever I do in the next ten years is preparatory to that . . . publishing? . . . business?"[28] Here his social discomfort and continuing outsider status played a key role in attaching him to Hadden. Hadden's confident and light manner attracted Luce, the first of many times when Luce felt the pull of men more at ease with power, privilege, and prestige. While Luce could cultivate relationships when they might prove to his advantage, he could never have pulled off Hadden's coup in getting a job with Herbert Bayard Swope at the *New York World*. Having sneaked into Swope's office to ask for a job, Hadden finally won over the skeptical editor by claiming, "Mr. Swope, you're interfering with my destiny."[29] Luce envied such confidence and the accompanying sense of entitlement. Though attracted to ideas and aware of the talents of the poets, he shared Hadden's tendency to counterpose the effete and ineffective intellectual with the worldly and sophisticated man of action. He admired men such as Benjamin Disraeli and Theodore Roosevelt, who could successfully balance intellectual interests with political power. Like these heroes, Luce increasingly gave pride of place to politics. While he remained enamored of intellectuals, he never again identified himself as one.

Together this "strangest of partnerships" launched a magazine empire that would place this attitude toward intellect and action at its heart.[30] *Time* magazine owed much of its success to its ability to keep a recurring tension in balance, one aptly symbolized by Luce's seriousness and Hadden's frivolity, by Luce's awe of intellectuals and Hadden's disdain. *Time* sought simultaneously to inform and entertain. At a time when the news market was segregated between serious newspapers and journals of opinion, such as the *New York Times* or the *Literary Digest*, on the one hand, and tabloids such as the *New York Daily News* and the *Graphic* on the other, *Time* positioned itself between the poles.[31] *Time*'s credibility depended on its ability to serve as a guide to contemporary politics and culture. Its readability depended on its ability to present information in a distinctive medium and entertaining idiom. Taking intellectuals and ideas seriously shored up its credibility; its distinctive style simplified and therefore diluted its content. Ideas were thus simultaneously deployed and domesticated. The magazine Luce hoped would educate and edify middle-class readers proved better at exploiting and assuaging their cultural insecurities.

Organizing and Managing the News

Though the first golden age of magazine publishing ended in the 1920s with the rise of entertainment competition from movies and radio, the early years of the decade were still a propitious time to start a magazine. Low postage rates and decades of technological innovation, including rotary printing presses, conveyor systems, and multicolor picture reproduction, lowered costs and increased capabilities. Capital was relatively easy to raise, and with radio in its infancy, magazines faced no competition for rapidly increasing national advertising dollars. A white-collar middle class swelling in size provided both a target for national advertisers and a market for new magazines.[32] Reaching this expanding middle class and exploiting its needs and insecurities proved a durable key to success, but advertisers were far quicker than publishers to recognize and take advantage of the opportunity.[33] The character of a new white-collar readership was barely understood by most publishers and its importance was largely ignored.

The three great magazine success stories of the decade, *Reader's Digest*, *New Yorker*, and *Time*, all owed their prosperity to this expanding middle-class market.[34] Of the new magazine impresarios, however, only the *New Yorker*'s ever-surprising Harold Ross had a clear sense of the market he was trying to reach. Noting that many large New York retailers did not need the national advertising they purchased as much as they needed targeted advertising in a few markets, Ross recognized an opportunity for a magazine catering to the urban sophisticate. If he could reach these readers, a modest circulation would translate into huge advertising revenues. To that end, he tailored his magazine's content to an urban milieu by exploiting the decade's Jazz Age culture and consciously catering to his readers desire to differentiate themselves from the provincial middle class. Ross made this separation explicit in his famous prospectus, when he announced the *New Yorker* was not for the "little old lady from Dubuque." It was a formula that underwrote the *New Yorker*'s success for most of the twentieth century.[35]

The founders of *Reader's Digest*, Dewitt and Lila Wallace, on the other hand, stumbled upon their success. They took an old formula, the eclectic magazine built on contributions culled from other sources, and updated it by trimming the collected articles down to their bare bones and including only articles they thought "constructive." The magazine prospered by providing the "little old lady from Dubuque" with an inexpensive condensation of articles appearing elsewhere, all of them selling an optimistic patriotism and a message of individual self-help. By providing a smattering of culture and entertainment to the middle class at a low price, the *Digest* became the most popular magazine in the world. Yet the Wallaces had originally conceived their magazine as directed toward a narrower readership: college graduates (predominantly women) with intellectual interests. Its extensive popularity caught them completely by surprise.[36]

Time's founders also aimed for an audience among the newly college-educated, though a broader audience than the *New Yorker*'s. As Hadden and Luce wrote in their 1922 prospectus, they sought to produce a magazine that "adapted itself to the time which busy men are able to spend on simply keeping informed." The audience they had in mind was the educated middle class, sophisticated or not. Estimating that there were already more than one million college graduates in the United States, *Time* was "aiming at every one of these."[37]

Time, the name they settled on after experimenting with *Facts*, would summarize the week's news in a series of departments. Their magazine would be pithy and brief, using a distinctive style and terse language to get the news "off its pages into the minds of its readers." From the beginning Hadden and Luce dispensed with a disinterested presentation of the news. Contrasting itself with the influential *Literary Digest*, which, "in giving both sides of a question, gives little or no hint as to which side it considers to be right," *Time* would give "both sides, but clearly indicate which side it believes to have the stronger position." It would have certain "prejudices" (a word perhaps inspired by H. L. Mencken's popular series of books of that title), including distrust toward the increasing size and cost of government, "a respect for the old, particularly in manners," and "an interest in the new, particularly in ideas." Overall, however, it would be less interested in advancing a specific politics, and more interested in its primary mission, "to keep men well-informed." In sum, the prospectus went on, "the magazine is one of news, not argument, and verges on the controversial only where it is necessary to point out what the news *means*."[38]

In practice, this meant a magazine that departed from the journalistic convention of giving equal space to opposing views, substituting the authority of a single voice in its place. To this end, the magazine would be written anonymously, as if produced by a single writer. The result was an innovation not properly understood at the time. Ever since the old partisan press had been eclipsed in the late nineteenth century, news had been separated from opinion. Among the higher-quality newspapers, news coverage sought impartiality while reserving advocacy for the editorial page. *Time*'s editorial judgments would instead be woven into its coverage. What read like a refreshing insistence on "telling it like it is" obscured a structure for managing the news.

Though the prospectus identified the potential audience as the college educated, Luce and Hadden had little knowledge of their readership. They conceived their magazine as an aid to the man too busy to wade daily through the *New York Times* or other comparable big city papers (each issue of which had as much content as the average novel, as a journalism professor of the day observed). For these readers, *Time* would provide a much-needed summary.[39] In this it would be distinctive both from the more issue-oriented *Literary Digest* and from the *World's Work*, which had pioneered many of the features of the news magazine, but combined lengthy articles of analysis with summaries of the week's happenings.[40]

Luce and Hadden had correctly identified the growing ranks of the college educated as an underserved market, but they misunderstood the needs of their audience. The vast majority of Americans suffered not from too much news, but from too little. For those from middle-sized cities where the local papers printed little national and almost no foreign news, *Time* came to function as a national newspaper. Luce and Hadden remained unaware that their magazine was filling this need until they traveled around the country and actually saw how little national and foreign news even a paper the size of the *Cleveland*

Plain Dealer carried. *Time*'s circulation was strongest in medium-sized cities, suggesting that its success stemmed more from its ability to provide national and international news to those who had previously done without than from its ability to summarize for those inundated with too much information.[41]

Such success was still years down the road, however, when the pair of twenty-three year olds polished their prospectus in early 1922. Renting a small office in New York, Luce and Hadden set to work in earnest. They drew on their connections for advice and money. They solicited and received feedback from Henry Seidel Canby, Herbert Bayard Swope, Walter Lippmann, and a number of other journalism notables. Their idea received a range of reactions, from mild encouragement to outright skepticism, but all those consulted recommended major alterations to the basic concept. Confident of their formula, however, they resisted all attempts to change it. Instead they used their contacts to master their areas of inexperience, including the intricacies of direct-mail campaigns, the mechanics of subscription drives, and the nuts and bolts of incorporation. Raising the necessary capital proved more difficult than expected. Thanks to their Skull and Bones connections, they had easy access to people with the necessary money, but neither Luce nor Hadden was an effective pitchman. Luce was too brusque and artless, and too honest about the risks. Hadden pushed too hard. He called his technique "the groining iron," named after a medieval torture implement, and exhausted prospects likely noted the aptness of the analogy. Eventually, with the help of Hadden's cousin (T. S. Matthews's friend from Princeton) Johnny Martin, they managed to raise $86,000 in capital and decided to take the plunge.[42]

The next step was hiring a staff. Hadden and Luce's early hires for *Time* drew extensively on their college connections. Of the first twenty *Time* writers, editors, and business managers, fourteen were from Yale. They were attracted by the pair's missionary zeal, and by the opportunity to write for pay in a growing and ambitious organization. Canby sent Luce and Hadden their first writer, Manfred Gottfried, a Yale senior and aspiring novelist. Gottfried later described why he chose *Time* over more-established outlets: "Canby had sent me to a series of editors. All their offices were grubby, and, what was worse, their attitudes towards their jobs seemed grubby . . . The office of Hadden and Luce was just as grubby, but their attitude was different. They were two young men who thought they had something useful and profitable to do and they intended to do it."[43]

With a staff and the necessary capital in place and a subscription list of 6,000, *Time* went to press. Total sales of the first issue were less than 9,000 and by year's end had yet to reach 20,000, despite prepublication hopes of a subscription list of over 25,000. Its competitor, the *Literary Digest*, held a circulation of over 900,000.[44] *Time*'s appearance was drab, the writing frequently fell flat, and the behind-the-scenes departments were often incompetent. Hiring some of Hadden's friends to handle the mailing led to the disastrous distribution of the first issues. An early issue of the magazine went to press with a blank back page after they failed to sell a suitable ad, breaking one of the cardinal rules of advertising (never leave the most valuable space blank). This provoked the advertising director to quit in protest. Nevertheless, the magazine's sales steadily climbed. By the mid-1920s *Time* was financially secure. In 1930 circulation passed 300,000, enabling Luce to start a second magazine, *Fortune*. By the end of the 1930s *Time* was the most important newsmagazine in America, and Time Inc. a media empire. The *Literary Digest*, on the other hand, had folded in 1938. It had been losing circulation to *Time* for years, and when its straw poll picked a decisive Landon victory over Roosevelt in 1936, it was doomed. (*Fortune*, on the other hand, had used its new poll to correctly predict the size of the Roosevelt landslide.)

Time succeeded thanks to a deft—if accidental—alchemy. It combined twentieth-century organizational principles with nineteenth-century cultural prejudices. Its structure was heavily indebted to the Fordist thinking of the era. *Time* organized both the production and the presentation of the news. It manufactured journalism according to assembly line procedures and it organized the news for more efficient consumption.[45] Putting together the magazine meant sorting through piles of *New York Times* clippings and reproducing them in summary form. A staff of female researchers did the background work and fact checking, the writers took the week's events and turned them into brief, readable, and compelling summaries, and the editors did the rewriting necessary for space and overall coherence. Hadden and Luce needed skilled writers, therefore, and those they hired were noteworthy for their literary aspirations and ability. In addition to aspiring young graduates, Luce and Hadden solicited contributions from earlier connections. The poets Luce met in Canby's class helped out: Archibald MacLeish contributed the education section, Steven Vincent Benét joined the staff, and John Farrar, the editor of the *Bookman*, often wrote literary columns. Other moonlighters included Mark Van Doren, who wrote the education column for part of 1924.[46]

Aspiring young writers were drawn to *Time* despite its anonymous journalism. For many of the established writers who contributed in the early days, the anonymity was probably a blessing. A Farrar or Van Doren could whip off the weekly column, collect his paycheck, and concentrate on other work. *Time* also attracted a number of writers who aspired to nothing more than joining the class of literary professionals that had arisen to meet the expanded needs of mass-circulation magazines. They avoided much of the drudgery of reporting, concentrating exclusively on writing, and earned a comfortable living at the same time. Nevertheless, the heavy editing and the need to adopt a house style did require a discipline many writers resisted. The early staff was characterized by high turnover with a small band of stalwarts churning out much of the copy.

Time's editors organized and presented the week's news in innovative ways. In so doing, they offered middle-class readers an easy means of familiarizing themselves with the key events in national politics, happenings in the rest of the world, and the latest developments in art, literature, music, theater, and a host of other fields. Employing a colorful, terse, and strong style that relied heavily on memorable descriptions and repeatable epigrams, *Time* always left the reader with a clear sense of what the magazine thought of the week's developments. By providing a weekly exercise in self-improvement, *Time* functioned like an updated Chatauqua, the adult education camps of the turn of the century that stressed cultural enrichment.[47] Like Chatauquas, *Time* provided its education in a lively manner designed to make reading it enjoyable. *Time* may have been good for you, but it went down more like ice cream than Castor oil.

Time's key innovation was to push the organization of the news further than anyone had before. Chaos is the law of nature, it used to be said, and order the dream of man. If so, nature was well reflected in the newspapers of the early twentieth century. They contained a great deal of information, all crammed together in an unwieldy mishmash. Reflecting the era's drive toward greater control, whether in economics (fixing the harmful effects of competition through consolidation and association), industry (Taylorism and its "rationalization" of industrial production), or personal behavior (Prohibition), *Time* organized the news for more effective and efficient consumption. By breaking the news down into component departments, *Time* provided an easy organizing framework, and also created space for departments such as religion or the media that were poorly covered in the daily newspaper.

Time summarized not just news, but cultural developments as well. Its cultural departments concentrated on providing overviews of the painters, authors, and musicians "most in the public eye," and lists of books to have read. The very first issue offered sketches of the members of the Algonquin circle, catching readers up on the ins and outs of New York's literary scene. It also introduced readers to "a new kind of literature abroad in the land, whose only obvious fault is that no one can understand it." Discussing James Joyce and T.S. Eliot, the article managed in one short column to convey that, to "those in on the secret" the new modernists represented the "greatest achievement in modern letters." Their work, however, was largely unreadable, *Time* claimed, quoting the last eight lines of *The Wasteland* to score this point. The style was justified, *Time* concluded, by a new theory of "literature as self-expression."[48] The overall effect of cultural coverage such as this was not only to keep readers up to date with what was happening in the most advanced circles, but also to equip them with a pleasing sense of superiority. This first issue's patronizing domestication of modernism reflected *Time*'s effort to bolster the shaky cultural self-confidence of its middle class readers. The magazine's concern with the cultural tastes of these readers mirrored one of the dominant trends of the time, as a national cultural machinery developed to shape and form middle-class tastes.[49] Unlike efforts such as the Book-of-the-Month club, however, *Time*'s quick and condescending summaries took the place of directly experiencing new artistic creations. In this it encouraged its readers to suspect that intellectual culture was essentially hollow. *Time*'s sniping at the ridiculous in modernist literature mirrored other 1920s efforts to abase upper-class culture before an allegedly democratic public.

A recurring characterization of journalism in the 1920s paired the two Walters, Lippmann and Winchell, as representative of the divided directions in which journalism was headed.[50] On the one hand, the reasoned and moderate Walter Lippmann represented the growing professionalization of journalism. He bemoaned the irrationality of a public unable to govern itself and called for professional experts to take over more of the administrative functions of democracy. The sort of managed society Lippmann envisioned required a reasoned, responsible journalism, speaking to the (educated) public in measured and considered language.[51] Luce shared Lippmann's gravity, his increasing trust in disinterested expertise as a bulwark against the highly interested and irrational vagaries of public opinion. Both viewed an enlightened journalism as a necessary precondition to progressive reform.

Walter Winchell, on the other hand, represented everything Lippmann and his colleagues wanted to eradicate in journalism. Loud, brash, self-promoting, Winchell emerged in the 1920s as the other most famous newsman in America. Contrasted with the patrician Lippmann, Winchell was proudly plebeian. He was, as Neil Gabler's insightful biography demonstrates, a voice for the disenchanted and disenfranchised. He symbolized the arrival and the ascendance of the masses in American cultural life. Winchell's gossip served to open the lives of celebrities to public scrutiny, fueling the decade's exaltation of success even as it cut the individual star down to size. The great power Winchell wielded over Broadway seemed to be exercised on behalf of the common people, though Winchell himself was accountable to no one as long as his column sold newspapers.

If forced to choose between Lippmann and Winchell, Hadden and Luce would surely have sided with the respectable Lippmann. They had solicited his advice from the beginning, and they conceived of themselves as engaged in a common endeavor. Indeed, Luce's justification for *Time*, with its emphasis on providing citizens with the information necessary for self-government, drew heavily on Lippmann's 1920 essay *Liberty and the News*. *Time* shared more with Winchell, however, than Hadden and Luce cared to recognize: the newsmagazine wed the seriousness of Lippmann to the gossip-propelled, snappy style of Winchell. Though Hadden disparaged the tabloid audience Winchell wrote for as "gumchewers," his interest in vivid language and his full-fledged embrace of the frivolousness of the 1920s marked important connections with the self-proclaimed Bard of Broadway.[52]

Hadden had long been interested in stylistic innovation. Though the early issues of *Time* did not properly reflect this (probably because of the pressures of getting the magazine launched), over time the magazine developed a distinctive voice that brought it both attention and criticism. Hadden drew on his own predilection for Homer, adapting the poet's double adjectives and inverted sentences. If Homer had his "high helmed Hector" or his "wine dark sea," *Time* wrote of "white-crested Senator Johnson" or, more commonly, used more abrasive descriptions such as "snaggle-toothed," "weed-whiskered," or "beady-eyed."[53] Hadden fully indulged his enthusiasm for slang, wit, epigram, and aphorism. *Time* shared these traits with the other notable magazine successes of the decade, mirroring the *Readers Digest*'s emphasis on brevity and the *New Yorker*'s penchant for wit. It combined the two to successfully ride the zeitgeist of the era. As Charles and Mary Beard aptly characterized the dominant cultural mood of the era, "to be brisk, curt, concise, telegraphic, and bright became the verbal mode of the hour."[54] The Beards could have had both Winchell and *Time* in mind when they penned those words. Both exploited the era's enthusiasm for wordplay to coin new compound words ("newsmagazine" had been one of the first) like "cinemaddict," which each claimed to have originated. Both employed euphemism to skirt the libel laws and give readers "the inside dope." For *Time*, "great and good friend" emerged as the house term for mistress, while Winchell employed "Adam-and-Eveing it." *Time*'s penchant for multiple adjectives (Homeric justification notwithstanding), its inverted syntax ("backward ran sentences until reeled the mind," in Wolcott Gibbs's famous *New Yorker* parody),[55] and its often sneering tone all paralleled the mood of Winchell's heyday.

Time's link to the tabloids also extended to its narrative structure. Drastically departing from the summary lead and inverted pyramid structure that made newspaper writing so deadly dull, *Time*'s articles borrowed the narrative technique of the story. Johnny Martin told newspaper editors, "Our writers are required to present in each piece of any length a story with definite literary form, a beginning, a middle and an end."[56] The respectable newspapers of the day provided information, not story. While the big city tabloids had adopted the storytelling model, in their emphasis on continuing scandals and crime stories, *Time* was unique in combining the two competing models. It sought to convey a weekly summary of information but relied on storytelling to capture attention and accomplish its goal of "getting the news off the page and into the reader's head." In so doing, it not only synthesized different modes of conveying the news, but it also brought techniques originally developed by the tabloids to a middle-class publication.

Though this balance between high and low contributed to *Time*'s success, the combination contained built-in instabilities. The cultural space Hadden sought for the magazine is suggested in his response to the advent of the *New Yorker*. The *New Yorker* prepublication announcement irked Hadden. He and his cousin Niven Busch wrote a review of the new magazine, quoting the opinion of a "real" old lady from Dubuque whom they had invented: "The editors of the periodical you forwarded are, I understand, members of a literary clique. They should learn that there is no provincialism so blatant as that of the metropolitan who lacks urbanity," and concluded, "They were quite correct, however, in their original assertion. The *New Yorker* is not for the old lady in Dubuque."[57] The review sought to separate *Time*'s audience both from the provincialism the *New Yorker* imputed to Americans outside the cultural hub of New York, and from the literary and intellectual crowd the *New Yorker* targeted.

But it was an open question whether the cultural space Hadden sought, separated both from the snobbishness of the intellectuals on the one side and the provincialism and materialism of the Babbitry on the other, existed in sufficient measure to allow the magazine to succeed. This may have been why Hadden seemed content with a modest circulation and actually sabotaged efforts to increase circulation in more benighted areas of the country. When *Time* conducted an extensive circulation drive in the south, Hadden, acting from a desire to needle his new audience, purposefully printed criticism of lynchings and addressed male African American southerners as Mr., setting off a chain reaction of angry letters and canceled subscriptions.[58] Luce took no such pleasure in offending readers, nor did he have any qualms about a readership of middle-class businessmen. While Hadden relished Sinclair Lewis's characterization of Babbitry, it seems to have offended Luce. Luce managed to move *Time* to Cleveland in 1925 to lower costs (he accomplished this while Hadden vacationed in Europe). There, he enjoyed mingling with the local business class as a much bigger fish than he had been in New York. Hadden, on the other hand, had a miserable time. In New York, Hadden had viewed the provincial middle-class businessman as a curiosity. In Cleveland, he was surrounded by them. Spotting a particularly noxious example of the self-satisfied, complacent businessman he would scream "Babbitt!" at him at the top of his lungs. His unhappiness in Cleveland suggests the pressures Hadden felt: disdaining the intellectuals clustered around the *New Yorker*, the *New Republic* and the *Nation*, yet desperately fearful of sinking into middle-class conformity. The Cleveland experiment did not last, and Hadden returned the magazine to New York City in 1927 (while Luce vacationed in Europe).[59]

If Hadden's behavior belied a fear he was editing a magazine designed to serve the class he despised, Luce had difficulties of his own with *Time*'s direction. Luce especially wanted *Time* to be taken seriously. While he viewed the newsmagazine as a business venture that could bring him wealth and prestige, and possibly a political career, Luce seriously believed his magazine should play a key role in creating both better-informed and culturally educated citizens. Unlike Hadden, Luce was not bothered that these better citizens would be drawn from the ranks of the business class. On the contrary, he believed that business might supply the educated, service-minded elite needed to take up the mantle of proper leadership the country needed. When Hadden died in February 1929 of a blood infection, the field was clear for Luce to take *Time* down a more serious and ambitious path.

The form and tone of *Time*, however, militated against its achieving Luce's high aspirations. As the magazine steadily increased in circulation it began to attract critics. Emphasizing *Time*'s tortured syntax, heavy reliance on descriptive adjectives of dubious taste, use of description to color the interpretation of individuals and events presented, and reliance on an anonymous voice that conveyed an unearned authority to its interpretation of events, critics claimed that *Time* sacrificed objectivity for both entertainment and the propagation of its politics. They pointed out the wide disparity in individual characterizations, which corresponded with *Time*'s opinion of the subject. Though the most notorious example, the use of "Jew Blum" to characterize the French labor leader and Prime Minister Leon Blum, dated from the 1930s, the basic technique emerged earlier. A more commonplace description was *Time*'s characterization of New York mayor Fiorello La Guardia as "fat, rancid, garlic-smelling."[60] Despite such evidence of editorial animus, it was difficult to detect a consistent politics behind *Time*'s style during its first decade. Though *Time*'s tone in the 1920s might have been more sneering than prejudiced, as biographer James Baughman concludes, by the end of the 1930s, criticism of *Time*'s distortions increased as political issues took on a greater importance.[61]

Criticism of *Time*'s failure to be objective left Luce unfazed. As he explained, "never, at least with my knowledge and consent, did TIME ever claim impartiality. TIME's charter is that TIME will tell—will tell the truth about what happened, the truth as it sees it. Impartiality is often an impediment to truth. TIME will not allow the stuffed shirt of impartiality to stand in the way of telling the truth as it sees it."[62] The qualifying "as it sees it" saved Luce from having to equate his magazine with objective truth, but the passage revealed his conviction that *Time* could better judge truth than its readers. It was, as Baughman observes, "a magazine of supremely confident young men," who never seemed to doubt their ability to correctly judge the events of the day, and to convey their conclusions not with the qualifications familiar to journalism, but with a voice of anonymous authority.[63]

The magazine dispensed with objectivity largely because of its own uncomplicated certainty. What Luce's view of journalistic objectivity meant, from the very beginning, was that *Time* would articulate the views of its editors. It is equally clear that these views would not be presented as opinion, but as fact. Though Luce never made this explicit, it was built into the structure of the magazine. Here is the key to *Time*'s success and its most troubling aspect: in summarizing it rendered a complex world simple; in presenting opinion as fact, it stripped the reader of his or her critical capacities. Setting out to equip citizens with the information necessary to govern themselves, it instead supplied them with the opinions they need not develop on their own. Luce desired more than to provide his readers with the information necessary for self-government. He intended to outfit them with the interpretive lenses that they would need to properly view the world. As an early in-house history of Time Inc. described the company's mission, *Time* intended to "Give the public the truth we think it must have."⁶⁴ This philosophy held a deep appeal for intellectuals looking for their own avenues to cultural influence and authority, but it would also prove to be the source of conflict between Luce and these same intellectuals when they proved unwilling to render the world in quite the way he wished.

The Tycoon's Own Magazine

By 1928 Henry Luce wanted his own magazine. He and Hadden had initially decided to swap responsibilities for the editorial and business ends of *Time* annually. In practice, however, Luce demonstrated a better grasp of financial affairs and was more comfortable in the milieu of businessmen, while Hadden's one year managing the business proved the organization ran better if he stuck to editing the magazine. From then on Luce handled most business matters and Hadden carried most of the editorial weight. Luce still had a voice in the content of the magazine, but it remained largely Hadden's show. Though its flip irreverence helped account for *Time*'s popularity and notoriety, it left Luce cold. By the late 1920s he was planning a new magazine, one nearer to his heart in content and style.

As a magazine intended to chronicle American industrial life, *Fortune* fit Luce's requirements. Its founding provided a perfect instance of sound business opportunity meshing seamlessly with the needs and desires of its proprietor. A business magazine seemed the obvious choice around Time Inc. The growing surplus of material for *Time*'s business department, despite repeated expansions of its space, prompted the original idea. Many of the unused items suggested larger stories to Luce, addressing issues too detailed and complex for *Time*'s summary handling.⁶⁵

The official history of Time Inc. credits Luce's decision to start a business magazine to his "intuitive sense of the way the current of society ran." But it was not Luce's intuition that was responsible for his success, here or elsewhere, but rather what he did with ideas others were talking about. The preeminent place accorded business in American life during these years could not escape notice, even by Calvin Coolidge. The president's declaration that "the business of America is business" served as both summation of an era and justification for Luce's magazine. *Fortune* was not even first into the field, as *Nation's Business* and *Forbes* had existed for years and *Business Week* (the old *System* reworked into a weekly) began publication in early 1929.

The existing business magazines, however, were entirely conventional, built around the interests of the small businessman or salesman who was presumed to make up the lion's share of the market. Newsprint paper reinforced their emphasis on covering business news of the moment and their focus on being of practical service to businessmen. *Fortune* positioned itself instead to capture the attention of the corporate world, to reach the growing numbers of upper managers and executives. Luce recognized that the current business magazines paid too little attention to this group. If reading *Business Week* was one more task for the busy businessman, reading *Fortune* would be a welcome respite from the office, an experience to be savored at home. As Luce wrote in the prospectus, "unless we are prepared to believe that America's industrialists are chiefly concerned with the technique of sales departments, with the stale Get-Rich-Maxims of onetime errand boys, the subject matter of such a magazine as *Forbes* must be thought piddling and inexpressibly dull."[66] In contrast, *Fortune* would seek a small but exclusive circulation. By setting out to "portray Business in all its heroic present-day proportions," *Fortune* was seeking to be the "Tycoon's own magazine."[67] Luce knew there were only a small number of potential readers available (although he underestimated how few), but he knew that advertisers would pay dearly to reach precisely this audience. Not only did the managerial elite have sufficient income to attract dealers in luxury goods such as boats, cars, clothes, and jewelry, but they also controlled the purse strings of their companies, making them a perfect target for corporate industrial advertising. Aiming at a growing business class that advertisers had trouble reaching proved the most important element in *Fortune*'s success. Celebrating this class and its achievements became the early raision d'être of the venture.

Luce and his staff built their magazine around the idea that business was now the "prime determinant of society."[68] The original name for the magazine, *POWER*, put this as plainly as possible. Given that it was "a generally accepted commonplace that America's great achievement has been business," as *Fortune*'s prepublication advertising announced, there was a pressing need for a magazine that could reflect business "in ink and paper and word and picture as the finest skyscraper reflects it in stone and steel and architecture."[69] *Fortune* set out to celebrate business in all its gaudy late 1920s excess. Formatted like an oversized art magazine (an imposing 11½ by 14 inches), printed on heavy, "wild wove antique" paper, hand sewn between heavy board covers, and needing twenty-seven separate presses to assemble the letterpress, offset, and gravure sections, each *Fortune* weighed in at more than two pounds an issue.[70] The monthly magazine was priced at an outlandish dollar an issue, at a time when the other business magazines cost less than a quarter.

Thomas Maitland Cleland, a well-known graphic artist who worked in a flamboyant Beaux Arts style, signed on as art director. Cleland executed the first cover himself, establishing the magazine's identity with an illustration of a giant wheel of industry mounted over a bustling sixteenth-century port. At the base of the wheel an allegorical female figure unveils cornucopia, herself presided over by an angel. Cleland deftly combined timeless images of abundance and fecundity with a historical depiction of the origins of our present "fortune."[71] He thus portrayed business as reaching back to our heroic past, as the author of our prosperous present, and as sanctified by God. Higher claims for business centrality are difficult to imagine.[72]

The aesthetic valorization of business continued inside the magazine.[73] In his drive to produce the world's most beautiful magazine, Luce knew he needed to find a way to make industrial production visually compelling. He found his answer in a series of images of Otis Steel taken by the young photographer Margaret Bourke-White. Though less striking and grandiose than her later work, the Otis Steel pictures amply displayed Bourke-White's gift for capturing the gargantuan size and scale of steel production and imbuing it with a stark, dark beauty. *Fortune* proved the perfect venue for Bourke-White to develop her style, a deft melding of corporate promotion and modernist aesthetics. Her emphasis on the beauty to be found in the size, scale, and shape of industrial production aligned nicely with *Fortune*'s identity. The cold formalism of her compositions, her tendency to deploy people only to enhance the scale of the machine, echoed *Fortune*'s early neglect of the human component of industrial production and, more generally, modernism's mistrust of the masses.[74]

Bourke-White's work was the centerpiece of early issues of *Fortune* (she was the only person credited in the table of contents for the first issue, as writers were not granted a byline). Two photographers who worked along similar lines, William Rittase and Russell Aikins, soon joined Bourke-White on the magazine. While their aesthetic was the most striking element in *Fortune*, it was only one of a number of visual styles the magazine employed. Luce experimented with new ways of conveying information graphically and developed an expansive definition of industrial society that allowed for the inclusion of subjects that lent themselves to visual depiction. Early issues included a ten-page spread on the use of color in industry, beautifully painted maps and photographs of art objects displayed in museum settings, including paintings, sculptures, jewels, and even the Peacock Throne of Persia. Almost every issue also included a full-page portrait of a corporate chieftain, frequently executed by the British artist Sir William Orpen at $15,000 apiece.[75] His style, and that of others such as E. H. Baker, stuck to determined modernist lines, occasionally employing a mild cubist effect. All of these visual styles cohered around a vision that glorified industrial life, emphasizing the immense size and earth-altering scope of production and the pinnacles of art available for consumption, all resting in the assured hands of business executives.

The writing in the magazine struck a balance among the celebratory, the hortatory, and the merely informative. Each issue contained a dozen or so major articles. The lengthiest tended to be the corporation stories, a form *Fortune* invented. These involved an in-depth look at a single corporation. Frequently accompanying these articles were profiles of the heads of the corporations. At least one of these in every issue tended to be of a major industrial producer, whose vast factories and furnaces lent themselves to the Bourke-White treatment. The other was often a service retailer such as a major hotel. The success of the corporation story quickly led to an expansion to a series of articles covering an entire industry, such as oil or cotton. These articles combined an in-depth look at one of the major corporate players in the industry with an overview of the defining characteristics of the industry as a whole. There was often at least one long analytical piece, beginning with Luce's own 10,000-word essay on the rise of branch banking. Other major efforts included examinations of the industrial base of American cities such as South Bend or Pittsburgh. Mixed in with such weighty fare were articles chronicling developments in business, such as the use of color in product design or George Washington Hill's assault on good taste in advertising. Both of these are characteristic examples, as they lent themselves to the visual display *Fortune* always sought. Lighter still were the frequent lifestyle pieces on yacht racing, wine, swimming pools, or how to live in Chicago on $25,000 a year.[76]

Luce's sense of mission prevented the magazine from devolving into a pure celebration of business accomplishment and wealth, even before the Depression forced changes in *Fortune*'s identity. Luce was careful in his choice of subject matter. He highlighted corporate leaders he felt worthy of emulation with extended profiles, while more powerful men, who failed to use their power as Luce thought they should, received colder notice. The existence of a business opportunity in the form of an under exploited market was not enough for Luce. Ever the missionary's son, he needed to justify to himself the larger purpose his new magazine would serve.

Looking at America in the 1920s, Luce was concerned with what he considered "the inadequacy of motive in modern life." America was the first nation in history whose people had enough to live on, but, Luce lamented, "the best of those 120 million cannot find enough to live *for*."[77] In the past purpose had been provided by war, the pursuit of personal honor, or dedication to a cause (usually religiously sanctioned). None of these retained a grip on the modern imagination, and Luce searched for "an attachment to a purpose which transcends a single life—" the equivalent of his own religiously inspired sense of purpose—that would be compelling in modern America.[78] The possibility he offered also reached back to the past. "America today," Luce lamented, "is the most amazing example in history of a civilization in search of an aristocratic principle." He borrowed the idea from one of his heroes, Disraeli, whom he quoted in every speech he made during these years: "England is not governed by an aristocracy; it is governed by an aristocratic principle which binds together all those whose nature it is to aspire and excel."[79] For Luce, the aristocratic principle, with its recognition of excellence and superiority, and its emphasis on the abilities of the individual and insistence that men were equal neither in skills nor morals, nor "in what they ought to receive from society or in the duties they should discharge," was the foundation on which all other values rested.[80] He was deeply suspicious of the leveling tendencies in democracy, a suspicion that grew over time and was given focus by his later reading of José Ortega y Gasset's *The Revolt of the Masses* (1932), another work he cited endlessly during the 1930s.

Luce thought business leaders were the natural candidates for a new American aristocracy. Business was what Americans believed in; it was what the best young men were pursuing. More important, business would never be run democratically. "Business need not be autocratic. But certainly business must be aristocratic. There must be a top and, if possible, the best men must get there."[81] Changes in the business world made the emergence of this aristocracy more likely. Power was being transferred from the old inventors and empire builders to the new corporate managers. Passing on were the horsetrader, the tinkerer, the drummer, the good-fellow, the boor. The engineer and the lawyer, "gentlemen" of "genius adapted to the needs of the age," who rose to the top of a corporate hierarchy through ability alone replaced the man owing his wealth to luck, inheritance, or shady activity.[82]

Previously business exalted competition and success, but it rewarded no higher purpose than serving the bottom line, expected nothing beyond amassing more and more wealth. The result: "we got an undifferentiated plutocracy and babbitry—a plutocracy without any common sense of dignity and obligation."[83] According to Luce, the new class of business leaders had a more finely tuned sense of their power and therefore their responsibilities. At times, Luce assumed that greater power would automatically bring social responsibility in its exercise. He claimed that "a few men will soon have the power to speak for an entire branch of our economic civilization. If they have the power to do so, it will soon follow that they have the responsibility and obligation to do so." As modern tycoons emerge into the public eye, "being well known, they will be depositories of public trust."[84]

Luce never fully explained why he believed public responsibility must follow from private power. Actually, he knew it did not: wielders of power should act for the public good, but the evidence that they often felt no such responsibility was too obvious for a good journalist to ignore. Therefore, Luce believed this new class of business leaders must be trained in the use of its power. America must find a way to make corporations "develop a deep sense of responsibility to the public . . . to find a way to develop a place for public conscience and public responsibility in all so-called private business." In essence, this was the core of all New Era economic thinking: the need to instill a new class of managers and corporate technicians with old values of social responsibility and stewardship. The best way to teach them this curious blend of economic rationality and moral obligation, Luce felt, was to "turn ourselves into a nation of critics—or, at any rate, there must be a broad aristocracy of critics whose consistent criticism shall be ceaselessly felt." We must sit as "highly interested judges and critics of the leaders in so-called private business."[85]

This is what made *Fortune* important. Luce wanted a magazine that would educate American business leaders to their responsibilities, showing them what an educated business aristocracy would look like: how they would dress, what they would read, what paintings they would hang on the walls of their homes and offices, and finally what they would think about key political and economic issues. He was appointing himself the role of business critic. He stated as much in the prospectus, where the critical function held pride of place in a list of *Fortune*'s many relationships with business. Yet his criticism was not predominantly, or even largely, a negative proposition. His magazine would praise more than it would blame. "We cannot effectively castigate the mediocre man unless we have it in us to honor the superior man," Luce wrote, and a large part of *Fortune*'s project would center on celebrating the emerging new breed of socially responsible business manager.[86] Celebration, of course, was more likely to sell than castigation.

A necessary corollary to this project was the idea that private business was a public interest. Luce picked up on New Era calls for a more socially responsible business leadership and pushed them to their natural conclusion. Luce's *Fortune* would look into American industry with "unbridled curiosity," announcing, "it is going to be the business of the public to know and to judge" the heads of major American corporations. Luce emphasized the need to "develop a place for public conscience and public responsibility in all so-called private businesses."[87]

Luce believed that the fear of publicity exhibited by corporate America was a relic of the past, more understandable in an era of business rapacity when corporations often had a great deal to hide. Now that the modern "tycoon" was emerging in positions of power, Luce believed, the business leader would no longer be "forced by his press complex to be kittenish as a Victorian subdeb or boorish as a lion in captivity."[88] Here Luce miscalculated. He underestimated the conservatism of most corporate leaders, who saw no reason to invite scrutiny and were quite happy with a business press that for the most part limited itself to publishing corporation press releases. His idea that modern corporations had little to hide was even further misguided. Even if they were more willing to court publicity, Luce's idea that the workings of private corporations were the public's business was unlikely to find support even among the most progressive of corporate chieftains.

Luce and his staff encountered business hostility toward publicity early and often while they planned their new magazine. In an era when trade names were usually left out of business reporting, the corporation story was a radical idea that most corporations found threatening. It was a large step from referring to Macy's only as "one of the larger New York department stores," the convention at the time, to lifting the roof of the retailer to detail its operations, management, finances, and prospects.[89] In the planning stages, the *Fortune* staff attempted a story about International Telephone & Telegraph. Even after the company refused to cooperate they managed to produce a fairly detailed picture of the workings of the company. They also hit on the strategy that would mark *Fortune* research: they would provide the subject company with a draft of the story in order to allow the company to make corrections of fact and argue over *Fortune*'s interpretation. Companies correcting *Fortune*'s often-fanciful estimates therefore supplied much of the factual material in the resulting stories.[90] Luce was able to pursue his belief that the public had a right to know about the inner workings of corporate America even without the willing cooperation of the American business leadership.

Like that other landmark of the late boom, the Empire State Building, *Fortune* was conceived in the shadow of the expanding stock market but unveiled in the harsh light of the Depression. Despite the bad luck of announcing the publication of a new magazine devoted to celebrating business the very week the stock market crashed, thus beginning a decade when the achievements of business civilization would seem pathetically remote, the Depression could not have occurred at a better time for Time Inc. In Briton Hadden, *Time* in the 1920s had an editor perfectly attuned to that adolescent, frivolous, smart-alecky era. Hadden would not have found the 1930s as hospitable either personally or professionally. While his death might not have been the "historical necessity" Dwight Macdonald claimed, it did clear the way toward making *Time* a more serious and, therefore, more influential, magazine.[91] The serious Henry Luce was far better equipped to guide *Time* and Time Inc. down this more sober and ambitious road.

With its lengthier articles of analysis, *Fortune* was already positioned to exploit the increasing interest in the world spawned by the Depression. Though again Luce did not recognize it at the time, forecasting that even if the Depression lasted a year they could ride out the storm, the Depression proved the best thing that could have happened to *Fortune*.[92] Corporate resistance to appearing in *Fortune* did little to impede the same managers from subscribing to the magazine. Despite its launch just three months after the crash, *Fortune* was an immediate success. Though Luce believed it unlikely that a circulation much above 30,000 was even possible, by 1935 there were more than 100,000 subscribers.[93] Advertisers were willing to pay dearly to gain access to these readers, giving *Fortune* enough advertising revenue to turn a substantial profit.

Circulation, advertising revenues, and profits all continued to climb even as *Fortune*'s editorial content changed. The economic catastrophe pushed the magazine to sharpen its criticism, to move away from its stance as business class celebrant, and to embrace its role as critic. Building on the groundwork laid before the Depression, Luce pushed *Fortune* to analyze and criticize business as never before. Beginning with a bold acknowledgment of the magnitude of the suffering in New York City, *Fortune* quickly took on the housing industry in a six-part exposé on why the building industries were inefficient and incompetent. Just before the 1932 presidential election the magazine published a feature criticizing the Hoover administration's failure to acknowledge the severity of the Depression ("'No one has starved'... which is not true" opened the article). Increasingly impatient and critical corporation stories followed, along with favorable reviews of New Deal legislation and even a remarkably friendly if condescending article on the Communist Party.[94]

There were clear limits, however, to how far *Fortune* would go in its criticism. Even when functioning with a great deal of editorial freedom, *Fortune* still needed to sell magazines, and much of its monthly content was nearly indistinguishable from its early, more celebratory issues. *Fortune's* claim that any human activity that made money was a legitimate subject for analysis (cockfighting, burlesque, divorce) undercut Luce's idea that business needed to be socially responsible.[95] Finally, *Fortune's* critical content depended on a shared understanding between Luce, his writers, and their audience. The increasing political polarization of the 1930s brought this understanding under increasing pressure. Many readers thought *Fortune's* criticism had exceeded anything that could be considered constructive, and Luce began to agree. The majority of the writers, on the other hand, sought to push the magazine's critical edge further to the left. The resulting internal conflict simmered at *Fortune* in the middle years of the decade before boiling over in 1936. The spillover ultimately altered the path *Fortune* would take, just as it reshaped the career paths of a number of its writers.

"The Audience to Which They Were Invited to Lecture"

Writers such as Archibald MacLeish, Dwight Macdonald, T. S. Matthews, and a host of other intellectually inclined young men, were arriving at a Time Inc. that bore little resemblance to the mass culture behemoth feared and reviled by 1950s critics. At the beginning of 1930 the corporation was still primarily *Time* magazine, a growing success, but still a small magazine of modest circulation and uncertain influence. The minuscule staff consisted of twenty-one writers and editors, a handful of researchers, and a small business office. *Fortune*, just preparing to begin publication in the weeks after the stock market crash, had an even smaller staff.

What the organization had was the air of success and the promise of importance. Henry Luce, with his intensity and energy, exhibited an undeniable charisma, and he attracted intelligent and ambitious writers to his organization. By and large, these writers came from the same class background and were educated at the same schools as Luce. When young intellectuals such as MacLeish and Macdonald started at Time Inc. their outlook on the world was very similar to his. Having been educated in the same schools, and associated with the same narrow stratum of American society, they had developed similar interests. Trained for cultural and political leadership, they were also attracted to the life of the mind. They were drawn to Time Inc. by their own ambivalence about the intellectual's detachment from and lack of relevance to American society and by their desire to participate in Luce's experiments in journalism. Though they might sneer at *Time*'s vulgarity or cringe at *Fortune*'s ostentation, they shared Luce's progressive, Lippmann-influenced assumptions about the function of the media. Luce's journalism offered an opportunity to help mold an educated public opinion. It promised influence and prestige. In short, it offered intellectuals a platform, and a voice sure to be heard by a large audience. These writers understood that Luce controlled access to this platform. From the beginning intellectuals recognized that their success depended on their ability to influence Luce.

By and large, the intellectuals who came to work for Luce clustered at *Fortune*. The business magazine offered greater scope for the writer's craft, fewer space and time constraints, and less editorial meddling. As the Depression settled in, it also offered a laboratory in which to study the workings and misworkings of American capitalism. How far *Fortune* and Henry Luce were willing to go in this critical project, to what extent they would lay the blame at the doorstep of American business, was at the outset an open question. Archibald MacLeish and Dwight Macdonald were among those newly politicized intellectuals at *Fortune* who would force an answer. In so doing they precipitated a crisis at the magazine, in the process clarifying their own ideas about intellectual identity and the complicated relationship between intellect and power.

In the mid-1930s, as the political sides began to be drawn at *Fortune*, Luce intervened in the venerable Time Inc. manner, with a memo. He reminded his writers that their readership was primarily businessmen: this was "the audience to which they were invited to lecture."[96] Luce had effectively pinpointed what provided many of his writers with their sense of purpose. Intellectuals of their generation may have disdained university professors for their pedantry and limited influence, but they were drawn to teach, to lecture before an assembled class. If the class contained an audience of business leaders that intellectuals found difficult to respect, it also gave them an audience of powerful and influential men. The intellectuals at Time Inc. wanted that audience almost as much as Henry Luce did, though they ultimately sought to teach very different lessons.

CHAPTER THREE

The Search for a "Radical Capitalism" at *Fortune* Magazine

> We are deluged with facts, but we have lost, or are losing, our human ability to feel them. Which means that we have lost or are losing our ability to comprehend the facts of our experience as poetry comprehends them, recreated and made real in the imagination.
>
> —Archibald MacLeish, "Poetry and Journalism"

The week the stock market crashed, Swedish Match king Ivar Kreuger's enigmatic face peered from the cover of *Time* magazine on newsstands across the nation. A brief article celebrated "the man who is behind the great Swedish trust" and detailed how he had recently extended his string of match monopolies by striking a deal with the German government.[1] The article praised him as a corporate wizard and the financial savior of European governments, echoing the chorus of acclaim Kreuger had been receiving in both the American and international investment communities. This faith proved grossly misplaced. Under Kreuger's direction Swedish Match had evolved from a leader in the match industry to a massive Ponzi scheme, allowing Kreuger to swindle financiers in America alone out of a quarter of a billion dollars. By 1932, with Kreuger no longer able to attract the additional capital necessary to keep his concerns afloat, exposure was unavoidable. On 12 March 1932 he shot himself to death. His financial chicanery emerged gradually in the months that followed. In retrospect, *Time* could not have selected a more apposite figure for the cover of an issue dated 28 October 1929.

This same issue of *Time* carried a three-page announcement for a new magazine "which shall represent business in ink and paper and word and picture as the finest skyscraper reflects it in stone and steel and architecture." The magazine was *Fortune*, and its editors were hoping their announcement would attract "those active, intelligent and influential individuals who have a relatively large stake in U.S. Industry and Commerce."[2] Presumably this audience was a bit too distracted that particular week to give *Fortune*'s announcement the attention it sought. Nevertheless, the magazine appeared as planned in February 1930, devoted to exploring and celebrating the centrality of business to American life. As the stock market slide tumbled the country into Depression, and Henry Luce's dark assessment that the slump could last as long as a year proved wildly optimistic, *Fortune* gradually altered course. The more celebratory content began to retreat to the back of the magazine, replaced front and center by a series of increasingly searching and critical examinations of the American industrial system. At its best, this reporting deftly combined factual content with literary presentation. The new approach fully emerged in a 1933 series of articles on Ivar Kreuger's rise and fall, penned by *Fortune*'s star writer, Archibald MacLeish.[3]

MacLeish began with an extended presentation of Kreuger's last day, titled "Overture Played on a Browning." The first paragraph powerfully conveyed MacLeish's style:

> The stair smelled as it had always smelled of hemp and people and politeness—of the decent bourgeois dust. After the linoleum smell of the ship and the harsh, acrid, dampish smell of the boat train the air had a friendly, almost an intimate taste. Mr. Kreuger breathed it softly as he went down around the caged-in column of the *ascenseur*.

The piece continued through Kreuger's last moments, conveying them from his perspective, complete with his final observations as he lay on the bed to shoot himself ("Looking up he saw the fat, gold stucco cherubs in the ceiling corners of the room. Odd witnesses!").[4] It was a tour-de-force of imaginative journalism.

MacLeish labeled the next month's installment "history rewritten by the accountants." Prefacing a methodical financial reconstruction of Kreuger's career, MacLeish claimed that only the accountants could "apply to rumor the hard edge of fact." *Fortune*'s analysis showed Kreuger to be more or less what he purported to be, a match producer, until he encountered the speculative frenzy of Wall Street in 1924. From that point on his efforts were entirely devoted to sufficiently cooking his books to put over a series of stock offers. Even this long litany of numbers was leavened with MacLeish's distinctive style. He offered evocations of Scandinavian cities stretching on for hundreds of words and extended his imaginings of Kreuger's last thoughts and movements. His third installment merged these two techniques to offer a convincing explanation for Kreuger's long success. MacLeish laid the blame on the decade's market mania and on corporate secrecy. By the late 1920s the New York investment houses were reaping great profits and had little incentive to question their source. The simple explanation Kreuger so often proffered to Wall Street, that his money was repeatedly funneled through endless chains of companies to avoid taxes, was readily and uncritically accepted by a financial community who viewed tax evasion as a moral imperative. The financial secrecy Kreuger's companies engaged in, including the lack of independent audits, allowed him to successfully hide his manipulations. Kreuger was now being criticized for this, yet American companies such as Allied Chemical & Dye, *Fortune* pointed out, engaged in precisely the same practices.

As the Kreuger articles demonstrated, the newly critical *Fortune* operated from two key assumptions in its expanding investigation of corporate America. First, *Fortune* maintained, business should operate in the public interest. Second, the public must have access to corporate information to guarantee good faith. In furtherance of these goals, the young literary intellectuals at *Fortune* developed a unique form of journalism: history as compiled by the accountant, yet written by the poet. Criticizing corporate leadership, sympathizing with struggling working-class and poor Americans, embracing the New Deal, and exploring the contours of modern America, they produced some of the most vivid and incisive reporting of the era. They also played an important role in legitimating a historic shift in American politics, away from the private and corporate control Luce had advocated and toward the acceptance of a new set of social rights protected by an expanded federal government. Luce initially embraced this new journalism, but the built-in tension between factual presentation and literary license eventually came to a head as the political stakes climbed in 1936. A struggle for control of *Fortune*, and by extension of *Time* and the newly launched *Life*, played out in the late 1930s, leading to changes in *Fortune*'s style of journalism and to the departure of many of the key participants.

Turning Poets into Business Journalists

Henry Luce was determined that his new magazine be well written. "There are men who can write poetry," Luce believed, "and there are men who can read balance sheets." Concluding, "it is easier to turn poets into business journalists than to turn bookkeepers into writers," Luce staffed the magazine with as many poets and aspiring creative writers as he could find.[5] This accorded well with previous hiring practice at *Time*, and allowed him to exploit the pipelines that already ran from literary Yale and Princeton to Time Inc.

First on board was Parker Lloyd-Smith, a poet and classicist from Princeton who had wound up as *Time*'s business writer. In family background, education, and literary interests, Lloyd-Smith resembled MacLeish, Macdonald, and Matthews. The son of well-to-do parents, educated in private schools, Lloyd-Smith wrote poems, short stories, and plays at Princeton (one cowritten with C. D. Jackson, another future *Fortune* writer), then took a job at *Time* while he pursued his writing.[6] Attractive, charming, and sophisticated, Lloyd-Smith impressed Henry Luce so much that Luce appointed him *Fortune*'s managing editor despite Lloyd-Smith's lack of experience in editing or in business. Intellectually curious yet diffident, a colleague described Lloyd-Smith as "physically indolent to the point of affectation."[7] Smooth and unflappable at work, he also had a serious and troubled side that emerged only in his searchingly mystical poetry.[8] He ran a fabulously unorganized office, regularly knocking the top half of the teetering pile of accumulated correspondence, memos, and manuscripts off his desk and into the trash to catch up on back work.[9]

His first writer was Dwight Macdonald, drafted from *Time*. For much of the year spent preparing the magazine for publication, Macdonald was the entire writing staff. At *Fortune* he wrote "competently and intelligently but with neither passion nor distinction," an editor remembered: "he was, those days, a wheel horse type writer."[10] Macdonald wrote best when stoked by a fierce sense of indignation. Even at twenty-three he recognized indignation was both a vice and a strength, and observed to a friend, "I can work up a moral indignation quicker than a fat tennis player can work up a sweat."[11] Yet in his early years at the magazine his work rarely provoked him deeply enough to elicit this distinctive style.[12] Despite his flickering fascination with business leaders, he had no "deep or living interest" in the magazine or its purpose, and he resented having to write for it.[13]

Macdonald, Lloyd-Smith, and various writers borrowed from *Time* did all the writing in the run-up to publication. Once enough advertisers were recruited to guarantee a viable launch, Luce recruited MacLeish. Arriving in November 1929, MacLeish quickly installed himself as the star of the staff. He took advantage of Luce's deference toward him to pick and choose assignments, avoiding corporation stories completely. MacLeish proved to be a talented and reliable journalist, turning in on time page after page of vivid prose. Long hours at a frenetic pace were the norm for writers at Time Inc., where even *Fortune*'s monthly schedule could not protect it from the chaotic scramble to get the magazine to the printers. Much of the writing and editing was done in the middle of the night. Not so with MacLeish, who could "just turn the switch and let her run."[14]

In the months following the inaugural issue, with circulation and advertising revenues both growing steadily, a larger staff was slowly assembled. Lloyd-Smith transferred Macdonald's friend Wilder Hobson from *Time* in early 1930. An excellent slide trombonist and the author of an important early book on jazz, Hobson's skillful but undistinguished prose made him a reliable but perpetually disappointing fixture on the magazine. Edward Kennedy, a small, quiet, binge-drinking alcoholic but also a prolific and vivid writer, showed a unique ability to handle the corporation stories that immediately emerged as *Fortune*'s trademark and that most other writers tried to avoid.

The young poet and novelist Russell Davenport made the last unlikely addition to the first year staff. In the late 1920s he had used astrology to make a sizable amount of money in the stock market, and then followed his astrologer's advice to get out before the crash. He then turned the advice into fiction, publishing a novel, *Through Traffic*, which predicted the crash. Davenport, a descendent of the John Davenport who cofounded the New Haven colony in 1637, had followed Luce at Yale. He, too, had made Skull and Bones, largely through his literary endeavors, and after graduation he worked for *Time*. He left to pursue a love affair out west, the failure of which provoked more poetry. Returning to New York, he married Marcia Gluck Clarke, the daughter of singer Alma Gluck and later a successful novelist in her own right. Despite the money made speculating, Davenport was looking for work that would better connect him to the world of active affairs than had his novels. At *Fortune*, he quickly demonstrated an ability to wed his idealistically inflected writing to the requirements of the assignment. He was also unique among the intellectuals in openly professing his belief that *Fortune*'s journalism was important. Unlike the others, he never felt demeaned in addressing himself to a business audience, and was optimistic about the prospects of merging business and literature.[15] Davenport and Lloyd-Smith became fast friends, even drawing up plans for a corporation (called Davensmith, Inc.) "for the creation, promotion, and perpetuation of an American literature."[16]

The growing staff of literary eccentrics magnified Lloyd-Smith's managerial inadequacies. Luce responded by hiring Ralph McAllister Ingersoll away from the *New Yorker* to share the managing editor job (Luce was never able to fire an editor, if they were not up to the job they were shifted around or bumped upstairs). Ingersoll had joined the *New Yorker* six months after its debut, hired by Harold Ross partially because Ross spilled ink on Ingersoll's white suit during the interview ("Hell, I'll hire anybody!" Ingersoll heard Ross yell as he left the office). He was a key figure in helping the *New Yorker* survive its first years and developed some of its most lasting features, including the format for Talk of the Town. Ross let Ingersoll go when Luce called, declaring "Ingersoll, *Fortune* was invented for you to edit."[17]

Ross was right. A swift, smart, and decisive manuscript editor, Ingersoll was known for penning epic memos packed with critical analysis of his publications and ideas for improvement. MacLeish called him "far and away the best combination of editor, writer, idea man, administrative and business executive" at Time Inc. or anywhere else.[18] Furthermore, Ingersoll saw himself as self-consciously adopting "a career in both camps," living simultaneously as part of Park Avenue society and Greenwich Village bohemia.[19] His family background reflected the division: staidly influential Ingersoll's on one side, descendants of the flamboyant socialite Ward McAllister on the other. Ingersoll, too, had attended Hotchkiss and Yale, graduating in 1921. Expected to join the family business, he instead worked as a mining engineer in California, Arizona, and Mexico, an experience he turned into his first book, *In and Under Mexico* (1924). His access to upper-crust New York café society had been crucial in bringing the right tone of insider sophistication to the *New Yorker*. At *Fortune*, he enjoyed hobnobbing with corporate big wigs one evening (it was usually his job to meet with and charm the recalcitrant managers of the corporations *Fortune* was writing about) while throwing parties for his writers and the Greenwich Village artistic community the next.

Ingersoll helped recruit other serious writers over the next few years, including Louis Kronenberger, John Chamberlain, Robert Cantwell, Eric Hodgins, and brothers Charles Wertenbaker and Green Peyton. Ingersoll also hired James Agee, who had just graduated from Harvard in 1932 and was looking for work. Agee had struck up a friendship with Dwight Macdonald in 1927, writing him a letter praising some of the stories Macdonald had published in the *Yale Lit* and observing that "we evidently write and think remarkably alike." The letter, which Agee feared carried "all the unpleasant earmarks of a 'pickup,'" did result in a correspondence and in Agee's eventually enlisting Macdonald's help in finding a job.[20] On the strength of Macdonald's recommendation and a parody of *Time* Agee wrote for the Harvard *Advocate*, Ingersoll hired him in the summer of 1932.

Agee was a fiercely talented writer, generally thought by the staff to exceed even MacLeish in ability. Though he followed the familiar path from prep school and the Ivy League to *Fortune*, Agee came from a financially and socially humble family from rural Tennessee. He needed a job after graduation, and the pay at *Fortune* promised to be good, especially for the Depression. Agee also looked at *Fortune* as a compatible place to pursue his own writing. At the time he graduated, Agee was embarked on a long poem, the professed goal of which was "a complete appraisal of contemporary civilization."[21] By 1932, when Agee joined the staff, *Fortune* had expanded its scope, committing itself to essentially the same task.

In 1930 Agee had confessed to his friend Father James Flye, "I'm committed to writing with a horrible definiteness,"[22] an apt description of the intensity he brought to anything he wrote. Deadlines seemed to take on a literal meaning to him, as he drove himself relentlessly to finish his pieces on time while making them good enough to meet his own exacting standards. Years later, when a review for *Time* brought only a lukewarm reception from his editor, Agee stayed up all night rewriting it, knowing full well it was too late to get it into the magazine.[23]

Agee completed the group that, with occasional writing contributions from Luce, *Time*'s business manager Charles Stillman, or writers imported from *Time* such as foreign affairs writer Laird Goldsborough, produced *Fortune* for its first couple of years. As a group, they were extremely gifted, filled with literary ambition and a condescension toward business common among intellectuals but odd for a business magazine. Later managing editor Eric Hodgins aptly described the staff as "insane, unreliable, alcoholic, and, all in all, I think the most brilliant magazine staff ever to exist in America."[24]

Half Believing in *Fortune*

For most of these young writers, working for *Fortune* provided a necessary income. Aspiring to write their own poetry and prose, they nevertheless needed a job. Some, such as Parker Lloyd-Smith, worked to avoid a dependence on family support that they viewed as worse than work. Others, from less financially secure backgrounds, resented the necessity of holding a job at all. Macdonald complained to his friend Dinsmore Wheeler that he and Hobson were among the few of his college friends with "steady, desk-polishing, nose-grindstone-rubbing jobs in this lousy, filthy, clangorous, demented metropolis."[25] MacLeish, who with the collapse of his Carson Pirie Scott dividends now needed the job, wrote his editor, Robert Linscott, "This writing in the recesses of hack work is Hell. But we are as poor as the rest of the world this year."[26] As a group they found the balance between their own writing and their *Fortune* assignments difficult to strike. Most dreamed of escaping at least for a brief time, and all the writers did manage to take leaves of as long as six months to pursue their own interests. As the Depression continued and as their salaries increased, many feared their success at *Fortune* would trap them. After Luce called Agee's story on the Tennessee Valley Authority one of the best pieces of writing he had ever seen in *Fortune*, Agee confessed to his friend Father Flye, "I feel the well-known prison walls distinctively thickening."[27]

Despite this constant desire to escape, the writers took their work seriously. Even the young Macdonald, who complained more than the others, displayed pride in his work and an eagerness to be recognized by his boss. Though he felt that his work required too little of him ("The job in FORTUNE is very interesting, but how much does it take of me? By God, it's child's play"),[28] he could still work up his earlier interest in the vitality of business leaders. Secretary of Commerce Robert Patterson Lamont might seem "like most of the Big Business Leaders . . . a pretty dull fellow," but Macdonald described railroad man Leonor Frisell Loree as "masterful, powerfully built, very able, full of energy and given to speaking his mind on all occasions."[29] His old fears of the irrelevance of literature emerged in reflections on the diesel engine, which he had observed up close for an article. Extolling the power and efficiency of the engine, he concluded, "our machines are as effective as our artists are impotent."[30] He also recognized that few other intellectuals shared his interest in business. "The great in finance and industry have always impressed me more than they seem to impress most members of the intelligentsia," he mused in a letter to Dinsmore Wheeler.[31]

Despite this occasional enthusiasm, most of Macdonald's letters of this time convey his frustration with his work and his growing belief that he would have to break with *Fortune*. His mood about work turned darkest when he was most depressed, usually due to problems with women.[32] He disliked the house style, "all cut up, bristling with facts, so dynamic and vigorous that it makes your head ache—if you have any perceptions at all." Since *Fortune*'s readers were unlikely to be burdened by great perception, Macdonald concluded, the magazine would probably be a great success.[33] Nevertheless, he never felt at home writing in *Fortune*'s idiom, so heavy on facts and so light on interpretation. *Fortune*, he felt, had no room for the artist's imagination, a word he often used as a contrast with the magazine's mania for facts.

Even at his most frustrated and stymied, Macdonald, like the other writers, felt a strong attraction to Luce and a desire for his approval. Though he described him in letters as "Massa Luce" and "the Great White Father of the mad journalistic tribe," he recognized Luce's commitment and his success in enlisting writers in his project. Macdonald described Luce in a letter: "The man is a driver of the first order—not offensively so, however. He is human underneath it all, and if he drives his writers, he certainly drives himself even more frantically."[34] While getting *Fortune* ready for its initial publication, Macdonald had been spending his spare time launching another magazine, the *Miscellany*, a literary magazine he founded with friends F. W. Dupee and George L. K. Morris. When it first appeared in December 1929, Macdonald showed it to Luce, expecting him to be impressed by "this evidence of cultural enterprise on the part of one of his writers." On the contrary, Luce felt Macdonald had betrayed Time Inc.: "this is a twenty-four hour profession, you never know when you may get an idea for us, and if you're all the time thinking of some damn little magazine."[35] Luce never could approve of his writers seeking other outlets for their work, even though he was forced to accept it as the price of hiring talented writers. Though Macdonald never accepted Luce's contention that his job should be the sole focus of his interests (nor did most aspiring writers at Time Inc.), he was caught up in the force of Luce's drive. Luce's personality elicited from his writers a level of commitment to his project they would not otherwise have felt.[36]

Macdonald was the least committed of the writers. Others found more satisfaction in their work for the magazine, even while resenting its necessity. Ralph Ingersoll, *Fortune*'s managing editor, once complained that Archie MacLeish only half believed in the magazine.[37] The striking point is that he did half believe. While MacLeish never thought much of the businessmen who were the magazine's audience, he did acknowledge the importance of big business to American society, and therefore the importance of the task *Fortune* set for itself. At least until 1932 he even shared some of Luce's hope that business leaders might take a more effective leadership role in American society and that *Fortune* could be a force behind this process. Either way, MacLeish threw himself into his work for the magazine. From the very beginning he set out to recruit his literary friends for *Fortune*, including Stephen Vincent Benét, John Peale Bishop, John Dos Passos, and Ernest Hemingway.[38] Though all but Dos Passos wrote for the magazine, none of them took to the work. Hemingway grudgingly produced an article on the finances of bull fighting. As he wrote to his editor Maxwell Perkins, "Am doing it for Archy—how he got mixed up with them God knows . . . if ever a magazine sounded like useless balls this one does."[39]

While MacLeish complained of the work to Hemingway and his other literary friends, he simultaneously devoted more time and energy to it than the job required. Despite his financial agreement with Luce, he worked full time for *Fortune* much of its first few years.[40] Rather than accept conventional assignments, MacLeish regularly proposed more ambitious (and time-consuming) assignments for himself. These assignments provided him with an essential education. By the middle 1930s he had taken to goading radical friends by maintaining that *Fortune* was a far better social historian than the *New Masses*.[41] And far from disabling his own writing, his years at *Fortune* were the most prolific of his life. In addition to the hundreds of pages published in the magazine, he also published four collections of poems, three plays, a ballet scenario, a word and picture book on the effects of the Depression, and more than thirty other essays during his almost nine years there.

Searching for a "Radical Capitalism" Men Can Believe In

In its initial guise *Fortune* was neither political nor particularly critical, sticking to its original celebratory prospectus for its first year. *Fortune* turned its brand of investigation into the inner workings of corporations such as the Atlantic & Pacific Tea Company and American Telephone & Telegraph, industries such as petroleum and nitrogen, and industrial cities such as South Bend and Pittsburgh. It featured elaborate pictorial displays of art collections, Persian rugs, and fine jewels. These art pieces shaded in tone from didactic pieces on stained glass to lifestyles-of-the-rich-and-famous pieces on swimming pool design or yacht racing. Advocacy of branch banking or primers on antitrust law alternated with features instructing readers on how to live on $50,000 a year in New York City. The most ambitious segment of the year was a six-part series on the conception, construction, and use of a skyscraper in New York City, written by MacLeish. Even the investigative articles focused little attention on workers or unions, frequently substituting platitudes about contented workers for actual investigation. In the coal industry, for example, *Fortune* claimed local union leaders frequently called strikes despite a tractable management and a rank and file "bitterly opposed to interruptions in work."[42] The only article focusing on unions was a comic piece lampooning ridiculous work rules enforced by unions *Fortune* labeled "Burlesque tyrants."[43] Individual workers rarely appeared in pictures, except as framing devices for Bourke-White's shots celebrating industrial size and power. Criticism of corporations and corporate leadership was muted, though the magazine frequently observed the persistence of "obsolete" corporate concerns with secrecy and the lamentable frequency with which it encountered corporate leaders unencumbered by any sense of public responsibility.

By and large, the magazine's views reflected the worldview of the writers. Few had any direct experience with working-class Americans or knowledge of industrial working conditions. Early research trips to factories were led by corporate officials who had little interest in drawing attention to work practices and conditions and provided *Fortune*'s journalists with few opportunities to meet workers. The writers rarely seemed aware of the oversight.

Beginning in the first issues of 1931, however, *Fortune* began to engage the economic crisis more directly and make explicit the sort of capitalism, and capitalist leadership, it advocated. The year began with a three-part biography of Owen D. Young, the head of General Electric, written by Wilder Hobson. The profile was part of a wave of favorable publicity for Young in early 1931, with laudatory articles in *Colliers*, *Review of Reviews*, and *New York Times* sparking a movement to draft Young as the Democratic challenger to Hoover in 1932.[44] *Fortune*'s article praised Young as "the greatest living American businessman" for his efficient management and, more important, his application of an "industrial philosophy" stressing corporate responsibility.[45] The magazine approvingly noted Young's observation that "managers were no longer attorneys for stockholders; they were becoming trustees for an institution." It supported his claim that the public welfare was the aim of all corporations, and his conclusion that "after all, capitalism is only a vehicle by which civilization has gotten this far along the road. It is not an end in itself."[46]

Young, with his policy of maintaining high wages, his belief in corporate responsibility, and his emphasis on better industry organization and efficiency and less competitive chaos, was fully in line with the more liberal strains of the era's economic thought, what Young, Edward Dennison, Edward Filene, and Henry Ford were given to labeling the "new capitalism."[47] This conception of business as determined to place social utility above the bottom line appealed to Luce and his writers. The articles on Young first made explicit *Fortune*'s belief that private business was invested with public responsibility, a belief the magazine returned to repeatedly in future issues. *Fortune* also rarely missed an opportunity to praise efforts to bring order and direction to markets, criticizing the chaos of the housing industry, and awarding a prize for an article touting European experiments in social planning. It praised leaders who were interested in exerting leadership during the current crisis, even invoking Young as an example of a necessary corporate aristocracy, a description that likely came directly from Luce.

As *Fortune* became increasingly explicit in its praise of liberal corporate leadership, it became openly critical of other, less responsible corporate behavior. In April 1931 it published a rogues gallery of eight of the most spectacular failures of the Depression. "Some were reckless, some dishonest. Some are broke, some in jail. All are exhibits of depression," the magazine intoned.[48] Despite this increasingly apparent loss of patience with elements of American corporate leadership, however, nothing the magazine had previously published prepared the reader for the August 1931 issue.

The editors devoted the middle of the magazine to a sixteen-page spread on the "American Workingman."[49] Ostensibly an attempt to explain industrial workers to readers ("Who Is He? What Is He? How Does He Work and Live?" ran the subtitle), the piece instead juxtaposed representations of workers in bronze, paint, and pictures with *Fortune*'s fullest elucidation and justification of "the new capitalism." As with many *Fortune* articles, the artwork dominated the presentation, beginning with a collage of the hands of working men, clipped from assorted Bourke-White pictures. Following this disconcerting image of disembodied worker "parts" were more Bourke-White photographs, bronze sculptures of steelworkers, and paintings by Reginald Marsh and Thomas Benton.[50] Finally, on a page dealing with labor radicalism labeled "Reds," were three paintings from "artist-economist" Gerrit A. Beneker ("The Alabama Kid," "Constructive Radical," and "Men are Square") celebrating idealized industrial workers and farmers.

Rather than examine the worker as it promised, the opening essay instead explained what the magazine meant by the "new capitalism." MacLeish, who wrote the essay, called this new capitalism the "Doctrine of High Wages" after what he took to be its most important feature. MacLeish seized upon the fact the wages had not been immediately rolled back when the Depression struck, as in previous slumps, as his primary justification for announcing the triumph of the new capitalism and laying out its principles. Denying Ford's claim that high wages were merely a doctrine of economic expediency, MacLeish claimed its effects were necessarily social: "to replace a capitalistic class with a capitalistic society, a society in which labor, by virtue of its share in the profits of industry has a stake in the existing order. And its ultimate consequence must be the joint control of industry by workman and employer." Calling the new capitalism as radical as Stalinism, MacLeish concluded:

> The economic duel so generally prophesied for the next generation will not be fought between Communism and Fascism . . . . The economic duel will be fought, if it is fought at all, between a radical capitalism with its purpose to make men productive in order that they may be free, and an experimental Communism with its purpose to enforce men in order than they may be productive. And the judge of the outcome will be American labor.[51]

Appearing in the summer of 1931, when the administration's attempt to enlist major industrial leaders in a cooperative effort to keep wages steady was beginning to crumble, the article was clearly an attempt to intervene directly in this debate. *Fortune* presented business with an image to fear—organized industrial workers. The article, with its huge reproductions of red-tinged radical workers, threatened business and tried to goad it into adopting the sort of industrial policies *Fortune* now openly advocated. *Fortune* advanced a vision of a radically altered capitalism, a capitalism of shared risk ("One of the smuggest platitudes of the old capitalism was the contention that capital took all the risks . . . . There are workmen who have reason to know from their own experience that they also take a risk") that would yield shared benefits; a capitalism that could compete with communism on its own terms by offering industrial workers a stake in the system. *Fortune* again quoted Young: "No man . . . with an inadequate wage is free" (a sentiment MacLeish later improved upon: "Ask yourselves what reason there is in heaven or earth or out of it why a man earning five dollars a day should believe in capitalism in any of its forms").[52]

Accompanying the essay by MacLeish were a number of articles that functioned to make explicit the threat business leaders faced if they failed to take workers' needs seriously. If business did not seize this opportunity it was faced with losing the struggle for labor. At a time when organized labor was coming off a decade of defeat and rollback, a period of decline the early Depression merely deepened, *Fortune* announced the return of organized labor. In a profile of a relatively well-off Ford worker ("How to Live on $7 a Day"), *Fortune* noted that worker's horizons had changed in the past twenty years. American workers were not "workers in the social propaganda meaning of the term." *Fortune* decided, they were "*petit bourgeois* in their desires and middle class in their interests." But should unemployment threaten, this middle-class worker would revert back to his basic working class identity, he would again think of "unions and organizing and solidarity and strikes."[53] *Fortune* was presciently declaring the return of organized labor as a factor to be reckoned with, at a time when big business continued to discount its power. To further illustrate business blindness, *Fortune* ended the issue with a compilation of the explanations for the cause of the Depression offered by various prominent Americans. It included a liberal business perspective (Daniel Willard) and a senator crusading for regulation (James Couzens of Michigan), before allowing J. P. Morgan to speak for the "old capitalism": "I don't know anything about any depression. What depression is this? You know I really can't discuss anything."[54]

The maintenance of wages proved to be a thin reed on which to hang a radical redefinition of capitalism. When corporate leaders such as Ford and Young joined other corporations in slashing wages, *Fortune*'s justification fell away. It retained its belief in organization and the application of creative intelligence to industrial problems, but as it charted the severity of the Depression, it increasingly turned its attention to Washington. This helped convince MacLeish (though not Luce) of the bankruptcy of Hoover's faith in corporate leadership. In late 1931 *Fortune* began measuring the magnitude of the failure and looking to the government for answers in articles on federal farm relief and Hoover's Committee for Unemployment Relief.[55]

By 1932 *Fortune*'s ambitious new journalism of exposure and interpretation had emerged in full. Departing from the standard journalism practice, urged by Hoover, of minimizing the effects of the Depression, it repeatedly exposed its severity. Government efforts to react to the prolonged economic slump soon came under *Fortune*'s expanded purview, with articles appearing on Congress, the Reconstruction Finance Corporation, and the Fourteenth Amendment. The magazine grew increasingly impatient with business, excoriating the housing industry in a six-part exposé. Finally, *Fortune* added international coverage with a lengthy consideration of the

Soviet Union, announced with a striking Diego Rivera cover depicting a Soviet train.[56]

Previous explanations for *Fortune*'s change of direction have attributed it entirely to Luce. Macdonald, for instance, claimed the change occurred because "Luce was journalist enough to see that the New Deal was news and that big business, temporarily, wasn't."[57] MacLeish, looking back years later, believed there must have been an editorial conference, guided by Luce, that resulted in a radical reconstruction of *Fortune*'s mission, an expansion of its scope from business to American industrial civilization, broadly conceived.[58] There is no evidence, however, of any such conference or explicit change in policy. *Fortune*'s new direction, revealed in its searching analysis of the magnitude of the Depression, its favorable reception of the New Deal, its increasing skepticism of the leadership of corporate America, and its openness to the labor movement, emerged piecemeal over time and was largely the result of the collaboration between MacLeish and Ingersoll. MacLeish himself was the moving spirit in expanding the magazine's scope, as Ingersoll later acknowledged. MacLeish's ability to determine his own assignments and his growing interest in the causes and effects of the Depression were the motive force. Once Roosevelt came into office, MacLeish exploited his contacts with the administration and his lawyer's expertise to undertake the majority of *Fortune*'s early analysis. While MacLeish's views were shared by many of the writer's on the magazine, the change in subject matter in 1932 through 1934 largely mirrored MacLeish's changing ideas.[59]

MacLeish's poetry and *Fortune*'s journalism developed along parallel paths in the early 1930s. In retreat from the introspection of the 1920s, with its tight focus on the individual, MacLeish's early work at *Fortune* showed him how industrial life snared the individual in larger social forces beyond his control or influence. As he observed in a notebook in 1931, "the necessary effect of Industrial Civilization has been to make every member of the community dependent in one way or another upon every other . . . . And it is a matter of history that a surplus of the metal silver in India may so depress the currency of South American countries that men in Collinsville Connecticut won't eat."[60] The economic interconnectedness of human society and the inability of unregulated economic markets to provide either security or stability were themes MacLeish pursued in *Fortune*, emerging most directly in his series on the chaos, inefficiency, and incompetence of the housing industry. In industrial America, he concluded, the individualism so celebrated in the nineteenth century was virtually meaningless, replaced by a dense web of economic connection. Machines made men obsolete, giving the lie to platitudes about individual initiative.

For poetry to remain central to human experience, MacLeish concluded, it needed to reflect this new social reality. In an essay on the recent course of poetry, published in July 1931, he observed that the two major poetic responses to industrialism had been glorification of the machine and a retreat into the extreme individualism of the "excessively personal, self-searching, painful and sometimes beautiful poems of the Hamlet mood." Both were dead ends, he declared. Instead, he advocated a poetry not of man but of mankind, "Not myself, my soul, my glycerine-dropping eyes, but these unknown and nameless men, anonymous under this sky, small in the valleys and far-off and forever there."[61] Having caught a "refracted glimpse" of a "new image of man" in Diego Rivera's Mexico City frescoes, MacLeish hoped to provide "an image of mankind in which men can again believe."[62] As he wrote this he was completing *Conquistador*, his first major attempt to speak of man in the aggregate, and writing his extended essay on the "American Workingman" for *Fortune*.

Though increasingly aware of the way industrial society mounted a serious challenge to individualism, MacLeish did not follow this line of thought to the determinist dead end at which so many arrived in the 1930s. He consistently fought the determinism of the right and of the left, of the market and of the party. This, not the social engagement of the poet per se, was what MacLeish attacked in his widely misunderstood 1932 poem "Invocation of the Social Muse."[63] Published in the *New Republic*, his inflammatory labeling of artists as "Whores" following the troops, and the obscurity of his ultimate position, sparked a controversy over the proper role of the intellectual. Critics consistently miscast him as defending the extreme independence of the artist, a view that has prevailed among historians. Richard Pells, in his generally reliable survey of 1930s intellectual trends, attributed to MacLeish the view that writers embracing social causes had "invariably compromised their talent, trying to turn literature into a vehicle of mass expression at the expense of personal creativity."[64] What MacLeish objected to, however, in his invocation and elsewhere, was the poets' subsuming of his art in the specific political struggles of Europe, the revolutionary ideologies of fascism and communism.[65] MacLeish sought a new social role for the poet, even in the early 1930s, but his conception looked backward to an age when the poet guided from above, not forward to a day when the poet marched arm in arm with the proletariat.

Ordinary people might be subject to distant economic forces they could neither influence nor understand, MacLeish believed, but business leaders and intellectuals were not. Though keenly aware of the irrational and immoral results of free markets, he retained a confidence that markets could be brought under human control. In essence, he was repeating Walter Lippmann's progressive era calls for mastery. Describing the Depression as a failure of intelligence, he claimed "Men have understood more complicated things than money."[66] He retained a New Era faith, worked out in *Fortune*, that economic markets could be controlled, organized, and regulated, though he found little hope that American industrial leaders were up to the task. "A sadder, stubborner, more timorous, whistle-in-the-graveyard lot never before lived on earth," MacLeish wrote to a friend, characterizing the American capitalist class.[67] Government control of industry might seem the only available alternative, but as late as 1932 he still entertained the idea that business leadership might be enough, that business could institute the necessary reforms itself. In a letter "To the Young Men of Wall Street," MacLeish reiterated his castigation of business leaders for having "ignored the necessity of giving the economic order shape and structure and human hope." "Only the credulous hope anything further from the generation now in control (more or less) of American capitalism," he concluded. Yet he made plain his belief that a new generation of leaders, following in the footsteps of *Fortune*'s hero, General Electric's Owen D. Young, could provide the necessary leadership. He called on a new generation of capitalists to "create an idea of capitalism which men will support with their hope rather than their despair."[68]

MacLeish realized that American business leaders were too caught up in trying to keep their companies afloat to concern themselves with creating a new justification for capitalism. Nor were the capitalists he encountered at *Fortune* likely to effectively convey such a vision, even if they could conceive of it. The task fell more properly, he believed, to the poet, whose currency was the imagination. Or, equally, to the poet in the guise of the journalist. Thus, in the early 1930s, in both his poetry and his journalism, MacLeish worked to develop a vision of America in which workers and capitalists alike could believe.

Facts: "Telling Them What the Hell's What"

While MacLeish's developing interests fueled *Fortune*'s expansion of its field of analysis, Ingersoll supplied the rationale for the change. A prolific memo writer, Ingersoll, like Luce, was prone to imbue every policy with an elaborate justification. With the Depression of paramount importance, business seemingly helpless to respond, and calls for government intervention growing, Ingersoll cannily decided to turn *Fortune* into what he called a "journal of free inquiry." No longer an appendage of business, *Fortune* would stand "on the sidelines, simply writing history." As he put it in an internal memo in 1934, "our function should be neither that of prophet nor of expounder but that of the stern complete factual authority giving the reader the material with which to answer the questions the politicians will be batting back and forth over his head. They will be talking about 'liberty lost' and 'the forgotten men.' We will be telling them what the hell's what."[69]

This progressive era faith in presenting the facts and allowing them to dictate the response provided the foundation for *Fortune*'s new approach. Arousing an audience to action through a careful marshaling of facts had been the technique of the turn-of-the-century muckrakers, and *Fortune* led the way in updating this technique in the documentary mode that later emerged as the decade's characteristic form of expression. "Truth," Roy Stryker said, "is the objective of the documentary attitude," and Ingersoll claimed truth could be discerned through the investigation and presentation of information. Like the muckrakers, however, this emphasis on facts often served to camouflage the emotional dramatization and political agenda that accompanied it.[70]

This approach was already on display in MacLeish's major article on unemployment, appearing in September 1932, just two months before the presidential election. *Fortune* titled the piece "No One Has Starved," Hoover's claim minimizing the suffering caused by the Depression, but added the subtitle "Which Is Not True." The actual magnitude of the suffering has not been known, the magazine claimed, because of the country's inability to accept the truth. "Since the facts were never frankly faced as facts, people came to believe that unemployment was relatively unimportant." Statistics proved otherwise, *Fortune* maintained, as a detailed calculation of unemployment figures demonstrated. *Fortune* relied on this presentation to convey the magnitude of the problem. A striking Reginald Marsh painting of massed anonymous men led the article and accompanying pages of photographs of the unemployed further set off MacLeish's article. The text contained the evidence while the pictures brought home its emotional meaning.[71]

Factual inquiry became the entering wedge for *Fortune*'s most critical work. Forceful presentation of unexpected information caught the reader's attention and established a firm basis for *Fortune*'s critical conclusions. MacLeish began his six-part inquiry into the disarray of the housing industry by the application of statistics to a novel. Ever since Sinclair Lewis's novel *Babbitt* had appeared, George Babbitt had represented "in his person and his possessions, and particularly in his house and his bath, the house and the bath of the average American of our time." But looking at the financial information Lewis supplied, MacLeish established that George Babbitt was better off than 98.9 percent of his countrymen. Examine the facts, MacLeish concluded "and Babbitt becomes a novel of the richest 1 per cent." The ground was set for a look at the inadequate housing endured by the rest of America, the cumulative marshaling of statistics building to an emotional force comparable to that achieved by Jacob Riis's groundbreaking *How the Other Half Lives*. The remaining five installments in the series exposed the lack of organization, planning, and association that rendered American housing inadequate and the housing industry, in MacLeish's words, "bogged, bound, and helpless." [72] The series was such a success it was later published in book form.

Fortune's famous March 1934 article "Arms and the Men," an exposé of the European munitions industries that helped prompt the Nye Hearings in Congress, employed this technique to great effect. The magazine used the cold justification of financial numbers to launch a moral inquiry. The article began:

> According to the best accountancy figures, it cost about $25,000 to kill a soldier during the World War. There is one class of Big Business Men in Europe that never rose up to denounce the extravagance of its government in this regard—to point out that when death is left unhampered as an enterprise for the individual initiative of gangsters the cost of a single killing seldom exceeds $100. The reason for the silence of these Big Business Men is quite simple: the killing is their business.[73]

The article then went on to inquire into what became of the $25,000 per dead soldier: who profited, by how much, and why.

The cool juxtaposition of death and financial profit made "Arms and the Men" powerful investigative journalism. It is important to note, however, that *Fortune*'s justification for the exposé rested on the premise that war was a business. Because people profited from the killing, it fell within *Fortune*'s purview. This became a common strategy in *Fortune*, but it also legitimated racier content. The magazine justified articles on the divorce industry in Reno, cockfighting, the mass production of debutantes, birth control, and a pictorial of stripper Gypsy Rose Lee by claiming that all were businesses and as such were appropriate subjects for *Fortune*.[74] Few readers probably needed the justification, but the effect was important. While *Fortune* deployed the idea that business was imbued with a public interest, its tendency to define "business" as the ability to make money made the opposite claim: businesses that made money were legitimate regardless of their social utility.

Facts Made Real in the Imagination

The necessary corollary of *Fortune*'s factual content was its packaging of information as forcefully and effectively as it could. In so doing it experimented with a wide range of techniques for conveying reality more directly, immediately, and effectively. From the very first its visual presentation had been almost as important as its text, and in *Fortune*'s early forays into political issues the pictures often carried the emotional content left out of the article.[75] In 1933, however, MacLeish led a drive to push the limits of *Fortune*'s fact-inflected prose, seeking a more forceful melding of information and literary presentation.

MacLeish suggested what the writers had been trying to accomplish in a series of lectures delivered at the University of Minnesota in 1958. Speaking just a few years before the emergence of the "new journalism," MacLeish attacked what he viewed as the increasingly strenuous separation of journalism and literature. Journalists, he claimed, strove "towards an admirably dispassionate objectivity which presents the event in the colorless air of intellectual detachment at the cost of its emotional significance." The resulting journalism failed to engage the reader. Poetry, on the other hand, reacting against this tendency "turns more and more to the emotional significance divorced from the event." Taken together, MacLeish concluded, "we are deluged with facts, but we have lost, or are losing, our human ability to feel them. Which means that we have lost or are losing our ability to comprehend the facts of our experience as poetry comprehends them, recreated and made real in the imagination."[76]

MacLeish's words provide a good summary of what *Fortune* sought to accomplish in the middle 1930s. In part, this had always been *Fortune*'s mandate—to provide business with its own literature. But as the magazine became more piercingly analytical, the meaning of that literature changed.

No longer merely an accouterment of business life (bringing culture to the busy businessman), it now sought to employ literary technique to make its description of America more compelling. *Fortune*'s effort to "integrate journalism and literature," in Ingersoll's words, became an effort to represent American civilization in a way that facts alone could not.[77] This is what MacLeish attempted in his series on Ivar Kreuger, history as written by the accountant and the poet. Other writers were compelled by this project, appreciating the creative freedom it provided them. Here was the leeway needed to make business their own in giving full license to their literary talents.

This is how James Agee began an article on the Tennessee Valley Authority in October 1933:

> The Tennessee River system begins on the worn magnificent crests of the southern Appalachians, among the earth's older mountains, and the Tennessee River shapes its valleys into the form of a boomerang, bowing it to its sweep through seven states. Near Knoxville the streams still fresh from the mountains are linked and thence the master stream spreads the valley most richly southward, swims past Chattanooga and bends down into Alabama to roar like blown smoke through the floodgates of Wilson Dam, to slide becalmed along the crop-cleansed fields of Shiloh, to march due north across the high diminished plains of Tennessee and through Kentucky spreading marshes toward the valley's end where finally, at the toes of Paducah, in one wide glassy golden swarm the water stoops forward and continuously dies into the Ohio.[78]

Agee then described the regions surrounding the valley, the cities of Asheville, Knoxville, Chattanooga, and Paducah, the small towns, the farms, the mountains and their people. He detailed the rich natural resources, their wasteful depletion, and the deep poverty that enveloped the region. Only after pages detailing the natural and human world of the Tennessee Valley did he move on to a consideration of the TVA and the vexing questions of private versus public power. The effect was profound: political questions receded as readers were reminded of the ultimate stakes: the people and the land they inhabited. The article did not slight the factual analysis *Fortune* required. Instead, it deepened it by placing it in a human context. The article became one of Luce's favorites, resonating as it did with his belief that business must be a means to larger ends.

The effort to effectively represent American reality sprang up in all sorts of articles. In September 1934, *Fortune* discovered "The Great American Roadside," that just emerging world of highways, barbecue stands, and clapboard transient shacks, just months before Frank Capra's "It Happened One Night" exploited the same world. Again written by Agee, the article tried to describe what he called "incomparably the most hugely extensive market the human race has ever set up to tease and tempt and take money from the human race." He chalked it up to American restlessness, but, in a foreshadowing of a concern at the heart of *Let Us Now Praise Famous Men*, Agee wondered about his ability to convey the truth behind this generalization: "the truth is, it isn't at all easy to say right." He tried, with the typical combination of detailed factual information (including a rigorous breakdown of every penny spent by the average touring American) and poetic description ("the spreaded swell and swim of the hard highway toward and beneath and behind and gone and the parted roadside swarming past"). Agee actually poured a great deal more energy into this attempt to make his language convey a reality difficult to apprehend, but *Fortune* had no space for the extra 10,000 words he wrote.[79]

During the middle 1930s, article after article in *Fortune* began with a long descriptive passage, where the author pushed his ability to capture the reader's attention and accurately sketch the shape of his subject. Luce supported the experimentation. Though he occasionally complained that the language sacrificed too much clarity for poetic effect, complaining, for example, in the Kreuger stories that "Arch was not edited into enough plain explicitness," he applauded the general tenor of the work.[80] It accorded with his skepticism of objectivity and appealed to his desire to make his magazines effective. Luce the journalist knew MacLeish's pieces were read and discussed, while his own lengthy and turgid account of banking sunk without comment or effect. Prose that stuck in the reader's mind by appealing to the emotions and the intellect, Luce believed, was more effective than a cold, clinical recitation of facts.

The mixture of journalism and poetry practiced by the writers at *Fortune* contained the same tension between factual presentation and emotional manipulation that characterizes all documentary effort. The writer's description and dramatization of the material became paramount, resulting in more overtly political content as the writers were radicalized. Ingersoll never admitted to the tension, claiming a naive faith in *Fortune*'s objective pursuit of the truth. In later years he described his vision of what *Fortune* in the 1930s had been in typically grandiose terms: "The essence of the dream . . . was the dream of freedom in the enquiry, freedom to tell it as it is—or at least, as honest men saw it—to go wherever the truth should lead, whatever shibboleths it might challenge, and not ever to take sides when battling in such corrupting arenas as the political."[81] As a skilled political infighter, however, Ingersoll's use of this get-the-facts discourse seems constructed to legitimize the magazine's travels to the left.

Taking Sides in the Class War

For Ingersoll, his writers, and even Henry Luce, the "plain facts" as they were presented in the magazine increasingly pointed toward specific conclusions. Unemployment was far worse than Hoover or business wanted to admit. American industry was too chaotic and unorganized to marshal the necessary response, and business leaders continued to mouth the same tired platitudes from the past. Republicans had no effective response to the problem. As MacLeish wrote in an analysis of the hatred of Roosevelt, "the Republican Party has displayed the minimum of intellectual activity consonant with continued life," a sentiment that echoed Luce's own statement that conservatives "had not had an idea since the Civil War."[82] Ingersoll summarized the conclusion the magazine reached: "the great corporations of America were responsible for the American economy but they had proved themselves helpless or irresponsible or both when the heat had come on."[83]

Once examining the causes and consequences of the Depression and the government response was established *Fortune* policy, guided by Ingersoll's documentary approach and the experimental impulses of the writers, the other writers quickly followed MacLeish's path of politicization. As *Fortune* pushed to examine the reality of corporate America, it began to radicalize writers that had remained personally inured to the effects of the Depression. The more the magazine paid attention to management's labor policies, the more it found itself in sympathy with labor. As Ingersoll remembered, "It was in these contacts that we rich boys learned for the first time what a Hell of a time the working people of America had had—and were still having—in the depression."[84] Wilder Hobson, for example, mild-mannered and genially conservative, came back from covering a strike in a company-owned coal town completely horrified. Politically awakened, he soon helped lead the unionization drive at Time Inc. and became the first head of Time's Newspaper Guild branch.

Though Luce was never radicalized, he walked along the same path to the left for a while. He, too, saw the failure of corporate America to respond effectively to the crisis. Though he retained hope that the necessary corporate leadership would emerge, he was not optimistic. He briefly flirted with fascism, championing its interest in reviving such "ancient virtues" as "Discipline, Duty, Courage, Glory, Sacrifice," but soon acknowledged the brutality of Mussolini's Italy.[85] He supported the early New Deal, since its emphasis on industrial organization and cooperation seemed like extensions of his New Era economic beliefs. In 1934 Luce listed two minimum principles conservatives must acknowledge if they were to be taken seriously: "a livelihood must be guaranteed to every man," and every "man, woman, and child" must live in a dwelling that "conforms to some minimum standard of decency." He fully expected the government to establish and enforce the necessary standards. Though later a harsh critic of the New Deal, in the middle 1930s his major complaint was Roosevelt's criticism of business. Luce asked that "the President should lead Big Businessmen as he leads others by courage and hope."[86] In 1933 and 1934, *Fortune*'s belief that corporations were public institutions with public responsibilities and its corollary conviction that they had failed to meet their responsibilities, erected a tent big enough for Luce, Ingersoll, MacLeish, and the other writers to all comfortably stand under.

Interestingly, Macdonald, eventually the most radical of *Fortune* writers, proved less immediately susceptible to this process than the others. He enjoyed writing the occasional "muckraking" piece, but in general his journalism had little impact on his political thinking. In January 1932 Macdonald wrote a piece on the Berkshire Knitting Mills and their fight against union pickets in Reading, Pennsylvania, a city then under socialist administration. The story Macdonald submitted was openly skeptical of the union's aims and admiring of the company's intransigence. The company managers "are obstinate, no question about it," Macdonald concluded. "They run their mills exactly as they think best, which, as we have seen, is very admirably indeed."[87] In letters written while researching the story he noted the local happenings but was not particularly struck by the struggle. He was more animated in his discussion of his own finances ("Of late I have taken a great interest in the stock market . . . speculation pure and simple").[88] For Macdonald, political radicalization came from outside *Fortune* and was driven primarily by meeting Nancy Rodman, his future wife and a woman of strong political convictions.

They met in the spring of 1934, as Dwight was getting to know Nancy's brother Selden Rodman and the circle around Alfred Bingham's independent, quasi-socialist, magazine *Common Sense*. Dwight was taken with Nancy, and though he initially resisted her politics, complaining of being dragged to "drearily long-winded left-wing political meetings," he was soon won over by the hard-headedness and clear thinking of the Communist interpretation of the New Deal.[89] He put his new interest in radical politics to work in *Fortune*'s September 1934 profile of the Communist Party. The idea to write up the party had been Ingersoll's, who had picked up two hitchhiking Communists and was intrigued by their intelligence and commitment. Macdonald produced a long overview of the party and its opponents, before venturing a typical *Fortune* conclusion: "the Reds are 'trouble makers' and 'fomenters of rebellion,' but they can make trouble and foment riots only when the capitalist system has done gross injustice to some social group. By leading the oppressed classes and making their grievances articulate, the Communists force the capitalist system to adjust its most glaring inequalities." The overall tone of the article was superior and amused, excoriating the Communists for their fealty to Moscow, their addiction to theoretical wrangling, and their relentless factionalism (he profiled the Trotskyites, Gitlowites, Lovestoneites, and Weisbordites, who "I'm told consist of Weisbord and his wife").[90] He denounced the Communists' enemies in less amused tones, ridiculing their apocalyptic reaction to a nonexistent threat. This combined tone of indignation and supercilious amusement came naturally to Macdonald. In preparing the article he had spent a day with Walker Evans (whose pictures illustrated the article) at a Communist camp "to see the Communists at play." He found the experience "came near making a fascist out of me." He disliked the "herd" living, the close proximity of so many people, the bad music, soiled plates, and bathing in a "dirty pool." By "Sunday noon we could stand it no more and we stole away to the Westchester Embassy Club . . . where we bathed in a clean if capitalistic pool and drank a couple of Tom Collinses in capitalistic solitude."[91]

The experience did nothing, however, to shake his developing conviction that Communism offered the only "way out of the mess our society is in."[92] He was skeptical of Stalin from the first, but, convinced of the failure of liberal democracy to reform itself and of the contradictions within capitalism that made its continuance impossible, he saw Communism as the only possible alternative. Macdonald tried to bring his convictions to bear at *Fortune*, meeting with Luce in an attempt to convince him to make the magazine even more critical and socially responsible. Luce mollified Macdonald personally and assured him that his political convictions would be respected, but made no concessions. Soon thereafter Macdonald took a six-month leave to work out his developing political ideas.

When he returned to work in 1935, sporting a red Trotskyesque beard ("Everyone in *Fortune* dislikes it, everyone outside of *Fortune* admires it," he wrote) Macdonald was caught up in the increasingly political atmosphere of the magazine. With the New Deal under increasing pressure from the left and organized labor asserting itself, the writers at *Fortune* continued to push their critical project. Macdonald began to think he might turn his *Fortune* work into something worthwhile.[93] He knew he wanted "to analyze, to discriminate, even to think if necessary, and to put it all down in writing as skillfully as I can." For the first time he considered whether he could do this at *Fortune*, and determined to make the attempt.[94] During his leave he had read Adolf Berle and Gardiner Means's *The Modern Corporation and Private Property* for the first time. He soon put it to work in his next big assignment, a profile of Republic Steel. The piece was a typical *Fortune* corporation story, though it contained extensive treatment of individual workers (Republic's labor policies, however, were barely mentioned). The content was mildly critical of the company, though it missed few opportunities to laud Tom Girdler's "vital" leadership (Macdonald later regretted that he had "panegyricised Girdler and his money men").[95] Macdonald began his summary section by noting "an indictment cannot be drawn against Republic and its management by anyone unwilling also to draw an indictment against the whole U.S. corporate system."[96] He then proceeded to indict American corporate management for overstepping their legal role as trustees of the stockholders. Managers such as Girdler acted like earlier capitalist owners, making decisions for the corporation, and then engineering the necessary stockholder approval. The hopes of liberals such as Berle and Means, that the divorce of ownership from managerial power would make management more "disinterested," were misplaced. Corporate management's power remained unchecked.

Macdonald's draft had been more overtly critical. When Girdler read the draft (*Fortune* let all cooperating companies see a draft to correct factual mistakes and argue interpretation) he exploded, labeling it "Socialism" and threatening to pull Republic's advertising. After an editorial fight in which Macdonald enlisted Luce's aid, MacLeish was called in to rewrite it. He managed to retain the basic tenor of Macdonald's criticism yet placate the other editors (though not Republic). Macdonald was pleased with the result, though he was also determined not to let the editors eviscerate the critical edge in his writing the next time. He also appreciated MacLeish's help ("For all his lousy poetry, MacLeish has his uses around here as a left-wing social force.") He was seriously reconsidering the importance of his *Fortune* work, musing "I feel that FORTUNE can be made somewhat more critical and socially conscious." [97] To that end, he joined MacLeish, Hobson, and Eric Hodgins (who now shared the job of managing editor with Ingersoll) in an effort to combat what they perceived as *Time*'s biased coverage. Macdonald compiled a lengthy dossier of examples of *Time*'s distortion of the news, especially as it treated organized labor, to attach to the indictment penned by MacLeish. The effort met with indifference.[98]

Macdonald pushed his politics further in his next assignment, a corporation story on the company a previous generation of muckrakers had made their names assailing, U.S. Steel. It was the most ambitious and important corporation story *Fortune* ever attempted. Macdonald was forthright in his goals, seeking to utilize *Fortune*'s distinctive journalistic technique in pursuit of a political agenda. Writing to Wheeler, he boasted, "I hope to so buttress my extremely unfavorable opinion of the Corporation with fact and analysis that even the average pachyderms of steel won't be able to topple it."[99] Indicating the capaciousness of *Fortune*'s critical conception, he was joined by Charles Stillman, the conservative business manager of Time Inc., who was every bit as eager to criticize Steel for its shortcomings.

"The Corporation," a "critical analysis of the world's biggest industrial enterprise," began in the March 1936 issue. For the first time, Macdonald experimented with the literary mode favored by other *Fortune* writers. He offered himself as the voice "who will sing the terror and power of American industry," penning a long poetic invocation of the steel-making process. The piece, while not as deft as the best work of MacLeish or Agee, effectively emphasized the ugly, destructive force of steel making, dwelling on its capacity to remake the world. Macdonald invoked "streams running bister brown around Pittsburgh," "the lichen of rust spreading over the stacks of steel," the molten iron "twisting and roaring through sanded channels, glutinously gobbling, bearing on its surface black rafts of slag." The accompanying photographs, by Russell Aikins, celebrated the scale and beauty of steel production, but Macdonald brought out the terrible power. *Fortune* photographs typically used tiny workers to frame the machines, in the Bourke-White manner, but Aikins and Macdonald drew attention to the device and to the man. Aikins's steelworker glowed, and Macdonald's descriptive section ended with a view from outside the plant, of "the monotonous immensity of their exteriors, without scale or meaning until a man walks by."[100]

Turning to analysis, Macdonald proposed to measure U.S. Steel by two standards: as a machine for making money and as a machine for serving society. The conclusions he reached were unequivocal: U.S. Steel had not made money and it had not served the interests of its stockholders, its employees, or its customers. The company was too big, it favored the status quo over innovation, its pricing policy was "the words are measured - artificial, wasteful, discriminatory, and noncompetitive."[101]

The first two installments of the article, where Macdonald pressed these points, were widely read and discussed. Felix Frankfurter, who had recently written for the magazine, was appreciative, and sent the article on to Louis Brandeis, who also thought well of it (Macdonald acknowledged, when he heard, that "few men's praise could be sweeter to me.")[102] *Fortune* received more mail for the Steel articles than for any previous work, and promised to devote a later issue to printing the commentary (it never did). U.S. Steel and its chairman of the board, Myron Taylor, were of course angry. The Morgan interests, who still controlled the board, had pressed Luce hard to cut the criticism, but the first two parts had run much as Macdonald wrote them.

The third installment, covering the corporation's labor policies, was assigned to Robert Cantwell at Macdonald's urging. The author of the fine proletarian novel *The Land of Plenty*, Cantwell seemed a good choice to continue the critical tenor of the article. Cantwell, however, Macdonald claimed, "lost his nerve, for complex personal reasons, and turned in a piece that was so diplomatic . . . that Luce saw it wouldn't do."[103] The piece was rewritten, and the published article pushed Macdonald's line of criticism further. *Fortune* ridiculed the welfare policy of the company for its proud boasting of furnishing employees with toilets and sinks. It claimed an "industrial democracy" was better served by the "strength and protection of a steelworkers' union" than such welfare work.[104] Macdonald's criticism, implicit in the first two pieces, that the corporation had defaulted on its social responsibility, was made explicit. U.S. Steel's great power brought responsibilities it had failed to uphold.

At this point the series was slated to end. Macdonald pushed for a final summary installment, weaving together the threads previously examined individually. He received the go ahead, and produced a lengthy analytical draft pushing an interpretation he signaled by leading the piece with a quote from Lenin: "free competition is the fundamental property of capitalism....Monopoly is the direct opposite of free competition....Monopoly is the transition from capitalism to a higher order." Macdonald concluded,

"The problem of the United States Steel Corp. is the problem of a quasi-monopolistic power in an economy based on the free market. The syllogism of Lenin quoted as the beginning of this article admirably expresses the paradox: competition logically leads to its antithesis, monopoly, and with equal logic monopoly leads to Socialism. It is the supreme contradiction of capitalism that its mightiest children are also its most dangerous enemies. Communism is being prepared more effectively at 71 Broadway [U.S. Steel headquarters] than in Union Square."[105]

This essay prompted an internal fight inside *Fortune*. Ingersoll, the editor for the entire story, had been fighting a running battle with Macdonald over each installment of the series and did not think the piece should run as written. He did try to broker a compromise, however, by giving Macdonald a byline for his critical interpretive essay, telling Luce that Macdonald's viewpoint was "an informed and intelligent one."[106] Luce shot down this idea, being opposed to any interpretive articles or "any conclusion which might be construed as a letting of Macdonald or any other individual member of the staff draw critical conclusions from our Steel series."[107] Eric Hodgins, who had generally sided with Macdonald in his fights with Ingersoll, again backed him, but not strongly enough to counter Luce. In the end Ingersoll rewrote Macdonald's piece, eliminating all the interpretive and speculative material and substituting a summary that kept faith with the tenor of the previous articles but pushed the conclusions no further. If the published piece little resembled the "rosy Valentine" to Steel that Macdonald bitterly described, it was a curiously tepid conclusion to the sustained critical analysis that preceded it.[108]

The struggle over the Steel series clarified the political divisions between the writers and editors. Luce had monitored the series throughout, pressed by the Morgan interests, Steel management, his own editors, and Macdonald. The flap over the final installment convinced him that *Fortune*'s position as independent critic of business was no longer tenable. He was bolstered by increasing outside criticism of *Fortune* as "paid with Moscow's gold." Even the *Fortune* advertising salesmen were up in arms, frankly asking Luce whether it was ethical to solicit advertising from business if the magazine was biased against it.[109] Luce considered all this before meeting with Ingersoll and declaring "What is going on in the steel industry and maybe in the whole country is war—war between capital and labor." If that was the case "then I've got to tell you there simply can't be any question about whose side *Fortune* magazine is on. *Fortune* has got to be on capital's side."[110] It was clear to Ingersoll the Steel series meant a permanent change for the magazine.

Macdonald was the first casualty. Even after the fight with Ingersoll and Luce, he had remained, hoping to patch together a compromise that would allow him to continue. Macdonald had invested a lot of himself in the Steel series, more than he ever had working for *Fortune*. Despite taking a "bad beating at the combined hands of J. P. Morgan, U.S. Steel, and *Fortune*" it was still difficult to leave a job he had only recently come to view as important.[111] That he was making $10,000 a year made the decision even harder. Overcome by "a state of psychic impotence," however, he left *Fortune* in June for a leave of absence that later became permanent.[112]

Macdonald fired a parting shot in a series of articles on Time Inc. published in the *Nation*. He described his old magazine as "a social phenomenon as bristling with contradictions as the capitalist system for which it speaks." Like Luce, he felt those contradictions could be resolved only if the magazine openly declared itself. He characterized the magazine as driving "madly ahead on its mysterious course, all sails set and the steering gear out of order."[113] Luce and Macdonald both wanted to impose a steering gear on *Fortune*. Luce wanted to tack to the right by acknowledging *Fortune*'s fealty to business. Macdonald attempted to steer it left by viewing the economy through the lens of Marxist economics. Ingersoll's big tent of journalists, engaged in the disinterested search for truth, threatened to collapse when the stakes were raised to the level of the class war in which both Macdonald and Luce believed the country was engaged. The time had come, both believed, for choosing sides.

Whither *Fortune*?

In 1937 Luce tried to force a major reconsideration of *Fortune*. No longer comfortable with the direction of the magazine's journalism, he now wanted to print an explicit acknowledgment of *Fortune*'s "bias in favor of free enterprise." He assigned Eric Hodgins, the sole managing editor now that Ingersoll had been promoted to publisher of *Time*, to write up a new "Respectus." Hodgins tried "everything except iambic pentameter" before admitting he could not offer a convincing reconciliation of bias and journalism. The writers were even more forcefully opposed. The emphasis on factual inquiry filtered through the writer's imagination had always been the bridge between Luce and his writers. As a writer put it in one of the flurry of memos discussing Luce's proposal, "an artistic conscience (*Fortune*'s should be that) does not have to 'believe' in the profit system any more than it 'believes' in the Chrysler Building. The profit system is a fact, not a cause." MacLeish followed up, claiming that "a truly objective journal," as *Fortune* had striven to be, could not have a preconceived commitment to any outcome of its research. "The advocacy of the point of view of the owners of big business is incompatible with the journalism FORTUNE has developed," MacLeish argued, and *Fortune* risked making itself a "journalistic joke" by operating from such a position. *Fortune* must remain a magazine *of* business, not *for* or *against* business.[114]

In the face of this opposition, Luce backed away from his hopes to see the magazine print his acknowledgment of subservience to business.[115] Nevertheless, the expansiveness of *Fortune*'s journalism slowly eroded. Macdonald left first. Agee's production for the magazine gradually declined, and MacLeish formally resigned in 1938. That same year Russell Davenport became the managing editor, and despite his personal literary aspirations, he was less interested in artistic experimentation than in pushing the magazine to embrace his own, more libertarian, political views. *Fortune* continued to be a sharp analyst, and sometimes a penetrating critic, of contemporary American society. But it was a more staid, more chastened magazine. It was never again the magazine it had been in the middle 1930s.

What, ultimately, is the significance of the efforts made by these intellectuals to turn Luce's business magazine into a vehicle of political and artistic experimentation? *Fortune* during its mid-1930s peak was an extraordinary magazine. MacLeish liked to boast to his radical friends that *Fortune* was a better social historian than the *New Masses*, and most of the time he was right. The magazine consistently produced incisive, provocative, compelling, and influential journalism. This journalism reached a powerful and influential audience. Among other accomplishments, it fueled a national debate on housing, spurred a congressional investigation of the role of munitions makers in the First World War, and helped convince corporate leaders to reach an accommodation with industrial unions. It is no surprise that Franklin Roosevelt paid close attention to the content of *Fortune*.

The magazine played a significant role in pushing political opinion to the left. *Fortune* accepted and propagated a series of assumptions—that business must place the public good above private ends, that social rights to housing and employment existed and must be met, that organized labor was a legitimate expression of the just needs and demands of workers, that free markets were but one means, and not necessarily the best means, to achieving a more democratic, more fair, more just society. These assumptions provided concrete support for the New Deal and its expansive new role for the government.

Historians have long attributed Roosevelt's "Second New Deal," beginning in 1935, to the "thunder on the left," a shorthand term describing the simultaneous rise of organized social movements such as the industrial unions of the CIO, expansion of farm-labor parties in the midwest, growth of socialist and communist political organizations, and appeal of populist voices such as Huey Long, Father Coughlin, and Francis Townsend.[116] In this telling, the pressure building on the left pushed Roosevelt to embrace the Wagner Act, and to launch a "Second New Deal" built around Social Security, the Works Progress Administration, and a "Soak the Rich" tax on wealth.

Too often overlooked, however, is the crucial legitimacy granted Roosevelt's program from elements of the mainstream that could have been expected to resist any such moves to the left. The entire political culture shifted left during the Depression years, and *Fortune* was an important voice in a mainstream political chorus that accepted, echoed, and even championed a new set of ideas about the expanded capabilities and responsibilities of the government.

Recent analysts have dismissed the aspirations of *Fortune*'s writers, describing the magazine as part of the "new corporatism," or as articulating a coherent ideology of corporate leadership, or of being part of a new "historic bloc" of capital-intensive corporations that seized control of the Democratic Party.[117] All these interpretations necessitate ignoring the political views of the intellectuals who produced the magazine, dismissing their struggles to see those views represented in the magazine, and underplaying the critical and political edge of *Fortune*'s journalism. These interpreters all proceed from the assumption that the 1930s marked the frustration of the left, the failure of grand aspirations for socialist or communist transformation. That the political road to the left in the United States proved a mild left rather than a sharp left, that the United States never achieved the social democracy (or, much more problematically, communism), longed for by many, should not eclipse the achievement of the New Deal in altering key assumptions about the role of government and the legitimacy of the corporation in American life. Nor should it denigrate, minimize, or eclipse the role of *Fortune*'s band of intellectuals in the articulation and legitimization of this new political culture.

Crucial to *Fortune*'s success was the self-identification of its journalists as intellectuals. Conceivably journalists could be expected to pursue the type of journalism expected by their editor and publisher. But Luce could not impose his own vision for *Fortune*'s journalism on his writers. Their primary commitment was intellectual: to exploring, understanding, and depicting the world they found. They held a commitment to their own intellectual independence, yet unlike later intellectuals who turned this independence into a fetish, they believed they could act unimpeded from within the interstices of a large institution. They were willing to fight to see their vision represented in the magazine. They succeeded less than they hoped, but more than might be expected, and enough to create a critical and important magazine. The experience indelibly marked their understanding of themselves as intellectuals.

CHAPTER FOUR

Intellectuals Visible and Invisible

> ... to speak of you as "tenant" "farmers," as "representatives" of your "class," as social integers in a criminal economy . . . to name these things and fail to yield their stature, meaning, power of hurt, seems impious, seems criminal, seems impudent, seems traitorous in the deepest: and to do less badly seems impossible: yet in withholdings of specification I could but betray you still worse.
> —James Agee, *Let Us Now Praise Famous Men*

Archibald MacLeish was a well-known intellectual in 1937, the year he left *Fortune* magazine. A Pulitzer Prize-winning poet, the author of numerous books, radio plays, and magazine articles, and one of the public faces of the Spanish republican cause, MacLeish was a controversial figure. Regularly denounced for his "unconscious fascism" by the Communist left, he was simultaneously tarred as the first "fellow traveler" by Representative J. Parnell Thomas. After leaving *Fortune*, MacLeish went on to a new career in public service, serving as librarian of Congress, director of the Office of Facts and Figures, and assistant secretary of state during the Roosevelt years. He published many more books, won two more Pulitzers, drafted the preamble to the United Nations charter, and constantly intervened in public disputes. In many ways, MacLeish served as the very model of a public intellectual for the rest of his life: prolific, visible, accessible, and consistently seeking to articulate the democratic promise he felt the United States needed to fulfill.

Dwight Macdonald and James Agee, on the other hand, labored in obscurity. Agee's great work, *Let Us Now Praise Famous Men*, earned mostly hostile reviews and sold fewer than 600 copies when it appeared in 1941. For the rest of the 1940s, he spent much of his time writing film reviews before moving to Hollywood to collaborate on scripts. Agee worked on a number of important films, such as *The African Queen* and *Night of the Hunter*, but remained little known when he fell dead of a heart attack in 1955, at just forty-five years of age.

Macdonald moved from *Fortune* into the world of left politics, associating largely with the anti-Stalinist Trotskyists. Engaged primarily in the internecine warfare of the left, he joined the editorial board of *Partisan Review* when it resumed publication in 1937. He broke with fellow editors Philip Rahv and William Phillips over the Second World War (Macdonald refused to support the Allied cause), and then spent the next five years publishing his own magazine, *Politics*. Well regarded in certain nonaffiliated left circles, *Politics* remained a small-scale affair, never growing much beyond 5,000 subscribers. After *Politics* folded in 1949, Macdonald supported himself on his old Time Inc. stock and the proceeds from freelance writing. By the late 1950s he was writing cultural criticism for the *New Yorker* and film reviews for *Esquire*. He never produced the full-length book that he had hoped to write for more than forty years.

Since their deaths, the reputations of all three have nearly reversed. Interest in Agee began growing almost as soon as he died. The novel he had never been able to finish, *A Death in the Family*, appeared in 1957 to warm praise and won the Pulitzer Prize. In 1960 *Famous Men* was reissued, this time to widespread acclaim. In the years since, Agee has been the subject of numerous biographies, critical studies, conferences, and dissertations.[1] His work has been collected in the Library of America, as close to an official canon as the United States possesses.[2] Macdonald's legacy has been less substantial, and more divisive, yet his work has received respectful attention in recent decades. His essays on popular culture continue to serve as touchstones of cultural criticism, even as they have been attacked for their elitism. His position as a key figure among New York intellectuals has guaranteed him a place in postwar intellectual history. Macdonald has received an excellent biography, two other book-length studies, and many serious examinations of his ideas. Collections of his letters and of interviews with him have both appeared in the last few years.[3]

MacLeish, on the other hand, has suffered a gradual, yet serious, critical eclipse. Scott Donaldson wrote a literary biography in 1992, now long out of print. MacLeish has received little attention since. A couple of his poems from the 1920s remain anthologized, but his work is rarely discussed in the academy. Every few years someone publishes a brief article pleading for MacLeish's importance, but these essays sink without even creating a ripple in critical opinion.[4] Richard Pells's authoritative two-volume survey of midcentury intellectuals in the U.S. contains detailed, probing consideration of both Agee and Macdonald. MacLeish is mentioned only in passing.[5]

Historical legacies are complicated things, with literary reputations waxing and waning for myriad reasons. Part of the explanation has to do with quality, as historians seize on the most penetrating, complex, or persuasive works of the past. Part of the explanation has to do with the issues, anxieties, and needs of our present era, as historians look to locate a usable past that can clarify our present problems. Part of the explanation is bound up in the difficulties in analyzing an author's audience. Their contemporary reputation is often correlated with the size and character of the audience they reach, a factor that historians, faced with the daunting task of measuring the size of audiences and the influence of particular works on readers, often ignore or underplay.

But in this case, part of the explanation also resides in a key difference in the assumptions about acceptable and unacceptable ways of pursuing intellectual commitments. MacLeish, Macdonald, and Agee each modeled different ways of being an intellectual. MacLeish's approach—that of the engaged intellectual who combines intellectual inquiry with practical application, sometimes from a position inside the government—has been denigrated and dismissed. Macdonald's approach—that of the intellectual as independent critic—has been championed and venerated, so much so that Agee's very different ideas about the proper place for the intellectual have usually been misunderstood as echoing Macdonald's. MacLeish sought to throw open and pass through the doors that separated intellectuals from political leaders, government officials, university presidents, media moguls, and the broad American public. Macdonald sought to keep those doors shut, lest the traffic between corrupt the values intellectuals held dear. The success of Macdonald and similarly minded critics helped leave intellectuals segregated from the main currents of American society, with MacLeish on one side of the door and Macdonald on the other. Here the metaphor breaks down, because it would appear that Agee was left standing with the intellectuals next to Macdonald. Yet this is accurate only if his ideas are misrepresented. To glimpse Agee's complicated ideas about how one should go about being an intellectual, the doors need to be thrown open. There we might find the small anteroom where Agee worked, practically invisible from the outside, in a place connected to the intellectual world on one side and the rest of American society on the other, but not truly a part of either place.

"A Time to Speak"

For his whole life Archibald MacLeish struggled to reconcile his desire to create art with his equally pressing desire to assume an active role in public affairs. MacLeish viewed these as competing goals, believing that he could either write a personal poetry, as he had quite successfully during the 1920s, or seek the public role for which his education and class background had prepared him. During his years at *Fortune*, however, experimenting with ways to combine the two, he made the transition from modernist poet to public intellectual.

In the late 1930s, MacLeish occupied a position unique in American political and intellectual life. Always a remarkably versatile man, during these years he was a well-known poet, playwright, essayist, political agitator, and public servant. Thematically, his work plowed a narrow furrow, as he consistently exposed the dangers posed by fascism and called for a positive democratic response. But he pursued these views in a wide range of forms, and he succeeded in putting his ideas before an immense audience.

On 11 April 1937, millions of radio listeners heard Orson Welles narrate the first verse play written for radio, MacLeish's drama *The Fall of the City*. The play was a parable, dramatizing how easily the people of an unnamed city were persuaded to accept passively the fall of their city to a conqueror in armor, an event they took to be their fate. Only when it was too late did the radio announcer intone that the suit of armor was empty, that the people had succumbed to fear and surrendered to a phantom. The night of its broadcast, one commentator noted, "more people heard the message of a single poet and a single poem . . . than at any other time in history."[6]

MacLeish followed this up with a second radio play, *Air Raid*, inspired by Picasso's painting *Guernica*, depicting the Nazi bombing of the Spanish city. Again he used a narrator to provide a realistic description of events. Debuting four days before Welles's use of the same technique in *War of the Worlds* caused widespread panic, MacLeish eschewed the specificity of that broadcast. Instead, he depicted the generalized horror of modern warfare, allowing listeners to feel the horror of death arriving anonymously from above, targeting soldier and civilian alike. In both plays MacLeish worked the same ground, concerned with the loss of individual agency and control, replaced in the first by men in the mass and threatened in the second by mechanized death.

Both plays were early forays into the antifascist politics that came to dominate the cultural front of the late 1930s. As an artist, MacLeish looked upon the rise of fascism with grave trepidation. He recognized the threat the Nazis posed to the freedom vitally necessary to art. He further recognized the threat fascism posed to democratic politics. Unlike many others in the antifascist vanguard, MacLeish did not see the future as a competition between fascism and communism. Nor did he see antifascism as necessarily an intervention on behalf of Soviet communism. As he wrote to Walter Lippmann in 1937, he believed the conflict between fascism and communism was "superficial and temporary" in comparison with what he believed was "the profound conflict between the conception of intellectual and moral freedom on the one hand and on the other, the conception of the totalitarian state." Communism and fascism posed equally dire threats to the autonomy of the individual and the artist. They needed to be opposed by a democratic renewal, a belief that led MacLeish to insist antifascism was insufficient. What was needed, he argued, was an expansion of reform aimed at the "realization of the potential strength of democracy."[7]

Personal reasons also drove MacLeish to react with so much vehemence and energy to fascism. In it he saw a threat sufficiently grave that it forced him to choose public engagement over private poetry, ending his struggles to reconcile the two. If the Nazis threatened to topple the core values of Western culture, then private art needed to be set aside. Its pursuit became irresponsible. Artists and intellectuals needed to fight to protect their values, not by picking up guns, but by deploying ideas in their own defense. Seeking a vital public role for the poet, MacLeish envisioned the antifascist struggle as a way to return "the poet to a position of common responsibility among the men and women of his time."[8]

MacLeish developed this argument in a series of addresses and essays in the late 1930s. Collected as *A Time to Speak*, their titles attest to his major concerns: "Public Speech and Private Speech in Poetry," "Question of Audience," "A Stage for Poetry," "Poetry and the Public World." These essays were directed against the isolationism still pervading the nation. While he was writing and speaking, Congress was passing a series of Neutrality Acts designed to decrease the ability of the president to aid one side in the growing conflicts in Europe and Asia. Congress narrowly failed to pass the Ludlow amendment, requiring a national referendum for a declaration of war, a measure supported by 73 percent of Americans.[9] MacLeish's essays were also interventions in the long-standing debate among writers about the relationship between art and politics. He wrote to counter the view that art must remain separate from the political concerns of the nation, while insisting that poetry need not be subordinated to the political program of a particular ideology.

MacLeish's developing position culminated in two addresses delivered in 1940 that generated a storm of controversy. The first, "The Irresponsibles," was delivered to the American Philosophical Society and printed in the *Nation*. In this essay, considered in greater detail below, MacLeish asked how history would judge those scholars and writers who stood on the sidelines in the face of the fascist assault on their culture. He followed it up with the second, a speech reprinted in the *New Republic* as "Post-War Writers and Pre-War Readers." Here, he addressed himself to postwar writers such as John Dos Passos and Ernest Hemingway. He celebrated their work, claiming that their furious assault on the way honorable ideals were manipulated and perverted in the cause of war had expressed a compelling reaction to the tragedy of the Great War. "They say what all of us after the war would have said if we could," MacLeish claimed. Nevertheless, he now charged these writers and others with doing their work too well. They had so effectively debunked the beliefs that had driven young men to their graves in the First World War that they left the current generation of young readers distrustful "of all statements of principle and conviction, all declarations of moral purpose." Writers such as Hemingway and Dos Passos rendered young Americans incapable of "using the only weapon with which fascism can be fought—the moral conviction that fascism is evil and that a free society of free men is worth fighting for."[10] The profound conclusions writers drew from the last war, MacLeish concluded, left Americans in the 1930s ill-equipped to fight fascists in the next.

The two essays, "The Irresponsibles" and "Post-War Writers and Pre-War Readers," were generally viewed together, and they brought a remarkable outpouring of calumny down upon MacLeish. Despite his flattery, Hemingway took the pieces personally, holding up his own direct involvement in Spain to claim that MacLeish must have a guilty conscience.[11] Edmund Wilson argued that Hemingway had hardly tainted such notions as courage, and scorned MacLeish's claim that books and ideas could accomplish as much as MacLeish assumed. If books such as Erich Maria Remarque's *All Quiet on the Western Front* were this influential, Wilson argued, then "the Nazis would not now be in France."[12]

Most critics did more than point to logical inconsistencies in MacLeish's argument. They painted his essays as symptomatic of the dangerous rise of totalitarian values in U.S. society. MacLeish might believe he was fighting fascism, they argued, but he was actually preparing us for its triumph. The true "literary irresponsible," concluded MacLeish's old nemesis, Edmund Wilson, was MacLeish himself, who seemed to forget "the class war . . . the fundamental conflict of the contemporary world."[13] Burton Roscoe claimed MacLeish was ladling out "totalitarian he-man hooey." MacLeish had the "same idea as Hitler," he just didn't know how to express it. MacLeish was "patrioteering," critics claimed, he was a "crisis patriot," one of the new "ideological policemen," another of the "frightened philistines." Morton Zabel summed up the critics position, claiming MacLeish had written "a moral pronouncement on the duties of the artist to the state."[14] For the political and literary left, from which most of this criticism emanated, MacLeish had misunderstood history. The values he saw as universal were merely the values of bourgeois society, the values of a dying class. The future was the conflict between fascism and communism. Calling for a defense of bourgeois culture necessarily aligned MacLeish with the fascists. Worse, calling for art to serve political purposes placed him in the company of Nazi propaganda minister Joseph Goebbels and his calls for art that would bring about a spiritual mobilization of the German people.

Dwight Macdonald made this point most clearly. As an editor of *Partisan Review*, Macdonald entered the fray in response to essays by the elderly literary critic Van Wyck Brooks. Once a champion of the radical writers of the 1920s, Brooks had hardened into a celebrator of American culture and a critic of modernism. In "Primary Literature and Coterie Literature," Brooks echoed MacLeish's call for a literature of engagement. He criticized writers he viewed as "mostly out of touch with the primary realities, for they had no real connection with the world they lived in; and their only responsibility was to their art." Brooks went much further, however, extending his arguments into a full-scale dismissal of modernist literature. Claiming modernist greats such as James Joyce and T. S. Eliot were driven by a "death-drive," Brooks linked literary decline to a spiritual crisis afflicting American society.[15] Despite the stark differences between the two (MacLeish would never dismiss the great modernists), Macdonald saw in Brooks the logical culmination of MacLeish's views.

Macdonald led the charge against what *PR* began calling "the Brooks-MacLeish thesis" in a lengthy essay titled, "*Kulterbolshewismus* and Mr. Van Wyck Brooks." Though Macdonald focused on Brooks, he made clear he viewed Brooks's ideas as an "amplification" of MacLeish's. Indeed, Brooks's paper was "the boldest statement to date of that cultural counterrevolution opened by Archibald MacLeish's attack on the irresponsibles." This was a shrewd debater's tactic, allowing him to use the far more inflammatory Brooks to discredit MacLeish. Brooks was seeking to enforce, Macdonald claimed, an "official culture." "The official approach to art has for its aim the protection of a historically reactionary form of society against the free inquiry and criticism of the intelligentsia," he concluded. "It is an attempt to impose on the writer *from outside* certain socio-political values, and to provide a rationalization for damning his work *esthetically* if it fails to conform to these *social values*." Brooks and MacLeish were subordinating literary quality to political utility. Thus, while Brooks had become "our leading mouthpiece for totalitarian values," MacLeish was equally complicit. For months *PR*'s letters columns echoed with hostile considerations of "the Brooks-MacLeish" thesis.[16]

By linking "The Irresponsibles" with "Post-War Writers and Pre-War Readers," critics made the charge that MacLeish was labeling the literature of the prewar era irresponsible because of its political content. By linking MacLeish's speeches with Brooks's far more intemperate attacks, they asserted that MacLeish was suggesting literature pass a political litmus test, that he placed artistic values below political intentions. Fueled by the hothouse political climate that prevailed during 1940 and 1941, it seemed credible to charge that MacLeish sought to use art politically in much the same way as had the Nazis. These tendencies combined to prevent "The Irresponsibles" from receiving the attention it deserved. The essay bears little resemblance to the caricature pilloried by writers on the left. It is actually a strongly argued assertion of the expansive responsibilities that properly fall at the feet of the intellectual.

MacLeish opened "The Irresponsibles" with a question that he feared would be asked by historians in the future as they worked "in the paper rubbish of our lives." Why did scholars and writers in the United States, "witnesses as they were to the destruction of writing and of scholarship in great areas of Europe," and "to the exile and the imprisonment and murder" of writers and scholars, not react more forcefully to the danger? Possibly these events were too distant to make much of an impact on the daily consciousness of writers, but similar forces were at work in this country and writers and scholars still failed to act in defense of their values. "Why did we not fight this danger" MacLeish imagined future scholars asking, "while the weapons we used best—the weapons of ideas and words—could still be used against it?"[17]

The answers given in the past, the answer Leonardo was supposed to have given Michaelangelo when he claimed "the study of beauty has occupied my whole heart," no longer sufficed. This crisis was different. It was more than a clash of armies, economic classes, or political systems. The practical person, concerned only with food and shelter, might be indifferent, MacLeish claimed, but "the scholar, the poet, - the man whose care is for the structure of the intellect, the houses of the mind" could not be, for it was "the scholar's goods" that were in danger.[18]

MacLeish posed the totalitarian threat in stark terms, not as a political or economic crisis, but as a cultural crisis. "Great numbers of men in various parts of the world," he wrote, "wish passionately and even violently to give up the long labor of liberty and to surrender their wills and their bodies and even their minds to the will of a leader, so that they may achieve at least the dignity of order, at least the dignity of obedience." "Whole nations of men" he continued, "have gladly and willingly released themselves, not only from their rights as individuals, but from their responsibilities as individuals, so that they are no longer compelled to feel or to respect the individual humanity of others."[19]

Was this really so different from early periods? The Western culture MacLeish saw imperiled had witnessed more than its share of political violence, of murder, inquisitions, torture, and the brutal suppression of dissent. Such violence, MacLeish argued, had always been justified in the name of truth, humanity, or God. What was new, however, was a "cynical brutality which considers moral self-justification unnecessary and therefore ... dispenses even with the filthy garment of the hypocrite."[20] Fascism substituted the cynical pursuit of power for morality. A political philosophy that subordinated ideas to military power, that labeled art degenerate if it did not confirm Nazi power, left no room for an independent intellectual life. Fascism assaulted truth, reason, and justification. This was the danger intellectuals faced and why they were peculiarly necessary to the defense.

Why did intellectuals fail to respond in the face of "the newly discovered techniques of deception, of falsehood as a military force, of strategic fraud?" It was not lack of wisdom or a failure of courage, MacLeish argued. Instead, it was due to "the organization of intellectual life in our time." Intellectual life had become divided between scholars and writers, he claimed, with neither accepting responsibility for the larger world of ideas. In previous times, the "man of letters," or intellectual, had been responsible for everything that touched the mind. Here MacLeish had in mind Milton (who "defended freedom of the mind in sentences which outlive every name of those who struck at freedom") and Voltaire (who "displayed naked to the grin of history the tyrants who were great until he made them small").[21]

In our present time, MacLeish argued, this intellectual had disappeared, replaced by more specialized scholars and writers. Specialization had not led to a decline in literary achievement. Unlike Brooks, MacLeish was not claiming contemporary writers were incapable of greatness. Indeed, he argued, "the time we live in has produced more first-rate writers than any but the very greatest ages."[22] The cost was in responsibility. Both scholars and writers had forsaken larger responsibilities when they accepted specialization.

The irresponsibility of the scholar, MacLeish argued, was the irresponsibility of the scientist. Scholars had become increasingly devoted to method, seeking detachment and objectivity in their quest to produce knowledge. It was not surprising, he claimed, that the principal contribution scholars had made to literary form was the Ph.D. thesis, "work done for the sake of doing work—perfectly conscientious, perfectly laborious, perfectly irresponsible."[23]

The irresponsibility of the writer, on the other hand, was the irresponsibility of the artist. Writers felt no responsibility to anything larger than their desire to strip away "the intellectual world ... the world of ideas, the world of judgments" and to represent the world as it was.[24] Art was its own justification. Devotion to the eternal values of art precluded involvement in the day-to-day political and economic struggles. Here MacLeish likely had in mind an exchange with William Butler Yeats from the previous year. In "Public Speech and Private Speech in Poetry" MacLeish had invoked a poetic tradition running back to Milton and Dante. It was time to revive that tradition, he argued, "to regain that conception of poetry in which a poem, like a war or an edict, is an action on this earth."[25] Yeats dissented, writing his 1939 poem "Politics" in response to MacLeish. In the closing lines:

> And maybe what they say is true
> Of war and war's alarms,
> But O that I were young again
> And held her in my arms.[26]

Yeats beautifully and movingly asserted the primacy of private concerns. But he would not be young again, and the world was headed to war. Events would move with or without the engagement of the poet. The present struggle, MacLeish believed, threatened the values that made private poetry possible.

It was the responsibility of the poet to speak to the political crisis. "Poetry alone imagines," MacLeish wrote, "and imagining creates, the world that men wish to live in and make true."[27] If, as he claimed, fascism represented the negation of the intellectual values at the core of Western civilization, then the poet's articulation and defense of these ideas were crucial weapons.

Scholars and writers, each operating in their specialized spheres, failed to accept their responsibility for the course of current events. MacLeish was calling for their unification, for the return of the intellectual who was ready to play a leading role in the events of the age. His insistence on political engagement followed from his belief in the power of ideas. For him, ideas, by illuminating the range of the possible and permissible, shaped the world far more pervasively than did political, or economic, or class, conflict. This belief led to his outsized sense of the role and responsibility of the intellectual. For MacLeish, both the poet and the scholar needed to transcend their isolated positions and act as public intellectuals, creating and clarifying the ideals that formed the foundation of a democratic and free society.

MacLeish was testing these ideas even as he wrote. In 1939 Franklin Roosevelt nominated him to head the Library of Congress. This presented him with a dilemma. The position would raise his stature, allowing him to regularly reach a wide audience. At the same time, it would prevent him from writing poetry. These misgivings led him to twice turn Roosevelt down. Roosevelt paid little attention to MacLeish's refusals. Playing to his desire to be of service, a need rooted in his family and emphasized during his education at Hotchkiss and Yale, Roosevelt charmed him into accepting. Pushed by Roosevelt, MacLeish envisioned the library as a useful platform from which he could extend the reach of his voice.

MacLeish was a controversial choice, both because he came from outside the librarian profession and because of his political activities (it was during his confirmation hearings that Representative Thomas smeared him as a "fellow-traveler" and tried to paint the Roosevelt administration as thoroughly infiltrated by Communists). But he was confirmed, and he became, according to historians of the library, one of the most important individuals in the institution's history. During his brief tenure, MacLeish oversaw a badly needed administrative overhaul of the library, establishing organizational structures and policies that remained in place for the next half century. He built bridges between the library and the literary community, bringing poets such as Robinson Jeffers, Robert Frost, Carl Sandburg, Stephen Vincent Benét, and Allen Tate to the library.[28] He also used the platform the library provided to become a national spokesman, to continue to proclaim his views on the struggle against fascism and the need for democratic renewal. The many addresses he delivered were published in 1943 as *A Time to Act*, a companion to his earlier volume that nodded to his change in profession.

MacLeish remained in government service for the duration of the war. In October 1941 Roosevelt added to his responsibilities, naming him head of the newly established Office of Facts and Figures (OFF), overseeing the dissemination of information concerning defense. There was a great deal of internal disagreement about what OFF should do, with many wanting it to be a public relations branch of the government, others expecting it to be a more benign version of the infamous Committee for Public Information, the agency led by George Creel that had pioneered inflammatory propaganda measures during the First World War. MacLeish saw it differently. He saw the agency as responsible for the distribution of as much factual information (such as, after Pearl Harbor, war production numbers, casualty reports, and war progress reports) as possible. Calling for "a strategy of truth," he adamantly opposed turning OFF into a propaganda agency. Unable to convince the War and Navy Departments to release the needed information, MacLeish became a lightning rod for press criticism. Eventually OFF's mission was changed in the bureaucratic reshuffling so common during the Roosevelt era, and MacLeish's role diminished.[29]

Despite the frustrations, in both jobs MacLeish had turned the institutions he headed into effective reflections of his views. Believing that the Library of Congress could enrich the national culture and act as a firm advocate for the widespread dissemination of knowledge, he fought against censorship and excessive deference to the secrecy demands of national security. Believing that the American public was poorly served by the distortions of the propagandist, he fought to turn OFF into an information agency that would provide the information citizens needed for self-government. In both instances he fought against what he called "nervous liberals," whose wavering commitment to their beliefs left them willing to compromise their faith in a free, open, democratic society and make concessions to more ominously authoritarian forces within the government and media.[30]

After leaving OFF, MacLeish spent the rest of the war serving in various capacities, including his job at the Library of Congress (which he maintained during his tenure at OFF). In 1944 he resigned from the Library hoping to return to writing. Roosevelt promptly named him assistant secretary of state. From that post MacLeish was heavily involved in the planning for the United

Nations. He helped to organize the San Francisco conference and to write the preamble to the UN Charter and the Declaration on Human Rights. He left government service when President Truman assumed office after Roosevelt's death.

Throughout his government employment, MacLeish managed to write a good many essays, speeches, and even plays, but he wrote no poetry. He consoled himself with the belief that his time working for government would serve as what he later called "a proper preparation" for the poetry to come. For a good while thereafter, the poems refused to come. His first postwar book of poems, *Actfive*, foundered on his struggles to find a consistent voice, alternating between the declamatory style of his public poetry phase and the private, more personal lyricism of his early works. Reviewers savaged his efforts.[31]

Despite the struggles with his poetry, he continued to intervene in the political issues of the day. He emerged as an early and forceful opponent of the anti-communist hysteria that resulted in congressional investigations and blacklists (earning him a 600-page FBI file for his troubles). Trying to encourage Henry Luce to speak out against the House Un-American Committee investigations, he wrote, "freedom is not something you have, it is something you do. The only way you can defend it is to exercise it."[32] MacLeish published poems and essays attacking the character assassination that constituted so much of the anti-communist agenda.

He also wrote a trenchant analysis of the impact of the early Cold War. In "The Conquest of America," MacLeish argued the United States had been psychologically conquered by its obsession with the Soviet Union. Again adopting the perspective of a historian looking back at the era in question, he rather hyperbolically began, "Never in the history of the world was one people as completely dominated, intellectually and morally, by another as the people of the United States by the people of Russia in the four years from 1946 through 1949." American foreign policy was a mirror image of Soviet policy. No U.S. politician could be elected without demonstrating his antipathy for everything Russian. Political proposals passed only after it was demonstrated the Soviets would dislike them. At precisely the moment when American power was unrivaled, he concluded, the United States had "contracted its national will to the dry negation of the will of others." MacLeish called for Americans to break free from these ideological binders. Returning to the themes that had animated him during his years at *Fortune*, he called for Americans to begin to "hammer out a political and industrial and economic order in which individual men—all men as individuals—should be capable of living and working in dignity and freedom and self-respect with an adequate opportunity for the realization of their full potentialities as human beings."[33]

Having found a voice as a political essayist, he struggled to regain his poetic voice. His literary standing fell. In his influential 1939 book *Modern Poetry and the Tradition*, Cleanth Brooks had made the case that MacLeish ranked with Robert Frost and W. H. Auden as the most important successors to Yeats and Eliot. Passing over candidates such as Wallace Stevens, William Carlos Williams, and E. E. Cummings, Brooks rated MacLeish's poetry higher than anyone had previously. It was the last time a serious and respected critic would make such claims for MacLeish's poetry.[34]

His 1948 book *Actfive* had been a disaster. In 1952 he published a *Collected Poems, 1917–1952*, a volume that was warmly received in the popular press and won a number of prizes. But the reaction in the literary quarterlies was far less positive. There the old complaints returned as critics claimed he was essentially derivative or he was too aggressive a self-promoter. Everyone agreed that his best poems had been published long ago.[35]

The reaction to *Collected Poems* set the tone for MacLeish's remaining years. Increasingly he functioned as a literary elder statesman. He was well regarded in the newspapers and the *Saturday Review*, but his popularity was never accompanied by the critical acceptance he sought. It was during these years that the conception of MacLeish as a popular but second rate poet took root. Both dynamics are visible in the reaction to his 1958 play, *JB*.

Hoping to reach the audience he had commanded in the late 1930s, MacLeish returned to themes he had developed in those years. Touring bombed out neighborhoods of London after the war, seeing the randomness that left certain buildings destroyed while others were left standing, he sought to make sense of the incomprehensible injustice of human experience. He eventually settled on a retelling of the story of Job, the biblical consideration of how one man could endure and explain the terrible afflictions that beset him. MacLeish transformed the biblical figure into J.B., a successful New England banker. J.B. is visited with a serious of tragedies, including the death of each of his five children, the last in an atomic blast that also destroys his wealth. J.B. is offered the comfort of three philosophies—religion, psychiatry, and Marxism—which all offer to explain away his troubles as the product of forces he cannot control. J.B. denies all three as offering a false comfort, comfort purchased by denying the free will of the individual. In the end, J.B.

concludes, the human capacity to love is all that can offer comfort. As J.B.'s wife, Sarah, speaks in the play's last lines,

> Blow on the coal of the heart.
> The candles in churches are out.
> The lights have gone out in the sky.
> Blow on the coal of the heart
> And we'll see by and by . . . .[36]

MacLeish's play made its way from the page, to the Yale University Theater, and eventually to Broadway in a production directed by Elia Kazan. It won rave reviews from the theater press, including Brooks Atkinson's influential review in the *New York Times*, where he gushed, "Looking around at the wreckage and misery of the modern world, Mr. MacLeish has written a fresh and exalted morality play that . . . seemed to be one of the memorable works of the century as verse, as drama and as spiritual inquiry.[37] *J.B.* ran on Broadway for more than a year, won MacLeish his third Pulitzer, won the Tony Award for best play, and became a staple of college repertoires for years thereafter.

The play, with its humanistic emphasis on the individual and its dismissive attitude toward religion, evoked a fair measure of religious controversy. An early performance was delivered to an audience of religious leaders, with MacLeish afterward engaging their criticism. In the early months of its Broadway run, MacLeish held seminars with audience members after the performance, discussing the play and the questions it raised with anyone who cared to stay. Discussion usually focused on a key passage, where God's indifference to the world He created is expressed in words quickly moving from pithy to poetic:

> If God is God he is not good,
> If God is good He is not God;
> Take the even, take the odd,
> I would not sleep here if I could
> Except for the little green leaves in the wood
> And the wind on the water.[38]

Critics outside the theater community reacted differently. They bristled at the quick transition from tragedy to a hopefulness born of love. As one critic bitingly put it, "MacLeish has not been able to avoid the greatest cliché of the fifties, the conviction that love cures boils."[39] The emphasis on love seemed a cowardly failure to face up to the real dimensions of the tragedy the play describes.

Unsurprisingly, Dwight Macdonald articulated this criticism most forcefully, linking MacLeish's play to middlebrow culture. In his lengthy analysis of "Massult and Midcult," Macdonald singled out four "typical" midcult products for special consideration. Along with Hemingway's *The Old Man and the Sea*, Thornton Wilder's *Our Town* (of which Macdonald concluded, "I agree with everything Mr. Wilder says but I will fight to the death against his right to say it in this way"!), and Stephen Vincent Benét's *John Brown's Body*, Macdonald provided a savage reading of MacLeish's *J.B.* He ridiculed MacLeish's "high-falutin'" aspirations, capitalizing its claims to be "Profound" and "Soul-Searching" and dealing with the "Agony of Modern Man." He contrasted the actual Book of Job with MacLeish's "forcible-feeble" style, and generally lampooned MacLeish's efforts throughout. His major complaint, however, was with the conclusion. The introduction of love in the conclusion—the idea that human connection was the only possible solace in an arbitrarily cruel world—was not even considered as a serious idea. Rather, Macdonald viewed it as a tremendous copout, brought in solely to "magically resolve the problems raised by the preceding two hours of conspicuously loveless dramaturgy."[40]

For Macdonald, *J.B.* is emblematic of what was so troubling about middlebrow culture. Prized by critics who should know better, popular with the educated classes, technically advanced enough to impress but never intimidate middlebrow consumers, these works provided a comforting ersatz culture in the place of the serious troublings of serious art. In its aspirations for universality, its consideration of serious and weighty matters, its insistence on spoon-feeding the audience the message of the work, and finally its conviction that love can solve all problems, Macdonald found *J.B.* to represent all the major characteristics of middlebrow culture. It was also typically anti-intellectual: Macdonald noted that the three false prophets who seek to comfort J.B. were all "men of ideas" and "repulsive bigots."[41]

Macdonald's criticism is more provocative than fair. The false prophets may be men of ideas, but they are also each peddling a specifically determinist creed. They each present their respective singular idea (God, psyche, class) as an escape rather than an engagement. In terms Christopher Lasch would later describe, it is they who are the anti-intellectuals.[42] And Macdonald's reading of the play's conclusion seems unduly colored by his need to fit *J.B.* into the middlebrow description he has developed. It is hard to see how the ending of the play resolved or even displaced the tragedies and the difficult questions raised previously. The "love" that MacLeish offers is hardly a panacea, and the last lines, "and we'll see by and by," hardly a fade-to-sunset happy ending. Yet it has been Macdonald's criticism, and similar criticisms by others, that have proven more influential over time. Esteemed in the "middlebrow" press, MacLeish never received recognition in the intellectual magazines.

After *J.B.*, MacLeish continued to live according to his own sense of his intellectual responsibilities. He wrote poems, plays, and essays that were both topical and aspired to universal themes. He intervened in the political issues of the day, remaining a critic of the Cold War, enthusiastically endorsing the civil rights struggles of the 1950s and 1960s, and maintaining a strong and vocal dissent against the U.S. war against Vietnam. Engaging McGeorge Bundy in a 1965 debate, MacLeish asked "Are we 'realistic' now? Hardheaded? Indifferent to those opinions of mankind which our progenitors put in the first sentence of their first communication to the world?"[43] He remained a public intellectual to the last. He thought of an intellectual as someone who kept up a "running quarrel with his time."[44] MacLeish consistently, admirably, held up his end of the quarrel.

The intellectual identity he established, and the responsibilities he held himself to, came at a literary cost. Throughout his life MacLeish reflected on Milton's example. It convinced him that a broad engagement with the world would deepen his art. "I think that whatever happens to a man committed to his art in his life, provided it really happens to him, can only be grist to his mill," he reflected, "because poetry does involve, must involve, the whole of human experience, not simply certain aspects of human life, certain emotional situations." He assumed his art would be enriched by his political engagement with the crises that defined his time.

In his own circumstances, however, MacLeish erred. His decision to place his poetry in the service of his politics, as he did during the late 1930s, his decision to set his poetry aside entirely, as he did during his wartime government service, both came at an aesthetic cost. The public poems he wrote had a certain success, due largely to his remarkable versatility. They were not his best work. As Louise Bogan, a fierce critic of his early public poetry, observed, MacLeish was "a private, a lyric poet through and through."[45] His public speech could not compare with the best poems of the 1920s, or the quite moving lyrical poems he wrote near the end of his life. Ironically, his poetic talents lay in precisely the private lyrics, the poems he found irresponsible during moments of political crisis.

Yet, if MacLeish suffered as a poet, he flourished as an intellectual. From the 1930s through the 1970s, motivated by a fierce conviction that ideas mattered, and a consistent faith in American possibility, MacLeish intervened in public disputes. In 1940 he wondered how historians would judge the intellectuals of the prewar years. Historical legacies are rarely as neat as he supposed they would be. The questions historians ask are not quite the questions MacLeish expected. Yet looking back at his record as a public intellectual, his positions have been almost invariably vindicated. He was right to warn of the fascist danger, right to believe in American possibility, right to be sharply critical of the failure of America to realize that possibility, right to oppose McCarthy, right to point to the pernicious political effects of subsuming our minds to the Soviet threat, right to champion civil rights, right to oppose Vietnam. Further, he was right to be troubled by larger issues raised by World War II, right to be worried about the capacity of the individual, right to be concerned with the impact of the war on the moral imagination of humanity, a point Macdonald essentially granted in his own considerations of these same themes. His voice, articulate and persuasive if not always profound, pushed American culture in beneficial directions. MacLeish's life as an intellectual came at a cost to his art and to his reputation as an artist. His historical legacy suffers as a result, and justly so. Nevertheless, his life as an intellectual brought benefits to weigh against the costs. MacLeish lived and wrote in his present, not our past. His actions in his time are worth remembering and recounting in ours.

Only a Hero Can Resist

World War II provoked Archibald MacLeish to assume a more active role, and in so doing to clarify for himself what it meant to be an intellectual. In publishing the essays in *A Time to Speak* and *A Time to Act* while serving in Roosevelt's administration, MacLeish extended the similar role he had played at *Fortune*, acting as both champion and critic of democratic capitalism. The war also pushed Dwight Macdonald to clarify his own ideas about the responsibility of the intellectual. Macdonald's political ideas were developing rapidly in the late 1930s, and the war became the crucial event in shaping his thought. Like MacLeish, he drew on his experiences writing for Luce's business magazine, though Macdonald learned quite different lessons.

Up until his difficult decision to leave *Fortune*, Macdonald seemed pulled between different desires. He wanted literary success, but he could never shake the conviction that artists and intellectuals were too divorced from power in American society. Macdonald's youthful infatuation with business leaders did not last, but his concerns about the powerlessness of art remained. Where his loyalties were once split between literature and business, after he left *Fortune* they were divided between literature and politics. Writing for and editing *Partisan Review*, he was able to pursue both, but during World War II he decided that the coercive power of the modern state threatened the individual as much as the corporation did. For Macdonald, this meant repudiating his position at *Fortune*. His years spent observing how corporations worked up close left him attuned to the ways powerful institutions conditioned and shaped the assumptions that governed thought. He became convinced that both needed to be opposed. It was the intellectual's role to criticize and oppose the corporation and the state, to act as the voice of an otherwise powerless individual conscience. Macdonald was at heart a critic, and the war years saw him emerge as a perceptive and articulate critic of the organizational life of the modern world.

Dwight Macdonald had little use for Archibald MacLeish, but he certainly would have approved of MacLeish's insistence that an intellectual keep up a "running quarrel with his time." Macdonald was a consummate quarreler. When Macdonald left *Fortune*, his first published writing was a series of analytical eviscerations of the Luce magazines for the *Nation*. It set a pattern he often repeated. His path to the political left led to the *Nation* assault on Time Inc. Embracing Trotskyism in 1937, Macdonald attacked the *Nation* from the pages of the Trotskyist *New International*. Writing for and helping to edit *Partisan Review*, he turned his growing dissatisfaction with the Trotskyists into a critical article on the *New International*. Breaking with *PR* over that magazine's support for World War II, Macdonald published his own magazine, *Politics*. Of course, he used its pages to criticize *PR*. From there he moved to the *New Yorker*, a magazine he had pilloried in his first *PR* column. In the *New Yorker*, where he remained from 1952 until the 1960s, he attacked the cultural ambitions of many of the magazine's readers.[46]

This pattern suggests that Macdonald made and shed strongly held opinions with equal regularity. By temperament and by inclination, Macdonald was a critic. His associations, beginning with *Fortune*, and then with the Trotskyists, the *Partisan Review* crowd, and finally the more generalized world of New York intellectuals, suggest Macdonald's generally underappreciated need to belong to a body of likeminded compatriots. Macdonald was happiest in an aesthetic or political splinter group, but where he found similarly inclined friends. This preference can be traced all the way back to his days at Exeter and his band of fellow esthetes. But also, Macdonald had a rare gift for picking fights among his new friends almost as soon as they were made. He was temperamentally incapable of finding a comfortable home in any group. Charitably interpreted, he never let friendship interfere with the pursuit of his convictions.

In many ways Macdonald functioned as a recognizable ideal type of intellectual. In taking on *Fortune*'s fealty to corporate elites, or the Trotskyist tendency to worship power, or the *New Yorker*'s deference to its audience's prejudices, Macdonald modeled the intellectually fearless critic, beholden to no one, having to trim his sails to no employer, free to interpret and describe the world he perceived. Macdonald's willingness to lacerate his friends and his enemies alike in scorching prose demonstrated both his independence and his integrity. The contrast with MacLeish, who criticized outsiders from his inside position, is clear.

Macdonald's position, valorized from Julien Benda to Edward Said, has much to recommend it. "It takes a constant struggle," George Orwell wrote, "to see what's in front of one's nose," a sentiment Macdonald echoed in a 1945 essay on "The Responsibilities of Intellectuals."[47] Macdonald had that gift, the ability to identify, analyze, and sometimes puncture the hidden assumptions that propped up political ideology and political practice. At his best, Macdonald identified these assumptions, whether it was the connection between collective responsibility and individual powerlessness during World War II, or the drive to sweeten and adulterate high culture before it could be thought palatable for middle-class appetites. He also wrote from his own assumptions, however, and generalized from his own experience. His struggle to find his own intellectual identity soon became an effort to turn that identity into a rather narrow conception of the intellectual's place in American life.

When Dwight Macdonald left *Fortune* in 1936, a relatively unknown and unemployed writer in a city filled with writers, he felt directionless. Desiring to write and pursue his developing political views, he initially planned to turn his series of U.S. Steel articles into a book. That plan quickly ran aground. His political involvements were developing so quickly that he soon decided an economic study was too detached from the vital questions that now captured his imagination. He also grew frustrated by his inability to write a book "in cold blood."[48]

For a very brief period Macdonald tried political journalism for the liberal weeklies. He wrote his 1937 three-part essay analyzing the Luce press for the *Nation*, depicting the magazines as "proto-fascist." But within the year Macdonald had moved so far to the left he was no longer comfortable or welcome at the *Nation* or *New Republic*. As he later observed, "The speed with which I evolved from a liberal into a radical and from a tepid Communist sympathizer into an ardent anti-Stalinist still amazes me."[49]

Like many intellectuals during the "Red Decade," Macdonald was initially drawn to the Communists as a political party of action. Alone on the left, the Communists seemed to be doing something in the face of capitalism's collapse. Coming to radical politics relatively late, however, Macdonald's flirtation was very brief. Reading Marx and Lenin in 1936, by 1937 Macdonald was active in the defense of Leon Trotsky, and emerging as a forceful anti-Stalinist. He was drawn to the Trotskyists because they shared the Communists' commitment but seemed insulated from the crimes of Stalinism. They also possessed Trotsky himself, the very model of an intellectual who made his ideas matter.

That same year Macdonald joined Philip Rahv and William Phillips as editors of a revived *Partisan Review*. Breaking from its roots as an organ of the John Reed clubs, the Communist Party's literary front, the new *PR* pushed a platform of anti-Stalinist political radicalism and cultural modernism. This suited Macdonald perfectly. He found the writers at *PR*, especially Rahv and Phillips, to be genuine intellectuals, especially as opposed to the political hacks they encountered among the Stalinists. Macdonald threw himself wholeheartedly into a world where political and cultural questions seemed equally urgent.

Through the political writing and wrangling of the left Macdonald began to find his voice. In addition to writing for and helping to edit *Partisan Review*, he began contributing to the Trotskyist journal *New International*. Macdonald quickly became a prolific contributor to the internal debates of the anti-Stalinist left. What he failed to find, even among the Trotskyists, was a comfortable political home. Unsurprisingly, Macdonald was incapable of submitting to any sort of political discipline. After his semi-willing acquiescence to the compromises of a business system he disliked, he could not agree to compromises in a political vision he believed in passionately. In his debut in the *New International* Macdonald invoked the Kronstadt rebellion, pushing Trotsky to provide a fuller explanation of his role in the suppression of the sailor's strike during the early years of the Bolshevik revolution. He was soon comparing Trotsky's angry response to the tactics employed by the Stalinists to stigmatize opposition.⁵⁰ Any political program Macdonald committed to needed to be worthy of his loyalty, it needed to possess virtues important to him: intellectual rigor, accountability for mistakes, and a basic fidelity to his standards of justice and morality. It was important for Macdonald to be on the right side of issues, and he had little patience with political compromise. Little interested in political organizing or party building, he spent most of his time criticizing Trotsky and his followers (so much so that Trotsky was reputed to quip, "Every man has a right to be stupid on occasion but comrade Macdonald abuses it").⁵¹

For a couple of years Macdonald tried to function within the Trotskyist movement as an internal critic. In 1939 he joined the Socialist Workers Party, the Trotskyist party led by James P. Cannon and Max Schachtman. Within months the Soviet Union invaded Finland, and Macdonald was denouncing the action as imperialist aggression. This placed himself in opposition to Trotsky's insistence on supporting the USSR as a worker's state bringing socialism to the Finns. It was characteristic of Macdonald's ambivalent relationship to the movement and the Socialist Workers Party.

Macdonald was far more at home at *Partisan Review*, engaged in the critical role of the intellectual rather than functioning as an unwelcome internal critic of a political party. In the late 1930s and early 1940s *PR* emerged as the intellectual home of the modernist, anti-Stalinist left. It attracted important writers and served as the crucial journal for what latter came to be known as the New York intellectuals. For a while Macdonald worked well with Rahv and Phillips, until a political dispute divided them as well. The cause was the growing likelihood of war in Europe. Rahv and Phillips joined the antifascists and supported war as a necessary evil. Macdonald, on the other hand, made the classic general's blunder: he determined to oppose the last war.

Taking his lead from Randolph Bourne, Macdonald resurrected Bourne's opposition to the First World War. Looking at the rapid transition from pacifism to support for the war that occurred in the United States in 1917, Bourne had noted that intellectuals had not just moved into support for Wilson's war. No, the intellectuals "are now complacently asserting that it was they who effectively willed it, against the hesitation and dim perception of the American democratic masses." The young progressives at the *New Republic*, and even the radical John Dewey, fell prey to the delusion that the war was their cause. They saw, in Bourne's words, "A war made deliberately by intellectuals!... A war free from any taint of self-serving, a war that will secure the triumph of democracy and internationalize the world!"⁵² In brief,

Bourne argued that the intellectuals convinced themselves that Wilson and the ruling class he represented were fighting for the same causes in which they themselves believed. The aftermath of the war showed how badly they had deceived themselves.

Macdonald saw much the same thing happening in 1939, with important magazines such as the *New Republic* and the *Nation*, and writers such as Van Wyck Brooks and MacLeish, pushing the United States toward a war with fascism. As Macdonald put it in his consideration of Bourne and the present crisis, "The intellectuals, in a word, want to crush fascism. The State Department thinks rather of Germany" and the threat the German state poses to U.S. economic interests. As a *Partisan Review* editorial had noted earlier that year, "it would appear that it is the peculiar function of intellectuals to idealize imperialist wars when they come and debunk them when they are over."[53]

Macdonald saw the entire war as a rehash of the Great War—the same competition between imperialist European states, the same ruling class control, the same intellectual cowardice, all tending toward the same likely outcome. Fascism did not pose a radically new type of threat. Rather, Macdonald saw it as a form of capitalism, a "union of advanced technology with reactionary social concepts."[54] Supporting the capitalist nations England, France, and the United States in their drive toward war with Hitler, as writers such as MacLeish counseled, was an unacceptable compromise with the lesser evil. Those who believed the war could be used to advance a radical or progressive political agenda were, just as they had been in World War I, mistaken. Macdonald went farther, arguing that fascism could only be defeated by an England or United States remade by working-class revolution. The task of the political intellectual was to "work with the masses for socialism which alone can save our civilization."[55]

Macdonald's views on the war were difficult to sustain. His "10 Propositions on the War," written with Clement Greenberg in the summer of 1941, interpreting the war along these lines, were roundly criticized, drawing printed objections from his fellow editors.[56] Given that the socialist revolution Macdonald called for was impossibly distant in 1941, critics correctly pointed out that Macdonald was essentially counseling inaction. Macdonald's opposition to the war has fared even less well over time. As Macdonald admitted only many years later, he was entirely wrong about World War II.[57]

Macdonald's lonely and misguided position, however, proved critically productive.[58] It led him to turn a critical eye to the impact the war was having on the United States. Unwilling to accept the war's rhetorical division of the world into, in the widely echoed phrasing of Vice President Henry Wallace, free and slave, Macdonald identified the ways the war revealed disturbing developments in the relationship between the individual and the state.[59] *PR* proved an unwelcome home for his analysis, however, and his ongoing opposition to the war caused a serious breach with his fellow editors. They continued working together until 1943, when Macdonald, losing a battle for control of the journal, left with plans to start his own magazine.

Using his wife Nancy's money and funds left over from his *Fortune* stock, Macdonald began publishing his own magazine, *Politics*, in January 1944. For a man who needed a small band of similarly minded friends to help stake out an unpopular minority position, *Politics* was the perfect magazine. Editorially, it was wholly Macdonald's. Though Nancy contributed crucial office management, and was a driving force behind the magazine's efforts to organize relief for European refugees, Macdonald edited and wrote a substantial portion of each issue.

Macdonald gathered together a number of intellectuals at *Politics*, forming what historian Gregory Sumner has described as the *Politics* circle.[60] These included European intellectuals such as Andrea Coffi (writing as "European"), Victor Serge, Niccolo Tucci, Simone Weil (though she died in 1943, the magazine published a number of her translated essays posthumously), and especially the Italian anarchist Nicola Chiaromonte. A number of young Americans also played important roles, among them C. Wright Mills, Paul Goodman, Daniel Bell, and Lewis Coser. It was Mills, then a young sociology professor sharing Macdonald's passion for politics and his contrarian sensibility, who suggested the magazine's name. Macdonald explained the choice in the first issue. In an era when calls for political unity during wartime served to delegitimize political opposition and debate in all the warring countries, Macdonald argued, "it would therefore seem useful to have a magazine which, beginning with its very title, will consistently emphasize the political reality of anti-political ideology and practices." From his first issue Macdonald drew links between both camps in the war, noting that the war was defined on all sides in ways in which "the power of the state can be extended and the more thoroughly can all society be politicized." The magazine would be Marxist, Macdonald declared, but the opening editorial employed little in the way of Marx's class analysis or historical materialism. Instead, the magazine took as its motto Marx's quotation, "To be radical is to grasp the matter by the root. Now the root for mankind is himself."[61] In other words, in the first issue Macdonald signaled his major concerns: the growing power of the state and the diminished capacity for individual resistance, the magazine's roots in the Marxist left, but also a dissatisfaction with traditional Marxism, which, contrary to that quote, often failed to put "man" at the root of analysis.

In *Politics*, Macdonald edited a remarkable magazine. He published trenchant analysis of the changes the war brought to the nation's political economy. Unlike other magazines, production levels did not concern Macdonald. He instead analyzed the likely long-term impact of the wartime economic mobilization. Macdonald described the creation of what economist Walter Oakes described as a permanent war economy, "organized along democratic/capitalist, not fascist lines." This permanent war economy, supported by liberals and labor, would stifle socialist or social democratic initiatives and preempt political alternatives by "first preparing for and finally waging World War III."[62]

Politics also covered social issues both at home and abroad. The magazine drew constant attention to racial issues, including the treatment of African Americans in the service and at home, and the internment of Japanese Americans. Macdonald published articles written by soldiers, especially African-American GIs who described discrimination in the Jim Crow army. He published articles advancing a feminist critique of American society, and an essay by Robert Duncan advocating for the equality of homosexuals. In all these ways *Politics* was a groundbreaking magazine.[63]

Most significantly, *Politics* focused on the impact of the war on the nation's moral imagination, examining the myriad ways the war brutalized the Americans who fought it and brutalized the sensibilities of those who supported the war. As Daniel Bell later noted, *Politics* held a "unique place in American intellectual history . . . [because] it was the only magazine that was aware of and insistently kept calling attention to changes that were taking place in the moral temper" of the nation.[64] Macdonald analyzed how soldiers were trained to kill, he documented how the press coverage of the war acted to legitimize brutality even as the same press expressed outrage at Nazi or Japanese atrocities.

Macdonald perceived the brutalization of modern society reflected in wartime mass culture. Always interested in popular cultural forms, Macdonald filled *Politics* with articles on movies, magazines, books, and radio, invariably pointing to the ways such commercialized products manipulated mass audiences. Warner Brothers' *Mission to Moscow*, painting the Soviet Union as a brother democracy, was a favorite target. On this level, distinctions between the popular culture of the United States, the Soviet Union, or Nazi Germany were less important than their shared manipulative strategies. Again and again Macdonald made the point that popular definitions of the war as a fight between a free world and a slave world obscured the disturbing similarities between how all modern states organized the populace for total war. As Macdonald's biographer Michael Wreszin notes, "it was the image of the machine, totalitarian and on the move, that governed Macdonald's view of popular culture."[65]

His most important conclusions coalesced in two essays. In the first, "The Responsibility of Peoples," Macdonald responded to the Holocaust with a meditation about what the conduct of the war had done to notions of collective responsibility. In the second, "The Root Is Man," Macdonald launched a strong critique of both Marxist historical materialism and progressive science, hoping to replace both with a radical politics that placed individual consciousness at its core.

In many ways Macdonald had been slow to respond to the atrocity reports coming out of Nazi-occupied Europe. Wary of horror stories pushed by the liberal, pro-war press, Macdonald discounted their plausibility. That changed once the Allied armies liberated the Nazi extermination camps in Eastern Europe. Then Macdonald became one of the first to give serious attention to the Holocaust and its significance. Looking at the end of the war, and doubtless spurred on by popular press articles that gave voice to deep anger at the German people and held the German people collectively responsible for the war, Macdonald launched an examination into "The Responsibility of Peoples."[66]

Trying to come to terms with systematic extermination as a national policy, Macdonald limned the distinguishing features of the Nazi "final solution." He described the Nazi "death factories," a world that saw "rationality and system gone mad." Looking at Maidanek, Macdonald perceived "the discoveries of science, the refinement of modern mass organization applied to the murder of noncombatants on a scale unknown since Genghis Khan." What impressed Macdonald, in other words, was not the sheer horror. Humans had committed horrible atrocities before. What was distinctive was the use of rational means, the rationality of the factory or the slaughterhouse ("as in the Chicago stockyards, no by-products were wasted"), for irrational ends. "What has been done by other peoples as an un-pleasant byproduct of the attainment of certain ends has been done by the Germans at Maidanek and Auschwitz as an end in itself."[67]

Making a shrewd though overdrawn comparison between Nazi anti-Semitism and American racism, Macdonald argued that anti-Semitism had been largely state policy imposed on the German people, in contrast to Southern lynching, a form of popular "justice" opposed (if often winked at) by the state. The implication was clear: the Holocaust was the result of the policies of Hitler and his state, not of the German people.

From the very beginning of his essay, then, Macdonald was describing the problem of Nazism as a species of the problem of modern society. He described the Nazi Holocaust as distinctive and new, but also as the worst manifestation of a rational, organized, political, and economic order common to all industrialized states. If the Holocaust was particular to Nazi Germany, the questions it raised were universal. "Modern society," Macdonald concluded, "has become so tightly organized, so rationalized and routinized, that it has the character of a mechanism which grinds on without human consciousness or control . . . more and more things happen TO people."[68] Macdonald quoted a U.S. air force lieutenant who had completed more than thirty bombing runs over Europe, describing himself as "a cog in one hell of a big machine." Macdonald argued that such feelings were widespread and recognized that it was necessary to soothe such anxieties. When 300 sailors died in an industrial explosion at the Mare Island Naval Base, the requisite admiral spoke of the "heroism" and "self-sacrifice" of the dead sailors. But, as Macdonald pointed out, their "heroism" was involuntary. "TNT offers no surrender terms," Macdonald pointed out. Besides, the sailors were drafted into service, and most were African Americans consigned to dangerous work because of their race and against their will. They were powerless.[69]

At the same time, Macdonald continued, ideas of collective responsibility were increasingly pervasive. Things might happen to people, but those same ordinary people were then held responsible for the actions of the state, actions they could not influence, let alone control. Or, as Macdonald put it, "as the common man's moral responsibility diminishes . . . his practical responsibility increases." Such was the necessary conclusion drawn from a world where terror bombing made no distinction between combatant and civilian, where the enemy was defined as a racialized other, where calls to exterminate the enemy were widespread.[70]

Macdonald examined in detail an anecdote that had appeared in the liberal daily *PM*, and had been discussed by Hannah Arendt in the *Jewish Forward*. An Allied reporter had interviewed a German paymaster in one of the liberated camps. The paymaster admitted people were killed, poisoned, and buried alive in the camps, but he held himself blameless. He was only a paymaster who had done his job, why was he responsible for the crimes committed? Why should the Soviets put him to death (as they soon did)? What had he done?

"What had he done indeed?" Macdonald asks. "Simply obeyed orders and kept his mouth shut. It was what he had *not* done that shocks our moral sensibilities." All this made the world "a complicated and terrifying place," Macdonald concluded. "Where can the common people look for relief from this intolerable agonizing contradiction?" he asked. "Not to their traditional defender, the labor movement," he concluded. Such a movement no longer existed in the Soviet Union, and it had been hopelessly co-opted in the United States and Great Britain. Instead, Macdonald counseled looking toward the individual, "to our essential humanity and to a more sensitive and passionate respect for our and other people's humanity."[71]

In a world in which ordinary people were caught up in the immoral activities of the state, "it is not the lawbreaker we must fear so much as he who obeys the law." "We Americans," he noted, "have a long and honorable tradition of lawlessness and disrespect for authority."[72] In other words, against the organizing and disciplining power of the state and the corporation, the only hope lay in active resistance, in noncooperation, in noncompliance.

The atomic bomb confirmed for Macdonald much of what he had argued in "The Responsibility of Peoples." Not only did its use as a legitimate weapon of war depend on the argument that Japanese civilians were morally responsible for the actions of their military rulers, but the enormous organizational effort to build the bomb, involving billions of dollars and hundreds of thousands of workers kept in the dark about their actions, also underlined his argument. He noted, "there is something askew with a society in which vast numbers of citizens can be organized to create a horror like the Bomb without ever knowing they are doing it."[73]

"The bomb," writes Michael Wreszin, "was the final catalyst precipitating Dwight's rejection of Marxism and 'scientific socialism.'"[74] For Marxists, the problems of injustice and exploitation resided entirely in the capitalist system, its sanction of private property, and the economic power of the bourgeoisie. But Macdonald's analysis of the war suggested an equally pressing problem: the power of the modern state—organized, rationalized, and beyond the influence or control of individuals. A radical politics, Macdonald concluded, must oppose the state and must defend the individual against the state. A socialism that hoped merely to capture and control the state promised no real liberation.

Macdonald now saw Marxism as an obstacle to new roots forward in American politics. Dissatisfied with the traditional left-right political dichotomy, Macdonald saw striking similarities between core assumptions of thinkers on both sides. In "The Root Is Man" he proposed a new political characterization, based on a distinction between Progressives and Radicals. Progressives were those who "saw the Present as an episode on the road to a better future," who "think more in terms of historical process than of moral values," who believe the application of scientific knowledge is the key to the creation of a better society. They included much of the political spectrum, ranging from the Marxist left to the New Dealers to moderate reformers to much of the Republican Party. The only political figures who did not accept these assumptions were certain ideological conservatives and reactionaries and, of course, radicals. Macdonald described radicals as the small group of "anarchists, conscientious objectors, and renegade Marxists such as myself," who reject the concept of progress, seek to limit the scope of science to its proper sphere, and "feel the firmest ground from which to struggle for that human liberation which was the goal of the old left are . . . [those] non-historical Absolute Values (truth, justice, love, etc.)."[75]

"The Root Is Man" was a long, often unsuccessful attempt to justify this view. The first installment was largely concerned with explaining Macdonald's dissatisfaction with Marxism. Here he gave eloquent expression to the problems with the scientific, progressive assumptions of Marxists (he often used the Marx of "The German Ideology" to great effect against the economic determinism of the later Marx and his followers). Macdonald had been working to this conclusion for the entire publication run of *Politics*, and his indictment was strong (not that it was likely to convince committed Marxists, who either sought to refute Macdonald by engaging in close textual disputes, citing chapter and verse in the sort of tedious, narrow reading that always drove Macdonald crazy, or by retreating to a species of "you can't make an omelet without breaking some eggs" pragmatism that Macdonald found morally repellent).

The second installment, delayed for months, presented Macdonald's philosophical elaboration on what it meant to place man at the root of analysis. This section was vague, confusing, and ultimately unconvincing, even to those who accepted Macdonald's rejection of Marxism. It revealed Macdonald's strengths as a critic and his weaknesses as a political philosopher.

Summarizing Macdonald's conclusions from the war, "The Root Is Man" deftly posed the most troubling questions of the era. It was no longer possible to believe, Macdonald concluded, that the sins of capitalist exploitation could be overcome by the capture of the state by the revolutionary working class. The threat to the individual came not just from the organized power of the capitalist class, but from the organized and administered power of the state as well. Macdonald described a stark future in such a world.

His answer, however, was less compelling. A political opposition based on individual consciousness described acts of individual protest, not an organized political opposition. Eternal verities such as "truth, justice, and love" were impossibly detached from real world political organizing or struggles for power. Essentially, "The Root Is Man" revealed that Macdonald had worked himself into a political corner, into a politics without a political program. For a while Macdonald flirted with anarchism, pacifism, and a sort of left libertarianism. His search for a politics rooted in individual consciousness led him toward a politics of individual liberation (one of many instances where his politics foreshadowed the politics of the new left). He experimented with nudism and tried to become more sexually adventurous. None of this, however, added up to a serious or satisfying political alternative.

Macdonald's political frustration—he was convinced of the correctness of his critical analysis and equally convinced of the hopelessness of a viable political alternative—contributed to the end of *Politics* in 1949. After that, his political involvement revolved mostly around opposition to the Communist Party in the United States, and the left liberals he saw as dupes of the Communists. Meanwhile, his interests turned increasingly toward cultural criticism. Having reached true political impotence, Macdonald put aside his old fears that literary critics were too detached from power. He believed he could play a significant role in critically analyzing American culture.

Expanding on his essays in *Politics*, Macdonald became a keen analyst of mass culture, and especially of the border regions between mass culture, middlebrow culture (what he often called "Midcult"), and high culture. Or, as he put it, "my subject is not the dead sea of masscult but rather the life of the tide line where higher and lower organisms compete for survival."[76] The competition involved high culture competing against its middlebrow rival. Midcult threatened high culture because, Macdonald argued, midcult seeks to have it both ways, "it pretends to respect the standards of High Culture while in fact it waters them down and vulgarizes them." Macdonald was insistent, "Midcult is not, as might appear at first, a raising of the level of masscult. It is rather a corruption of High Culture . . . [that] is able to pass itself off as the real thing."[77] Macdonald took it upon himself to expose midcult's attempt to pass as "the real thing," to act as the defender of high culture (by which he meant, especially, the achievements of avant-garde modernism). Just as the individual resister, the hero, might act against the state in defense of moral values, the intellectual could, and should, resist the homogenizing pressures of mass and middlebrow culture.

Macdonald saw many of the same managerial and organizational forces at work in both politics and culture, making the transition relatively seamless. A managed, organized, and administered politics was mirrored by a produced and administered mass culture. Under industrial capitalism, a mass culture had developed that was, like the corporations that dominated the economy, highly centralized and organized. Macdonald's developing analysis of mass culture depended heavily on the conclusions he drew from World War II. Just as the wartime state had the power to reshape the world beyond the individual's capacity to influence or alter it, mass culture producers such as the Hollywood studios or Time Inc. organized and controlled the production of culture. Individuals working inside such organizations were every bit as powerless as the soldiers and paymasters serving during the war. "As in politics," Macdonald wrote, "everything and everybody can be integrated . . . into the official culture-structure." For an example, he chose "the talented writers absorbed by the Luce organization since 1930."[78] And just as the only hope in fighting the trend toward increasingly powerful organizations lay in the resistance of the heroic individual, the only hope against mass culture was the resistance of the intellectual and the artist.

Writing about culture, Macdonald noted, "Individuals are caught up in the workings of a mechanism that forces them into its own pattern; only heroes can resist, and while one can hope that everybody will be a hero, one cannot demand it."[79] It was wrong to expect extraordinary acts of resistance from ordinary people, but Macdonald expected more of the intellectual and the artist. It was the intellectual's role to resist. The artist must resist the pressures of commercialization and the rewards of the market. The critic must resist the acceptance of midcult as acceptable high culture.

This line of thinking forced Macdonald to reinterpret his years at *Fortune*. Of course, he had essentially repudiated his work for the business magazine once he radicalized politically. But he consciously analyzed his role at *Fortune* only after he had developed his comparison between mass culture corporate producers and the organizing and disciplining power of the state. His former belief that he could work toward his own convictions through the pages of Luce's magazines became so untenable to him that he no longer recalled his efforts. He now described his *Fortune* years as an act of "selling out," as years spent as a "hack in Luce's stables." He claimed he was "tempted, morally, to keep selling out"—the money was good, he noted, ". . . but it had become neurologically impossible."[80]

In many ways Dwight Macdonald was an exemplary intellectual. He had a fierce critical intelligence. Any target that came into his sights was subjected to a rigorous undressing, as he pitilessly exposed the hidden assumptions that led inevitably to error. He was an effective enemy of the shoddy, the lazy, the easy, the formulaic, and the counterfeit in thought and culture. He wrote in an accessible prose style that was simultaneously easy to understand and uncompromising.

His vision of the proper vocation of the intellectual—independent and critical—is vital and necessary. The forces that Macdonald saw as threatening—the increased centralization, rationalization, and concentration of power, the distance between individuals and the institutions that structured their lives, the absence of fundamental moral values as a political foundation for radical politics, the power of corporations to structure the cultural life of the nation—were all powerful and disturbing. Though his was often a lonely voice raised against these particular threats, when he called for the intellectual to be independent, he joined a growing chorus. That the intellectual should be an independent critic, an individual willing to "speak truth to power," became an increasingly persuasive theme in the postwar years.

Over time, Macdonald's position came to be seen as the only viable position for the independent intellectual. Interest in ideas, in art, in serious criticism of American cultural practices, necessitated a protective separation from a society hostile to intellectual values. There is an irony here. In seeking to protect the intellectual from the forces of organization and bureaucracy that rendered the individual powerless, Macdonald consigned the intellectual to a specific, organized location: the intellectual as professional (and eventually academic) critic, acting as a cultural arbiter. Even an independent intellectual needs an income. The narrowed scope of legitimate, untarnished work meant the academy became the place for intellectuals.

One measure of the success of these ideas is their ability to absorb other possibilities, to obscure our understanding of intellectuals who had other ideas. Its success may be measured in the ease with which Archibald MacLeish is rendered irrelevant. Or the ease with which James Agee's complicated ideas about the place of the intellectual become reduced to a simpler echo of Macdonald's independent vision.

"In the Service of an Anger"

So pervasive were the assumptions Macdonald acted from that they have colored our understanding of James Agee. For decades Agee's ideas of intellectual life have been collapsed into an echo of Macdonald's. If the triumph of the independent intellectual meant the eclipse of MacLeish, it has left us unable to understand what James Agee thought it meant to be an intellectual.

Far more has been written about James Agee than about any other intellectual to work at Time Inc. So much, in fact, that Alan Spiegel has charted three "varieties of adoration," "the cults of Poor Jim, Saint Jim, and Plain or Country Jim." The most pervasive is "Poor Jim," the purveyors of which manage simultaneously to worship Agee and situate him as "a fascinating but characteristic species of the artist's career failure in mercantile America." In these accounts, Spiegel claims, "the poet flings the body of his genius on the altar of commercial America" when he "sells his talent to Henry Luce" and "fritters away his best years as a slavey on *Fortune* [and] *Time*."[81] Invocations of Poor Jim trace back to his friends, Dwight Macdonald and Robert Fitzgerald among them, who viewed themselves as complicit in Agee's failure to leave Time Inc.[82] Typical of the Poor Jim lament is Robert Phelps's introduction to the *Letters of James Agee to Father Flye*, where Phelps asked, "Why did he not write a dozen Chekhov-Shakespeare novels instead of a quarter of a million unsigned words for *Time* and *Fortune*?"[83]

The Poor Jim characterization arose from a number of sources. Agee's own ambivalence over his job contributed a great deal. Writing to Fitzgerald about his feelings for *Fortune*, he claimed, "It varies with me from a sort of hard, masochistic liking without enthusiasm or trust, to direct nausea at the sight of this symbol $ and this % and this *biggest* and this some blank billion. At times I'd as soon work on *Babies Just Babies*. But in the long run I suspect the fault, dear *Fortune*, is in me: that I hate any job on earth, as a job and hindrance and semisuicide."[84] The end of this passage suggests the second contributing factor: Agee's peculiar psychological intensity. His letters constantly reverberated with expressions of exalted intent followed by guilt and self-loathing for failing to live up to such lofty goals.

The Poor Jim view, however, necessitates ignoring or denigrating

Agee's own aspirations for his work at Time Inc. Critics too readily accept Agee's oft-expressed distaste for *Fortune* while minimizing the ambitions he entertained for his journalism. They fail to notice that Agee's anger at journalism was frequently inseparable from his own guilt and self-loathing. Laurence Bergreen's biography exemplifies this mistake. Bergreen concocts a largely fanciful account of Agee's consistent hostility toward Luce and his magazines that makes it impossible to understand why Agee worked so hard at a job he despised.[85] Agee's attitude toward *Fortune* and its journalism was far more complicated than critics such as Bergreen allow. Pained by much of *Fortune*'s content, frustrated by its editors, and repelled by its audience, Agee nevertheless believed the magazine offered important possibilities for his writing.

Agee's hopes for his writing at *Fortune*, and later *Time*, were tightly bound up with his view of the artist's place in society. Committed to an artistic avant-garde, critical of mass culture, and suspicious of acceptable art, Agee nevertheless remained fascinated with mass cultural media. As much as he denigrated Hollywood films, for example, as trite, formulaic, and commercially infected, he retained a faith that artistic sensibilities could still speak through them and audiences could be educated to appreciate them. The same held true for magazines. Cultural gatekeepers, on the other hand, earned his lasting enmity. "A good artist is an enemy of society," Agee wrote, and he fully expected society to try to disarm its enemies. Writing to Walker Evans about Evans's 1938 photographic exhibition at the Museum of Modern Art, Agee claimed, "The world has not the slightest idea what to do with these productions . . . can neither throw them away nor have them around, and so has invented a sort of high-honorable day nursery or concentration camp for them, so that they will not be at large."[86] Unlike his friend Dwight Macdonald, who sought to cultivate an aristocratic appreciation for high culture, Agee distrusted any social acceptance art managed to win.

The trick, therefore, was to avoid making art that would slide gracefully into the strangling embrace of polite society. Agee intended his work as a constant rebuke, a steady prick to the conscience of readers. Fighting the "emasculation of acceptance," Agee's goal was to create art and keep it at large. (In *Famous Men* he explained why "we make this book and set it at large.")[87] Agee's hostility extended to all acceptable locations for art and literature. He constantly sought evidence of art smuggled into unlikely places.[88] His distrust of high culture, however, left him without a clear idea of what to do with his own writing.[89] One difficult, quixotic, but necessary answer was to smuggle it into Luce's magazines. Just as he believed films of high quality could occasionally emerge from Hollywood studios (more frequently, great moments could occur within mediocre films), he hoped that work of deep humanity could emerge from within journalism. Agee took the project MacLeish had begun at *Fortune*—to combine poetic technique and language with searching moral inquiry in the hopes of better representing the world—as far as it could be taken in the magazine, and a then a great deal farther.

Understanding Agee's ideas about the place of the intellectual in American society then, and understanding how Agee acted in pursuit of those ideas, requires a detailed look at Agee's journalism. For both MacLeish and Macdonald, their years at *Fortune* played important but minor roles in their intellectual development. Their years working for Luce shaped them both in important ways, but other factors were more important to their ongoing development. For Agee, on the other hand, his journalism at *Fortune* is absolutely crucial.

Agee constantly pushed against creative boundaries in his *Fortune* articles. In the summer of 1935 he described the summer horse-racing scene in Saratoga. Envisioned by editors as a colorful chronicle of the mixing between gamblers and high society, Agee turned it into something entirely different. He composed what he called a "day-night poem," describing a typical twenty-four hours during the racing season. Transcending a simple sketch of personalities and recitation of statistics leavened with anecdotes, he situated the racing community within Saratoga's physical and social environment. Searching for new ways to represent the world, his stylistic experiments continued. Sentences lengthened dramatically with clauses piling on top of clauses. Descriptions of people he found in Saratoga ran to 250 words and more. The balance between statistics and descriptive evocation tipped increasingly toward Agee's circling attempts to depict the world he saw. Though *Fortune* planned to publish the article in August, just as the racing season was beginning, Agee insisted on carrying his story through to the end of August. He ended with a beautifully elegiac imagining of the day the last bookies and bettors departed town:

> And every next morning the streets are strangely empty as a new-made corpse of breath; . . . and swift and broad upon the lush elms and the kaleidoscopic slate shingles and the wild gables and the apoplectically swirled colonnades and the bare porches and the egregiously extensive and pitiable slums of this little curious city there settles, delayed a little

but by no means dispelled by Saratoga's other season, the season of waters, the chill and the very temper and the very cold of death.[90]

Suggesting the necessary insufficiency of a final absolution, Agee was also experimenting with the religious language and imagery that later permeated *Famous Men*.

Although the Saratoga article demonstrated what Agee could do with a topic that inspired him, he grew increasingly frustrated. The political awakening so typical at *Fortune* began to affect him. Writing to Father Flye in early 1936 of his growing interest in communism, Agee attributed it to "three years of exposure to foulness through *Fortune*."[91] Agee was never politically active, but he was looking for ways to reconcile his art with his political sensibilities. He tired of writing articles on the cultural interests of the affluent. Assigned a feature on orchids, Agee complained of having to value a "thing because it is the largest, the loudest, the most expensive." He disdained the orchid's snob appeal. His initial draft began:

> The orchid get its name from the Greek orchis, which means testicle; and there are those who condemn that title as understating the case, since to them the flower resembles nothing printable so much as a psychopathic nightmare in technicolor. It has also been favorably compared in sexual extravagance to the south apse of an aroused mandrill, and it sports a lower lip that qualifies to send the Bourbon Dynasty into green visceral spasms of invidious love's labors lost.[92]

Unsurprisingly, Agee's editors refused to publish the passage. Agee's criticism in the final draft was limited to noting that the orchid was "one of the most eminently useless commodities in existence during six of the most eminently lean years of an era."[93]

Articles like this left Agee feeling stultified. His desire, he told Father Flye, was to get "as near truth and whole truth as humanly possible," and to set "this (near-) truth out in the clearest and cleanest possible terms."[94] Writing to MacLeish, Agee declared his intention "to see and wring out on paper" the world, yet he despaired of ever getting material at *Fortune* worthy of the effort.[95] That changed in the summer of 1936, when his editors assigned him an article examining the lives of southern tenant farmers.

The story was intended for the magazine's "Life and Circumstances" department, which featured in-depth looks at the lives of working-class ans. William Stott, in his otherwise excellent account of *Famous Men*, dismisses the series for its "tone of heavy condescension."⁹⁶ Following Stott's lead, the "Life and Circumstances" articles have been viewed as "sensationalizing the distress of people struggling through the Depression." This misreads the articles (and *Fortune*). The series, conceived by Eric Hodgins, attempted to make the suffering of Depression and the experience of relief real to *Fortune*'s readers. The articles sought to replace myths about the causes and consequences of unemployment with individual experiences. One article, in particular, contained an insistence on the particular individuality of the subjects that foreshadowed one of Agee's own central concerns. Writing of Steve Hatalla, a construction worker laid off in 1931 and on various forms of relief since 1932, the magazine observed, "Steve is not the typical unemployed man . . . this, then, is not the story of unemployment and relief in the U.S. It is simply the story of Steve Hatalla."⁹⁷

Agee recognized the sharecropper assignment as the opportunity he had been awaiting. Immediately after learning of it, he wrote a hasty letter to Father Flye, informing him of the "best break I ever had on *Fortune*. Feel terrific responsibility toward story; considerable doubts of my ability to bring it off; considerable more of *Fortune*'s ultimate willingness to use it as it seems (in theory) to me."⁹⁸ That brief note proved brilliantly prophetic. Within hours of being given the assignment that eventually emerged as *Let Us Now Praise Famous Men* five years later, two of its most characteristic features were present. First, Agee was already seeking alternatives to the prevailing practices that he believed pried into and exploited the sufferings of others. He found this in his insistence on the irreducible humanity of the people whose lives he chronicled, evident in his later description of his work as "an independent inquiry into certain normal predicaments of human divinity."⁹⁹ Second, Agee's extreme self-consciousness, which he used to interrogate his own role in the narrative and to set it against what he saw as the unself-consciousness of the tenant farmers, was also there from the earliest moments. And Agee was right; *Fortune* would not be able to use the story he brought it.

Agee feared he might be paired with photographer Margaret Bourke-White. Despite her growing reputation elsewhere, Bourke-White remained *Fortune*'s star photographer. Though her 1937 collaborative book with Erskine Caldwell, *You Have Seen Their Faces*, was still a year away, Agee already perceived and despised the contrivance, dramatization, and manipulative social do-goodism in her work. His one assignment with her had not been a success.¹⁰⁰ Bourke-White already functioned as a useful stand-in for everything

Agee hoped to distinguish his work from. Hoping to forestall her involvement, he immediately asked that Walker Evans be hired. He and Evans had become good friends, united by shared aesthetic interests. Agee had a great deal of respect for Evans's photography and complete confidence in his ability to work along complementary lines. *Fortune* worked out an agreement with Roy Stryker of the Farm Security Administration, where Evans was employed. The FSA agreed to lend Evans to *Fortune* for the summer, in exchange for ownership of the photographic negatives after *Fortune* used them.

The account of Agee and Evans's trip south and the long road from research to the final publication of *Famous Men* in 1941 has been told repeatedly. Struggling to find the right sharecroppers to study, then staying for weeks with a family in Alabama, Agee spent two months collecting material (while Evans took somewhat less to make his pictures). Returning to New York already a month behind schedule, Agee spent months writing an article that *Fortune* refused to publish. After sitting on the article for a year, *Fortune* released it to Agee, who found an interested publisher (Harper and Brothers). After long revisions, Agee delivered a manuscript in 1939. Harper decided not to publish it, however, when Agee refused extensive changes designed to make the book more palatable to readers. Finally, in 1940, Houghton Mifflin agreed to publish the book if Agee would delete a small number of objectionable words. Agee relented, and the book appeared in 1941.[101]

Let Us Now Praise Famous Men is a book without peer in American literature. Though it grew organically out of Agee's writing for *Fortune*, it also contained an explicit repudiation of the magazine's journalism. A study of poor, southern sharecroppers, the book joined a long list of such documentary efforts from the 1930s. Yet, as William Stott showed, "it epitomizes the rhetoric in which it is made, and explodes it, surpasses it, shows it up."[102] Where documentary tended to be pragmatic and progressive, Agee was elegiac and pessimistic. Emerging from a socially meliorative genre that tended to view individuals as, in Agee's words, "social integers in a criminal economy," Agee wrote in a religious idiom that emphasized the divinity of each human being. His book contained exhaustive descriptions of the ephemera of human life, the houses, clothes, and meager decorations of the Gudger family, far exceeding any other such record. Yet it also featured astonishingly long flights of Agee's lyrical fancy, prose poems that continued page after page. Agee went to extraordinary lengths to establish the irreducible humanity of the families, and to protect them from the pity, condescension, and ultimate scorn of the reader. Nevertheless, he subjected them to his own relentless self-interrogation, weaving his own thoughts through their lives, even to the point of making them complicit in his sexual fantasies. *Let Us Now Praise Famous Men* was many things, but perhaps chiefly, it was a strenuous moral inquiry into the nature of confronting ourselves as we in turn confront others.

Agee and Evans's book has itself been subjected to countless interpretations, both appreciative and hostile. Yet nothing anyone has written about the book quite captures its contradictory fullness and complexity. It slights the book to focus narrowly on its relationship to Agee's journalism, but such a consideration does illuminate aspects of what Agee thought he was doing that otherwise remain obscure.

Unfortunately, though the typescript of the book exists, no copy of the article Agee submitted to *Fortune* remains. Explanations for why *Fortune* refused the piece remain speculative. Agee's friends blamed the magazine. Robert Fitzgerald, in a passage widely quoted, claimed the magazine had the "impertinence" to assign Agee the story but "did not have the courage to face in full the case he presented."[103] This simplified matters too drastically. A few things are known for certain. First, there was a change of editors at *Fortune* while Agee worked on his piece. New managing editor Russell Davenport canceled the "Life and Circumstances" series containing Agee's article.[104] This made it more difficult for Agee's work to see print in any form. Second, Agee had misgivings about both working his material into a form *Fortune* could use, and seeing it appear in the magazine. He was already deciding he would not compromise his vision of the material, and was beginning to consider turning it into a book.[105] Finally, in typical fashion, the draft Agee submitted was impracticably long (some estimates placed it at ten times the required length). Describing the growing draft to Evans, Agee observed, "This little number, now typed up, runs to a few over eighty pages. So now I tunnel under the cellar with dynamite. God damn."[106]

While it is impossible to know for certain what was in the draft Agee submitted, his previous experiments at *Fortune* allow for some informed speculation. Up until the sharecropper assignment, Agee used lengthy passages of precise yet poetic description to present a more complicated depiction of the world than normal journalistic methods allowed. In this, he followed the lead established by MacLeish and pushed further. Two of the characteristic elements of *Famous Men*, then, the lengthy passages of laborious description and the alternating poetic evocations of mood and environment, traced directly to his earlier *Fortune* work. An additional distinctive element of *Famous Men*, Agee's extreme self-consciousness about his ability to render the moral complexity of his subject, had also shown up in earlier articles. The article he wrote for *Fortune* likely pushed each of these techniques toward the summation Agee eventually achieved in the finished book.

Agee repeatedly insisted in the text of *Famous Men* that his method was an "effort to perceive simply the cruel radiance of what is." He called his writing an "effort to suspend or destroy imagination." In the most famous declaration of this intent, he wrote, "If I could do it, I'd do no writing at all here. It would be photographs; the rest would be fragments of cloth, bits of cotton, lumps of earth, records of speech, pieces of wood and iron, phials of odors, plates of food and of excrement."[107]

This sentiment expressed only one aspect of Agee's project. The exhaustive account of the contents of the Gudger house was Agee's attempt to make a clear, transparent, documentary record. Otherwise, however, there was hardly a passage in the entire book not woven through with his imagination. In a widely misinterpreted passage, Agee praised the camera as, "next to unassisted and weaponless consciousness, the central instrument of our time."[108] Usually read as an endorsement of the primacy of photography, Agee actually subordinated photography to his own consciousness, his distinctive contribution to the book (or, given the purposeful ambiguity of "next to," equated the two, as in the final text).[109]

Agee revealed his own presence in two ways. Most obviously, he continually intruded on the text. As the review in *Time* noted, the first thirty pages were "devoted largely to alienating the reader."[110] Agee is as much a subject of *Famous Men* as the families he depicted. More subtly, he revealed himself through the use of language. Agee's idiosyncratic and self-consciously literary prose implacably drew attention to his presence, to his role mediating between the reader and the tenant families. Combined with the lengthy descriptive passages, Agee's intrusiveness created the simultaneous impression that the text was both an objective record and a highly subjective account of a man attempting to grapple with the problems producing such an account raised. Agee never permitted readers to accept his account without questioning how he came to know what he reported, and what it meant to know this.

In addition to his extraordinary attempts to record the material world the tenant farmers inhabited, and his insistence on foregrounding his own filtering presence, the other distinctive element of Agee's text was its vituperative attack on journalism. Of the many beginnings in the book, one started:

> It seems to me curious, not to say obscene and thoroughly terrifying, that it could occur to an association of human beings drawn together through need and chance and for profit into a company, an organ of journalism, to pry intimately into the lives of an undefended and appallingly damaged group of human beings, an ignorant and helpless rural family, for the purpose of parading the nakedness, disadvantage and humiliation of their lives before another group of human beings, in the name of science, of "honest journalism" (whatever that paradox may mean), of humanity, of social fearlessness, for money, and for a reputation for crusading and for unbias, which, when skillfully enough qualified, is exchangeable at any bank for money . . . and that these people could be capable of meditating this prospect without the slightest doubt of their qualification to do an "honest" piece of work, and with a conscience better than clear, and in the virtual certitude of almost unanimous public approval.[111]

This passage, along with the other frequent attacks on journalism sprinkled throughout the text, must have been added in the later revisions.[112] It reflected a distance from *Fortune*'s journalism Agee did not feel in 1936. Yet the sentiments it expressed were implicit in Agee's journalism all along. And his terror did not prevent him from prying into the lives of these appallingly damaged human beings. Agee had different reasons than *Fortune*, and was filled with doubts about the purity of his intentions that the magazine was unlikely to entertain, but he pried into the lives of the Gudgers, Ricketts, and Woods families just the same.

Stott's argument about Agee's relationship to documentary—that "it culminates the documentary genre and breaks its mold"—applies with equal force to journalism.[113] "The very blood and semen of journalism," might be, as Agee famously characterized it in *Famous Men*, "a broad and successful form of lying."[114] Nevertheless, the struggle to make journalism speak the truth was still necessary. The simplification, sensationalism, and condescension that Agee abhorred in other documentary efforts necessitated the response he gave in *Famous Men*. The "lying" he found in journalism made telling the truth (contingent, subjective, radically filtered through the writer's consciousness, but closer to the truth because of this) all the more necessary.

Even after his frustrations with the tenant farmer story, Agee continued to seek to smuggle his own vision of journalism into Luce's magazines. In 1937 he submitted a massive application for a one-year Guggenheim Fellowship.

Rather than suggesting a single project, Agee submitted a brief outline of forty-seven different projects he planned to undertake. A number of them later figured into *Famous Men*. Many included different perspectives on journalism, including a proposed account of "high class people" on a cruise that he hoped to expand from "a technique . . . developed part way" in a *Fortune* article (again collaborating with Walker Evans).[115]

That same year he and Evans made a proposal that they be given extensive editorial control over some aspects of *Life* magazine. The idea, as Agee expressed it in a letter, was for *Life* to give them an office and a stipend to develop a type of photojournalism not beholden to the magazine's regular editorial and time pressures. Together, they hoped to accomplish "a great freezing and cleansing of all 'art' and 'dramatic' photography" and to convey "much more sharply than is customary its power as historian, arrester of matter and of meaning." Agee and Evans were again looking for a platform at Time Inc. from which they could pursue a critique of its normal journalistic content. "I grant it might be impossible to get out a weekly or run a whole magazine in this way," Agee concluded diplomatically, "but it might turn out to be very wise to create such a category of work as a non-conflicting part of the machinery of the magazine."[116]

Though the editors of *Life* turned down the offer, Agee returned to incarnations of this idea again and again. In the 1940s Agee wrote up "Notes and Suggestions" for a magazine devoted to the study of what is now called popular culture. In it he proposed "to contrive techniques for making clear to the average reader—gradually—what is true and what is phoney in a photograph or a public speech or a letter; without sacrificing or in the long run simplifying any standard or perception we have."[117] Though wary of the possibility of failure, Agee still hoped to pursue his exposure of the manipulative coerciveness of journalism. And he still sought to do so in the form of a magazine with a wide readership.

The closest he came were his years writing for *Time*. In his movie reviews for the *Nation* and *Time*, Agee worked to sift through the rote, familiar, unthinking, and accepted in order to glimpse those moments when film succeeded in getting close to the natural, the real, and the true. In an appreciation of filmmaker Preston Sturges, Agee argued the director's artistic success stemmed paradoxically from the restrictions Hollywood imposed on him. Agee speculated that given freedom, Sturges "would become a relatively helpless, perhaps melancholic, distinctly mediocre artist." Instead, working within the studio system, "his films are invariably and resourcefully, built in reference to a corrupt and half-mad environment."[118] This might serve as a suitable description of what Agee attempted as a journalist working for Time Inc. It was only by working within the corrupt and half-mad world of journalism that Agee could see and define what it was he opposed.

James Agee spent most of his writing life working for Time Inc. Maybe this prevented him from producing the writing his great talent always promised. Maybe. There were other forces conspiring against Agee's success, most of them emanating from inside his own skull. What Agee did accomplish, however, is worth commemorating. Agee produced writing of stunning complexity for mass-circulation magazines. He worked within the constraints of Time Inc. without letting those constraints force him to compromise his own vision. He pushed to pursue his own interests, despite formidable obstacles. Indeed, in *Famous Men* he turned those obstacles into a profound meditation on the nature of journalism and art, moving far beyond the simple hope that journalism and poetry could enrich each other that prevailed among intellectuals at Time Inc. John Hersey, a later interstitial intellectual at Time Inc., provided the best summary of what Agee thought he was doing at *Fortune*. "The special challenge for Agee," Hersey concluded, was "to try to set truth free in what he saw as the headquarters of lying."[119]

Figure 1 (right). The inaugural issue of *Fortune*, by Thomas Cleland, celebrating the centrality of industry to American progress, but appearing just months after the stock market crash. (FORTUNE is a registered trademark of FORTUNE magazine, a division of Time Inc. © 1930 Time Inc. All rights reserved.)

Figure 2 (below right). By 1932 *Fortune*'s covers often embraced a modernist aesthetic that subtly suggested a more critical attitude towards business, as this Paulo Garretto cover from February 1932 illustrates. (FORTUNE is a registered trademark of FORTUNE magazine, a division of Time Inc. © 1932 Time Inc. All rights reserved.)

Figure 3 (below left). Henry R. Luce in the early 1930s, well on his way to becoming one of the most significant media moguls of the twentieth century. (The Cleveland Press Collection, Cleveland State University Library).

Figure 4 (facing page). The Riverside Works at Otis Steel, by Margaret Bourke-White, part of the series that led to her becoming *Fortune*'s star photographer. (Margaret Bourke-White Collection, Special Collections Research Center, Syracuse University Library. Photo © Estate of Margaret Bourke-White/Licensed by VAGA, New York, NY).

Figure 5 (top right). Chrysler: Gears, one of Bourke-White's most famous early pictures, and one typical of *Fortune*'s treatment of the heroic size and scale of industry. (Margaret Bourke-White Collection, Special Collections Research Center, Syracuse University Library. Photo © Estate of Margaret Bourke-White/Licensed by VAGA, New York, N.Y.).

Figure 6 (bottom right). NBC Mural, Electric Generator, a typical Bourke-White stylized treatment of the repetitious patterns found on factory floors. (Margaret Bourke-White Collection, Special Collections Research Center, Syracuse University Library. Photo © Estate of Margaret Bourke-White/Licensed by VAGA, New York, NY).

Figure 7. Pouring ingots of rimming steel, a photograph by Russell Aikins used to open Dwight Macdonald's 1936 *Fortune* series criticizing U.S. Steel. (Industrial Life Photograph Collection, Baker Library Historical Collections, Harvard Business School)

Figure 8 (left). Archibald MacLeish in the 1930s, prize-winning poet, future government official, and *Fortune*'s star writer, who described writing for *Fortune* as an "essential education" (Alfred Eisenstaedt/Time and Life Pictures/Getty Images).

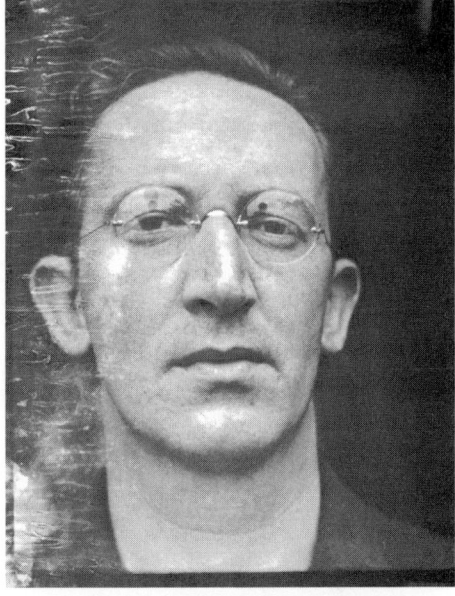

Figure 9 (top right). Dwight Macdonald, photographed by Walker Evans, wrote for *Fortune* from 1930 until 1936 before becoming an important radical intellectual and critic of mass culture. He claimed he quit *Fortune* because he "kept falling asleep in the act of prostitution," but the truth was more complicated. (The Metropolitan Museum of Art, Walker Evans Archive, 1994 [1994.254.2376] © Walker Evans Archive, The Metropolitan Museum of Art)

Figure 10 (bottom right). James Agee, photographed by Walker Evans, whose landmark book *Let Us Now Praise Famous Men* began as a *Fortune* assignment. In that book he described journalism as a "broad and successful form of lying," yet he used the techniques of the journalist to seek "the cruel radiance of what is." (The Metropolitan Museum of Art, Walker Evans Archive, 1994 [1994.254.11] © Walker Evans Archive, The Metropolitan Museum of Art)

Figure 11 (above). Walker Evans's photograph of the shopfloor at Kaiser-Fraser revels in the disorder, in stark contrast to the usual Bourke-White style. *Fortune* (March 1946). (The Metropolitan Museum of Art, Walker Evans Archive, 1994 [1994.254.1482] © Walker Evans Archive, The Metropolitan Museum of Art)

Figure 12 (facing page, top). Walker Evans, describing himself as a "leisured and untethered eye," depicted urban decay in Chicago, *Fortune* (February 1947). (The Metropolitan Museum of Art, Walker Evans Archive, 1994 [1994.254.1526] © Walker Evans Archive, The Metropolitan Museum of Art)

Figure 13 (facing page, bottom). Remnants of the Chicago 1933 Century of Progress International Exposition, which Evans described as "huddles of serio-comic sculpture…imploring someone to hack them to pieces." *Fortune* (February 1947). (The Metropolitan Museum of Art, Walker Evans Archive, 1994 [1994.254.1505] © Walker Evans Archive, The Metropolitan Museum of Art)

Figure 14. Walker Evans's photographs of vintage office furniture offered a rebuke to the sleekly organized and managed modernism of the postwar era. *Fortune* (August 1953). (The Metropolitan Museum of Art, Walker Evans Archive, 1994 [1994.252.16.31] © Walker Evans Archive, The Metropolitan Museum of Art)

CHAPTER FIVE
======

The Intellectual as Insider at Time Inc.

> . . . our great job from now on is not to create power but to use it.
> —Henry Luce (1940)

In 1937, T. S. Matthews, who had spent the previous seven years trying to balance reviewing books for *Time* with his own attempts to write, decided to accept a job as editor of *Time*'s critical departments. Despite publishing a novel, his career as a writer had not unfolded the way he had planned. When the offer to edit came, Matthews was ready to channel his intellectual energies in another direction. Recognizing his new job could mean "a long, perhaps a final, goodbye to any hopes of writing," Matthews believed the opportunities editing offered would balance the sacrifice of his literary aspirations.[1] By assembling and managing a staff of gifted writers, Matthews intended to make *Time* more intellectually respectable and at the same time use the magazine as a platform for their views. His decision to become an editor was a product of his deep conflict over the writer's life and his desire for influence. In essence, Matthews put aside his own writing in pursuit of personal power and the possibility of producing a new kind of literary journalism. His career tested how much influence an intellectual could have in Time Inc.'s corridors of power.

That same year, Russell Davenport faced a similar decision. Having spent the 1930s writing for *Fortune*, he, too, was offered an editorial position. Unique among intellectuals at *Fortune*, Davenport had never scorned the magazine's business audience. He had, however, dreaded the anonymity of Luce's journalism. Davenport had labored throughout the 1930s on a long experimental autobiography, part prose and part verse. Accepting Luce's offer to edit *Fortune* meant setting aside this project. To Davenport, it "meant a definite break with the kind of life I intended to lead . . . that of an independent writer who might fairly be described as an 'artist.'"[2] In exchange, the job offered him a commanding position on the podium of capitalism's conscience. Trying to decide, Davenport left the only copy of his autobiographical manuscript in a taxicab. Feeling a sense of relief, he accepted Luce's offer. Davenport spent the next fifteen years intermittently struggling to speak his mind with all the authority of Luce's magazines behind him.[3]

Matthews and Davenport chose to deepen their commitment just as Macdonald, MacLeish, and Agee were stepping away from Luce's journalism. For Macdonald, MacLeish, and Agee, *Fortune* in the 1930s had offered intellectual opportunity and nurtured dreams of influence, but ultimately the magazine proved too narrow politically or artistically for the full pursuit of their interests. Their own writing remained of primary importance. Their ambivalence toward intellectual life was real but limited; their desire to turn *Fortune* to their bidding was halting and secondary; their belief in its importance eroded easily. They could better pursue their interests, they decided, elsewhere.

Matthews and Davenport reached the opposite conclusion. More politically in tune with Luce than Macdonald or MacLeish, less artistically ambitious than MacLeish or Agee, Matthews and Davenport found common ground with Luce. Neither Davenport nor Matthews accepted the idea that intellectuals and the American mass audience were irrevocably divided. Neither could countenance Macdonald's decision to edit and write for *Partisan Review*, in essence exiling himself to what Paul Gorman terms "the Siberia of the cerebral."[4] Matthews had previously left the *New Republic*, a magazine with many times the circulation of *Partisan Review*, because he felt too ineffectual writing for a limited audience. Though often disdainful of *Time*'s middle-class readers, he remained committed to the magazine's journalism, believing with Luce that its content could be more serious and respectable. A more intellectually rigorous magazine, Matthews assumed (unconsciously echoing Luce), would yield a better-educated, more civilized readership. Davenport respected the business leadership addressed by *Fortune*, and hoped for real engagement between intellectuals and businessmen. He explicitly advocated a more active role for intellectuals, similar to what MacLeish experimented with in the 1930s.

Both Matthews and Davenport spent the 1940s trying to make Time Inc. embody their hopes. Both found they could work with Luce and reached influential positions within the organization. Both struggled with the relationship between intellectual work and practical power, and with the complicated relationship between intellectual honesty and journalistic practice. Both, however, were ultimately frustrated by their inability to realize their larger ambitions at Time Inc., due to the degree to which their success depended on sustaining Luce's support.

Despite these similarities, the two men hoped to accomplish different things at Time Inc. Matthews strove to change *Time* magazine. He believed a synthesis of poetry and journalism could produce both better poets and a better magazine. To that end, he hired as many talented writers as he could, hoping to use the magazine to spread the influence of the intellectuals with whom he surrounded himself. Sharing Luce's belief in the necessity of better educating *Time*'s readers, Matthews envisioned *Time* as a purveyor of intellectually rigorous content. Davenport, on the other hand, better exemplified Luce's suspicions of intellectuals and his faith in middle-class values. Considering himself an intellectual, Davenport was nevertheless suspicious of other intellectuals whom he deemed too critical. Seeking to use Time Inc. as a platform for his own views, he advanced a sharply attenuated concept of intellectual life. Where Matthews sought to expand the influence of intellectuals, Davenport ultimately strove to domesticate them.

The projects they pursued at Time Inc. separated Matthews and Davenport from the other intellectuals in the organization. Neither could be described as an interstitial intellectual. Both were identified too directly with the organization for which they worked. Matthews sought to create an environment at *Time* where other intellectuals could work interstitially. Davenport, on the other hand, hoped to use Luce's magazines as a vehicle for his own views. His view of the proper role for the intellectual involved a close identification of the intellectual with the goals of Time Inc. Together, they explored the opportunities and risks facing intellectuals who tried to climb the corporate ladder at Time Inc.

T. S. Matthews: The Intellectual as Editor

T. S. Matthews's career holds a fascination beyond that justified by his work. In a sense, he was but one of the many talented and eccentric young writers, now forgotten, who made Time Inc. distinctive in its early decades. He is important not because he was a "typical" intellectual at *Time* (there was no "typical" experience for intellectuals at Time Inc.), but because he wielded more power at Time Inc. than any other intellectual. He also embodied many of the tensions intellectuals, especially those that gathered at Time Inc., struggled with in heightened and extreme form. Convinced of their own superiority, especially to the middle class they were both a part of and apart from, writers such as Matthews nevertheless were painfully aware of their marginality. Championing modernist art that held little appeal to a mass audience, disdainful of middle-class taste, they longed for connection with their fellow citizens and felt the pull of a class ethos that stressed ideals of service. Driven by matters of intellect, they also felt the appeal of a life of action, holding and wielding power rather than merely writing about it. Yearning for independence materially and intellectually, they were keenly aware of their own dependence.

Matthews's career was a study in these contradictions. His sense of his own superiority and his desire for influence left him susceptible to fringe groups that validated his self-importance with flattery. His quixotic pursuit of power at Time Inc., the country's preeminent purveyor of culture to the middle class, rested uneasily with an aristocratic disdain for middle-class taste. Financially independent, he nevertheless consistently depicted himself as dependent and supplicant, adopting metaphors of gender dependence that drew on, then inverted, a pervasive understanding of high culture as masculine and mass culture as feminine.[5] Unable to write the serious books he wanted to, increasingly conscious of his failure to make a decided impact in the literary world, his quest for intellectual prestige gradually became a search for more tangible power.

Seeking that power at Time Inc., Matthews rose through the ranks to be *Time*'s managing editor through most of the 1940s. Ultimately frustrated by his inability to convince Luce that *Time* should alter its structure to separate fact from opinion, Matthews nevertheless succeeded in making important improvements. He elevated the tone of the magazine, curtailing the stylistic tics that had been the magazine's trademark for its first two decades, but that both Luce and Matthews viewed as an obstacle to the influence they desired. Through his commitment to his writers, he also created a hospitable work environment for a number of intellectuals. Receiving crucial support from above, writers such as James Agee, Robert Fitzgerald, Louis Kronenberger, and John Hersey were able to pursue their own interests in the pages of *Time*, while receiving support for independent work as well. The years Matthews edited *Time* marked the high point for intellectuals writing for the magazine. Facing opposition from other editors, Matthews protected and nurtured writers who otherwise would not have been welcome. When he left, he took with him the last hope that serious intellectuals could find a consistent platform at *Time*.

Matthews joined *Time* in the fall of 1929, recruited away from the *New Republic* by his college friend John Martin to write and help edit the six-year-old magazine. Matthews put in a few arduous months writing three sections of the magazine and acting as late man, where he guided the last pages to press every Monday night. The transition from the *New Republic* was difficult. He worked three months without a day off. He struggled to master the curious rhythms of *Time* style and resented the relentless editing of his writing. Worse, he found it impossible to take the magazine seriously and viewed his fellow writers as little better than ill-informed, overconfident savages. His dreams of influence at *Time*, which had helped him make the break from the *New Republic*, were quickly dashed by both the pace and the content of the newsmagazine. Matthews quickly decided to tack away from the magazine and back toward his independent intellectual aspirations. Rather than pursue the career path Martin had laid out for him, culminating in a highly paid assistant managing editorship, Matthews chose to write just the book department. It meant less money, but freed him from the long hours in the office. Matthews expected the job would leave him enough time to focus on his own writing.[6]

He spent the next seven years writing *Time*'s book reviews. He set his own hours, only appearing in the office once a week to drop off his copy and pick up the next load of books. He soon grew frustrated with the constant reading (eight books a week), and the lack of time for his own sustained work. Becoming a competent journalist gave him a "certain satisfaction," but he longed to "write something that would be more acceptable to myself."[7] In 1932 he arranged for a six-month leave of absence and set sail for the Mediterranean island of Mallorca, where he and his wife planned on renting a cottage. He expected to spend the time writing a novel about Katherine Mansfield's life. Matthews and Mansfield had both been involved with the Russian mystic G. I. Gurdjieff during the 1920s. Though Matthews had drifted away from the Gurdjieff cult in the late twenties, he maintained an interest in its teachings, and was taken with Mansfield, who had spent her last years at Gurdjieff's Institute for the Harmonious Development of Man in Fontainebleau. Matthews felt their shared experiences opened up insights into Mansfield's life and work that others had missed.

Matthews's Mansfield project was pushed aside by a chance engagement with the literary gathering around the English writer Robert Graves and his

American lover, the poet Laura Riding. Matthews again became involved in an intense intellectual circle, one that dominated his life for much of the decade. The Graves and Riding connection validated Matthews's sense of his own abilities, and encouraged his ambitions. Despite the creative and commercial failure of his novel, *The Moon's No Fool* (1936), his literary hopes remained high.[8]

In 1935, hoping for more time to write, Matthews recruited the young literary leftist Robert Cantwell to split his job at *Time*. Cantwell had published two books, including the well-regarded proletarian novel *Land of Plenty*, and was reviewing books for the *New Outlook*. The New York book review community admired Cantwell for his Jamesian cadences and discerning criticism. Matthews thought Cantwell might appreciate the opportunity to earn good money half of the year at *Time*, and Cantwell agreed. Each would spend six months of the year writing *Time*'s book reviews and have the rest of the year for independent work. They continued the arrangement for two years. Neither was able to produce much other writing during their leaves, however, and they both invested themselves more deeply in their work at *Time*.

After only a few weeks on the job Cantwell was writing letters to Matthews, expressing his surprise that he was beginning to like the work, but fearing he might end up in the arms of "Canby's sirens" (a reference to Book-of-the-Month Club judge, *Saturday Review of Literature* editor, and all around middlebrow maven Henry Seidel Canby). Matthews downplayed the threat, claiming the column was more dangerous to him than to Cantwell, and arguing "I don't think even such a limited platform as *Time*'s book page is to be sneezed at." Advising Cantwell to adopt Matthews's own attitude toward the editors, he counseled his partner to "remember you're better than they are, and gradually they'll admit it."[9]

They also discussed Luce and his demand that writers work for Time Inc. full-time. Matthews observed that Luce needed to have writers of impressive reputation but was distressed when they insisted on writing for outside magazines. Luce wanted "us to comport ourselves like eunuchs and yet get virilely excited" by the work at *Time*. Chalking it up as one of the many contradictory elements of their boss's personality, he advised Cantwell not to take Luce's admonishments seriously.[10] Cantwell remained unconvinced, not wanting to anger Luce and thus risk a job he was beginning to regard as necessary.

Matthews later claimed he recognized the "danger" Cantwell was in, the danger of choosing a transitory journalism over the permanence of literature. At the time, if Matthews did think in these terms, Cantwell's choice did not worry him. Matthews was beginning to take journalism seriously. Driven partly by frustration at his inability to write a good book (his novel had sunk without a trace), and goaded by Riding, he began thinking about the possibilities within journalism. At the same time MacLeish and Agee were experimenting with language in *Fortune*, Matthews was developing a belief "that poetry and journalism must marry, to produce clearer poetry and sturdier journalism."[11] He began by considering whether the book department could be improved. He shared these thoughts with Cantwell, and hoped for his assistance.

Convinced that the project was important, Matthews worried that he lacked the power within *Time* to make the changes needed. Writing to Cantwell, he reached for a suitable metaphor for his situation at *Time*. "This marriage that *Time* wants you to take so sacredly is not quite romantic enough," Matthews observed, "it's an arranged match, a marriage of convenience, simply an economic arrangement. If you can forget it's your wife who has all the money you can do your share without too much heartburn, but now and then she gives you a thorough-going rap with her velvet-gloved iron paw."[12] Matthews had already ceased to think of his job at *Time* as simply an economic arrangement, if he ever had, but the marriage metaphor did suggest his discomfort with his lack of control, and his understanding that power ultimately resided in control of the purse strings. This understanding of himself as dependent and supplicant, and his presentation of his situation in gendered terms, deepened as his involvement with Time Inc. intensified.

During the years Matthews was writing the book department, *Time* was becoming increasingly important. The magazine's circulation continued to sharply increase, doubling between 1930 and 1936, and reaching nearly a million readers a week by the end of the decade. It gained growing respect from professional journalists, especially in the face of the fiercely partisan attacks on Roosevelt that filled so many daily papers. Though hardly championing the New Deal, it provided a far more balanced guide to domestic politics than many newspapers. The magazine still suffered from problems, especially in foreign affairs, where it concentrated inordinate attention on European royals while complacently dismissing Hitler and the Spanish Civil War.[13] But throughout the 1930s, *Time*'s success served to validate Matthews's journalism.

Despite his growing journalistic ambitions, which he decided to pursue in earnest at *Time*, Matthews viewed turning his back on his literary ambitions as a "lowering decision." "I had thought I wanted to write," he observed, "I hadn't wanted to, evidently, enough to do it—and there had been plenty of opportunity in the last few years."[14] Matthews countered this feeling in a familiar manner. His sense of his own superiority to the people on *Time* hardened. He consistently denigrated the quality of the magazine and especially the abilities of the writers. At the same time, he rapidly developed high aspirations for his work, convincing himself of the importance of journalism and the necessity of improving the quality of the writing in *Time*. Given control in 1937 over the "back of the book"—the cultural departments in the back of the magazine—these two justifications combined in his avowed objective. Convinced *Time*'s cultural coverage offered a field for his displaced literary aspirations, Matthews decided, "I wanted to make the rest of the magazine look sick."[15]

Matthews spent his first few weeks as cultural editor assessing the abilities of his staff. The previous regime of Martin and John Shaw Billings had been suspicious of culture and vigorously policed the back of the book for signs of literary pretension. Combined with *Time*'s habit of assigning writers subjects they were ignorant about, Matthews found he managed "a Religion writer who hated religion, a Cinema writer who despised the movies, a Music man who said he hated music, an Art man who knew nothing about pictures."[16] It was not as bleak as Matthews made it sound. In Books he had Cantwell and Calvin Fixx, a dependable writer who could be relied on for workmanlike, if uninspiring, reviews. In Theater he had Louis Kronenberger, a gifted writer recently transferred from *Fortune*, where he had displayed a light touch and easy manner better suited to theater reviews than assessments of steel pricing policies. And the Art writer, Robert Fitzgerald, may have appeared to be ignorant of art, but he was a poet and scholar with much the same critical sensibilities as Matthews. He had started as Matthews's assistant in books, but his copy was so literary that Billings had banished him to Business for two years. Matthews had brought him to write about art as one of his first moves, and together they set about using the department to explain why Braque's "The Yellow Cloth" had been worthy of its recent first prize at the Carnegie Art Show. The change in tone of the Art page, and "the raising of its standards" was applauded by both the editors and the readers (according to the appreciative letters that followed).[17]

This experience confirmed Matthews's sense that the back of the book afforded him a serious opportunity. "In effect," Matthews observed, "they formed a magazine within the magazine; as far as I was concerned the cream of it . . . . My ambition was to capture or rescue *Time*'s vital organs—which *Time* didn't know were vital—and make them beat and breathe as they should." He set about making the critical departments "civilized and respectable."[18] At this point, in 1937 and 1938, Matthews's aspirations for *Time* remained entirely cultural. He disliked *Time*'s sneering tone of condescension toward culture and its unwillingness to treat art with the space and consideration it deserved. He hoped to make the magazine more serious, civilized, and respectable, a triumvirate of cultural aspiration that appears repeatedly in his discussions of the magazine. He wanted good writers who shared his basic cultural predilections and prejudices.

Matthews had remained aloof from the 1930s debates over the social requirements of literature. Despite his youthful revolutionary aspirations, he had always been more interested in literature than politics. Matthews had left the *New Republic* just before the political departments again became the most vital part of the magazine, and during his years reviewing for *Time* he displayed little interest in the politics of a thoroughly political era. But as Europe headed toward war he, too, began to concern himself with what Lionel Trilling called "the dark and bloody crossroads where literature and politics meet."[19] The drift of the world toward war gripped the literary circles around Matthews, including the Graves and Riding coterie, and he began connecting his journalism with the impending crisis.

A shakeup at *Time* opened the door to greater involvement. In early 1939 Ingersoll announced he was leaving *Time* to start *PM*, a leftist New York daily newspaper. He took a number of *Time* writers with him, and the departures sparked a great deal of uncertainty about what would happen to the magazine. Matthews stepped into this breach. Though he still considered the magazine "barbarous," it now "had possibilities that hadn't been apparent to me before."[20] Newly convinced of the magazine's potential importance, he discovered that the Ingersoll exodus had created a vacuum at the top. Among the writers still at *Time* were a number of like-minded men, including Fitzgerald and Cantwell. Enlisting their support, Matthews hoped to take over the magazine.

The success of this project, Matthews realized, rested on the shoulders of Henry Luce. Could he be won over to the type of journalism Matthews had in mind? Matthews had never thought much of Luce. His first impressions of Luce had come from Martin, who always believed his cousin, Briton Hadden, had been the brains behind *Time*'s success and that Luce had merely been lucky enough to have inherited Hadden's work. To the extent that *Time* magazine was simple and vulgar, Matthews assumed, Luce must be too. But Matthews and Luce were in some ways quite similar. Both had a strong faith in the power of mass magazines to educate their audience. Both believed in the power of carefully crafted words to change history. Both took the importance of culture as an article of faith. Both were convinced magazines should be operated in the public interest. Matthews was to be pleasantly surprised when he got to know Luce.

In the summer of 1939 Matthews arranged a meeting with Luce. Along with *Time* writers John Osborne, Charles Wertenbaker, Robert Fitzgerald, and Frank Norris, Matthews met with Luce in his apartment in the Waldorf Towers. The group peppered Luce with questions about his journalism, his personal beliefs, his intentions for Time Inc., and his financial stake in the company. According to Matthews, they were quickly "impressed by him and by his straight answers and also by what he seemed to believe about journalism." The meeting went on for hours and eventually spilled over into three evenings. For the last meeting, which was to serve as a summary of final principles, Luce cut the ground from under them. They had prepared a list of final questions, but when Luce arrived they found he had typed up a lengthy summation of his journalistic ethics and beliefs. As Matthews remembered, Luce "somehow lifted the whole argument from the area of suspicion and 'I want to know' to a general discussion of journalism" and he ended with a "statement of his journalistic beliefs." Matthews and his compatriots came away greatly impressed with Luce and convinced they shared ideological ground with him.[21]

No copy of Luce's memo remains (Luce himself collected them before leaving, fearing they would wind up in Walter Winchell's column). The only accounts of the meeting are Matthews's memoirs, the official Time Inc. history, and an account in Charles Wertenbaker's 1954 novel, *The Death of Kings*.[22] Unfortunately, Matthews's account skimps any specific discussion of what Luce claimed to believe. But Matthews came away from the encounters convinced he could work with Luce in remaking *Time*. As Matthews recalled, "I jumped to the enthusiastic conclusion that all that ailed *Time*—its crude smartness, its horrible lapses in taste, its generally brummagem quality—all these flaws could be mended if only *Time* and Luce got better acquainted."[23] Matthews clearly believed he had Luce's imprimatur to work to make *Time* a more serious, respectable, civilized, and therefore influential magazine. These words, Matthews's own, suggest his own assumptions about journalism, his audience, and the responsibilities he felt as an intellectual and as the product of America's upper class. He shared these assumptions with Luce. They were the basis of their common understanding and the underpinning of Matthews's rise to power at *Time*.

This account was essentially borne out in *The Death of Kings*, where the press lord Louis Baron enlisted a dubious band of progressives on his news magazine *Beacon*, with an inspiring speech that played simultaneously to their political commitments and to their outsized sense of their own importance. Dwight Macdonald, in his demolition of Wertenbaker's novel, argued the book failed because it treated the delusions of "such addlepated heroes" as Robert Berkeley (the Matthews figure) as high tragedy, when they were better understood as farce or pathos. Maybe. Viewing his own experience at Time Inc. with bitterness, Macdonald had already begun to erase his commitment to the journalism Luce practiced. He acknowledged "we took ourselves pretty seriously, I suppose, when I worked for Luce on *Fortune*," but then immediately qualified his seriousness to apply solely to the "grubby details" of the magazine. Anyone who might continue to invest work for Luce with importance and meaning warranted only Macdonald's derision, and by focusing on Wertenbaker's overwrought prose, Macdonald was able to dismiss the whole phenomenon of serious people taking *Time*'s journalism seriously, calling it a "liberal soap opera."[24] In Wertenbaker's tin-eared prose, Baron provided nothing but bombast, and his audience, the idealistic young intellectuals-cum-journalists, responded with a pretentious seriousness and a gullible acceptance that was impossible to credit. Yet Luce in person was capable of inspiring precisely the level of commitment Matthews felt, as Macdonald knew from personal experience. By playing to a shared belief in the importance of intellectual leadership and journalistic responsibility, Luce restored a sense of mission to writers such as T. S. Matthews who had lost touch with their intellectual ambitions as their literary hopes faded.

What Luce wanted in 1939 was a better, more influential magazine. The conception and publication of *Life* preoccupied Luce during 1936 and 1937. In 1938, naming himself editorial director of *Time*, *Fortune*, and *Life*, Luce determined he would reacquaint himself with the other magazines. He took over as publisher of *Time*, giving himself responsibility for the "general character, tone, direction, ambition, and ideals" of the magazine.[25] Concerned with the growing portents of war in Europe, Luce looked to turn his magazine into a more effective platform for his views. In 1940 he further distanced himself from Time Inc.'s business affairs, handing oversight of business operations to Roy Larsen. As Luce wrote to Larsen in April 1940, "our great job from now on is not to create power but to use it."[26] Luce's determination to strengthen *Time* and to use it to further his own beliefs helps explain why he devoted as much time and energy as he did to meeting with a small group of *Time* writers and editors. To carry out his plans, he needed to win the support of the talented writers and editors he assembled. Reflecting on the meetings, Luce concluded, "I felt I convinced them that I indeed had a serious purpose."[27] He was also increasingly convinced Matthews was the man to help make *Time* more sober and responsible, to supply the literary finish it lacked, and lay to rest for good the stylistic mannerisms of the past.[28]

After the meetings with Luce, Matthews immediately set about trying to recruit others to his vision of a new *Time* magazine. Attempting to enlist Cantwell in early 1940, Matthews explained his change of heart. Previously believing "*Time* was Martin, and therefore really contemptible," he had now found that "*Time* was Luce" and the discovery, Matthews wrote, "hit me with the force of a revelation." Newly convinced journalism could be a "respectable, and more than respectable, whole-time job" he had discovered Luce to be "a damn-good man to be doing it with." The remainder of the letter sketched Matthews's sense of who else shared their appreciation of *Time*'s possibilities and how they could recruit others to their task. "What I contemplate," Matthews confessed, "is winning to our view of journalism other men in *Time*."[29] Matthews succeeded in convincing Cantwell and others, establishing a small coterie of friends on the magazine who, in Matthews's words, "shared my hope that, once I was on the bridge, we could take over the vessel."[30]

Where Matthews hoped to sail his new ship, however, was impossibly vague. Considering journalism "a necessary tool of democracy," he felt that its democratic mission had been insufficiently realized. Journalism was a "blunt instrument" in the hands of people whose professional standards were far too low.[31] Lamenting the increasing percentage of newspapermen on *Time*'s staff, Matthews hoped an infusion of gifted amateurs could result in an "intelligent, well-written, civilized, humane" magazine. "The trouble with journalism," Matthews believed, "was that you didn't have enough poets in it." By hiring poets as journalists, Matthews hoped "it would improve their poetry by making it more lucid and concrete and would also give journalism . . . respect for language and an ability to write well, and a care to write well."[32]

Underpinning Matthews's project were a number of unspecified assumptions. He believed that clear writing necessitated clear thinking. Intellectuals, therefore, would write better, more persuasive journalism than "mere" newspapermen. Matthews was less interested in the particular political content promulgated by his writers than in making *Time* into an outlet for intellectuals to combine journalism and poetry, writing about the news with clarity and imagination. Unwittingly, he was resurrecting the project pursued on *Fortune* in the 1930s, but without the political content that had both fueled that project and brought about its demise.

Matthews set out to recruit the best writers he could find, and he worked hard to keep them happy at *Time*. He gave added responsibilities to Cantwell, Kronenberger, and Fitzgerald. He soon brought Agee back into the Time Inc. fold, hiring him to write book and then film reviews. John Hersey, Theodore White, Whittaker Chambers, and later Irving Howe joined the staff while he was *Time*'s editor and found greater freedom under Matthews than when writing for other editors. Matthews continually watched for new intellectual talent, scouring the liberal weeklies and literary reviews for writing he admired, and hiring as many fine writers as he could. He recruited Irving Howe in typical fashion. Noting that Howe's savage reviews in the *Nation* reminded him of his own acerbic work for the *New Republic*, Matthews wrote Howe to ask if he could be persuaded to write similar pieces for *Time*. Though Howe had little respect for *Time*, Matthews convinced him to accept.[33]

But Matthews's hopes of staffing the whole magazine this way failed. The poets who could write well and also function as responsible journalists, as MacLeish had at *Fortune* ("a veritable Donne and Bradstreet," Kronenberger called him), were few.[34] Instead, most were "personnel problems," producing great work but sporadically and rarely on time. Matthews's description of them is worth quoting at length:

> In many cases, they were "hard to work with"—touchy, suspicious, arrogant, unpredictable. Their working habits were spectacularly individual. When they worked, they often worked all night, then disappeared for indeterminate periods. They were not only subject to temperamental tantrums but prey to fits of despair; and they had no feeling about going to press, one way or the other. They sometimes missed the target completely, or failed to pull the trigger. But when they did make a hit, it was often a bull's-eye. They were regarded by the rest of the staff with mingled contempt and awe. I loved and cherished them.[35]

As brilliant as his writers could be, the magazine could not survive more than a few at any one time. In what he called a "sad compromise," Matthews settled for a small coterie of great writers supported by a backbone of "people you can count on, even if what they wrote wasn't very exciting."[36]

Writers were only one of the difficulties Matthews faced. Hoping to steer his ship in a new direction, he soon found to his chagrin it was all he could do "to keep it plying back and forth on schedule, on its regular run."[37] The terrific pressure of putting out a magazine every week without fail left little time for bold new ideas, or for the concerted efforts necessary to make a dramatic improvement in the magazine's content or conception. The process left Matthews convinced they were making progress, but depressed over the final state of each issue. The results pleased Luce, who appreciated the improvements Matthews had made, even going so far as to write him a most uncharacteristic note of praise. Luce wrote, "Well, I guess some people would know how to put out a better current events magazine, but—I wouldn't."[38] Matthews remained convinced, however, that he knew how to put out a better magazine, and in an odd inversion of typical workplace convention, constantly badgered Luce with memos detailing all the ways the magazine was inadequate. In effect, he criticized Luce for being so easily pleased, and Luce resented the implication. A rift began to form between them.

Matthews also faced a great deal of internal opposition, above and beyond the back seat driving suffered by all managing editors. As early as 1938, business managers were articulating a complaint that became increasingly common throughout Matthews's years editing the magazine. "The trouble with *Time*," wrote subscription manager and Luce confidant Pierre Prentice, in an internal memo, "is that it is edited by too many young men who smoke pipes." What the magazine needed, Prentice and others claimed, was precisely the opposite of what Matthews provided. *Time* needed good, hard-hitting journalism, written by "men who are excited about the news."[39] What it had gotten under Matthews, Prentice claimed in a 1943 assault, was writers who thought of themselves as writers instead of journalists and who were too interested in producing an edifying magazine when readers wanted a more entertaining magazine. Matthews was adamant that Prentice's position was an evasion of their responsibilities and a recipe for a mediocre magazine.[40] Eventually Luce so tired of the argument between Matthews and Prentice that he called a halt to the whole thing, pleading that "noses for news lie betwixt ears for music."[41] Prentice's criticism was part of a climate of anti-intellectualism at *Time* that grew steadily throughout the decade. Increasing numbers of higher-ups at *Time* had business and journalism backgrounds and a disdain for literary pretensions. The influence of businessmen such as Prentice, Charles Stillman, and Allen Grover grew, while the men who successfully climbed the corporate ladder began to resemble John Shaw Billings. Named editorial director of Time Inc. in 1944, after having been *Life*'s managing editor for eight years, Billings was an efficient administrator, a staunch conservative, and a man boastful of his lack of creative abilities. In such a climate, Matthews's cultural interests became increasingly anomalous.[42]

Matthews also faced political opposition, especially from Luce. Matthews had been a consistent liberal Democrat, at least since his early socialism, and he was not shy about reminding Luce of their political differences. Indeed, his letter of acceptance of the managing editorship pointedly listed among his attributes that "I hate the Republican Party."[43] Luce had clashed with Matthews repeatedly over the 1940 election, when Matthews's criticism of the Willkie campaign as national affairs editor contrasted sharply with the pro-Willkie partisanship of *Fortune* and *Life*. Luce's attempt to influence Matthews's handling of the election led to Matthews's offering his letter of resignation. Luce refused it, papering over their political differences for a while, but they resurfaced every four years when *Time* faced coverage of another presidential election. Each passing election brought more internal pressure to favor the Republican candidate, both from Luce and from the decidedly Republican cast of managers and editors. Though many of the writers remained Democrats, Matthews was the sole Democrat left in a position of power at Time Inc. by the 1948 election.

Despite feeling intellectually and politically besieged, and despite having a wavering commitment to the journalism *Time* practiced, Matthews continued to pour his energies into the magazine. He did so because he knew it could be a better magazine, and he remained committed to providing an outlet for the intellectuals at *Time* whom he had recruited and now protected. Matthews did improve the magazine dramatically. Early in his tenure, he described what he expected. A good *Time* story, Matthews wrote, would be "clear without being flat, readable without being libellous, intelligent without being snobbish, critical without being cruel."[44]

Under his leadership, *Time* became a different magazine by the late 1940s than it had been in the 1930s. If it retained the simplistic self-confidence of its early years, and the same slippery mixing of opinion and fact, it had shed most of its sneering tone, what Edmund Wilson accurately described as its "jeering rancor."[45] The verbal tics so characteristic of *Time*'s first two decades—the inverted syntax, the mock-Homeric adjectives, the relentlessly coined neologisms—were all purged. In 1937, even back-of-the-book reviews were still larded with awful sentences such as this, from a review of the movie "You Only Live Once": "Too vivid in his mind is the manner in which he, innocent, was railroaded into his present plight."[46] By the middle 1940s, such writing was gone. Copy under Matthews's editing was clearer, simpler, crisper, and more forceful.

Time's cultural departments took intellectual life seriously. Though hampered by the serious space constraints embedded in its nature, *Time* dispensed with the combination of suspicion and condescension toward culture that characterized it in the early years. Still dismissive and hostile to some intellectual currents, notably existentialism, *Time* nevertheless rid itself of the knee-jerk ridicule of modernism that marked its first decade.[47] In its pages, James Agee wrote appreciatively of James Joyce, employing Joyce's life as "almost a Bible of what a great artist, an ultimately honest man, is up against."[48] Agee and Robert Fitzgerald cowrote a review of Henry Miller's novels *Tropic of Cancer* and *Tropic of Capricorn*, despite the fact that neither novel was legally available in the United States. *Time* justified its review by claiming these were books that would hit the "Man-in-the-Street . . . where he lived, if he could get them."[49]

Previously, *Time*'s movie reviews were brief plot summaries with critical comment limited to noting what scenes would be crowd-pleasing and complementing a film for featuring the best fight scenes of the year. When Agee was moved to film he began the most personally rewarding work of his career. Films had always been Agee's deep love; they were a passionate man's chief passion. Writing film reviews for *Time*, and later the *Nation*, Agee reinvented the film review as a legitimate critical activity. Expressing, in the words of David Denby, "a disgust for false piety and a demand for emotional truth," Agee's film reviews became essential reading for many writers. [50] Before Louis Kronenberger took over the theater department, reviews were often more like theater notices, complete with a mention of whether New York critics had liked it or not. Kronenberger's reviews, on the other hand, were widely admired in the theater community.[51] All told, the critical departments under Matthews were better written and more intellectually ambitious than at any other time in the magazine's young history.

The difference was manifest in more than just the cultural departments. The political coverage in *Time*, while still sparking a great deal of criticism, often justified, was at its best during this decade. Between the fascist flirtations of the 1930s and the Cold War consensus of the 1950s, the political coverage of the 1940s was a definite high-water mark for *Time*. In addition to improving the tone and minimizing *Time*'s tendency to editorialize by insinuation, Matthews's experiments with blending poetry and journalism often paid off. *Time* under Matthews occasionally published striking examples of what may be called political literature. Certainly Agee's longer articles for *Time* fit this characterization.[52] Additionally, in "The Ghosts on the Roof," Whittaker Chambers presented the diplomacy at Yalta from the vantage point of the deceased Russian tsar, sitting on the roof of his old palace, arguing with Clio, muse of history.[53]

The best example, however, was Agee's brief, brilliant essay on the dropping of the atomic bombs. Preparing the first issue of *Time* to appear after the end of World War II, Matthews realized that they had covered all the political angles, but had neglected to consider the atomic bomb itself. He called in Agee, and gave him twenty-four hours to write a lead essay. The essay Agee wrote appeared in the August 20, 1945 issue of *Time*.

Calling dropping the bomb "the greatest and most grimly Pyrrhic of victories," Agee claimed "the bomb rendered all decisions made so far, at Yalta and at Potsdam, mere trivial dams across tributary rivulets." He nodded to the political complications likely to follow from the bomb's use, and he sketched the implications of entering a new age. He concluded,

> When the bomb split open the universe and revealed the prospect of the infinitely extraordinary, it also revealed the oldest, simplest, commonest, most neglected and most important of facts: that each man is eternally and above all else responsible for his own soul, and in the terrible words of the Psalmist, that no man may deliver his brother, nor make agreement unto God for him.
>
> Man's fate has forever been shaped between the hands of reason and spirit, now in collaboration, again in conflict. Now reason and spirit meet on final ground.[54]

This brief essay stood as a rebuke to much of the mood of postwar celebration, a rejection of the comfortable assumption of moral superiority so easily adopted by Luce, and a signal of what the journalism to which Matthews aspired might look like. Describing Agee, Matthews once wrote, "By the seriousness of his intention, a seriousness that pervades his writing as veins and arteries branch through a body, he makes us feel like the liars we are."[55] Not strictly journalism, pieces such as these fully justified Matthews's faith that journalism and poetry could be wed, using literary skill to provide his own take on "information" as "facts in perspective."[56]

Matthews's greatest achievement, however, did not appear directly in the magazine's pages. His commitment to the intellectuals he recruited and admired, men such as Agee, Fitzgerald, and Kronenberger, was greater than his commitment to the magazine. It was this ranking of his own responsibilities that justifies describing him as an intellectual. His deepest allegiance was to his best writers and the writers recognized it. As Kronenberger remembered, Matthews's "primary interests were literary and cultural, and his primary sense of obligation went toward staff members he respected." He provided his writers with a "sense of being reassured and even protected from above."[57] This reassurance allowed them to pursue more ambitious work than they would have otherwise done. Furthermore, Matthews's attitude toward the writer's obligation to *Time* was the opposite of Luce. Luce wanted the writers to commit to *Time* wholly. He resented it when they published their own work elsewhere.[58] Matthews recognized that their primary allegiance was elsewhere and he did what he could to allow them to pursue their independent intellectual aspirations. Matthews insulated writers from the political and anti-intellectual pressures at *Time*, allowing them pursue their own interests in the pages of the magazine without having to constantly defend their work. Arguing that writers such as Agee, Chambers, and Fitzgerald "were in journalism, but not altogether of it," he took responsibility for trying to find outlets for their skills.[59] When Chambers wrote "T. S. Matthews' contribution to the humanity of *Time*, both in the intellectual and personal sense of the word, cannot be overstated," this was what he had in mind.[60]

To write as an interstitial intellectual, as Agee and others did, required a measure of editorial support and encouragement. Matthews's great gift as an editor was to provide that support without trying to shape the content of what was written. If his lack of political conviction limited his ability to remake *Time* in some ways, it also enabled the magazine to achieve a deeper, more afflicting journalism than a political perspective would have allowed.

Though Matthews made important improvements at *Time*, and made it a more hospitable atmosphere for the interstitial intellectual work he cultivated, he did not remake the magazine as he hoped. Ultimately, the problems at *Time* that Matthews hoped to solve were built into the structure of the magazine, and Matthews could not, try as he might, alter that structure. All attempts to change *Time* eventually led back to the difficult question of how the magazine treated news and opinion. From the magazine's earliest issues, it had lacked clearly labeled editorials and simultaneously avoided any attempt to present the news objectively. Instead, it strove to convey the news and, at the same time, give the reader a clear indication of "which side it believes to have the stronger position."[61] Often, however, the magazine did not clearly state its position, but rather allowed its handling of the issues to suggest its position. Luce was comfortable with *Time*'s continual sly assertion of political opinion and interpretation into its news coverage. For him, the original formula—of publishing no signed opinion pieces but simultaneously eschewing objectivity—retained its force. The failure to mark a clear line between opinion and news was not only unproblematic, it was constructive. Luce had always conceived of his magazines as vehicles of popular and middle-class instruction, and he believed "objectivity" was an evasion of journalist's responsibility to properly educate their audience. As he sought to wield more influence, *Time*'s formula was ideal. For Matthews, *Time*'s larding its news with "surreptitious opinion," was the heart of the problem. He pressed Luce to decide whether *Time* was going to be "purely a news magazine or follow a definite political line. The present compromise, in which it often appears to be a newsmagazine with tendentious hints inserted between the lines, is not, it seems to me, a permanently possible compromise." Matthews believed that his post as editor of *Time* held "more responsibilities for good and evil, more need for courage and clarity than any other editorial post in the U.S." and believed that abuse of this responsibility was structurally built into *Time*.[62] This conflict only deepened as Luce's politics moved to the right. By the late 1940s, Matthews was frustrated by his inability to exercise more control over *Time* and was looking for new projects that might give him the freedom and autonomy he lacked.

Russell Davenport: The Editor as Intellectual

Whereas Thomas Stanley Matthews viewed his job at *Time* as a project of improvement, Russell Davenport undertook a very different task. If Matthews was trying to elevate the intellectual level of *Time*'s readers, Davenport might be described as seeking to bring the intellectuals down to the readers. Conceiving of himself as a man of ideas, Davenport nevertheless scorned other intellectuals, especially disliking their disdain for the readers of Time Inc. magazines. Over time that scorn became a full-blown rejection of intellectuals, whom he felt had failed to lead society. Davenport stepped into that breach. He wrote intending to provide intellectual leadership to the middle class he viewed as the backbone of American democracy. In so doing, he developed a sharply attenuated picture of how an intellectual should operate.

The desire to combine intellectual leadership with practical influence fueled Davenport's rise at *Fortune*. He used his appointment as managing editor to push his views in the magazine and he used *Fortune* as staging platform for the launch of Wendell Willkie's 1940 presidential campaign. When Willkie lost the election, Davenport returned to Luce's magazines, again seeking to use them as a megaphone for his ideas. Encountering political resistance from Luce, Davenport spent the rest of his life alternating between independent work that left him free but ineffectual, and employment for Luce that gave him a large audience but imposed constraints he found onerous. Davenport sought a suitable perch from which he could pursue his vision of intellectual life, clarifying American ideals from squarely within the mainstream.

Russell Davenport's family had deep New England roots, tracing its lineage back to John Davenport, who cofounded New Haven colony in 1637. Born to well-to-do parents (his father was a distinguished metallurgist who managed the Midvale and then the Bethlehem Iron Companies and his mother was from Main Line Philadelphia and the founder and headmistress of a girls' school), Davenport's youthful career resembled that of the other intellectuals who first gathered at Time Inc. He alternated between a series of private schools and trips to Europe before enlisting in the army and becoming a twice-decorated ambulance driver during World War I. After returning to the states after the war, he went to Yale, where he followed the familiar path of literary accomplishment to campus eminence, editing the *Yale Lit* and being tapped for Skull and Bones. After graduating he broke the mold by heading west in pursuit of a love affair, writing poetry all the while. When his relationship collapsed Davenport rejoined his literary peers by leaving for France. After living the life of the literary expatriate, he joined the stream of writers who returned to New York at the end of the decade, moving to the city in 1929. He quickly published a novel (*Through Traffic*, 1929), which received little notice. Later that year he married Marcia Gluck Clarke, daughter of the singer Alma Gluck and soon to be a popular novelist in her own right as Marcia Davenport. Looking for a way to link his writing with more practical endeavors, Davenport took a job at *Fortune* just month's after its initial publication, in the summer of 1930.[63]

Like fellow *Fortune* writers MacLeish and Macdonald, Davenport felt the pull of competing impulses. He wanted to follow his literary muse, but he wanted also to achieve an influence unattainable through poetry. He spent the 1930s alternating between stints writing for *Fortune* followed by leaves spent pursuing other writing projects. Unlike the other intellectuals on the staff, Davenport believed unambiguously in the business magazine's importance from the very beginning. He viewed it in terms remarkably similar to Luce: industrial might was America's central accomplishment, yet it had not been properly valued or understood. Especially complicit in this, in Davenport's view, were the intellectuals. They were responsible for interrogating and interpreting the American experience, but they had instead been content to reject business civilization out of hand. The proper role for the intellectual, Davenport felt, was as artistic interpreter and chronicler of the American industrial landscape.

The tension between intellect and action that worried many writers, especially during the 1930s, worked differently on Davenport. Unlike MacLeish, he never felt the pull of a literary life divorced from the larger currents of American life. He never joined in the familiar renunciation of America as philistine, pecuniary, materialist, and anti-intellectual. In 1932 he penned a lengthy rebuttal to MacLeish's "Letter to the Young Men of Wall Street." Rhetorically depicting himself as one of the young businessmen MacLeish addressed, Davenport rejected the contention that businessmen had failed to provide a vision of capitalism worth believing in. He observed that there is "a fundamental, and perhaps disastrous division between us, as representatives of the most exciting civilization so far devised, and you, its artists." He complained that MacLeish expected industrialists to provide the justification for the system they led, when the act required was an act of imagination, the creation of which was properly the realm of the artist. The intellectuals, however, had gone over "to Pound's side" in their rejection of American life. Essentially MacLeish and Davenport were making the same argument, calling for an intellectual and artistic justification for capitalism and expecting it to come from the poets. The difference came in the position they staked out for themselves, MacLeish self-consciously speaking as a poet withholding his identification with business, Davenport identifying with the businessmen and inviting the artists to join in a common endeavor. Both, of course, worked in adjacent offices in the Time Inc. building when they wrote their letters.[64]

Established as early as 1932, these were the animating themes in Davenport's life. Convinced that the intellectual should function from within business civilization, he consistently rejected the idea that the artist should stand apart from American life. He also found it impossible to envision an America where private business was not the cornerstone of political and economic freedom.⁶⁵ Despite these beliefs, during most of the 1930s he refused to commit himself to Luce and his journalism. He worried about sublimating himself into Luce's organization, afraid of compromising his own ideas and reluctant to give up on his hopes for fame and influence. And despite his belief that the proper place for the intellectual was precisely *Fortune* magazine, he continued to harbor independent aspirations. Accepting Luce's managing editor offer in 1937, Davenport consciously set such ambitions aside. From that point on his intellectual exertions, including his poetry, were inseparable from dreams of practical influence.

Davenport had been a popular writer at *Fortune*, long on personal charm and possessing a crisp intelligence. As managing editor, his deep enthusiasm and dedication were infectious, inspiring writers and researchers alike to endure the long hours and chaotic conditions in which he thrived. As Louis Kronenberger remembered, Davenport often left the office after closing each issue "beaming with exhaustion."⁶⁶ His staff shared the exhaustion, if not the exultation, as Davenport's editorial brilliance was matched by an organizational incompetence extreme even for *Fortune*. Luce provided the last word on Davenport's methods, when he completed a long night putting an issue to bed for Davenport by quipping, "My God! If *Fortune had* a system, it would have broken down tonight."⁶⁷ The chaos, however, was tempered by his vision for the magazine. As *Fortune* writer John Jessup remembered him, "Davenport was in important ways the best managing editor *Fortune* ever had; in unimportant ways, the worst."

Davenport sensed the possibilities for influence at *Fortune* better than anyone had except for MacLeish. As managing editor, he had more power than MacLeish had been able to wield as a writer. He immediately set about using and expanding that power. Davenport was a writing editor, a common breed at *Time* but unusual at *Fortune*, who tended to rewrite every important piece that appeared in the magazine. His aggressive editing rankled *Fortune* writers unused to having their material handled so roughly. The office tension deepened as it became clear that Davenport's editing sought to impose an editorial unity and push an editorial point of view not shared by the writers and researchers. Under his pencil *Fortune* spoke with a more nearly singular voice, a strong departure from the cacophonous clamor of previous years, but the turmoil behind the scenes remained.

From the beginning of his tenure Davenport looked for ways to unify

Fortune and to have it declare its, or rather, his, beliefs. The struggle over *Fortune*'s stance toward business that had begun in the wake of the controversy over Dwight Macdonald's series on U. S. Steel continued in 1938. Luce still wanted to see a declaration of support for free enterprise in print. Davenport had initially opposed Luce in 1937, but a year later he had come around to Luce's position. For the next few years Davenport made repeated attempts to square the circle reconciling journalism with a bias for business.

Davenport seized on Luce's contention that the magazine was distrusted by business. To remedy this situation, he advocating dispensing with the journalistic formula that had guided *Fortune* ever since Ralph Ingersoll took the magazine over in 1931. Ingersoll had continually depicted *Fortune*'s job as presenting business with the facts about industrial America and letting them draw the conclusions. If the facts pointed out that big business had failed the American stockholders, employees, and consumers alike, as in the case of U. S. Steel, so be it. *Fortune*'s conception of itself as a fact-finding, and therefore truth-telling operation, had been central to its critical edge. In a 1937 editorial luncheon, however, Davenport complained that while "*Fortune* had developed into an excellent fact-finding agency . . . no one knew what its beliefs were." The answer, he maintained, was the formation and publication of a definite editorial policy. Once again, the staff could not be convinced.[68] The exchange that day continued afterward, eventually prompting MacLeish's valedictory memo, imploring Luce and Davenport not to scrap the old *Fortune* formula. "I submit," MacLeish concluded, "that the advocacy of the point of view of big business is incompatible with the journalism *Fortune* has developed."[69]

Unable to convince his writers, Davenport pursued his goal with his own pencil. In February 1938 *Fortune* began running a series of editorials under the title "Business and Government." These were the first avowed editorials to appear in a Time Inc. magazine, breaking with Luce's long-standing injunction against separating opinion from content.[70] Davenport dreamed up the idea, solicited a vague approval from Luce, wrote the copy, and went to press with it as quickly as he could. As he described their origins to an angry MacLeish (who believed Davenport had caved in to Luce), "this whole concept of having an editorial in *Fortune* is my concept, and my particular project. I conceived it; I sold it to Harry in theory; and at the first opportunity I acted without any knowledge on his part of what I was doing and without his approval."[71]

The original series concentrated on the conflict between big business and the New Deal. In the introductory editorial, Davenport described the misunderstandings that separated the two groups. The conflict emanated not from fundamentally opposed interests, Davenport claimed, but from a failure to understand the actual situation. The misconceptions each held resulted from "a lack of knowledge and information concerning the other side." *Fortune*, under Davenport's leadership, proposed to rectify this situation. As Davenport concluded, "The liberal—the salutary—path lies somewhere between the two. And that path is the one *Fortune* intends to explore." This editorial was of a piece with Luce's whole project—positioning *Fortune* to instruct business (now expanded to include government too) on its proper conduct. It also essentially built the magazine's support for the free enterprise system into the editorial direction of the magazine. It refrained from issuing the sort of blanket statement of support Luce advocated, but instead placed *Fortune* as arbitrator between government and business.[72] In subsequent editorials, Davenport developed an idiosyncratically libertarian strain of argument. Like Luce, he accepted much of the New Deal, especially the erection of a social safety net and the recognition of labor's right to organize, but he harshly criticized the anti-business rhetoric of the administration. He also worried that the New Deal exacerbated the monopolistic pressures that threatened competition. He championed competition as economically integral to recovery while epitomizing and protecting American freedom.

Davenport used the editorials to promulgate his views of the properly responsible conduct of business and the properly restricted role of government at a time when his political views were developing rapidly. Davenport had grown up in a typically old-money Republican family, at home among the social elite of Philadelphia and friendly with the du Pont family. His years at Yale and in Europe had done little to alter his politics, and when he began writing for *Fortune* his political thinking ran along familiar tracks. He found himself at home among the well-educated, politically naive, somewhat supercilious young men writing for *Fortune*. The Depression and New Deal politicized Davenport along with everyone else on the magazine. Though he never traveled as far to the left as MacLeish or Macdonald, Davenport joined in the early embrace of Roosevelt. He shared in the prevailing criticism of the timidity of business leadership, applauded the government's early initiatives, and supported the growth of organized labor. He joined the Time Inc. affiliate of the Newspaper Guild, and pressed MacLeish to join as well. Like Luce, however, Davenport found the administration's rhetorical attacks on big business unfortunate and disturbing. He had little patience with far-reaching criticisms of American capitalism, being convinced that economic and political freedom were inextricably linked. He supported New Deal regulation where it brought necessary order and stability and opposed it where it seemed likely to squelch initiative or hamper innovation.

The appearance of the Business and Government editorial in *Fortune* sparked consternation. Writers were whispering that Davenport's editorials had been written at Luce's instruction (Davenport's letter to MacLeish had been an attempt to quell these rumors). Worse, the research department threatened an outright rebellion. In April 1938 the research staff handed him a lengthy memo, protesting what they called "a progressive undermining of what we have previously felt to be the foundation upon which *Fortune* rests." They feared that *Fortune*'s group journalism (the method by which researcher, writer, and editor cooperatively produced the finished articles), was undermined when Davenport rewrote all the material from his own point of view and in accordance with the editorials he was also writing.[73]

Davenport denied the validity of most of the charges, claiming the editorials were less of a departure than the researchers seemed to think. "The editorial policy," Davenport claimed, "is the *explicit* statement of what has been *implicit* in *Fortune* all along." In describing how the magazine might reach different conclusions from the *Nation*, Davenport stated, "*Fortune* is a product of and had always been dedicated to, an economy based upon the profit system. The typical *Fortune* article is an implicit affirmation of that fact."[74] Davenport went further in a memo setting editorial policy regarding business news for the entire company in early 1940. *Fortune*'s championing of free enterprise was now taken as a given, and Davenport struggled mightily to reconcile advocacy of business with the journalist's responsibility to try to be objective. Davenport argued that editorializing for limited government in *Time*'s business coverage would be inappropriate, "*But Time Inc. is determined not to editorialize for unlimited government in its business news.*" Aware that this might not be clear enough, Davenport concluded "we are not confronted with the simple problem of playing fair (though we should always try to do that) but with a life-and-death struggle concerning which we have inevitably taken one side."[75] Davenport had been led astray by his growing distrust of the New Deal. Journalistic objectivity, or collecting and setting down the facts, were all well and good during normal times, but the present circumstances, Davenport believed, required their suspension. Convinced of the gravity of the historical moment and supremely confident in his political beliefs and judgment, Davenport sought to shape the content of the Luce magazine's to further his politics. He did so with Luce's support.

Despite the grumbling of the staff, Davenport was happy with the platform Business and Government provided him. He regarded it as "doing a great deal toward the advancement of intelligence in regard to business" and hoped it could "mold business opinion and even academic opinion."[76] He also sought other ways to make the magazine and himself more influential. He was the driving force behind the *Fortune* Round Table, in which businessmen, government officials, labor leaders, and academics came together to discuss and debate issues such as the relationship between government spending and free enterprise, or taxation and spending. The goal was to reach some common ground from which constructive action could be taken. The assumptions underlying the Round Table—that competing interest groups in fact shared common interests and that those commonalities could be made clear to all parties with the proper guidance—reveal both Davenport's faith in business leadership as necessary and benign, and his conviction that intellectuals must play a vital role in clarifying common interests.

Davenport soon got to test these beliefs. At the fourth Round Table on full employment, in August 1939, Davenport first met Wendell Willkie. He responded to Willkie immediately and was soon telling friends, "I have just met the man who ought to be the President of the United States."[77] A midwestern utility owner known primarily for his fights with the Roosevelt administration over the rights of private utilities to compete with government-subsidized competition, Willkie was just beginning to attract notice as a possible presidential candidate. Davenport invited Willkie to spend a weekend at his summerhouse, during the course of which Davenport's admiration for Willkie deepened. Willkie was exactly the sort of liberal businessman *Fortune* had been looking for. Willkie recognized the need for government regulation, yet was concerned to preserve the necessary conditions for private competition whenever possible. He supported the social welfare programs of the New Deal, but believed they could be run in a more efficient, businesslike manner. Most important, he was a foreign policy internationalist, who attacked the isolationists in the Republican Party and talked boldly of expanding American markets and democratic institutions across the globe.

Over the next months Davenport relentlessly pushed Willkie to make a run at the nomination, serving as an informal political advisor. In early 1940 he succeeded, and together they wrote up a platform, which Davenport published in *Fortune* under Wendell Willkie's name as "We, the People." The piece was accompanied by a Davenport editorial challenging the American people to be worthy of Willkie. ("The principles he stands for are American principles. They are progressive, liberal, and expansive. One cannot dare to doubt that they will eventually prevail. But whether they will prevail in terms of political candidacy is a question that depends upon the political *sophistication* of the American people.")[78] In the article Willkie laid out a political platform, advocating the return of power to the people (although he seemed chiefly to have had in mind the curtailment of the power of the Securities and Exchange Commission and the Federal Communications Commission), the running of government on business principles, and the acknowledgment that America had a great deal at stake in the developing European war.[79] The essay was reprinted in *Reader's Digest*, and Willkie's credibility climbed rapidly.

This rhetorical strategy, speaking past the political parties and directly to the people, laid the blueprint for Willkie's pursuit of the nomination. With Davenport's help, Willkie secured the support of important journalists, who pushed his candidacy in print. Willkie avoided the primaries, entering the convention as a dark horse, but with powerful interests ready to support him. When Dewey proved to have inadequate support, Willkie swept to the nomination.

The Willkie campaign that followed was the high point of Davenport's life. Davenport served, in the words of Willkie biographer Steve Neal, as "the central figure in Willkie's campaign, his chief strategist, speech-writer, alter ego."[80] The campaign was Davenport's best opportunity to see his ideas turned into a practical political program. Wendell Willkie was the perfect vehicle through which Davenport could realize his vision of a responsible, business-led liberalism. Unfortunately for Davenport, Willkie lost the election, depriving Davenport of the opportunity to put his political visions to work.

The defeat of Willkie, a defeat many blamed on the chaos of Davenport's campaign management, daunted Davenport but did not shake his confidence. If anything, it deepened his commitment to tempering intellectual work with practical politics. It also sharpened his antipathy toward other intellectuals. Still considering himself a "man of ideas," he nevertheless now disparaged American intellectuals for their failure to exert the leadership he expected of them. America was in need of spiritual guidance, and American intellectuals could offer nothing but materialist ideologies while simultaneously satirizing the needs and aspirations of their fellow citizens. Davenport had pursued this theme before the election in a *Fortune* editorial stressing the urgent need for spiritual leadership. Curiously, Davenport found unlikely support for these views from Lewis Mumford. Having read Davenport's editorial condemning the church for abdicating its responsibilities to exercise spiritual leadership in troubled times, Mumford wrote to express his agreement.[81] Calling it "one of the few things that have been written during the last year that give me any hope for our country," Mumford praised Davenport's diagnosis of the problem, but pushed him to look beyond the church for leadership. Given the gradual "shift in spiritual authority from the ecclesiastical organizations as such to the writers and artists and philosophers outside these organizations," Mumford noted, the intellectuals must be looked to on "behalf of reason, justice, charity, and other universal values." Unfortunately, "the writers of our time have left conscious ethical values and standards outside their scheme." "The American intellectuals stand condemned," Mumford concluded, "as the clergy stand condemned: and for the same reason, his faithlessness to the spirit and his failure to hear, to see, to bear witness, to speak out boldly those truths which belong to no country, those truths which must ultimately unite mankind or permit it, by their absence, to descend once more to the level of snarling beasts, who have not even a beast's concern for their own kind."[82]

Mumford's letter delighted Davenport, who wrote back to share his conviction that American intellectuals lived in a world where "all the values were distorted." He had left that world when he abandoned poetry to write for *Fortune*, a place where he again found himself "part of the stream of America."[83] This friendly exchange of letters masked the profound differences between Mumford and Davenport. For Mumford, American business values were one of the materialisms that had seduced the intellectual, while to Davenport, subscribing to these values served as a test of intellectual legitimacy. Nevertheless, Mumford and Davenport felt a shared antipathy toward most other intellectuals. Davenport, drawing support from Mumford's letter, drew toward the conclusion that intellectual values needed to be rescued from the intellectuals.

In the wake of the Willkie campaign, and with the clouds of impending war growing ever darker, Davenport renewed his attack on critics who had chosen to disdain rather than embrace America and its economic system. In his "Case Against the Intellectuals," Davenport indicted the American intellectuals for failing to lead. He assumed the power to lead America was there for the intellectual to wield, but they had refused the offer. Summarizing the intellectual's role over the last two decades, Davenport argued, critics "had left it [business] a headless monster in the twenties: now, in the 1930s, they blamed it because it had no head." He suggested, rather extraordinarily, that the Republican Party and the business leadership of the twenties, would have deferred to the leadership of writers if it was offered in the properly "productive" spirit. As naïve as this view was, it revealed Davenport's vast faith in the power of the project he was involved with at *Fortune*. It was time, he suggested, for the intellectuals to forsake their outsider role and their negative criticism, and to take up the mantle of leadership, in effect, following the path Davenport himself had trod. "Insofar as I am able to speak for my generation," Davenport concluded, "I am proud to speak for it. We may have been lost for a while, but now some of us are back in action."[84] The familiar distinction between intellect and action was here deployed to cover a political divide: the only possible excuse for the "debunking" of the twenties and the radicalism of the 1930s was a failure of intellectuals to fully engage with their country and act on that engagement.

Here Davenport followed an argument made in more sophisticated terms by MacLeish in his infamous essay "The Irresponsibles," in which he criticized American intellectuals who had refused to recognize the political struggles in Europe as their struggle.[85] Both Davenport and MacLeish tended to make criticism seem irresponsible. For Davenport especially, responsible criticism required acceptance of American political and economic systems. Taking American capitalism as a given, criticism could then emerge from within this framework. Such simplicities increasingly intruded into Davenport's thinking. He wanted to lead intellectuals, yet he found it difficult to consider himself one or to avoid blanket criticisms of American intellectuals. Such criticism was always rhetorically launched from outside their ranks.

Davenport did not find it easy, however, to act with the autonomy he desired from his position within Time Inc. Returning to *Fortune*, he sparked growing animosity among the writers and researchers who resented his tendency to consider *Fortune* his personal platform. During the Willkie campaign, Davenport had tried to quash a pro-Roosevelt article by John Chamberlain (written at the insistence of liberal staffers, to balance Davenport's pro-Willkie piece). In response, head researcher Patricia Divver had wired him a rebuke, "Who do you think you are—the Editor of *Fortune*?"[86] Such resentment increased when he returned in just the sort of amorphously defined position that Luce often settled on.

After a few months on *Fortune*, Davenport moved to *Life*, where he soon launched an editorial page in that magazine. His editorials sparked resistance inside the magazine and controversy outside. *Life*'s managing editor, Dan Longwell, had been opposed to the editorials from the start. After reading Davenport's early drafts, he penned a response, "I've read and pondered these and I swear Harry is going to have to convince me that LIFE should have an editorial page."⁸⁷ Davenport won Luce over, however, and Longwell was forced to acquiesce to the editorials. Having won the battle, Davenport almost lost it again with one of his early efforts. In October 1942 he penned "An Open Letter from the Editors of *Life* to the People of England" in which he blamed England for dragging its feet in opening a second European front because of its imperial preoccupations. The British perceived the editorial as threatening a separate peace ("If you cling to the Empire at the expense of a United Nations victory," Davenport declaimed, "you will lose the war. Because you will lose us . . . ") and a protracted round of meetings between British officials and *Time* editors failed to smooth the waters.⁸⁸ Eventually, Luce wrote a private letter in which he disavowed Davenport's views. Feeling pressure from all sides, Davenport remained uncowed. Writing to Luce, he apologized for dragging him into this trouble, and offered to resign. Gambling that Luce would refuse, Davenport then imposed conditions for staying, pushing for more autonomy and independence. If Luce wanted "the most important editorial page in America," then he must allow Davenport to have complete and sole responsibility for the content and strategy of the page.⁸⁹ Davenport's gambit left Billings "flabbergasted," and he warned Luce not to cave in to Davenport's demands for an editorial page "over which I (or you) surrender editorial veto power."⁹⁰

Davenport won his bet, however, and continued to write the page. A year later he was pushing for more, trying to convince Luce he should have a byline. Arguing that "an article with a signature gets around better" and that "I can be more effective if I am known (to some reasonable extent) to have a position of my own," Davenport was clearly looking for a way to speak to Luce's vast audience, but to do so in his own voice and name.⁹¹ He succeeded in speaking in his own voice, but failed to convince Luce to allow him to attach his name.

Despite writing the editorial page for the nation's most widely read magazine, Davenport was unsatisfied. His editorials occasionally provoked discussion, but they failed to capture the public imagination the way he hoped. Nothing he wrote compared in impact with Luce's own famous editorial, "The American Century," published in 1941. He continued to chafe at writing anonymously. In early 1944 he finally gave up, leaving Time Inc. due to a bitter dispute over the coming election. Davenport had decided to support Roosevelt because of what he viewed as the Republican Party's abandonment of Willkie's internationalist sentiment and return to its isolationist roots. Davenport went public with his views, appearing on an election eve radio broadcast to encourage other Republicans to join him in voting for Roosevelt.⁹² Luce viewed such actions as treasonous in someone he had entrusted to speak with the editorial voice of Time Inc.

Davenport's departure left acrimony on both sides. Writing to MacLeish soon after he left, Davenport described the departure: "Anyway, I couldn't say what I wanted to say in prose, and I couldn't say anything at all in any medium for Henry R. Luce."⁹³ Davenport was again thinking of writing poetry, and upon leaving he devoted himself to completing a long poem summing up his feelings for America. In it, he hoped to demonstrate the type of artistic work he believed American intellectuals should practice.

Davenport published the poem, *My Country*, in late 1944. The poem was structured as a meditation on the meaning of America interrupted by various attempts to eulogize a dead soldier. The first lines sounded Davenport's twin themes: that America's great achievements were achievements of action, and that the country lacked a literature or culture equal to its achievements.

> America is not a land of ease.
> We have not paused from action to beget
> Heroic simile and song and frieze;
> We have no empire of the mind as yet.

Americans have been the "sons of enterprise and sweat," the "builders of dynamic things." Their great productivity, in Davenport's rendering, emanated from the freedom guaranteed by the country's democratic political institutions (though at times he ascribed it to general invocations of the American way of life, sketched in the familiar Norman Rockwell manner). That soldiers were currently dying to protect these freedoms made the proper understanding of their nature and origin crucially important. Davenport asked "who will speak the words to honor the dead?"⁹⁴ He supplied answers from three figures, the dead man's sister, teacher, and buddy. The sister and buddy served as emotional bookends, used to invoke the pain of learning of his death and the wonderment that he died while others survived, surrounding the teacher's elaboration of the meaning of freedom. The teacher's description, the centerpiece of the poem, reiterated the descriptions of freedom by Davenport that opened and closed the poem.

The real answer to who would speak for the dead, of course, is that Davenport would. Both in its content and in its example, *My Country* provided a blueprint for the role Davenport envisioned for intellectuals. It also revealed the myopia of his vision. Ironically, for one who so frequently complained of the materialist doctrines and spiritual poverty of American intellectuals, he tended to celebrate material struggle and long for spiritual unity. Though he defined freedom as "struggle and strife," Davenport had no real appreciation for intellectual strife. Fundamentally, freedom meant the freedom to pursue economic interests. The struggle and strife was in the economic sphere, not in the realm of ideas. Intellectuals were useful primarily because they could animate and make meaningful abstract concepts such as freedom.

The poem was greeted harshly by literary critics. Despite a formal ambitiousness and sound technique, its rhetorical mode and avowed patriotism grated on ears tuned to more dissonant chords. Davenport's old friend F. O. Matthiessen objected to the naively positive depiction of American life, telling Davenport, "the parts of your poem that are the weakest are where you give a too easily glowing, almost poster or magazine-cover view of American life." *My Country* lacked, Matthieson claimed, the "more organic grasp of the tragic tensions" in human life.

Matthiesson correctly noted that intellectuals such as himself were not Davenport's intended audience.[95] Davenport wrote for the same audience that purchased the Luce magazines, the educated middle class. He wanted an audience of government officials, business executives, and community leaders. Davenport later defined the audience he sought, writing "we have in mind those millions of persons who do not pretend to any special learning outside their professions, but who are forced by the exigencies of democratic life . . . to provide a certain leadership . . . These intellectually unspecialized but generally intelligent people are the custodians of our moral values, and . . . of our policies of state . . . . If the U.S. is too understand freedom, it is in their minds and hearts that the understanding must live."[96] Davenport seems to have achieved his goal, as the poem sold very well, earned praise from most middle-class magazines, and provoked a flood of fan mail from business leaders, university presidents, and journalists. Dwight Eisenhower kept a copy on his desk thereafter.[97]

Pairing Davenport's case against the intellectuals with his example of what the poet should produce, it is clear he strove for an intellectual class without intellectuals. He envisioned intellectuals as a leadership caste, depicting American ideals, instructing American audiences, but from squarely within the mainstream of American values. He refused to acknowledge that such values might be contested. In 1956 *Time* ran an article applauding the eclipse of the intellectual as a "Man of Protest" and his recent replacement by the intellectual as a "Man of Affirmation." *Time* applauded those intellectuals who accepted a particular conception of America as a nation of freedom and opportunity, a beacon of hope to the rest of the world.[98] They described what is now often characterized as the consensus intellectual. More properly, the label consensus intellectual might be reserved for writers like Russell Davenport. It is a label he would have worn proudly.

Magazine X: The Anti-Intellectual Magazine for Intellectuals

Matthews and Davenport, despite similarities in their background, interests, and aspirations, and despite a common interest in imbuing their work at Time Inc. with intellectual substance and meaning, led quite different lives within the company. Matthews functioned anonymously, controlling the content of *Time* magazine through his aggressive editing and his placement of like-minded intellectuals on the staff. He sought to exercise power and influence behind the scenes. Davenport, on the other hand, had little interest in working with other writers. First at *Fortune* and later at *Life* he sought a platform from which he could propound his ideas. He dreaded the possibility of personal eclipse, seeking the large audience Time Inc. could deliver without the sacrifice of name and identity writing for the magazine usually required. Both men had a measure of success in the early 1940s, but both also failed in their grander aspirations. They had distinctively different ideas about intellectuals and their purpose. For Matthews, intellectuals were necessary to improve and humanize Luce's magazines. His concern was primarily with intellectual life, secondarily with the use to which intellectuals could be put. Davenport, on the other hand, hoped to use intellectuals to further the political and ideological goals of the magazines. In 1947, Matthews and Davenport were brought together on a project that held great personal appeal and that tested their respective ideas about the place of intellectuals in America and at Time Inc.

Luce planned to publish a new intellectual magazine. Stocked with contributions from prominent American and European writers, the new magazine would depart from Time Inc.'s usual method of anonymous staff production. Striking a middle ground in content between serious little magazines such as *Partisan Review* and *Politics* on the one hand and popular yet slighter magazines such as *Harper's* and the *Atlantic* on the other, Luce's venture would open up a new audience for serious, ambitious, and important intellectual fare. As one of its planned editors, John Chamberlain, put it, the magazine would continue and sustain "a real resurgence of interest in high philosophy and in the fundamentals of art, music, nature, economics, play, history, psychology, and sex."99

The project had originated with Willi Schlamm, a gnome-like refugee from Austria. Schlamm, described by one colleague as the man Peter Lorre built his acting career portraying, arrived in New York in 1938 and, after writing for the *New Leader*, found a job writing for *Fortune* in 1941.100 In Vienna, he had begun as a journalist for the Communist *Rote-Fane*, until he broke with the Party in 1929. He then edited the liberal pacifist journal *Weltbuhne*, before emigrating in the wake of Munich.101

At *Fortune* Schlamm became the latest intellectual to exert a substantial influence over Luce. Luce had always been susceptible to intellectual infatuations. He had been in awe of MacLeish ever since he followed his career at Hotchkiss and Yale. At *Fortune*, Luce had been intimidated by Parker Lloyd-Smith and regularly deferred to MacLeish. In the late 1930s, Davenport seemed to exert a similar influence. By the early 1940s Luce's attention had been increasingly drawn to the international arena. He began to seek out intellectuals with international expertise, especially European immigrants. These were years when Luce would entertain, as Alfred Kazin remembered, "any overcharged thinker with a mission."102 The Austrian economist Peter Drucker and the American head of the Foreign Policy Association, Raymond Leslie Buell had preceded Schlamm in Luce's estimation. By 1945 Schlamm's combination of anticommunism and the conviction that only spiritual values could successfully oppose Communism's soul-deadened materialism attracted Luce. (This was the same combination Luce discovered in Whittaker Chambers and other defectors from the Communist faith.) Schlamm pushed Luce to publish an intellectual magazine and secured Luce's approval.

In 1945 Schlamm came up with an initial prospectus. His goal was a magazine that would be a superior version of the existing monthlies *Harper's* and the *Atlantic*. It would resemble the little magazines such as *Partisan Review*, but pitched to a wide audience. He sought an audience of serious, literate, and concerned people who were troubled by, and anxious to understand, the postwar world. The magazine would help organize the intellectual lives of thoughtful Americans. This trick was possible, Schlamm believed, because he would shun the anti-American sentiments that repelled most Americans and insist on contributions that were useful. He sought the same audience Davenport had defined—serious, literate people, concerned with the state of the world. Excerpts from Schlamm's prospectus for *Magazine X* provided a sense of what he envisioned.103

Schlamm envisioned a magazine that featured earnest, intelligent exploration and debate oriented around a series of principles or propositions. The first, and most important principle, asserted that "man is the meaning, not the 'raw material' of history." This meant that "to the same extent that man is history-made, history is man-made." This was a necessary assertion, Schlamm believed, in the face of the threat posed by communism and bureaucratization more generally. Schlamm, like Luce, was also concerned with the ease with which the masses could be politically manipulated, as the success of fascism proved. To that end, Schlamm committed the magazine to defending "fundamental personal rights" that were not subject to majority consent. And he insisted that such rights derived from a set of values that were "simply true." In sum, his prospectus promised a magazine that would clarify an American alternative to both determinism and to the dangerous susceptibility of the masses to political manipulation.[104]

The prospectus also revealed Schlamm's deep antipathy for American intellectuals. His writing dripped with condescension for them. Blaming intellectuals for their climate of disillusionment after the First World War, he expected a similar outbreak after the Second. *Magazine X* was designed to be a serious alternative to the "adolescent despair" that was all that could be expected of American intellectuals. Schlamm proposed "a magazine for grown-ups," which sold "food—not drugs; substance—not package." In shunning "brilliant irresponsibility" it would be "anything but a magazine for intellectuals" (who Schlamm defined as "professional users of words, carriers of cocksure confusion, propagandists who don't know what they want and yet, they want it so madly!").[105]

Schlamm's idea of an anti-intellectual magazine, written by intellectuals but not for intellectuals, was perfectly pitched both to alienate intellectuals and appeal to Luce. Rosalind Constable, a literary young woman employed at Time Inc. to work with Schlamm, wrote a blistering attack on Schlamm's prospectus. Calling it "bombastic, arrogant, ignorant and old hat," Constable correctly noted the absurdity of publishing a magazine "calculated to antagonize the very people whose cooperation we should enlist."[106] Dwight Macdonald made the same point in his "Memo to Mr. Luce," published in the October 1945 issue of *Politics*. Calling "Project X" an "anti-cultural cultural magazine," Macdonald wondered how Schlamm proposed to attract the contributors he seemed determined to offend at every turn.[107] As an interested stockholder, Macdonald mockingly advised Luce to avoid such a dubious investment.

For Luce, however, Schlamm's magazine promised to provide exactly the sort of leadership Luce desired. By eliminating "Menckenism, 'debunking,' and adolescent despair," and substituting a "civilized respect for fundamentals, and mellowing experience," Schlamm could fence out irresponsible intellectuals while providing a pulpit for discussion of ideas he considered at the core of the modern dilemma—religion, freedom, responsibility, order.[108] Despite the pumped up rhetoric, Schlamm succeeded in compiling an impressive roster of contributors. The initial issues were to set to feature Simone de Beauvoir, Erich Fromm, Andre Gide, Arthur Koestler, George Orwell, and Reinhold Neibuhr. In addition to these well-known intellectuals, Schlamm had lined up a number of academics who he believed had important things to say and could write in the clear style he demanded. Finally, the magazine would use local talent, lining up Robert Cantwell on the New England mind, Whittaker Chambers on Dostoevsky's *The Possessed*, and T. S. Matthews on Edmund Wilson's career.

Despite the impressive lineup, Luce recognized Schlamm's limitations. The authors Schlamm had secured were too heavily waited toward Europe. Schlamm had not been successful in attracting important American contributors. Luce also knew the magazine could not succeed if it maintained the avowedly anti-intellectual tone struck by Schlamm. Luce decided to bring in T. S. Matthews to evaluate the project and, if it seemed worthwhile, to take it over. Matthews jumped at the opportunity. He described his response to Luce's offer this way: "Rachel was the girl I wanted to marry. I've served seven years and got Leah. I'd rather have Rachel."[109] With Luce acting as Laban to Matthews' Jacob, Matthews took a break from *Time* in the summer of 1947 to evaluate the work Schlamm had completed and to "answer the $64 question: have we got a magazine?"[110] Matthews's sympathies, split between intellectual culture and Time Inc., positioned him perfectly to evaluate the project on its merits. The memo Matthews produced struck a far different tone from Schlamm's. Whereas Schlamm wasted no time insulting all existing intellectual magazines, Matthews recognized that their magazine, "springing from the dubious parentage of Time Inc.," would "have to be better quicker and for a longer time" before the public would be convinced "that the only ax it wants to grind is cultural." Matthews's summary shared Schlamm's basic values, but toned down the offensive rhetoric. Schlamm's attack on the "self-appointed aristocracy of snobs who aspire to rule the masses" was replaced with a simple statement that the magazine would object to "intellectual and artistic snobbery (including intellectual dishonesty and vulgarity of all kinds)."[111]

Matthews concluded that the magazine could become "a magazine of high standards in literary quality, intellectual honesty, and moral integrity," but it faced formidable obstacles. Matthews believed the magazine could only succeed if Schlamm could be persuaded to accept a subordinate role. In addition, Matthews worried about the possibility of corporate meddling. Using advertising as an example of a subject the magazine would have to address, "it would presumably have very definite criticisms to make—criticisms which might very well effect" Time Inc. advertisers. To succeed, Matthews warned, *Magazine X* would require an unprecedented amount of freedom ("a perhaps unusual amount of faith, an unwonted length of rope, will have to be given to the editors").[112] Eventually, Matthews concluded the magazine would never be granted the necessary independence. He decided "I didn't want to have anything to do with it because it would have been much too tied to the apron strings of Time."[113] He went back to Leah, but retained the hope that, like Jacob, he might someday earn Rachel too.

With Matthews bowing out, Luce needed someone else to step in to Schlamm's place. The perfect candidate had already presented himself. In March 1947, Russell Davenport had written Luce a letter, reestablishing contact after nearly three years. Davenport wrote Luce, he claimed, because "it would be fun to know what goes on these days in that great brain of yours, against which I have so often beaten my mutilated wings."[114] He also wanted to sketch ideas he was developing for gathering together "a small group of men and women" to pursue and propagate the important issues of the day. Since 1944, Davenport had been involved in a number of organizations bent on developing a liberal agenda for the Republican Party and pushing the party to the left. The letter to Luce was an opening move in involving Luce in similar efforts. The same day he wrote to Luce, he also wrote to former *Fortune* colleague Eric Hodgins, complaining of "young men such as Luce, Paley, and Whitney, all of whom I know quite well, who have boundless assets and power, yet who are content" to leave the world as it is. Davenport wondered, in typical form, whether "the fault lies *primarily* with such creatures as you and me, who are supposed to be men of ideas, and whose role therefore is to animate such resources and give them something to work for."[115] Luce quickly responded and informed Davenport of his plans for *Magazine X*. When Matthews pulled out, Luce offered the editor's job to Davenport.

Davenport proved a more compatible match with Schlamm than Matthews. He shared Schlamm's criticism of American intellectuals and a similar vague assurance that spiritual matters were becoming central to American culture (as Schlamm wrote in the introduction: "Theology is about to become once more an immensely practical public concern").[116] Davenport's contribution, he felt, was to deepen its content. He defined *Quest*—the new title—as the response to a grave need, a response to the darkness that "hangs over almost all human enquiry." The magazine would be an antidote, an embodiment of "the search for Truth in its human form." It would begin from the assertion that "men, not things, constitute a civilization." The truths he had in mind were not exclusively philosophical. Indeed, Davenport believed that the current crisis was a crisis caused by the human embrace of reason above all other means of apprehended the world. Looking for a rekindling of "faith, inspiration, intuition," he turned to the artist, for it is "through the arts that man can come closest" to satisfactorily answering the questions of the age. The magazine would be structured around this quest, with a "philosopher editor" responsible for keeping the project on course.[117] With Davenport performing this role, Schlamm and a third house intellectual, John Chamberlain, would continue to line up additional submissions.

Ultimately, however, the bridge Luce was trying to build between intellectuals and his media empire was set afire from both ends. Macdonald's attack in *Politics* set the tone by which intellectuals observed the progress of *Magazine X*. Despite the fact that Macdonald was working along somewhat similar lines—his essay "The Root Is Man" shared a common insistence on making man the starting point of political action—his distrust of the "Lucepress" was too all encompassing to grant *Magazine X* any legitimacy.[118] Without the cooperation of the New York intellectuals, Davenport and Chamberlain struggled to find high quality American submissions. Their efforts to tone down the anti-intellectual tenor of the project failed to make up for the growing antipathy for Luce and his magazines among intellectuals.[119]

The situation was no better within Time Inc. Schlamm, Davenport, and Chamberlain presented the first three dummy issues to a board of Time Inc. editors in late 1947. The project elicited scorn and derision from a number of Time Inc. figures, including Billings and Longwell. Prefacing his remarks by noting that he had no real interest in magazines of this type and never read them, Billings nevertheless felt competent to deliver an attack on the entire venture.[120] Matthews was the only one present to offer unqualified support (he recalled the others as "sharpening their knives" to eviscerate a venture so dear to the "men with pipes").[121] The evening made clear that those with intellectual ambitions for Time Inc. were now an embattled minority. Despite a later memo by John Chamberlain, defending the magazine and declaring the likes of Billings incompetent to judge the matter, Luce's confidence was shaken.[122]

Though he let the editors go forward through the fall, in January 1948 the decision was made to scrap the project. The official history of Time Inc. attributed the decision to worries that the magazine would burden management and fears that Luce would not devote sufficient time to it.[123] This is another way of confirming Matthews's impression. Luce and his senior management were unwilling to let Davenport, Matthews, Schlamm, or anyone else have the responsibility for publishing an intellectual magazine over which Luce could not exercise editorial control. A magazine printed by Time Inc., but not written by Time Inc. staff writers, and not subject to line-by-line editorial control, was unacceptable.

The failure to publish *Magazine X* marked a significant disappointment for both Matthews and Davenport.[124] Matthews returned to *Time*, continuing to push Luce to make the necessary commitments to improve the magazine. By this time Luce was tired of his complaining. He recognized and appreciated how much Matthews had improved *Time*, but could not agree with him that the magazine needed a major renovation.

Also, their political differences were becoming increasingly difficult to hide, and Matthews tired of the constant battles with Luce over election coverage. He stuck it out until the 1952 election. For the first time he found himself fighting Luce's pressure from above and the efforts of pro-Republican political writers from below. Struggling to repair a writer's subtle attack on Democratic candidate Adlai Stevenson (the writer had praised Stevenson, but had chosen examples that deliberately undermined the praise), Matthews precipitated a major fight. During the argument, writer Max Ways yelled at Matthews: "The trouble with *Time* is, it's too fucking fair, and you're the one that does it."[125] Though Matthews considered this a tribute, such defensive battles were wearing him down.

Reflecting on his career, Matthews recalled the final question he and his colleagues had posed to Henry Luce in 1939 when they were trying to gauge his beliefs. Matthews had asked Luce "under what circumstances would you consider using *Time* as a political instrument?" Luce responded in the sort of high-flown terms that so impressed Matthews: "When the Republic was in danger." The Eisenhower election campaign confirmed that Luce now considered the republic to be threatened as long as the Republican Party was out of power.[126]

Matthews intended to resign, but was forestalled by Luce, who instead sent him to England to devise a new edition of *Time* specifically tailored to the English market. It is possible Luce approved Matthews's English project as a way of easing him out, a common strategy at *Time*, where editors were never fired, just sent abroad to develop new projects. At the time, however, Matthews believed it to be a serious opportunity, and spent the next six months developing an ambitious prospectus for a new kind of *Time* magazine. Matthews proposed a three-part structure, beginning with news ("with no slanting whatever, just straight news"), followed by a middle section of signed opinion pieces, and concluding with signed cultural reviews. As he worked, Matthews "got really quite keen on it," believing he finally had the opportunity to create his Rachel after all. After keeping him waiting for months, Luce finally cabled his refusal to launch the magazine. A furious Matthews cabled back, "If you weren't going to kiss me, why did you keep me standing on tiptoe so long?"[127] In contrast to the traditional view of mass culture as feminine and high culture as masculine, an understanding Matthews used in his earlier writings, he now represented himself and high culture as completely supplicant, dependent on a mass culture embodied by Henry Luce.

With that, Matthews's career at Time Inc. came to a close. Matthews remained in England, a country he found more congenial than his native America. He devoted his time to writing, publishing a biography of T. S. Eliot, an analysis of British newspapers, a pair of memoirs, and a series of volumes of poetry. Matthews had spent twenty-two years working for Time Inc., rising from a reclusive book reviewer to the most powerful man at *Time* magazine apart from Henry Luce. In later years Matthews was bitter about his experience. In his memoirs he presented a distanced account of himself, taking a bemused look back at how seriously he had taken the whole endeavor. He viewed the effort as quixotic and the results as disappointing. Measured against his own standards, it would be difficult to reject his self-judgment. Yet, *Time* was a better magazine while edited by Matthews than it was in the years before or after his tenure. And, Matthews did effectively make *Time* an hospitable work environment for a series of writers. He had built and protected an environment in which other intellectuals could work interstitially, writing for *Time* but driven by their own interests and interpreting the world according to their own lights. This might be a meager accomplishment when measured against his own grandiose expectations, but for the writers involved, it was an accomplishment nonetheless. Without his protection, James Agee, Louis Kronenberger, John Hersey and many others would have been unlikely to find *Time* a hospitable venue for their work.

Russell Davenport also remained at Time Inc. after *Magazine X* fell apart. Despite his disappointment, Luce's magazines still offered him the best available opportunity for bringing his views to the audience he desired. For the next few years he continued to work on new projects with Luce. In 1948 Davenport inaugurated the *Life* Round Table, which he described as "a democratic device for the exploration of important questions by many minds." Gathering together panels of experts and ordinary people along with a moderator, the assembled group would then engage in "enlightened conversation" on the topic at hand. The first issue discussed "The Pursuit of Happiness." The feature became so successful that Time Inc. produced a pamphlet helping people organize similar round tables at home.[128] Later Round Tables considered modern art, housing and the movies. The Round Table was an ingenious application of the Luce mission—helping ordinary citizens grapple with important issues in an effort to better understand and engage with their world. Though in print the round table functioned as the democratic initiative it purported to be, behind the scenes it was not beyond manipulation. In the aftermath of the 1948 election (a debacle to Luce and Davenport), when Davenport considered Dewey's failure attributable to his unwillingness to debate the issues that mattered to Americans, he made a remarkable proposal. Writing to Luce, he noted "that Time Inc. can play a useful, perhaps a historic role. I, for one, would be glad to put the Round Tables at the disposal of the Republican Party (in a kind of unofficial way, of course) for the purpose of searching answers to issues. If this is not done, the Democratic answer—more and more state control—is bound to prevail indefinitely."[129] Davenport, like Luce, was torn between the desire to provide their readers with the necessary tools to govern themselves better and a determination that the American people should see the world the same way he did.

In Davenport's last major effort for Luce, he set down his fullest statement of how America should be seen. Davenport edited (and finally earned a byline for) a single-subject issue of *Fortune* in 1951, later published in book form as *U.S.A.: The Permanent Revolution*. The volume summed up America history, developed a more traditionally American alternative to the welfare state, and reiterated the familiar call for business to lead the way in bettering America and extending the American way of life throughout the globe. The volume had all the earmarks of Davenport's great strengths and weaknesses as a writer. In a poetic invocation of what America had to achieve, he could be moving, as when he wrote:

> The individual lives surrounded by darkness. He is a mere candle. The task of the permanent revolution is to increase the light of every candle, so that one light may reach to another and the darkness may thus be dispelled. Here in this land, we have gained some elementary steps . . . . Yet in pursuit of real freedom we have yet to gain more than we have won . . . . We have not begun to gain freedom from hate, the freedom that is born of love.[130]

At the same time, Davenport persistently confused the best American ideals with the rather messier reality of American life. Unsurprisingly, this mistake occurred most consistently when considering the changing nature of business leadership. The sort of liberal business leadership *Fortune* and Davenport have been advocating for years was declared to exist. U.S. capitalism had now become "popular capitalism," where "the influence of Main Street has become vastly more important than the control of Wall Street." Corporate leadership had been ceded to socially responsible and responsive managers, the only element in modern society that had yet displayed "the sense of responsibility that ought to go with the [economic] power."[131] Such a rose-colored myth, no matter how movingly invoked, demonstrated the limitations of the intellectual as Man of Affirmation, on display in *Fortune* magazine.

Davenport never did sever fully his connections with Luce. In 1952, just two years before his death, he was still writing Luce letters hoping for continued space in what, Davenport wrote, "I continue to think of as 'our' magazines."[132] Davenport had never been able to resist the attraction of Luce's magazines, even as he failed to keep Luce devoted to the same liberal Republicanism he embraced. He had remained true to his own conception of intellectual life: seeking to clarify the meaning of America to a particular middle-class audience. Like Matthews, he failed in his grandest ambitions both in politics and at Time Inc. Unlike Matthews, however, Davenport had succeeded in using Luce's magazines to propagate his own ideas. He had succeeded in his endeavor because of his own writing gifts, his strengths as a political infighter, and because of the degree to which he articulated Henry Luce's own beliefs. Davenport could function as an intellectual at Time Inc. into the early 1950s, but only as an Intellectual of Affirmation, and even then he worked without the freedom necessary to intellectual life. Davenport's sharply attenuated vision of intellectual life ultimately led him to repudiate the critical self-consciousness integral to the intellectual's calling.

CHAPTER SIX

Journalism and Politics at *Time* Magazine

I: poor: blind in the sun: I have seen
With these eyes those battles: I saw Montezuma:
I saw the armies of Mexico marching the leaning

Wind in their garments: the painted faces: the plumes
Blown on the light air: I saw that city:
I walked at night on those stones: in the shadowy rooms

I have heard the chink of my heel and the bats twittering:
I: poor as I am: I was young in that country:
These words were my life: these letters written

Cold on the page with the split ink and the shunt of the
Stubborn thumb: these marks at my fingers:
These are the shape of my own life. . . .

We were the lords of it all . . . .
—Archibald MacLeish, *Conquistador*

Protesting heavy-handed editing of a cherished story, a senior writer complained to Henry Luce:

> I cannot tell you how much this affair has disturbed me . . . .For it strikes at the heart of my continued usefulness to Time [Inc.]. The increasingly agitated theme among the abler men around here is: Has

a man who has something to say and the ability to say it any real place at Time? Do not hacks do the job better?[1]

This was the question intellectuals who worked for Henry Luce repeatedly asked themselves: has the writer with something to say any real place at Time Inc.? The question took on an added urgency in the 1940s, as a new generation of young writers arrived at *Time* magazine. Raised in the political crucible of the Depression, spending their college years watching the rise of fascism in Europe, these were young men whose ambitions differed markedly from earlier intellectuals at Time Inc.

Never susceptible to the idea that intoxicated an earlier generation, that literature existed above and apart from politics, these young writers conceived of intellectual life as inseparable from political involvement. To choose sides—over the New Deal, over Roosevelt, over fascism, over Spain, over Stalin's purges, over Hitler—was the implacable imperative of their youth. Their literary models were no longer the heroes of the 1920s, writers such as Mencken, Eliot, and Joyce, but instead the novelists of political commitment, men such as Dos Passos, Malraux, and Silone. Their literary ambitions turned away from poetry (though they often wrote poetry, it was a private affair, a dalliance reserved for friends or kept in journals). Instead they sought an active engagement with the world and its crises. Deciding that journalism might suit their requirements, they strove to meld the techniques of literature and journalism. Unconsciously building on the experiments of MacLeish and Agee at *Fortune* and the narrative structure already employed at *Time*, they pushed journalism in new directions, seeking to depict the world with a greater complexity and conviction than traditional journalism. John Hersey, eager to write for *Time* and to see the war up close, summarized their beliefs, claiming "the devices of fiction could serve journalism well and might even help it aspire now and then to the level of art."[2]

Time, with its focus on the world's politics, was their natural destination, just as *Fortune*, charting the turbulent waters of a drifting capitalism, had been the location of choice during the 1930s. Young writers came to *Time* hoping, in the words of one of their number, Theodore White, to "see history made," and they expected to alter history's shape with their reporting. As White remembered, he and his fellow journalists believed "we could make events march in the direction we pointed, if we pointed clearly enough."[3] Having read MacLeish's *Conquistador*, writing in the years when Henry Luce's "American Century" took shape, they too felt they could be "lords of it all."

John Hersey, whose account of the atomic bombing of Hiroshima stands as a high point of journalism, and Theodore H. White, whose books on presidential campaigns created a new form of political reporting, were the best of the new breed of writer at *Time*. They differed from earlier *Time* writers not only in their backgrounds and aspirations, but also in the journalism they practiced. Until the late 1930s, *Time* was still a rewrite magazine. Reading the week's news, men in offices at Rockefeller Plaza rewrote events as if they had been there. A man who had never been closer to the event than the account in the *New York Times* wrote descriptions of the ominous weather at a dignitary's funeral. With the magazine's growing success, and the clear importance of world events, *Time* began to develop its own news bureaus and hire its own reporters. White was hired as a foreign correspondent in Chungking, Nationalist China's capital during its war against Japanese invasion and Communist insurgency. Hersey roved the world, covering the war in China, the South Pacific, Africa, Italy, and Europe. He joined writers such as Charles Wertenbaker (a *Fortune* veteran), John Osborne, Richard Lauterbach, Frank Norris, and Walter Graebner to form the core of *Time*'s war reporting team.

Hersey and White thrived in their roles, though reporting raised difficult dilemmas for each. Hersey surpassed conventional war coverage by experimenting with fictional techniques to convey factual events. He became Luce's star reporter, filing important stories for *Time* and *Life* that he turned into three successful wartime books, including his Pulitzer-Prize winning first novel, *A Bell for Adano*. Groomed as a likely successor to Luce, he struggled to balance the satisfaction of writing with the power offered by editing. White's dilemmas were different. Hired as *Time*'s man in Chungking, his industrious reporting quickly made him another Luce favorite. At age twenty-four, his war reporting earned him the first correspondent byline in *Time* history.[4] Conceiving of himself as a participant in China's resistance to Japan, he struggled to work out an acceptable balance between his conflicting obligations as a reporter and a participant.

Both Hersey and White caught the attention of Henry Luce with their intelligence, dedication, and their connections with his beloved China. Luce wanted to recruit both of them for New York editor jobs. Young, talented, able to influence Luce, Hersey and White were in the best position among the younger writers at *Time* to carve out the space they desired, to practice journalism as they believed it could be developed, and to pursue their interests in the pages of an influential weekly news magazine. They were determined to find out what place *Time* might have for men of ability and ambition.

Their ambitions clashed, however, with those of the man who wrote the memo questioning whether serious writers had a place writing for Henry Luce's magazines. The disgruntled writer was not a member of this generation, though he arrived at around the same time. He was Whittaker Chambers, the ex-Communist and former spy, who spent the nine years between his break with the Communist Party and his testimony against Alger Hiss working for Time Inc. An intellectual deeply suspicious of other intellectuals, Chambers viewed journalism as a means of exculpating his sins and a vehicle for awakening Americans to the dangers of communism. Older than the other new writers, he was also clearer in his own mind about what he wanted to achieve at *Time*. If writers such as Hersey and White came to *Time* looking to test their ideas against, in White's words, "the truths of visual observation," Chambers arrived convinced he already possessed the truth.[5] His task was to make every issue of *Time* trumpet that truth: that the United States was inextricably involved in a fatal fight between Christian civilization and Communism. Chambers began by insinuating anti-Soviet cracks into virtually every review he wrote. "Every week," a friend noted, "that mortar goes off in the last five pages of *Time*."[6] Promoted to edit foreign news on the strength of his great ability and Luce's growing anti-communism, Chambers fought the young correspondents in the field over how to interpret the events closing the war.

Driving the struggle between Chambers on one side and Hersey and White on the other were different perspectives on the Soviet Union. Their fight prefigured the ideological struggles of the Cold War. Hersey, White, and other reporters in the field, often battling censorship, tried to reduce complex and chaotic events into well-digested stories. They often operated with a respect for Communist wartime accomplishments, skepticism about Soviet intentions, and a deep hope that postwar peace could be preserved. Chambers, acting from a conviction the Second World War was just a prelude to a Third, edited to cast the worst possible light on Soviet intentions and interpreted all world events as primarily driven by the undeclared war between Communism and the West. His ability to win Luce to this view ultimately spelled the end of Hersey and White's aspirations at Time Inc. Chambers would not, however, enjoy his victory for long. The postwar climate of anti-communism that he had helped foster eventually made it untenable for Time Inc. to employ a confessed former spy.

The so-called "Chambers war" was also a fight between different conceptions of journalism and different definitions of how intellectual life should be lived. It provides both a stirring account of three individuals struggling to balance their own political, literary, and intellectual commitments, and also a snapshot of the changing journalistic climate as the Second World War gave way to the Cold War. It reveals how three different writers struggled to come to terms with contradictions between their political commitments and their commitment to truth. Chambers's fervent anti-communism, and his willingness to act on his belief that the ends justified the means, made him seem the least ambivalent, but over time his dogmatism diminished. In his last years, after the Hiss affair, Chambers seemed to repudiate his earlier willingness to subordinate ideas to ideology.

Despite their common opposition to Chambers and an enduring friendship, Hersey and White had quite different ideas about how journalism should be practiced. For both, journalism was more than a ticket to a ringside seat as history was made. Hersey wanted to experience cataclysmic events in personal terms. He was always drawn to the individuals trapped inside large events and his collected work adds up to a stirring testament to the varieties of individual experience under inordinate pressure. White, on the other hand, was attracted to men with power. His fascination with leadership subordinated ideas to personality, and his desire to influence events led him to confuse the world as it was with the world as it ought to have been. White shared these characteristics with Luce and his publications.

The developing Cold War, which emerged in the pages of *Time* magazine before it in fact existed, brought changes in the political climate that altered how journalism was practiced. Ironically, journalistic experimentation flourished during the Second World War, when the exigencies of total war would seem to have precluded them, only to virtually disappear during the peace that followed. The developing conflict with the Soviet Union brought a much more thorough constriction of the acceptable range of both political opinion and journalistic form. After 1946, the spaces available at Time Inc. for literary-minded journalists such as John Hersey, intellectually ambivalent journalists such as Theodore White, and even politically sympathetic journalists such as Whittaker Chambers, were drastically curtailed.

Time's Attractions

Most of the intellectually ambitious young men who went to work at Time Inc. in the late 1930s and early 1940s joined *Time*. They formed a less cohesive group than the earlier gathering at *Fortune*. They came to *Time*, not to *Fortune*, primarily because of the changing political situation. The rise of fascism, the Spanish Civil War, and the Japanese invasion of China meant that international affairs loomed as more immediate and compelling problems than the ongoing economic ills that had dogged America throughout the decade. The increasing appeal of *Time* and the diminishing attraction of *Fortune* were also due, however, to changes in climate at both.

By 1938 *Fortune* no longer attracted the same types of literary writers as it had in its earlier years. The magazine's changing politics scared off intellectuals who resided on the left. Though Luce had failed to make *Fortune*'s new attitude toward big business explicit, the tenor of the magazine's coverage of business, government, and labor had all moved to the right by the end of the 1930s. Russell Davenport's editorials explicitly embraced an increasingly libertarian economics that provided a foundation for persistent criticism of New Deal policies. Treatment of labor grew more critical, a trend accelerated by the wartime need for all sectors of America to make sacrifices for the common war effort. *Fortune*'s detailed reporting on industrial production provided the high point for the magazine during the war years, as it effectively focused attention on the key variable in America's victory. Though the magazine focused on all impediments to war production, its criticism most frequently came down on inefficient government and recalcitrant labor leadership.[7]

More conservative men replaced the liberal intellectuals who departed in the late 1930s. Davenport played an active role before and after the Willkie campaign. The Board of Editors, established during Davenport's tenure to keep the magazine editorially consistent, was comprised of men far to the right of the previous writers. The Board included Raymond Buell, who chaired the *Fortune* Roundtable and advised Luce on foreign affairs, John Jessup, who later became long-time editorial writer for *Life*, Charles J. V. Murphy, and John Chamberlain. The presence of Murphy and Chamberlain underline the magazine's changing politics. Murphy joined *Fortune* in 1936, after having been a reporter for New York newspapers and a freelance journalist. His desire was to be a magazine journalist; writing for *Fortune* was his greatest ambition. He was distressed by what he perceived to be the radicalism of the staff, refused to join the Newspaper Guild, and soon fell in with the fiercest anti-Communists at Time Inc., Whittaker Chambers and Willi Schlamm among them.[8] Despite his conservatism, Murphy found a welcome home at *Fortune* for thirty-four years, most on the Board of Editors. Chamberlain had been an eager liberal during the early New Deal years, writing the best-selling *Farewell to Reform*. By the late 1930s he began abandoning his anti-business liberalism. In its place developed a lionization of the "vigorous and exciting personalities" of the boardroom, whom he later argued in *The Enterprising Americans*, had been the real heroes of the Depression.[9]

In this climate, the room for a writer on the left was narrow. The experience of John Kenneth Galbraith was illustrative. Galbraith wrote for *Fortune* intermittently from 1943 to 1948, arriving after his stint as "price czar" (controlling prices in the Office of Price Administration) ended in the summer of 1943. Seeking a job outside government, *Fortune* seemed a good fit for Galbraith. He found a number of good friends on the magazine. Reporting on the practical workings of business made an indelible mark on the young economist. He later claimed that he developed at *Fortune* "a lasting immunity to the banalities of the neoclassical textbook economics." He also worked out the analysis of the technostructure that appeared in his book *The New Industrial State*. Galbraith credited Henry Luce's editing for making him an effective writer. (It appears Luce agreed: in later years he frequently told people he had taught Galbraith to write and had regretted it ever since.)

But Galbraith found himself constrained by a regime of self-censorship. He continually considered whether a particular section of an article was worth the predictable struggle with the editors. Usually, he lamented, it was not worth the fight. Though Luce would pass material if he could be convinced, the process was exhausting, and his editors were frequently less flexible than he was. Instead of protracted struggle, Galbraith resorted to carefully couching his views in language sly enough to pass the editors, "overlooking the near-certainty that it would slip by all . . . readers as well." Such a narrow outlet for his work did not suit Galbraith, and when new opportunities in government appeared, he took them.[10] For intellectuals with less technical fascination with economics, *Fortune*'s appeal waned.

Life was a far different magazine than *Fortune*, popular where *Fortune* was elite, and brief where *Fortune* was dense. The size of the audience might have an appeal, but in its early years *Life* attracted few writers. Its content was more frivolous than the other magazines, and was editorially tailored to attract the widest possible audience. Luce once noted that the role of *Time* was to make enemies, the role of *Life* to make friends.[11] The war brought a new seriousness to the magazine, and with it a willingness to risk offense. Though the magazine continued to be primarily a visual medium, Luce took advantage of the circulation to publish his editorials in *Life*, not *Time* (including "The American Century"). Writers, too, found an outlet for longer pieces in the magazine, illustrated with pictures. The normal path, however, was for correspondents employed by *Time* to write lengthier pieces for *Life* and maybe *Fortune*. *Time*, therefore, was where ambitious writers started.

In the 1930s, *Time*'s political coverage had been an embarrassment to the writers on *Fortune*. In 1936 MacLeish, Macdonald, and Eric Hodgins, had spearheaded a campaign to convince Luce that *Time* was reflexively anti-labor and generally biased against the left.[12] In 1937 MacLeish engaged *Time*'s Foreign News editor, Laird Goldsborough in a lengthy war-by-memo over their differing conceptions of the Spanish Civil War. Goldsborough, who described the Franco forces as "men of property, men of god and men of the sword," challenged MacLeish to define "fascist" whenever *Fortune* used it to describe the Franco forces. MacLeish replied that he would be happy to oblige if *Time* would define "'red,' 'reddish,' 'pink,' and 'pinko.'" MacLeish and Ralph Ingersoll, then *Time*'s publisher, peppered Luce with anti-Goldsborough memos, but were rebuffed.[13] In 1937, Goldsborough's columns, which historian Robert Herzstein aptly describes as characterizing Europe as "non-threatening, violent, amusing, and, above all, distant," were in line with American opinion.[14] After seeing the crisis in Europe at first hand, however, Luce's thinking changed. In December 1938 Goldsborough was given a "long overdue" one-year sabbatical. He never appeared in print in *Time* again (though many years later he jumped to his death from a Time Inc. office window).[15]

With Goldsborough out of the way, and the leftish Ralph Ingersoll in charge, *Time* changed rapidly. European events were now depicted as having immediate significance for American readers. Taking European politics seriously meant developing a network of correspondents. The assignment appealed to many *Time* men eager to escape the New York offices and see the crisis in Europe firsthand. *Time* soon established news bureaus in major world capitals, and editors in New York now took their material from correspondent cables instead of the *New York Times*. As the number of bureaus climbed, and the number of established writers leaving New York for overseas posts increased, jobs were easier to find for aspiring young writers. John Hersey was one of the many ambitious young men to join *Time* in the wake of Goldsborough's dismissal and Ingersoll's expansion of the staff.

John Hersey: Making War Journalism into Literature

Of all the intellectuals close to Henry Luce, John Hersey might have been the one for whom Luce had the highest expectations. A "mishkid" like himself,

Hersey shared a deep connection to China few other men at Time Inc. could understand. Tall, good looking, intelligent, and earnest, Hersey must have seemed to Luce like a young MacLeish. Hersey came to *Time* intent on making his mark, drawn to *Time*'s proximity to the events shaping the world. He was both ambitious, working hard to climb *Time*'s corporate ladder, and courageous, risking his life to report the war in person. Hersey's journalistic impulses—to see events firsthand and explore how people made sense of terrible events—were underwritten by intellectual aspirations. Intensely fascinated by the moral costs of survival, he experimented at *Time* and *Life* with new ways of conveying the emotional experience of war. He hoped to use the techniques of fiction to minimize the reporter's mediating presence between reader and event. The success of these experiments, developed in his wartime books, brought him popular and critical acclaim. They also forced him to decide between his professional aspirations at *Time*, where he was seen as a likely successor to Luce, and his artistic ambitions.

John Hersey was the son of Chinese missionaries, born in Tientsin, China in 1914. His childhood was spent in China before he moved to the United States in 1925. He enrolled at Hotchkiss on a missionary son's scholarship and from there followed the traditional path to Yale, arriving on campus in 1932. There, sports and social activities loomed as his primary interests. Active in campus politics, a member of the football team, and an editor of the *Yale Daily News*, Hersey was tapped for Skull and Bones. This event led him to reflect on his own growing ambitions. "Is ambition altogether reprehensible?" he asked, in a letter to his parents. "If there was no ambition there would be no 'great' men." Like many young college students, his aspirations remained vague. He had already displayed literary talents, and he assiduously wrote fiction and poetry, but he resisted allowing his ambitions to be "turned into intellectual channels." He feared the results would make him "stuffy and pedantic."[16]

After a year studying English at Cambridge, and another year as Sinclair Lewis's personal secretary, Hersey settled on journalism as the field best suited to his interests. He thought of *Time* as "the liveliest enterprise of its type," and wanted "more than anything, to be connected to it."[17] He received a job on the magazine in 1937.

Starting at the bottom, writing in the least desirable departments, Hersey gradually made an impression and moved first to the book department, then to the political desks. By 1939 his writing was beginning to be noticed and he soon attracted Luce's personal attention.[18] Hersey had always been conscious of Luce's presence at *Time*, never failing to note to his parents when Luce was around ("Harry Luce is editing this week, and the fur is certainly flying").[19] Luce invited especially gifted young writers to lunch, and Hersey got his first invitation in January 1939. During the lunch Luce outlined how Hersey might go about working his way into foreign news (Hersey's goal) and then even higher in the magazine's hierarchy. Concluding his account of the lunch, Hersey noted "All of that, of course, makes it important for me to do a good job on every little 10 line story I write."[20]

Luce and Hersey's relationship developed quickly, especially after Hersey's trip to China for *Time* later in 1939. By the outbreak of war, it was increasingly clear within Time Inc. that Hersey would be able to go as far as he wanted on the magazine.[21] Hersey's own ambitions still focused entirely on Time Inc., a place he described to White as "this strange and wondrous organization."[22]

When the war finally began in December 1941, Hersey was caught in New York. Eager to contribute to the war effort, he undertook to write a book detailing the disastrous fall of the Philippines. Hersey's *Men on Bataan* appeared in June 1942, one month after the fall of Corregidor. Alternating chapters sketching MacArthur's biography with accounts of the men who fought under him, the book, as biographer David Sanders aptly describes it, was "peculiarly the work of a *Time* staffer habituated to the practice of reducing piles of notes and cabled material to truncated columns."[23] It also perfectly exemplified the patriotic mood of the day, as Hersey justified the book in terms of the morale work he intended it to do: "You ought to know about them [the *Men on Bataan*] for they are like you. They have reacted as you will react when your crisis comes, splendidly and worthily, with no more mistakes than necessary."[24] Hersey's book gave a good approximation of the sort of journalism practiced by *Time* and expected by the nation in those days: journalists were not neutral chroniclers of events (an idea that always made Henry Luce mad) but interpreters of events, whose clear duty went beyond keeping readers informed to keeping their morale high. Unsurprisingly, *Men on Bataan* met with a chorus of praise and large sales.[25]

By the time the praise appeared in print, however, Hersey was already in the Solomon Islands, making the transition from desk chair to field journalist. On October 9, 1942, Hersey observed the third battle of Matanikau River, Guadalcanal. He accompanied an American marine unit in a failed attempt to push the Japanese back from the banks of the river. Even though he noted "it flatters the action a little even to call it a battle," he hoped to use it as "an example of how battle feels to men everywhere." He produced a clear and vivid account of the battle, but strained for literary effect and lapsed into hortatory declamation. He littered his narrative with similes (machine gun fire "like a knife tearing into the fabric") and analogies ("a regular crunch-crunch-crunch that reminded me of all the newsreels I had seen of feet parading"). Concluding his account of this brief, inconclusive battle, Hersey made an awkward profession of his "new faith in U.S. chances of winning the war in the visible future."[26]

Though the article garnered warm praise at Time Inc., Hersey could see its weaknesses. He was increasingly conscious that the journalist "is always mediating between the material and the reader." Awareness of the reporter's presence distanced the reader from the events described. Reworking his account of Matanikau, he began to experiment with "the devices of fiction in doing journalism, in the hopes that my mediation would, ideally, disappear."[27] Obscuring the reporter's presence meant stripping his stories of simile, metaphor, and analogy and relying on straight description. When he expanded "The Battle of the River" into the book *Into the Valley*, he ruthlessly purged these figures of speech.[28] He increased his use of dialogue dramatically. Interspersing a biographical study of the commanding officer, he switched scenes deftly to build suspense and tension. These techniques drawn from fiction made the account more immediate and gripping without alerting the reader to his efforts.

Hersey had not entirely effaced himself from the text. He included his own observations of combat, and occasionally reminded the reader of his presence as a reporter. In the *Life* article, he had mentioned a marine, awaiting orders in an exposed position, suddenly whispering "Jesu, what I'd give for a piece of blueberry pie."[29] A quick, hushed debate over the best kind of pie followed, before the men moved on. In his book, he admitted he had prompted the exchange with an explicit question: "what would you say you were fighting for?" He used their discussion of pie as a typical invocation of the way of life they were fighting to defend: "home is where the good things are—the generosity, the good pay, the comforts, the democracy, the pie."[30] Hersey was still a long way from achieving the extreme absence of authorial mediation of *Hiroshima*, but in 1943 he was already experimenting with the techniques he would employ.

Into the Valley was another popular success, but again Hersey took no time to relish the acclaim. Traveling from the Pacific to North Africa, Italy, and finally Russia, he wrote a number of important articles for *Life*, *Time*, and *Fortune*. He cabled battle reports from the landings on Sicily, and covered the fierce fighting on Okinawa. He continued to experiment with the techniques of fiction in his journalism. Occasionally he was able to fictionalize his reporting explicitly, as in a 1944 article for *Fortune*. Trying to assess the patriotism of Russian intellectuals and its effect on their art, Hersey imagined a conversation with a fictitious Russian writer. In a famous *Life* article, "Joe Is Home Now," he created a composite character combining the experiences of dozens of returning soldiers into a narrative of one soldier's difficulty returning to civilian life. In many other articles, he stuck to more traditional journalistic approaches, but still worked on tightening his writing and simplifying his descriptions to heighten their immediacy and power.[31]

Hersey soon pushed his experimentation to its natural conclusion, turning articles into his first novel. In an article for *Life*, he explored the American effort to administer Italian territory taken from the fascists. He wrote a descriptive account of the efforts of an Italian American major to establish order and wean the population from fascism in a liberated Italian town. He decided to rework the material as fiction because he was frustrated by his inability to report in detail on what he saw as General Patton's disastrous personal rule in the Italian campaign. He also thought he might be able to get closer to important truths about what America faced in the aftermath of the war. Returning to New York, working "in a sort of white heat," he wrote *A Bell for Adano* in a one-month vacation from *Time*.[32]

Though the book centers on a simple dichotomy between the virtuous Major Joppolo (the book opens: "Major Victor Joppolo, U.S.A. was a good man") and the power-drunk General Marvin ("a bad man"), the more interesting characters are those whose essential nature is less clear cut and pedantic.[33] Men such as Sgt. Borth, whose surface cynicism rings truer than his surprising sentimentality, or Captain Purvis, who struggles to reconcile his professed sense of propriety with his willingness to pass responsibility, were more complex than the one-dimensional protagonists. In these and other characters, Hersey explored how men behaved in crisis, their actions upsetting their carefully constructed sense of self. Though these characters were suggestive of his own maturing interests and ability, the book's success was driven by its thinly veiled attack on Patton, and its depiction of a good American easily helping the Italians remake themselves as American democrats. The book enjoyed good reviews, wide popularity, and won the Pulitzer Prize.

During the first two years of the war Hersey had gone from an obscure writer for *Time* to a prize-winning novelist and highly successful journalist. In his journalism he developed the techniques he would later employ to such notable effect. He also explored the two themes that characterized his best work, the strains of survival and the moral dimensions of warfare. Survivors always attracted Hersey's attention. He explored how people behaved under great stress, intrigued by what such tension revealed about their convictions and character. Again and again he found evidence that people's sense of their own identity was often at odds with how they behaved when put to the test. He began to grapple with these questions during the war, his treatment growing in power and sophistication as he experimented with new ways of conveying the facts of journalism with subtlety and force. These efforts later culminated in his two postwar masterpieces of survival, his account of the aftermath of the dropping of the first atomic bomb (*Hiroshima*), and his novel about the Jewish ghetto in Warsaw (*The Wall*).[34]

Hersey's success increased his value to Time Inc. Despite carping from Clare Booth Luce, who resented his workers publishing outside his magazines, Luce's respect for Hersey grew. Luce and his managing editor, T. S. Matthews, hoped to keep Hersey working for the magazine, grooming him as an eventual successor to Matthews. In late 1943, after the success of *A Bell for Adano*, Matthews wrote Hersey, assuring him he was "next in line for permanent succession." Matthews told Hersey "it's apparent to anyone with one eye . . . that you can go about as far as you want to in this shop, if you want to." Writing as an editor who wanted "the best damn staff in journalism," Matthews hoped Hersey would "decide that your future lies here, and not in the world of the successful book writer."[35] Matthews's encouraging words likely had an impact on Hersey. He retained an interest in editing *Time*. In 1944 he had a long talk with Luce concerning his future at Time Inc. Luce wanted him to stay in New York as an editor, but Hersey was determined to remain a writer in the field for as long as the war lasted. Instead of a desk job, he pushed to be *Time*'s correspondent in Moscow, taking him to the one theater of the war he had not yet visited and allowing him to see the Soviet Union up close. The trip would also, he hoped, remove him from the growing tensions in New York between Whittaker Chambers and some of *Time*'s writers, including Hersey's protégé, Theodore White.

Theodore White: Luce's Favorite Journalist

One of the best-known journalists of the postwar era, Theodore White was in many ways the perfect Luce journalist. Despite their differences, Luce and White shared a deep commitment to China, a belief that strong, powerful, charismatic men made history, a weakness for confusing what ought to be with what was, and decidedly ambivalent feelings toward intellectuals. They also both believed, as White put it, that they could make events march in the direction they pointed, if they pointed clearly enough. White became Luce's star journalist in China, as they united in an effort to bolster U.S. support for the Chinese in their fight against Japan. As the war dragged on, however, White's opinion about the character of the Nationalist Chinese government darkened, and a growing rift developed between him and Luce. White's reporting often succumbed to wishful thinking, but no amount of hope could blind him to the tremendous problems in China. Trying to convey what he saw, White fought an intense battle with Luce over Time Inc.'s coverage. Ultimately, White was forced to go outside *Time* and *Life* to tell the story. As a result of the changing political climate of the late 1940s, White was no longer welcome at Time Inc. The man who best embodied Lucean journalism could no longer work for Henry Luce.

Ironically, it was unlikely that Theodore White could have gotten a job with *Time* at all if he had applied in the usual manner in New York City. In the late 1930s, Time Inc. employed few if any Jews on its editorial staff. It continued to hire most of its writers from the staff of the student newspapers at Yale and Princeton, a practice that changed only when *Time* needed its own reporters to cover world events.[36] Even then, *Time* remained an editor's magazine, and the editors in New York were overwhelmingly Protestant products of elite universities. White had graduated from Harvard, but also from Hebrew school and the streets of Boston.

Theodore H. White was born and raised in the Jewish ghetto of Dorchester, three miles from the Boston State House. He grew up in deep poverty, in a household divided between his bookish, radical father and his far more practical grandmother. Teddy emerged an odd mixture of both, possessing literary sensibilities yet linking his father's failure to responsibly provide for his family with his disdain for money and his scholarly and literary aspirations. In later years White described his father as having had "a family of four children to support, though he cared little about money, except to buy books."

While other future *Time* writers were publishing family newspapers (such as the *Hersey News*) and later writing poems and stories for school newspapers, White hawked newspapers on Boston's streetcars. Eventually, he earned enough money to enroll at Harvard in 1934. Interested in history, adept at languages, and lacking a clear sense of what he wanted to do, he signed up for courses studying Chinese language and history. There he encountered the man who was to exert greater influence on his career than any other: China specialist John King Fairbank. In later years the doyen of American China studies, Fairbank was then a charismatic young scholar, adept at kindling enthusiasm in his students. Fairbank taught his students that history was happening now, in a China caught in the grips of revolution. Since the overthrow of the Manchu dynasty in 1911, China had been convulsed by changes that had swept away the old Confucian civilization, leaving in its wake a struggle of competing political parties and warlords. During the 1920s the Nationalist or Koumintang party, under Chiang K'ai-shek, overcame the competing warlords and the rival Communists to establish nominal control over the country. When the Japanese aggression of the 1930s culminated in war in 1937, Chiang was again fighting, this time splitting his efforts between resisting the Japanese invaders and prosecuting a renewed civil war against the Communists. The outcome, Fairbank convinced White, would determine the shape of Asia for decades. Fairbank's courses, White remembered, "inflamed my itch to be off, away and out—to China, where the story lay."[37]

On graduation White headed for China on a traveling fellowship.[38] Crossing the Atlantic on the SS *President Roosevelt*, he took time to reflect on where he had come from and where he was headed. Noting that he had been shaped by two competing traditions, his Jewish Erie St. home and the Protestant New England institutions that educated him, White recognized that the ideas he had developed at Harvard were about to collide with reality. Up until now, he wrote, his ideas "have been tested only in conversation; they have not yet been tried against the bitterness of personal ambition; or against the truths of visual observation." He looked forward to the test, but not without trepidation. He worried that "my ideas are squirming, soft things, live and vital and honest—but unformed, unprotected by a hard shell."[39] White's reflections marked his growing sense of intellectual seriousness. He thought of history as a means to test his ideas. He also inaugurated a favorite metaphor for the relationship between ideas and action. For the remainder of his life, things he admired—men, actions taken, difficult decisions—were hard, tough, gutsy. Ideas—and the intellectuals who worked with them—were soft, weak, pliable.

Arriving in China, White landed a job as a propagandist for Chiang K'ai-shek's Nationalist government in Chungking. He had come to China to fight fascism, help China, and see what "history was all about," and this job would allow him to do all three.[40]

White arrived in Chungking, Nationalist China's latest war capital, in April 1939. Chungking was a small city, built on steep cliffs hundreds of feet above the Yangtze River. Chosen because it was defensible and stood guard over the rich Szechuan hinterland, the city had had no wheeled vehicles as late as 1928. Within a month of White's arrival, the Japanese bombed and machine-gunned the city, committing what was then "the largest mass slaughter of defenseless human beings from the air." The cooperative and defiant atmosphere in the city instilled White with a love of the Chinese and a deep loathing for their Japanese attackers. White spent much of his time meeting and cultivating officials of the Chinese government, and grew impressed with their intelligence, dedication, and competence. Most had attended American universities, and White admitted, "it was not only their cause that captured me, but also the fact that they were, apparently, so very American."[41] He also developed an admiration for Chiang.

As impressed as he was by the contacts he made, his job proved frustrating. He chafed at not being able to honestly report all that he witnessed. In the spring of 1939, an opportunity to become a real reporter presented itself. John Hersey arrived in Chungking, collecting material and looking to hire a stringer for *Time*. Hersey offered the job to White and he accepted.[42]

As excited as White was to be working for *Time*, he quickly recognized its problems. Writing to Hersey in 1939, he complained that the articles he saw in *Time* "seemed to be compounded of at least 50 percent imagination, and a good dash of misinformation." He warned Hersey against portraying the Chinese as "white as angels" for fear it would lead to disillusionment when the truth came out. He also complained of the difficulties in getting his material past the strict censors of Chiang's government. Hersey wrote back, counseling him to be tolerant of factual mistakes (since verification was so difficult from the *Time* offices), but to alert them to mistakes in interpretation.[43]

The great advantage of writing for *Time*, White discovered, was the lack of a deadline. Where reporters for newspapers needed to file on a regular basis, he could spend weeks collecting background stories for *Time*, and then send them off in a bunch. This allowed him to travel far more extensively than other correspondents, and within a few months he had taken a leave from his Ministry job and headed to the front to see the war firsthand. After weeks touring the country, White returned to Chungking with enough firsthand material for a long *Time* article (winning him the first byline to appear in the magazine for one of its own correspondents) and a growing conviction that there was a fatal divide between the war as seen from Chungking and as experienced in the villages across China. "I could no longer see Chiang K'ai-shek or his Americanized administration as a real government," White decided, "They had no control of events."[44] Despite this realization, his reporting dwelled on the heroic resistance of the Chinese under Chiang's leadership.

For the remainder of the war, White was Henry Luce's star reporter in China. He excelled in supplying the "anecdotes, personalities, episodes, and names" on which *Time* thrived.[45] He provided vivid accounts of fighting in the months before war broke out in Europe. He rapidly developed a sophisticated understanding of the complexity of the situation—the divide between the government and the peasantry, the pathologies of inflation and corruption spread by the war, the rivalries between different American military leaders over how best to use Chinese armies, the conflict between resisting Japan and continuing a civil war against the Communists—and the difficulties in conveying this to American readers through censorship.

In May 1941 Henry Luce toured Asia, spending ten days in China and meeting White for the first time. They got along famously. White's fellow reporters, knowing him well, placed bets on how long it would take before he was calling Luce by his first name. The winner correctly predicted seven words: "Welcome to China, Mr. Luce. Now Harry . . . "[46] Luce was famed for satisfying his endless curiosity (and easing his social awkwardness) by firing questions at his reporters about everything he saw, expecting quick, factual answers. White fielded the questions, then quickly steered the conversation away from a flunky answering Luce's questions to a long disputatious assessment of China's prospects. And so these two men, one tall, powerful, rich, emotionally distant, and "Presbyterian-right," the other short, poor, gregarious, and "Jewish-left," formed a deep attachment over their mutual love of China and conversation.

At the end of the ten-day tour, Luce told White to pack his bags; he was taking him back to New York as Far Eastern editor of *Time*. White returned to New York in the summer of 1941, seeing *Time* from the inside for the first time. He also had the novel experience of living in New York with money, returning to visit his family in Boston as a successful young reporter, and spending his weekends socializing with the Luces. He enjoyed the life, especially his surprising new social milieu, but was anxious to return to China. When Japan attacked Pearl Harbor in December, White was happy that the entire country had now joined him in the war he had been fighting for the last three years. He headed east as fast as possible.

It took him more than six months to get back to Chungking, being diverted first to Australia and then to India. In India he met General Joseph Stilwell, who was soon transferred to China and played a key role in the drama that was to follow. When White finally made it back to China, he plunged back into his life as a war correspondent. *Time* published more coverage of the war in China and more profiles of Chiang and his ruling elite than any other major outlet in America. White wrote virtually everything the magazine published.

White appreciated the exposure he was getting, but fretted over where his career was headed. He worried that his relatively anonymous work in *Time* would never attract the proper notice. Writing to his mother and sister, he noted "Somehow no one who works for Time & Life seems to acquire a national reputation—you're always one of Mr. Luce's boys." He also had to defend *Time* against his sister's complaints that it was anti-labor, and her worries that his friendliness with Clare Luce meant he was changing his politics. White assured her he was still "New Deal and Roosevelt, all the way down the line," and that *Time* was "yards more liberal" than any other American publication on Asia.

Nevertheless, he was growing increasingly concerned over how *Time* was handling his reports. By 1943 he had come a long way from his early adulation for Chiang K'ai-shek and his government. The war was going poorly, the early camaraderie of Chungking had been destroyed by inflation and corruption, and it was painfully clear that Chiang was unaware of the true state of affairs in his own army. Despite the growing problems, in July of 1943 White received a cable from *Time*, letting him know the magazine was eager to print any good news he could provide. The cable wished that "maybe truth is that . . . pattern is one of good news rather than bad and if so it will now need your special attention." White wrote to his mother, "Well, you can imagine how difficult it is writing in a country where there is almost nothing but bad news, and your outfit wants only good news."[47]

The questions of how the news should be handled and interpreted, what the American people should be told, and the equally vexing issue of where his responsibilities properly resided, troubled White. Following up on an offer from Random House, he tried to write a book covering the Chinese resistance to Japan, but ultimately asked Random House not to publish it. Nothing he had written was untrue, yet the entire book seemed fraudulent to him. He had consciously conceived it and written it as an attempt to draw attention to China and bolster American support for Chiang and his government. The only way to do this, he found, was to self-censor all the truths about the corruption and incompetence that thoroughly infected Chiang's government. "Whether it was ethical journalism or not to suppress facts of interest to the American people," White pondered, "I do not know."[48] Yet, he must have known, for he soon thereafter made the decision not to publish. When he finally did write a book on China, he included the full indictment of Chiang and his government, convinced exposure was the only hope for reform, and reform the only hope for survival. Nevertheless, this tension between the truth and its effect was one White could never quite resolve in his work.

Struggling to find his own voice, pushed by his magazine to depict a courageous China under a heroic leader resisting Japan, yet pulled by events to acknowledge China's grave problems and Chiang's deep limitations, White was under great stress in 1943. In the winter of that year, a terrible famine in the Honan province resolved his dilemma. White described the Honan famine as "the most indelible" mark on his thinking.[49]

Famines have long been a part of Chinese history. In 1943 one struck Honan, an agriculturally rich province that had been crippled by two years of drought. In early 1943 disturbing reports began to reach Chungking about the extent of the suffering in Honan, so in February White left Chungking to see what he could learn. Reaching the famine areas, he witnessed horrors beyond his imagining. People were dying everywhere he looked. Calculating village by village, county by county, White estimated that millions had already perished, with another five million in imminent danger. But numbers that large "become statistics," White lamented, "thus forgettable." What stuck in his memory were the nightmarish scenes he witnessed. The bodies of refugees strewn along the sides of railroad tracks, having fallen from the roof of trains headed to safety. The parents selling their children: four hundred Chinese dollars for a nine-year-old boy (girls went cheaper, purchased by brothelkeepers who toured the famine districts). Worse still were the tales of cannibalism reported everywhere he went.[50]

The Japanese invasion was behind the disaster. The Chinese had cut the dikes on the Yellow River to stop the Japanese, halting their advance but also disrupting the areas ecology and ruining the transportation lines that might have brought relief. Nature then added to the tragedy, with a rainless summer leaving fields without wheat and millet. All that was obvious. But the government's incompetence and corruption, White discovered, greatly exacerbated the problems. Chungking's response was to remit the grain tax, a gesture White rightly labeled as either ignorance or hypocrisy. Taxes had already been collected, meaning the government was excusing taxes on crops not yet planted, for peasants unlikely to be around when the taxes came due. Everywhere he went White found army commanders selling confiscated grain back to starving refugees at exorbitant prices. He saw officials deducting taxes before handing out relief supplies to starving peasants. He witnessed corruption and cruelty beyond what he thought possible. And returning to Chungking, he witnessed the efforts taken to keep the extent of the suffering from Chiang K'ai-shek, and Chiang's willingness to ignore reports of serious suffering.

White, with a little luck, managed to circumvent the normal censorship channels and transmit the entire story to *Time*, which broke the story in March 1943. At the time Madame Chiang K'ai-shek was traveling in the States. Incensed by the story, she appealed to Luce (whom she knew well) to fire him. "He refused," White noted, "for which I honor him."[51] Back in Chungking, White had trouble getting any Chinese officials to hear him. With the help of the widow of Sun Yat-sen, he procured an audience with Chiang. The generalissimo refused to believe him ("They see a foreigner and tell him anything," Chiang remarked), but changed his mind after seeing pictures of dogs eating corpses.[52] After that heads rolled (literally) and relief began to reach Honan. Thankful that Chiang had finally acted, White was nevertheless convinced his government was too corrupt, incompetent, and distant from the people to effectively compete with the Communists.

White's eventual success in reaching Chiang was powerful evidence of the effect his reporting could have. In the wake of the famine and his changing assessments of Chiang's likelihood of holding power, White decided to write a new book about China. Writing to Hersey, he declared, "I feel now that there is no good to come of this government; that some one must once and for all lay the full picture before the American people."[53] He recognized that it would spell the end of his career at *Time* and hurt Luce, but he felt compelled to make the American people face the truth. Until he could write the book, however, he intended to force Time Inc. to print the full story of the crisis in China. In early 1944 White flew to New York to convince Luce to let him write a major piece for *Life*, detailing the situation and providing a critical overview of Chiang and his regime for the first time. White worried he would not be able to win Luce over, but after a good stretch of wrangling, White's article appeared in the May 1st issue of *Life*.

In retrospect, White considered the article a compromise. Writing to fellow journalist A. J. Liebling, he noted it had constituted "the first major reportage on the dishonest [sic] and incompetence of Chiang's government that appeared in any large American periodical" but that he had been forced to lay the blame on Chiang's administrators rather than the generalissimo himself.[54] At the time, however, White felt the flush of his victory. Writing to Luce from China, he noted, "I was told that you would never let anyone publish anything like the things I wanted to say" but he felt "my own professional and personal integrity was a stake." The fact that Luce had deferred to White's determination made it, for White "a god-dam inspiring experience."[55] Luce had conceded the article, but they continued their argument in an exchange of dense memos.[56]

Each wrote a long memo, tracing the history of Chinese reform efforts and their relationship to the West, seeking to understand current Chinese dilemmas as the culmination of deep-running historical currents. The exchange revealed much common ground between the two, especially concerning the current situation in Chungking, but also laid bare the one area of major disagreement. Luce chastised White for not recognizing that reform in China needed to emanate from indigenous sources. It could not be imported whole cloth from the West. The source of Chinese reform, Luce believed, must be Confucianism. White pointed out that Confucian ideology was essentially static. Blaming it for the failure of the Orient to keep pace with the Occident since the seventeenth century, he also held it to be inadequate to deal with the revolutionary upheaval gripping China. Their dispute had practical implications. Luce counseled letting Chiang get his own house in order, according to his own ideas, with full American support (Luce believed this support China's due, partially as exculpation for the failure of Westerners to live up to their Christian ideals in China). White saw this as a guarantee of failure. "If the Koumintang goes consistently more reactionary," he argued, "they will force everyone in society—all the intellectuals, almost all the peasants, plus all the factory workers, into the hands of the Communists." Communist effectiveness had to be counteracted with meaningful reform (land reform and democratic rights) or the Communists would continue to gain.[57]

After his article in *Life*, and this exchange with Luce, White hoped to continue reporting China's problems with the same honesty in *Time*. He believed American pressure on Chiang posed the only possibility for forcing reform on Chiang's regime. Pressure might also force Chiang to use his armies to fight the Japanese, rather than husbanding them for the coming civil war with the Communists. To make this case in *Time* seemed of the utmost importance to White. His prospects were greatly diminished in August 1944, however, when Luce appointed a new editor of foreign news, Whittaker Chambers.

Whittaker Chambers: Searching for a Cause

Whittaker Chambers's background was unlike that of any other intellectual to work for Henry Luce. In fact, it might be fair to say that Chambers, whom Alfred Kazin memorably described as the only American in *The Brothers Karamazov*, was unlike any American. In turns a Christian Scientist, a Coolidge Republican, a "Profanist," a Communist, an Episcopalian, a conservative, and a Quaker, Chambers was driven by a deep need to find a system of ideas in which he could believe. As believer, apostate, revolutionary, spy, defector, witness, and intellectual, he struggled through different roles to match ideas with action. Despite these wildly various beliefs, his life had a curious unity. Characterized by a Manichean sense of struggle, by Dostoyevskian emotional and psychological turbulence, Chambers was an intellectual who spent most of his life seeking to escape that role. Convinced that action trumped ideas, believing with Marx that the intellectuals had merely interpreted the world when it needed to be changed, he joined the Communist Party. Consciously turning his back on intellectual life, he went underground. Eventually breaking with the party over the purges, he took a job at *Time* magazine where he impressed some with his intellectual powers but appalled others with his conspiratorial obsessions. But even as a critic for *Time*, he conceived of his writing as action taken in a war against Communism. He continued to believe that ideas were merely tools to manipulate for the task at hand. In editing *Time*'s Foreign News section, Chambers attempted to expose and discredit Communism, distorting and manipulating the reports of correspondents to support his single-minded interpretation of world events. Yet he also used *Time* to explore the roots of his opposition to Communism, and eventually entertained a broader range of ideas. Chambers's career at Time Inc. posed a number of paradoxes. In some ways the most successful interstitial intellectual at *Time*, he was also the most fiercely anti-intellectual. Desiring to make *Time* a place for "a man who has something to say and the ability to say it," he set out to destroy the spaces other writers had created for themselves. Whittaker Chambers charted the extreme edges of the distinction between intellect and action, and the possibilities and problems for intellectuals working interstitially.

Chambers grew up on Long Island's south shore, in a troubled family divided between an insecure mother who craved social respectability and an aloof and reserved father, an artist, who met the conventional world with a sneer. Unpopular in school and without close friends, Vivian (his given name was Jay Vivian Chambers) lived largely through his imagination and the books he read at home. Victor Hugo's *Les Misérables*, a novel he read over and over again as a youth, became the Bible of his boyhood. Chambers committed to memory Hugo's foreword: "so long as ignorance and misery remain on earth, books like this cannot be useless."

In 1919 Chambers graduated from high school a Republican, a Christian Scientist, and a young man more at home with books than with any of his classmates.[58] Whittaker Chambers (as he now called himself, leaving Vivian behind forever) entered Columbia in the fall of 1920. There he found intellectual companionship for the first time. He discovered other students with bookish interests, who exposed him to a new world of literature and politics. They introduced him to "what was pulsingly alive—subversive, dangerous, intoxicating—in literature and ideas." Reading Tolstoy, Dostoevsky, Ibsen, and the other giants of late nineteenth century European literature, arguing fiercely with young men who included Meyer Shapiro, Herbert Solow, and Lionel Trilling, Whittaker Chambers had finally found a home.[59] For the first time he was among people with similar interests, who could stimulate and exasperate him.[60]

The time he spent with his new friends was more important to him than his more formal education. He found many of his classes worthless and most of his professors the subject of pity. He described seeing a professor "slumped, less from collapse than from organic ineffectualness, against a wall of the room."[61] Fittingly, the professor taught "Contemporary Civilization." One professor, however, stood out from the rest. The poet Mark Van Doren, impressed with Chambers's intellect, encouraged him to be a writer. Chambers later observed, Van Doren "infected me with the idea that the literary life is the best in the world and that to be a poet is the highest calling known to man."[62]

Chambers devoted himself to literary life at Columbia. Doing the minimum work necessary to stay in school, he threw himself into writing for campus literary publications. He helped relaunch a defunct journal, *Morningside*, with a long story, "The Damned Fool," which took up more than half the inaugural issue. Adopting the structure of Conrad's *Heart of Darkness* (men sitting quietly, reviewing and assessing one man's self-sought death in a quixotic pursuit of glory), the story was interpreted as a criticism of the ideals that drove men to fight, much in the vein of postwar literature. Few of those who praised it recognized Chambers's yearning for a cause to believe in, and the romantic attachment he felt for the fool's errand. "The Damned Fool" was less an indictment of belief, than a measure of the extremity of Chambers's need for belief. As Sam Tanenhaus properly observes, for Chambers "language is purely instrumental, as it is for prophets and propagandists."[63] Words had measurable effect, or they were merely self-indulgent. Chambers consistently fought against a conception of intellectual life existing solely on the plane of ideas. He resisted the idea that Don Quixote, tilting at windmills, was the archetype of the intellectual. Instead, Chambers wrote, "not Quixote, but Joan [of Arc] is its effective assertion. Not words, but the play of fire." "An idea was the starting point of an act," Chambers claimed, or it was nothing.[64] This stance earned him a measure of deference and respect among the budding intellectuals at Columbia.[65]

Shedding his rather tenuous religious faith and his more tenaciously held Republican politics, Chambers had as yet nothing to replace them except a new found devotion to literature and a developing picture of himself as a poet. In typical fashion, he viewed his decision to become a poet as a break with everything else. "The idea that I was a poet carried with it the strong implication that nothing else mattered—how I was to live, what obligations I might have to the community or my family."[66] This was a familiar formulation of intellectual life in the early 1920s, not far different from that developed by writers such as MacLeish, Macdonald, and Matthews in the same years. Unlike other writers of this generation, however, Chambers continued to look for a deeper level of commitment and belief than literature demanded.

The more time he spent at Columbia, the more his old belief withered away, as yet replaced by nothing but cynicism and rebelliousness. Elected editor-in-chief of the *Morningside* for his junior year, inspired by the upheavals emerging in modern literature (*The Wasteland* was published and *Ulysses* suppressed in 1922), Chambers hoped to launch his tenure with a major statement. Deciding the magazine must escape lyricism to embrace cynicism, Chambers announced the issue as launching "profanism." Derived from the latin *pro fano*, or outside the temple, the "Profanist dares to look at life unhesitatingly and dares to represent it without veils," Chambers wrote in his lead editorial. "Profanism is the healthiest sign of the determination of Columbia men to wipe away the lactic droolings of the late century and accept something more nearly approaching reality than the ethical, religious and materialist hypocrisy of modern life." Beneath the surface cynicism of his writing, Chambers was fighting a deep despair. As Tanenhaus notes, Chambers was "less a blasphemer than a tormented doubter, hungry for a sustaining faith."[67] He had already concluded that none of his professors, not even Van Doren, could supply that faith.

Leaving school, Chambers continued his search. In 1924, rummaging through used book shops in lower Manhattan, Chambers came across *The Soviets at Work*, a pamphlet printing a speech Lenin had given just months after the Bolshevik coup. Arrested by the brutal force of Lenin's language, the experience marked a major transition for him. "This was not theory or statistics," Chambers later wrote, "this was the thing itself."[68] During an era of confusion and despair, when those he admired could do nothing except chart and interpret the futility of modern life, Lenin had acted with clarity and force. He had taken a system of ideas and made it real. Lenin had ushered in a new world, sweeping aside the rotting and putrid world in which Chambers suffered. On February 17, 1925, Whittaker Chambers became a member of the Communist Party.[69]

Though he joined the party rather quickly after discovering radical politics, his commitment deepened over time. The crumbling circumstances of life at home furthered his radicalization. His family life, always difficult, had taken on a nightmarish intensity since he had left Columbia. His grandmother now lived with the family. Her mental instability made any semblance of a normal home life impossible. On more than one occasion Whittaker had to stay up all night, protecting the family against the knife-wielding old lady. His mother grew more desperate, aware that her family's pretensions to middle-class normality failed to mask serious problems. His father remained aloof and absent. His brother, Richard, had quit college and was descending into depression and alcoholism. Richard talked of suicide, even trying to interest Whittaker in a suicide pact. Eventually, Chambers acted as Richard's keeper. He watched over him, saving him from one suicide attempt, and providing Richard with an outlet for his anger and frustration. Most nights Chambers returned from work to listen to his brother and keep him from harm while he drank himself senseless. One evening, when he did not return from the city at the normal time, Richard stopped waiting. He went home, drank a quart of whiskey, and stuck his head in the gas oven. The suicide, Chambers decided, "was the beginning of my fanaticism." Displacing his brother's anguish onto society, he concluded, "that any society which could result in the death of a boy such as my brother was wrong and I was at war with it."[70] From that time on his sole significant interest was the Communist Party.

Given his interests and abilities, Chambers gravitated to the intellectual work of the party where he could write. In 1931 he published the first of a series of proletarian short stories in the *New Masses*, "Can You Make Out Their Voices?" A dramatization of the real storming of an Arkansas town by five hundred farmers demanding food, Chambers wove into the story a fable of a homespun Bolshevik, Wardell, who quietly and forcefully organized the protest before being jailed. The story was an early entrant in the emerging proletarian literature genre, but carried a power and authenticity rare in such work. His farmers were complicated, real individuals, and their political actions rose realistically from their situation. The revolutionary hero Wardell seemed simultaneously believably real and mythically ideal, a dirt farmer whose homespun thinking naturally evolved into political struggle.[71]

The story created a huge stir, garnering Chambers praise across the literary left. He followed up with three more stories, none as effective as the first but each continuing his powerfully poetic rooting of politics in the material experience of the proletariat. Collectively, they made him, as Joseph Freeman later wrote, "the hottest literary Bolshevik." Chambers became a minor literary star, emerging from his seclusion of the late 1920s, when radical politics were discredited, into the intellectual flirtation with Communism of the early 1930s. By the spring of 1932, Mike Gold offered him the editor's position on the *New Masses*. The magazine was publishing some of the biggest names in American literature, including John Dos Passos, Langston Hughes, Katherine Anne Porter, and Edmund Wilson, and Moscow wanted to ensure the magazine's political message remained intact. Chambers was the perfect choice.[72]

As his friend, and soon-to-be Time Inc. writer Robert Cantwell, noted, Chambers became a "fiercely orthodox Marxist critic to whom everything not on the party line was outside the pale."[73] Not only did he purge heretical writing from the magazine, he used its pages to push his conception of the role of intellectuals in the movement. In his first issue, he wrote an open letter "To All Intellectuals":

> You are either pioneers and builders of civilization or you are nothing. You will either aid in moulding history, or history will mould you, and in the case of the latter, you can rest assured that you will be

indescribably crushed and maimed in the process. And the end will be total destruction. History is not a blind goddess, and does not pardon the blindness of others. In history, defeat is the penalty of blindness or apathy—and sometimes annihilation.[74]

In ferocious language reminiscent of Lenin, Chambers put writers on notice that he intended to judge them by their actions, not their words. After editing only three issues, Chambers got to act on his own advice. He was recruited into the Communist underground.

After his frustrations at the *Daily Worker*, Chambers felt "elation at the knowledge that there was one efficient party organization and that it had selected me to work with it."[75] He spent the next six years as an underground spy, complete with assumed identities, stolen documents, and clandestine meetings. He lived for seven years with no fixed name or address. As careful as he was in clandestine work, he could not keep himself from maintaining contact with his old friends. For intellectuals such as Lionel Trilling, his underground work was the "openest of secrets while it lasted."[76] These were the years when Chambers got to know Alger Hiss, for whom he functioned as courier, copying documents Hiss stole and forwarding them to his superiors in New York. These were the events with which his name would forever be linked, but while he carried them out he was one small link in a thriving Soviet espionage ring. By all accounts Chambers was happy in the conspiratorial milieu of the underground man. But as the years passed, his confidence in Communism wavered. Disturbed by the purges and the growing rumors that men and women he had known and trusted were being murdered by Stalin's secret police, the NKVD, in 1939 Chambers decided to leave the party.

Breaking with the party, Chambers spent some months in hiding, fearing retribution. He knew that the best way to protect himself was to make himself as visible as possible. Though he could make money doing translation work, he wanted a writing position on a magazine, where his name would be in print. He appealed to his old friend Cantwell, who explained Chambers's Communist background (though not his spying) to T. S. Matthews and inquired about a job. Matthews read one of Chambers's old *New Masses* stories, found it full of "murky flashes of rather sinister brilliance," and agreed to try him on book reviews.[77] Chambers always claimed he clinched a permanent position by beginning a review of a war book "One bomby day in June. . . ."[78]

Chambers quickly established his reputation at *Time* as a brilliant writer and an odd, suspicious man who disdained the open-door camaraderie of *Time*. Working in his office behind a closed door, refusing all offers for dinner or drinks, dressed in a dour gray suit, Chambers carried with him an "air of suppressed melodrama," in Matthews's apt description.[79] He soon had co-workers wondering whether he was "on call as a pallbearer" or an "enthusiast of a sternly cheerless sect."[80] His writing attracted more favorable notice. Clever turns of phrase won a certain attention, but his deft cover story on James Joyce's *Finnegans Wake* made his name at *Time*.[81] Co-workers began to be curious about the enigmatic Chambers. A colleague in books finally prevailed on Chambers to have lunch with him, whereupon Chambers embarked on a trip to a distant restaurant that involved convoluted elevator and subway rides, a walk through the entirety of four floors at Macy's and more taxis before they finally ducked into a crowded restaurant. Days later Chambers confessed to the young reviewer that he had been convinced he was being led into a NKVD ambush. Stories such as these only fueled the growing amusement at Chambers's paranoia.[82]

Not everyone at *Time* found Chambers odd and amusing. Within weeks the Communists on staff (there were quite a few, including a number of researchers and a couple of writers) began a whispering campaign against him. In his memoir *Witness*, Chambers complained of being smeared as "a crank on the subject of Communism," and as suffering "from a delusion that the Communists were after his life."[83] No doubt much of the whispering was malicious, but both charges were true. Chambers was in fear for his life, and for the majority at Time Inc., who knew little or nothing of his background, the charges necessarily appeared ridiculous. More important, Chambers purposely set out to use his reviews to attack the Soviet Union at every opportunity. He wrote in *Witness*, "I never missed an opportunity to jab at Communism in my stories."[84]

The third sentence of Chambers's review of John Ford's film *The Grapes of Wrath*, for example, was a typical jibe: "Pinkos who did not bat an eye when the Soviet government exterminated 3,000,000 peasants by famine, will go for a good cry over the hardship of the Okies." This implacable hostility toward all things Soviet, and the broad brush with which he smeared liberals and leftists as pinkos, earned him the enmity of many at Time Inc.

Chambers constant sniping, however, did not bother Henry Luce, who soon recognized his other gifts. Indeed, that review of *The Grapes of Wrath* first attracted Luce's attention. Chambers picked up on Ford's reworking of Steinbeck's novel in a more populist, less political vein. Neatly taking the movie away from Tom Joad, Chambers placed Ma Joad at the movie's core, celebrating her as "the incarnation of the dignity of human being, and the courage to assert it against odds."[85] Luce called the review the best to ever appear in *Time* (though he often failed to read the back-of-the-book) and invited Chambers to his first editorial lunch.[86] Luce and Chambers soon became close, united by their antipathy for Communism and the New Deal, and by Chambers's deepening religious faith (in September 1940 he was baptized an Episcopalian).

Chambers also shared Luce's conviction that journalism could and should serve as an essential educational tool. Unlike Luce, however, his attitude toward journalism was essentially Leninist. Convinced of the latent power of Luce's magazines, Chambers self-consciously set out to use that power to educate *Time*'s readers about the true nature of Communism. Sharing Luce's educating impulse, but unencumbered by Luce's sense of fairness or his fear of getting too far ahead of his readers, he out-missionaried the missionary. As Malcolm Cowley summarized what Chambers had told him of his intentions, "he learned the technique of the [Communist] movement, and now he is going to apply that technique to destroy it."[87] Chambers viewed his journalism as propaganda deployed in a campaign.

In addition to his jibes at Communism, Chambers resumed his war on the intellectuals whenever possible. Writing in January 1941, he attacked the "literary liberals" who had flirted with Communism during the 1930s. Noting Lenin's observation that, when the train of history takes a sharp turn, those without a firm grip are thrown off, Chambers described the shifts in Stalin's policy as leaving intellectuals "spattered all over the right of way." He labeled American intellectuals as "fundamentally skeptical, maladjusted, defeatist." Suggesting their criticism arose primarily from personal problems, he claimed that their enthusiasm for Communism was solely due to its treatment of the writer as a "privileged employee of the state." He attacked writers for their flirtations with Communism and their failure to see it for what it was. Many of the writers Chambers criticized, including Lewis Mumford and Archibald MacLeish, had never entertained any enthusiasm for Communism. Others had been fellow travelers, never approaching his own level of involvement with the party. Underneath the political smear, Chambers's real complaint, as always, was the dilettantism of the intellectual. "Substituting a good deal of intellectual inbreeding for organic contact with U.S. life," intellectuals felt free to lightly pick up and discard political identities as if they were trying on clothes. As the fashions changed, out went one wardrobe of political platitudes, in came another. Again, Chambers had himself made these same changes, and more besides. But he felt the need to distinguish between his own anguished political conversions and those of others. He had toiled and suffered for his beliefs, and he sought to make others suffer as well.[88]

Chambers enjoyed the freedom of writing the back-of-the-book, but he hoped to write Foreign News, where he could directly influence how the magazine handled the Soviet Union. He was given opportunities, but his insistence on giving every article an anti-Soviet slant made a prolonged stint in Foreign News impossible. Despite the wartime alliance with Stalin, Chambers insisted on treating the Soviets not as "friendly allies, but cynical and treacherous enemies."[89] Even Matthews, who liked Chambers and appreciated his talent, was disturbed by his lack of perspective. He kept Chambers away from stories bearing on the Soviet Union and stripped his copy of the continuing attacks.

Chambers's skill, and his deepening relationship with Luce, guaranteed him other opportunities at Time Inc. Recognizing that his attacks were purely negative, he began to explore how he might clarify the alternative to Communism. By 1942 he was convinced the world faced a simple choice, "Belief in God or Belief in Man." Asserting the primacy of man, to Chambers, led inevitably down a slippery slope to Communism. Christian religious faith was the only force capable of combating Communism, and Chambers set about making this clear wherever he could.[90] Conversations on this topic with Luce led to an assignment organizing and editing an ambitious series of essays for *Fortune*, meant to clarify the philosophical basis of our civilization and the war effort. For almost three years, long essays by philosophers filled the pages of the business magazine.

The early essays, by William Ernest Hocking, William Pepperell Montague, Jacques Maritain, and William A. Sperry, were all variations on Chambers's theme. Rather than a political struggle between liberalism and totalitarianism, the war was reworked as a spiritual struggle against scientific thinking that had displaced the human soul with reason. Nazism and Communism were direct results of the replacement of spirit and faith by reason and science. Chambers's summary of Hocking's inaugural piece set the tone. Claiming the "enfeeblement" of man's religious sense as a result of experimental science, he wrote that Hocking "indicates the lonely dilemma of modern man, who, faced with the concentrated power of the totally secularized state, has lost the only power that can be brought against it—the power of the human soul." What was needed to meet the totalitarian threat, Jacques Maritain claimed, was nothing less than a "new Christendom."[91]

After the initial four-barreled attack on secularism, subsequent essays were more varied. Chambers published a rebuttal to the first four by biologist Julian Huxley (Aldous Huxley's brother) that was so dismissive of religion and so uncritically accepting of science as to skirt caricature. Huxley noted with relief that science "makes it possible, and necessary, to dispense with the idea of God," and claimed "the only cure for the insufficiency of science is more science."[92] His piece was a singular departure. Reinhold Niebuhr, sounding his familiar warnings about America's too optimistic view of human nature and possibility, was more typical.[93]

In addition to the *Fortune* series, Chambers earned a promotion to back-of-the-book editor in 1942. He now controlled thirteen departments. Though he still preferred Foreign News, the critical departments provided him with ample opportunity to editorialize as he edited. He relished the job. His desire to control every word of copy led him to rewrite much of the review section each week. He worked long hours even by *Time*'s standards, usually staying in his office for the thirty-six hours before publication, napping on his office couch, bolting meals at his desk, smoking packs of cigarettes, and downing endless cups of coffee. The pace, along with the weekly commute to his Maryland farm, wore him down, but he refused to rest. When staffers expressed concern to Luce about his health, Chambers perceived it as an "attempted putsch," and worked even harder to retain control. In October 1942, his loyal assistant, Calvin Fixx, had a heart attack under the strain, and in November Chambers himself collapsed. After an eight-month break, mostly spent in bed, Chambers returned and by 1944 had regained his previous position. He was a senior editor (one of seven) and shared the back of the magazine with Wilder Hobson. Despite this position, and his delicate health, Chambers still hoped to edit Foreign News. In August 1944, he got his chance.[94]

The Chambers War: Prelude to the Cold War

Allied forces advanced everywhere in 1944. In early summer Soviet armies entered Poland and Romania. The Americans and British regained a position on the European continent in June and began pushing through France toward Germany. As victory became near certain, questions about the nature of the postwar world moved front and center. Crucial to answering these questions were the prospects for maintaining the wartime alliance with the Soviet Union. Time Inc. had joined in the general wartime climate of cooperation with the Soviets, recognizing their heroic fighting during 1943 and producing an entire issue of *Life* devoted to celebrating the country. The issue led off with an editorial by Joseph E. Davies, the ambassador Roosevelt had sent to Russia on his *Mission to Moscow*. *Life*'s editors even presented a specially bound issue to Stalin, inadvertently translating the inscription as "To Comrade Stalin from the workers of *Life* magazine."[95] Luce had approved the positive coverage, but as the war drew to a close and Soviet armies moved west, his suspicions of Stalin intensified. He was also disturbed by the rosy assessments of Soviet intentions he was reading in *Time*, especially from Moscow correspondent Richard Lauterbach. When the Foreign News editor John Osborne left for Europe in late July, Luce and Matthews named Chambers to replace him. Matthews had misgivings, but Luce hoped Chambers would throw cold water on overly optimistic assessments of the Soviets.

Finally landing the "one section of *Time* I felt really equipped to edit," Chambers wrote Luce that "in dealing with international affairs, I feel like a man in a dark but familiar room: I may bump against the furniture, but I'm usually sure where the door and windows are . . . . I want to sit here and figure out history."[96] But Chambers already believed he had history figured out. His first lead story, ironically titled "Mission to Moscow," plainly made the case that the Soviets were busy installing a puppet regime in Poland. Every issue that followed pounded home Chambers's litany of beliefs. The Soviet Union was a "monstrous dictatorship," "a calculating enemy," bent on "conquest of the free world." The first steps were already taking place in Central Europe and China. The Chinese Communists, far from being "agrarian liberals," were the number one section of the Communist International after the Russians.[97] Making this case, however, required Chambers to ignore the reports *Time*'s own correspondents sent in, which often did not support his interpretation. It forced him to mislead his own researchers, some of whom he suspected of trying to undermine his position, by handing out fake assignments. It led him to evade *Time*'s fact-checking systems, as he threw away carefully gathered research to rely on material accumulated from newsletters put out by organizations such as the Polish Exile Catholic Society. All told, Chambers turned Foreign News into a weekly argument against the Soviet Union, rather than a weekly summary of world news.[98]

Chambers's methods and his columns soon brought down a chorus of criticism. Researchers complained of his methods. *Life*'s cable editor Filmore Calhoun wrote to Luce, arguing, "I read the incoming cables and I am amazed to see how they are either misinterpreted, left unprinted or weaseled around to one man's way of thinking."[99] Allen Grover also complained to Luce, and carefully collected the cables for comparison.[100] Angry reactions soon followed from correspondents overseas, beginning with Walter Graebner in London, Charles Wertenbaker in Paris, and even the conservative C. D. Jackson attached to Eisenhower's headquarters.

Theodore White in Chungking and John Hersey in Moscow were initially insulated from much of this feud. Published issues of *Time* were difficult to come by, often not arriving until they were months old. Contact with the New York office by cable made office gossip difficult. In addition, both Hersey and White were preoccupied. Hersey had arrived in Moscow in August as an editor-at-large for *Life* in addition to handling the Moscow bureau for *Time*. He had only been there a few months, working hard to pick up the Russian language, when he received a cable from Luce calling him back to New York to become a senior editor of *Time*, honoring "the spirit of our long conversation on the subject of your career."[101] Hersey did not want to leave his post in Moscow, but he was now forced to decide his future at *Time*. Did he want to set aside his writing career to become a top editor at *Time*, with the ultimate goal of becoming managing editor and steering *Time* in the journalistic directions he choose? As such, he could guarantee that other journalists found the autonomy and independence within Time Inc. to foster the creative work he had pioneered. Or did he want to remain a writer, hoping to continue balancing his own intellectual interests with the assignments available at *Time* and *Life*, and trusting that the political climate at *Time* would not become untenable?

After an exchange of cables with Luce, Hersey decided to refuse the promotion. Moving from his conviction that he wanted to continue writing for the duration of the war, he decided he would always prefer writing to editing. His interests, he told Luce, were "primarily humanistic rather than political," and his temperament too emotional to make him a good editor. In addition, he reiterated to Luce that he was a democrat ("both with and without a capital D"), and he honestly noted that he expected his political differences with Luce to make things difficult for him and for *Time*. Hersey told Luce he meant by his refusal "to disavow the long-range ambition of becoming *Time*'s Managing Editor," but he hoped to continue as a writer for Time Inc. for the foreseeable future.[102] Though his preference for writing over editing drove his decision, he clearly knew the political winds were blowing against him in New York.

A long cable from Dick Lauterbach, Hersey's predecessor in Moscow who was currently in New York, caught Hersey up on the developments since

Chambers had taken over Foreign News. Lauterbach told Hersey "the beefing about Whit has grown. But his influence has also grown." Lauterbach believed Luce was backing Chambers because he was convinced ("Luce is acting on a 'Hunch'") that, though Chambers was wrong about Soviet actions now, in two years "everyone will bow low and say, you were right."[103]

When Hersey received back issues of *Time*, in early December, they confirmed the fears raised by Lauterbach. Writing to his wife, Hersey complained, "They [Chambers and staff] seem to want to go out of their way to take cracks at Russia. Some of the things they said were partly true, some few of them I myself have felt here, but to work so hard to hit at Russia in . . . damn near every story in the magazine, seems to me to do plenty of disservice at this particular moment."[104] Though the magazine's political slant convinced him his decision had been the proper one, it made him despair nonetheless. Hersey hoped for some sort of postwar cooperation between the great powers, and he saw Chambers's editing as a deliberate attempt to sabotage such hopes. In protest, he let New York know he was refusing to supply material for Foreign News. Though he continued to argue the magazine's political line with the editors, (eventually telling Luce that there was as much truthful reporting in *Pravda* as in *Time*) Hersey concentrated on writing for the less politicized *Life* from that point on.[105]

White's battles with Chambers and the editors in New York were both more direct and more tense. Despite Allied victories along all other fronts, the war in China turned against the Nationalists in 1944. Chiang had convinced Roosevelt to support the plans of American General Claire Chennault, who believed air bases could be set up to launch long-range attacks against the Japanese. When the bombing runs began to hurt the Japanese, they quickly struck at the air bases. Just as Chennault's rival Stilwell had predicted, the Chinese army proved incapable of defending the bases, and the Japanese army quickly overran the Chinese and moved deep into China's hinterland. Faced with the possible collapse of major Chinese resistance, Roosevelt needed to strengthen Chiang's armies immediately. This necessitated, Stilwell believed, reviving the United Front between the Chinese Communists and Chiang, freeing up Chiang's best troops (then occupied watching the Communists) and providing military assistance to the Communists (the only effective opposition to the Japanese). Finally backing Stilwell, in July Roosevelt cabled Chiang demanding Stilwell be given "command of all Chinese and American forces" in the theater. He reiterated the demand in September, threatening the immediate end of all U.S. aid if command was not transferred to Stilwell. Chiang resisted, bolstered by

Roosevelt's own emissary, Patrick Hurley, who, though sent to placate Chiang yet support Stilwell, had instead acted to back Chiang and undermine Stilwell. By October Roosevelt faced a stark choice: support Stilwell and risk a rupture with Chiang, or back Chiang and acknowledge Chinese contribution to the war against Japan would be minimal. With the war against Japan progressing well on all other fronts, Roosevelt could do without substantial Chinese gains. On 18 October 1944, Roosevelt recalled Stilwell.[106]

Following events from the crumbling Chinese front, White had been convinced Stilwell was right. American policy must be directed toward reforming the Chinese government and its army, White believed, or Chiang would eventually lose the struggle with the Communists. White witnessed the Stilwell debacle firsthand, invited by Stilwell to hear his side of the story. The general allowed White and Brooks Atkinson of the *New York Times* to read through the cables he had received from Washington, hoping to win a battle by press he had already lost by policy. Stilwell made clear that Chiang had never been interested in fighting the Japanese, that he had hampered all efforts that might either risk his own troops or strengthen the Communists, and that the war contribution of the Nationalists had been riddled with corruption and incompetence. White wrote up the entire story and gave it to Atkinson to take home on Stilwell's plane, thus beating the Chinese censorship. Bitter about Stilwell's defeat, White at least felt he had done his part to get the story out.[107]

Back in New York, Chambers had to decide how to cover the Stilwell recall. He assigned the story to Fred Gruin, a trusted ally, but Chambers was responsible for the article. He had supplemental material gathered from Washington, but White's report was the smoking gun. Yet Chambers viewed White (and Hersey) with deep suspicion. He "made no secret of the fact that everything he received from Hersey or White went right into his wastebasket," a colleague remembered, "Half the time he wouldn't even bother to read their dispatches."[108] In *Witness*, Chambers went out of his way to list Hersey and White as among the "top names" of those who opposed him and "continued to feed out news written from the viewpoint that the Soviet Union is a benevolent democracy of unaggressive intent, or that the Chinese Communists are 'agrarian liberals.'"[109]

As Thomas Griffith argues, this was a "preposterous misrepresentation of the reporting" of Hersey and White.[110] Virtually everything White wrote on China explicitly warned against believing the Chinese Communists were merely agrarian liberals.[111] He also had few illusions about the Soviets.[112] He felt the Soviets, and by extension the Chinese Communists, could be negotiated with along realist lines. For Chambers, on the other hand, negotiations with Communists were futile. Their differences made it very unlikely Chambers would use White's smuggled copy.

Stilwell's recall earned the cover of the 13 November issue of *Time*. Praising Stilwell for his long service to China, the article quickly turned into a defense of Chiang and an attack on critics of his government as leftist apologists for Communism. Written by Gruin and Chambers, the article noted the persistent criticism of Chiang now cropping up in the American press only to attribute it to "leftists," "liberals" and Communist sympathizers. Dispensing with criticism from such suspect sources, *Time* could pin down the important issues. "Stripped to the bare facts," *Time* reported, the situation was this: "Chungking, a dictatorship ruling high-handedly in order to safeguard the last vestiges of democratic principles in China, was engaged in an undeclared civil war with Yenan, a dictatorship whose purpose was the spread of totalitarian Communism in China." The war against Japan, supposedly the heart of the issue, was a sideshow. Stilwell had complained that Chiang had no interest in resisting the Japanese. *Time*, on the other hand, claimed the Chinese Communists had won a great victory because "the Nationalist Government has refrained from throwing its full strength against them."[113] In conclusion, the article stated the stark alternatives for the United States: back Chiang fully and unquestioningly, or face a Communist China in the arms of the Russians.

White was outraged when he finally read Chambers's cover story. Though he knew Chambers had written the article, he blamed Luce. With White's own firsthand reporting available, Luce "let the story be edited into a lie, an entirely dishonorable story." [114] He fired off a forty-five-page protest to Luce, documenting the article's errors, and threatening to resign. Luce tried to conciliate him, and eventually White relented, staying on in the belief "perhaps they will be forced to tell the truth in the future if I do threaten them with resignation. They are so important that if I can get them to tell the truth it is worth almost any personal indignity."[115] White had more stories he wanted to report, and he needed Luce to get them in print. Immediately after Stilwell had been recalled, White seized a rare opportunity to travel to Yenan and evaluate Chinese Communism up close.

White returned impressed by what he had seen. Never deluded into believing the Chinese Communists were mere agrarian reformers, or taking their professions of democracy at face value, White nevertheless witnessed a Communist movement characterized by the openness, dedication, efficiency, and commitment totally absent in Nationalist China. He wrote up his experiences, and *Life* published his article "*Life* Looks at China" in December. Published when hopes for cooperation between the Communists and Nationalists were high, *Life*'s editors noted, "dire adversity might at least temporarily solve the deep-rooted ideological differences."

White portrayed the Communists as a dedicated and disciplined military movement, but one whose ideology had been tempered by pragmatism. The Communists successfully built support on their record of resistance to Japan and their ability to provide peasants with land. White made it clear that the Communist commitment to openness and "democracy" were policies of political expediency. Nevertheless, friendship between the United States and the Communists was possible for the same pragmatic reasons class warfare had been downplayed in Communist controlled territory.[116]

Despite this apparent victory, White could not get anything past Chambers and into *Time*. In 1945 he wrote a lengthy memo of criticism to Tom Matthews, noting that ever since the Stilwell cover, *Time*'s reporting had been "indistinguishable from the official propaganda of the Koumintang party." *Time* published Chiang's promises of reform as if they were accomplished facts, never criticized him personally, and made no mention of the "concentration camps, secret police, tortures, [and] ruthless censorship" by which he maintained his regime. Chambers's totally inadequate characterization of all this as "high-handedness" in the Stilwell cover marked "our last recorded independent criticism." White then set down how he thought *Time*'s coverage should proceed. Beginning with "a strict adherence to the facts," *Time* should treat the Nationalist government as it did other governments. Coverage should include constant measuring of government promises with reality, vigilant exposure of corruption, and persistent championing of civil liberties and criticism of their curtailment. *Time* should endeavor not to take sides in a civil war with Communism, but document the struggle fairly from both camps. Despite his attempt to win the right to report the war as he saw it, White's memo had no discernible effect.

By early 1945 the fights with *Time*'s editors were taking their toll on White. Though *Time* had given him a large raise, praised his combat copy to no end, and courted him to keep him on board, the fundamental disagreement remained. As he wrote at the time, "their political treatment of my copy is something worse than vicious." Writing to his mother and sister, he confessed, "I feel like a prostitute; it hurts the first time you lose your virtue; and after that it gets easier and easier; the only thing that grows in you is your shame and contempt of self." He hung a sign over his desk in the press hostel in Chungking, reading, "Any resemblance between what is written here and what appears in *Time* magazine is purely coincidental."[117] In his darkest moments, he distanced himself from his profession, claiming "I never decided nor wanted to be a writer. For me, always, the most important thing was seeing history made, and writing is just the penny that I pay the world for the opportunity to see what is going on."[118] Though, like Hersey, White was increasingly discouraged, he was not yet ready to give up on Time Inc.

The fallout from the Stilwell cover further deepened the divide between Chambers and the correspondents. Writers besieged Luce with memos criticizing Chambers, forcing him to undertake a general review of Foreign News. Luce concluded that events "seemed to have confirmed Editor Chambers about as fully as a news-editor is ever confirmed" and that Chambers "did a brilliant job" of charting Communist policy. Though conceding that Chambers too often conflated "the general revolutionary, leftist, or simply chaotic trends" with specific Communist activity, Luce's memo amounted to a stout defense of Chambers, his methods, and his political line. Luce did act to appease his disgruntled writers, however, creating an International News section to handle worldwide diplomatic developments. *Time* would contain two separate sections covering world news, an odd experience for readers, but an expedient compromise for Luce.

Though Chambers was angry at the "emasculation" of Foreign News, he continued to seek more effective methods to spread his message. He wrote *Time*'s cover story on Stalin in the run-up to Yalta, interpreting the Soviet ruler's policies as measured steps to advance the political revolution that now had the Soviets poised "on the threshold of global dominion."[119] In the wake of Yalta, in March 1945, Chambers submitted to Matthews a far more ambitious article. His draft was unlike anything *Time* had run before. Seeing the lack of news coming from the conference as an opportunity, Chambers penned a "political fairy tale," speculating on Yalta's meaning. He imagined a dialogue between Clio, muse of history, and the ghosts of Tsar Nicholas II and his family. Clio, observing the big power conference from the roof of the Tsar's old palace, was shocked to find that Nicholas had become a Stalinist. Nicholas had come to admire Stalin, who had brought unprecedented expansion to the Russian empire. The dead tsar lauded Stalin's use of international social revolution, "the mighty, new device of power politics which he has developed for blowing up other countries from within." By these methods, the tsar's family exulted, Europe and Asia were in the process of succumbing to Stalin. They believed England and America would soon follow. Here Clio demurred, for "America and Britain . . . will not become Communist states. More is at stake than economic and political systems. Two faiths are at issue." Despite the mysterious ability of the Americans to hold out, Clio foresaw "more wars, more revolutions, greater proscriptions, bloodshed and human misery" if the leaders below were unable to come to terms.[120]

Reaction to the piece was immediate and furious. Chambers's opponents on the staff tried to keep Matthews from running it, and Matthews himself debated the issue for a week. He recognized it as politically inflammatory and out of step with American opinion. He also appreciated the essay's power and Chambers's creativity. This was the type of journalism Matthews believed in: clear, powerful, and provocative. It was also clearly opinion.[121] Chambers had found a way to publish an editorial in *Time* without having to insinuate it between the lines of news coverage. Matthews ran it, after forcing one revision. Chambers "agreed to lop off the end" he recalled, "which described the Soviet Union and the United States as two jet planes whose political destiny could be fulfilled only when one destroyed the other."[122]

Luce's backing of Chambers, followed in short succession by the cover story on Stalin and "Ghosts on the Roof," made the winner of "the Chambers war" clear. Chambers, however, was not able to enjoy his victory for long. In the fall of 1945 his overwork again caught up with him, and he suffered increasing chest pains and blackouts. Luce and Matthews insisted Chambers take a six-month leave of absence. When he returned to *Time* in 1946, Foreign News had passed into other hands.

For years historians, sifting through the memos and articles of "the Chambers War," have sided with the correspondents. W. A. Swanberg views the Chambers affair as a prominent example of what he argues was a pervasive pattern of Luce allowing his personal prejudices to justify systematic manipulation of the news to fit his agenda.[123] Though later historians have rightly judged Swanberg's account overly hostile, they agree with his assessment of the Foreign News skirmish. Historians have generally criticized Luce for, in the words of Robert Herzstein, putting "aside his obligations as a reporter," when they clashed with his faith.[124] The encouragement of Chambers was the prime example of Luce's journalistic failings.

The collapse of the Soviet Union, however, has inspired a revision of Cold War history. Verification and documentation of the extent of Soviet espionage in America and the complicity of the Communist Party of the

United States has pushed historians to claim, "the historical context of postwar anti-communism in the United States must be rewritten."[125] Ardent anticommunism, emerging as a litmus test of political respectability, excused the means by which it was pursued.[126] At its nadir, such revisionism has attempted the rehabilitation of Senator McCarthy.[127] But more respectable scholars have accepted the same assumptions.

Sam Tanenhaus, in his otherwise excellent biography of Whittaker Chambers, resuscitates Luce's view that events validated Chambers's conduct. Arguing Chambers's "guesses caught the drift of history far better than the reports he was getting," Tanenhaus claims Chambers interpreted political developments through the lens of Leninism. "That lens collected its light from a narrow range of the spectrum," he argues, "but the beam it threw on events was stunning in its clarity." Tanenhaus limits his criticism to observing that Chambers was "not above crimping the evidence to suit his thesis."[128] His tepid criticism inadequately describes Chambers's willful manipulation and suppression of material.

Criticism aside, Tanenhaus defends Chambers as understanding "as well as any other American . . . that the postwar world would be formed in the crucible of 'power politics.'"[129] To be sure, Chambers was right to be skeptical of Soviet professions of good will, and his criticism helped move Americans away from the more unrealistic assessments of Soviet intentions. But his opponents at *Time* came closer to understanding power politics than he did. White's advocacy of tough negotiations with the Soviets, not trusting them to comply but impelling them when possible, defined realistic power politics. His conclusions that the Communists better understood and exploited peasant grievances and that Chiang must agree to reform or perish, were more in line with traditional notions of power politics than Chambers's apocalyptic vision of airliners destroying each other. Chambers saw the world as a Manichaen struggle between Communism and the West, not as a carefully calibrated competition between rival powers. What is more, Chambers was convinced Communism would be the triumphant ideology. The twentieth century would not be Henry Luce's American century, Chambers believed, it would be Karl Marx's Communist century.[130] When Chambers left the Communists, he believed he was "leaving the winning side for the losing side." Writing in *Witness* in 1952, he continued, "Almost nothing that I have observed, or that has happened to me since, has made me think that I was wrong about that forecast."[131] If Chambers was right, he was right for the wrong reasons. Tanenhaus's attempt to link Chambers with the realism of

George Kennan ignores the apocalyptic element pervasive in Chambers yet absent in Kennan.

Worse than his selective characterization of Chambers's views, Tanenhaus's justification cannot escape the argument that the ends justify the means. Even accepting Luce's view of journalism—that objectivity is not only impossible to achieve, but irresponsible as a goal—Chambers blatant suppression of facts he knew to be true, and his substitution of stories he knew were likely to be false, violated the ideals Luce professed. That Luce championed and supported Chambers's behavior merely demonstrated that journalistic ethics eroded easily in the face of political conviction. Despite his professed intention to seek the truth, Chambers edited as a political act, often at the expense of veracity. He did not seek to understand the world. He sought to convert it.

Fallout: Three Paths Away from Time Inc.

The trajectories of the three principal protagonists of the "Chambers War" diverged after 1944. Each remained at Time Inc. for a while, not willing to easily relinquish their hopes of speaking to Luce's audience in their own voice. All, however, left by 1948.

Returning to Time Inc. after his leave, Chambers was assigned to a new "Special Projects" department. Inaugurated in 1946, it met Matthews's desire for stories requiring "a particular seriousness and deliberation of treatment not always possible in the hurly-burly of reporting the week's news of the world."[132] Matthews assigned his two best writers, James Agee and Whittaker Chambers, to the new department. The two unlikely companions became good friends, united by religious temperament, cultural interests, and a preference for writing through the night in the quiet Time Inc. offices. Both were intent on pursuing their own idiosyncratic interests, yet both were committed to working through their ideas in Luce's mass magazines. Maybe it was the removal from the Foreign News political pressure cooker, perhaps the influence of the skeptical yet sincere, apolitical yet committed Agee, or possibly the inescapable awareness of his own mortality, but Chambers's writing underwent a dramatic change in tone..

Describing the mysterious origins of the spirituals sung by Marian Anderson, Chambers wrote:

One simple fact is clear—they were created in direct answer to the Psalmist's question: *How shall we sing the Lord's song in a strange land?*

> For the land in which the slaves found themselves was strange beyond the fact that it was foreign. It was a nocturnal land of vast, shadowy pine woods, vast fields of cotton whose endless rows converged sometimes on a solitary cabin, vast swamps reptilian and furtive—a land alive with all the elements of lonely beauty, except compassion. In this deep night of land and man, the singers saw visions; grief, like a tuning fork, gave the tone, and the Sorrow Songs were uttered.[133]

This passage, from *Time*'s Christmas cover story on Anderson, suggested the power Chambers's writing could achieve once the Soviet bugaboo was expelled from under the bed. Religious faith remained his central concern, but here Chambers presented its musical expression and emotional resonance rather than its political necessity. The story provoked such an outpouring of praise that *Time* took the unusual step of identifying Chambers as the author.[134]

Other important stories followed, all stemming from Chambers's particular interests. He summarized Arnold Toynbee's *A Study of History* in March 1947, helping to start the Toynbee craze that made his long, dense book a bestseller. Chambers wrote on Kafka, finding his life "terrible, not because its vicissitudes were overwhelming, but because, as in most life, they were endurable." He wrote the cover story for *Time*'s twenty-fifth anniversary issue on theologian Reinhold Niebuhr, the "troubler of [our] peace." In all these essays he effectively introduced difficult writers to middle-class Americans, yet simultaneously made the ideas of these authors his own. He also wrote ambitious essays of his own. For New Year's 1948, Chambers published a conversation overheard with the Devil in a New York nightclub (the Hotel Ninevah and Tyre). The fanciful interview, a homage to his literary hero Dostoevsky, let Chambers take some easy jabs at Communism (the Devil was pushing his 500-year plan). Underneath the humor, however, ran a serious indictment of the secularism of modern society.[135]

In 1947 Chambers also began a history of Western Civilization for *Life*. For the lavishly illustrated series, Chambers wrote long articles on the Middle Ages, Edwardian England, and the age of exploration among other topics, all carrying his own pessimistic stamp. The series broke down over his treatment of the Reformation. The article provoked, Chambers told Luce, "a head-on clash of historical viewpoint—between the economic interpretation of history and the humane interpretation of history." The *Life* editors, with the support of series historical advisor Jacques Barzun, "tore out whatever gave life to the piece," Chambers complained. This experience provoked Chambers to question whether he had any place at Time Inc. He asked Luce whether "a man who is struggling to express thought and feeling that is against the average editorial grain and which Time formulas and pressures were perhaps never intended to contain" should part company. Despite the heated rhetoric, Chambers had no intention of ceasing to write for Luce. Telling Luce he was the "intellectual enemy" of the liberals at *Life* (as he viewed them), he insisted "I am not subtracting myself from the struggle." Before the imbroglio over the *Life* piece was settled, Chambers was called to Washington to testify before the House Un-American Activities Committee. The Hiss case ended his career as a writer for Time Inc.[136]

When not writing in New York, Chambers led a quiet life on his Maryland farm. He once described his farming as an attempt to live in the interstices of modern life.[137] He meant to live according to his beliefs, even if he endured an environment hostile to their realization. No biographer is likely fully to come to terms with the complicated and contradictory character of Whittaker Chambers. Clearly, however, he meant his life to be a rebuke to the comfortable obliviousness he believed tragically crippled so many lives. The same determination marked his writing.

In his last years at *Time* Chambers began to evolve a more modest self-conception. The testimony against Alger Hiss, interrupted this process. Chambers's massive memoir, *Witness*, was marred by the conspiratorial convictions arising from his inability to see Communism clearly. In his last years, however, in writings he expected few to see, he revealed that his continuing search for truth had taken more modest, less certain paths. He could now write, "I may not claim for the larger meanings of what I say: this is truth. I say only: this is my vision of truth, to be checked and rechecked . . . against the data of experience." No longer so confident that beliefs required absolute commitment to be effective, he began to develop a truly conservative distrust of those too confident in their own understanding of truth. In a passage he wrote just before his death in 1961, Chambers summed up his views: "Thus at the end, or with the end in sight, truth alone becomes the compelling need and the quest for truth the only worthwhile occupation, while those engaged in it achieve that good humor of the spirit which most of those achieve who are engaged in any engrossing labor."[138] The quest for truth, not instruction in truth, became his final preoccupation. In the end, Chambers seemed to have accepted that he was an intellectual after all.

John Hersey continued to write for *Life* after he turned down the senior editor position. His enthusiasm for *Life*, however, quickly waned. Whereas

Life's confidence in its writers (Hersey claimed he wrote articles for *Life* that no single editor had read from start to finish) had once been a serious attraction, he now felt a constant pressure to justify and defend his political judgments. In 1946 he was looking for alternatives, and managed to make separate arrangements with *Life* and the *New Yorker* to send him to Asia. Given the long-standing hostility between the two magazines, the deal was almost guaranteed to cause problems.

The arrangement called for Hersey to supply the same number of stories for each magazine. Despite previously calling his work for *Life* "more satisfying to me than anything I had previously done at Time Inc.," Hersey clearly came to prefer writing for the *New Yorker*.[139] He now found writing for Luce politically constraining. The *New Yorker*, in contrast, encouraged him to experiment stylistically much as he had during the war. The rigorous editing of Harold Ross and Wallace Shawn forced Hersey to examine and justify his prose as never before. Luce noticed the difference. He accosted Hersey's wife at a party, angrily asking her why John's best pieces were appearing in the *New Yorker* instead of *Life*.[140]

For *Life*, Hersey wrote a couple of light, human interest stories, and an analysis of a Chinese peasant village that struggled to come to terms with the peasants' timeless distrust of all government authority. For the *New Yorker*, on the other hand, he produced some of his best journalism, including a brilliant indictment of American sailors' racist condescension to their Chinese allies.[141] He also wrote a parallel study of a Communist village, analyzing why the Communists had succeeded where the Nationalists failed.[142] The *New Yorker* article's crisp description and acute analysis far outstripped the *Life* article's gauzy prose and evasive interpretation.

Hersey's summer of 1946 may have been the most productive summer a single reporter ever had. In addition to the three slight but lengthy stories in *Life*, he wrote seven major articles for the *New Yorker*, all of remarkable quality. And then there was *Hiroshima*. When Henry Luce saw the entire 31 August 1946 issue of the *New Yorker* dedicated to Hersey's account of the atomic blast, he was livid.[143] In a fit of pique, he canceled a lengthy Hersey spread scheduled to run in the next issue of *Life*.[144] Years passed before Hersey's work could again appear in the magazine.

Hiroshima was Hersey's masterpiece. Its flat, uninflected tone should not obscure his craft in producing the powerful effects it contained. The structure of the account, following the experiences of six survivors of the first atomic bomb, was adapted from Thorton Wilder's *Bridge over San Luis Rey*. The literary techniques he employed—including extensively reproduced dialogue, regular switches between subjects to both increase tension and recreate the confusion and chaos of the blast, the slow opening up of time as the account progressed—all had been developed in his earlier wartime reporting. Though Ross and Shawn influenced the final copy (Hersey estimated working on the piece with them for twenty, ten-hour days), the techniques employed were Hersey's own.[145]

The success of *Hiroshima* allowed Hersey to choose what writing to pursue next. He chose fiction. Despite his great success as a reporter, Hersey believed fiction was superior to nonfiction. He was fond of quoting Santayana on the novel, "the argument is dramatized, the views become human persuasions, and the presentation is all the truer for not professing to be true."[146] In a 1949 *Atlantic* article, Hersey wrote a manifesto for the type of fiction he thought should be written, and that he intended to write himself. It was also a requiem for the pursuit of truth he had undertaken at *Time*. "It is an ironical fact," Hersey announced, "that the great industries of mass communications . . . have somehow failed to communicate clearly one thing: human truth." Imaginative literature, Hersey had concluded, "comes closer than any other to being able to give an *impression* of the truth." Hersey had no intention of abandoning the questions that had interested him as a journalist, or the events currently altering the world. He advocated what he called the "novel of contemporary history," treating through fiction the most important events then occurring. Hersey had just completed his second novel, a documentary history of the Warsaw ghetto, and he envisioned fiction that mattered to the reader, making him or her better capable of dealing with the most intractable problems of the world. For such fiction to be successful, it needed to maintain rigorous standards, above all avoiding the pitfalls of journalism. Hersey strove to use the virtues of journalism—"directness, clarity, fleetness of the metrical foot"—while avoiding its sins—false certainty, glibness, cliché—for the rest of his writing life.[147]

Just as his journalism borrowed fictional techniques, his fiction leaned heavily on journalistic practice. This borrowing led him to be considered as a forerunner of the "new journalism" of the 1960s. Hersey nevertheless remained convinced a sharp distinction had to be maintained between fiction and journalism. The remainder of his career was spent patrolling the border between the two.[148]

Despite his commitment to literature, Hersey continued to write journalism occasionally. He published myriad profiles over the years, and undertook an in-depth account of the race riots in 1967 Detroit. His novels continued to rely heavily on the techniques of nonfiction, as he continually played with different approaches to the realist novel. *The Wall* appeared as an imaginary archive of papers collected by a resident of the Warsaw ghetto. *The Child Buyer* purported to be congressional hearings before "the Standing Committee on Education, Welfare, and Public Morality." Finally, Hersey's monument to missionaries in China, *The Call*, was presented as a historical recovery of David Treadup's life. From Hersey's early journalism to his mature novels, he strove to make sense of contemporary events, to get as close to truth as possible, and to convey what he discovered as effectively as possible. That pursuit, he decided in the late 1940s, was not consistently possible within the institutions of mass culture.

Despite his frustrations, Theodore White was too committed and stubborn to give up easily. He continued to struggle with Luce, kept reporting the events he knew *Time* would carry, and kept alive plans to publish his interpretation in a book as soon as he returned to New York. As he summed up his situation with Luce: "I used him for the next two years and he used me, warily, suspiciously."[149] After finishing out the war in China, he returned to the States to write the book he had long planned. Taking a six-month leave from Time Inc., he wrote *Thunder Out of China* (1946) with Annalee Jacoby.[150] Though he knew the book's relentless criticism of Chiang's government would likely prevent his return to China and anger his boss, he still intended to return to *Time*. Writing years later, he described himself as a "born organization man," who believed "he could have it both ways—that he could say what he wanted to say, and yet enjoy the comfort and benefits of the parent organization that disagreed." Though it had been difficult and only sporadically successful, this was what he had been doing since 1943. After finishing the book, he returned to Luce to receive his next foreign posting.

Luce demurred. The posting White requested was part of the problem. White wanted Moscow, to see and decide for himself about the Soviet government.[151] Luce, misunderstanding the motivation for White's criticisms of China, distrusted his politics. Luce was also angered by his inability to control his best writers. First Hersey's best writing began to appear in the *New Yorker*, and now White was publishing a book depicting events in China in precisely the manner Luce had worked so hard to keep from his readers. In White's words, Luce felt "all too many of his bright young men had used *Time* as a personal mount, had galloped to fame on the magazine's back."[152] In this vein, Luce posed a question to White: did White want "to work for Time Inc." or did he want "a career as a foreign correspondent"? Luce wanted to know if White would put the organization's good ahead of his own, even asking him if he would consent to working the rewrite desk in New York for a year. White refused to acknowledge that he "belonged to *Time* magazine." When Luce could not get the answer he wanted, he wrote White a brief note, telling him there was no longer a place for him at Time Inc.[153]

Soon after the break with Time Inc., White found out his book had been chosen as the main selection of the Book of the Month Club. He now had the financial wherewithal to sustain himself without his lucrative *Time* salary. Heavily courted by other magazines, he refused a highly paid post with the *Saturday Evening Post* to write for the *New Republic*. Under Henry Wallace's leadership, White hoped to pursue "a new journalism, a liberal journalism, [that] could paint the nation's postwar portrait free of prejudice." The experience disappointed him. Finding that the magazine functioned as Wallace's campaign journal, he was surprised to discover "there was less freedom to deviate from the line of the *New Republic* than from the line of *Time* magazine."[154]

By the time he quit in 1947, the political climate had changed so dramatically that he could no longer find a position writing for a mainstream magazine. *Time*, which had praised *Thunder Out of China* as "obviously sincere" and generally fair on publication, now viewed the book and White as apologists for the Communists. By 1952, during the depths of the McCarthy era, the book was purged from the U.S. army library in Germany and burned. White was summoned before hostile congressional committees, and his brother was denied security clearance as a researcher at MIT because of his association with the well-known subversive Theodore White.[155] Columnists in *Time* were referring to him as "pinko Teddy White," and Luce even told the *St. Louis Post-Dispatch* that "he had to fire Teddy White because he was a communist."[156] All this on no better evidence than White's harsh criticism of Chiang. Political opinion on China was now reduced to simple dichotomy: analysts needed to choose between Chiang and Mao. By having criticized Chiang, White was viewed as having championed Mao.

White left for Europe, where he was reduced to freelance work. Comparing it with Time Inc., he declared "there's much less freedom in writing as a free-lance than as a wage-slave" because "your master is the market and you've got to write the kind of crap the market wants." Possibly forgetting his bitter struggles with Luce, he missed having a "boss who can protect you."[157] Eventually White stitched his freelance coverage of postwar Europe into another best-seller whose mainstream political analysis, combined with the waning of McCarthyism, ushered him back into the center of American political analysis.[158]

White remained the consummate insider journalist for the remainder of his career. In 1961 he published a groundbreaking account of the 1960 presidential campaign, a book credited as ushering in "a new era in the history of the media and American politics."[159] He joined the staff of *Collier's* magazine, a job he considered "the equivalent of one of the great chairs of History at Harvard, Princeton, Columbia, or Yale." He was happy to return to an institutional home, but the magazine was struggling and folded not long after he joined. Frustrated by "the exasperation of most reporters—the exasperation of being pinned to the facts, when the facts cannot tell the story," he wrote two best-selling novels.

Theodore White's journalism suffered from the same problems that bedeviled Henry Luce and Time Inc. Just as *Time* had long celebrated individuals as newsmakers, White was susceptible to the personality of charismatic men such as General Stilwell in the 1940s and John F. Kennedy in the 1960s. This veneration often blinded both to the limits of personal leadership and to the degree to which leaders were subject to historical forces they could not control. Like Luce, he set expectations for leaders that guaranteed eventual failure and disappointment. Committed to such leaders, both had difficulty presenting them accurately. Chiang K'ai-shek was the preeminent example for both. White's coverage of the Japanese surrender demonstrated the problem on a smaller, more vivid scale. Covering MacArthur's speech, he decided "out of respect" to quote the "Lincolnian phrases, not the McKinley purple."[160] White's reporting replaced the actual MacArthur, a man whose best characteristics were inseparable from his most insufferable, with the man White thought MacArthur should be.

As Joyce Hoffmann observes, both White's novels featured "men with the power and authority to make life-altering decisions on behalf of people for whom they have been given responsibility." White's 1960 novel *The View from the Fortieth Floor* drew on his experiences at the dying *Collier's* and his memories of Time Inc. In the novel, Ridge Warren, hired to save a dying magazine, spurned the heartless corporate calculus of advisors to protect the people who built the crusading magazine. Warren, who shared characteristics with Luce, was interested in the intellectuals on his staff, and a bit in awe of their learning, but never doubted they were too weak to face the tough but necessary decisions he mastered. Warren was a hero who thought with his guts, in Dwight Macdonald's apt phrase, making the tough decisions, White wrote, "for whatever reason his guts tell him."[161]

At the foundation of all White's work was this profound ambivalence toward intellectuals. In this too, he resembled Luce and his magazines. Though impressed by the intellectuals he encountered, and careful to demonstrate his own mastery of "intellectual volleying," he also exhibited a marked hostility toward intellectuals in general. Advising his younger brother on what career path to choose, White insisted "DON'T BE AN INTELLECTUAL. This is the age for men who can do something."[162] Discussing his novels, White complained they brought him into contact with a world that "reeked of culture, was choked with pretension."[163]

White was attracted to leaders who displayed intellectual interests and a respect for learning, but who clearly subordinated ideas to power. In the 1960s White wrote a series for *Life* on intellectuals who had been effective in seeing their ideas translated into tangible public policy. Believing them to be the new men of power, he labeled them "action-intellectuals" to distinguish them from the "out-intellectuals" who were marginal and powerless. White quoted Richard Goodwin: "the ultimate commitment to ideas is to act on them."[164] Despite the emphasis on specific men and the power they wielded, White worried that it was "egg-heady and intellectual as Hell" and might, therefore, alienate readers.[165]

The subordination of intellectuals to the realities of political power was a distinguishing characteristic of the Cold War consensus. White's distinction between action-intellectuals and out-intellectuals nicely, if inadvertently, described the acceptable options for postwar intellectuals. By the mid-1960s, when he wrote his analysis of intellectuals, White had worked his way back into the Time Inc. fold. It was emblematic of the narrowing of acceptable opinion in the 1940s, however, that even Theodore White could not then work for Henry Luce.

CHAPTER SEVEN

Interstitial Intellectuals and the Liberal Consensus

> One has to live consciously and self-consciously, in the involvement and in the alienation.
>
> —Daniel Bell

The years immediately following World War II were hard on the aspirations of radical and liberal intellectuals alike. The initial moments of postwar hope were quickly dashed on the rocks of the strengthening Cold War consensus. Republicans controlled Congress after the 1946 elections, and seemed poised the retake the White House. Labor faced hostile amendments to the Wagner Act and a bitter internal fight over Communists in the ranks. Attention increasingly focused on the international containment of Communism. Even Harry Truman's reelection did little to stem the tide, as domestic reforms stalled and international tensions increased.

In 1950, in the flashpoint city of Berlin, the Congress for Cultural Freedom was formed, enlisting intellectuals directly in the fight against Stalinism. Dwight Macdonald's political iconoclasm (and the power of personal conviction that led him consistently, if misguidedly, to oppose WWII) gave way to the necessity to enlist in the fight, as he, too "choose the west" in 1952.[1] The *Partisan Review* symposium of the same year, significantly titled "Our Country and Our Culture," demonstrated the strength of the growing consensus. There, *Time* theater critic Louis Kronenberger insisted that "Our first question in America must be 'Are you against Communism?'" while in the very next sentence he congratulated the participants on how "we oppose regimentation of thought on political grounds."[2] Kronenberger's naiveté notwithstanding, with HUAC investigations ongoing and Senator McCarthy looming on the horizon, American political thought grew increasingly circumscribed.

Paralleling the constriction of political culture, it looked increasingly as if the opportunities Time Inc. offered intellectuals were disappearing. The departures of John Hersey and Theodore White, both Luce favorite sons, meant the defeat of the liberals at *Time*. Whittaker Chambers's reduction of every conflict to a struggle against monolithic Communist expansion became *Time*'s bedrock foreign policy assumption. *Time*'s coverage of the 1948 election, while fairer than previous campaigns due to the overwhelming conviction that Dewey would win easily, remained biased against Truman. Partisan slanting of election news in favor of the Republican candidate returned with a vengeance in 1952.[3] *Life*'s reliance on *Time*'s political reporters and its subordination of writing to pictures made it equally inhospitable to liberal or radical intellectuals. Luce's decision to pull the plug on *Magazine X* foreclosed any possibility of a new vehicle, less beholden to his own political ideology. Even *Fortune*, usually the most receptive to writers and unorthodox thinkers, seemed less likely to encourage the independence needed for intellectual work. In 1948 the business magazine announced it would now be written explicitly on behalf of free enterprise, repudiating its agnosticism of the previous two decades.

A number of so-called "Luce novels" appeared in the postwar years, reinforcing the conviction that Time Inc. had become inhospitable to critical intellectuals. Written by former *Time* writers about a thinly disguised Time Inc., each agonized over the self-loathing writers felt as their integrity was compromised and their political power evaporated. These novelists agreed that intellectual integrity was now impossible at Time Inc. and that meaningful work could only occur outside mass culture corporations. The disaffected heroes of their novels invariably broke with the magazine in the final pages, moving on to rediscover earlier political convictions or to write novels exposing the enervation and defeat felt by mass culture workers. Writers that remained were nothing more than, in Kenneth Fearing's scathing description, "gelded birds in gilded cages." Arising directly from the frustrations of being an intellectual at Time Inc., these novelists analyzed the dilemmas writing for Luce posed.[4]

These novels also shared an anxiety common to postwar intellectuals disturbed by the impact of totalitarianism and mass culture on the political agency and humanity of the individual. These fears were omnipresent, from

Max Horkheimer and Theodor Adorno's linking totalitarianism to mass culture to Dwight Macdonald's parallel concerns about diminished human responsibility in bureaucratic society and the devastating cultural effects of "Masscult and Midcult." Concern for the fate of the individual in modern society was, among intellectuals, the prevailing anxiety of an anxious age.[5]

Yet neither the theorists of mass culture and nor the novelists of individual resistance should have the last word on intellectual life in mass culture America. Even as these writers fretted, intellectuals were again at work on *Fortune* magazine. Despite its explicit new fealty to free enterprise, *Fortune* again proved a more hospitable environment for intellectuals than *Time*. For one thing, the magazine did not focus on international affairs, making it peripheral to Luce's war on communism. To the extent that the Cold War atmosphere effected *Fortune* at all, it actually made it more critical of American business. The defense of capitalism against communism in the form of the aggressive free enterprise campaigns of the late 1940s and early 1950s required a socially responsible capitalism to counteract any possible argument that communism provided a materially superior standard of living to common workers.

Ironically then, *Fortune*'s declaration of support for the free enterprise system, which earlier intellectuals had fought to prevent because it threatened *Fortune*'s independence, launched another of the magazine's provocative and critical phases. *Fortune* between 1948 and 1956 entertained a variety of stances toward business. The more-or-less official line was Russell Davenport's vision of a business-led alternative to the New Deal. In the "Greatest Opportunity on Earth" articles and the "U.S.A.: The Permanent Revolution" special issue and book, Davenport called for business to take the initiative in seizing reform from the New Deal. A liberal business leadership, accepting its obligation to provide social security to its workforce, could achieve the needed reforms that the New Deal addressed without endangering the sources of American freedom. In effect, this was Luce's dream of an enlightened business class combined with Davenport's emphasis on the liberating power of capitalism. Davenport provided a blueprint for the 1950s corporate liberal consensus and the heart of the progressive variants of the free enterprise campaign.

Within *Fortune*'s own pages, however, dissenters abounded. The October 1948 issue, which announced that *Fortune* would henceforth be written on behalf of free enterprise, also introduced Daniel Bell's new Labor department. Each month Bell would chart the dilemmas facing labor, constantly attending to the gaps between labor's incendiary rhetoric and its pragmatic actions, between labor as an institution and as a social movement. Bell's columns were widely regarded by insiders as the best labor reporting in America. In *Fortune*, Bell's attention to ongoing conflict and hostility between labor and management threw water on Davenport's more optimistic expectations of cooperation.

A more direct assault on the Lucean defense of free enterprise came from William H. Whyte in highly publicized *Fortune* columns, collected in the books *Is Anybody Listening?* and *The Organization Man*. Exploring and exploding myths about American business, Whyte examined corporate life to find disturbingly authoritarian and conformist pressures where Davenport and Luce saw freedom and democracy. Though operating from similar assumptions (probably crucial to his acceptance in *Fortune*), Whyte offered a compelling counternarrative to the 1950s consensus. If Bell hoped for a revitalized labor movement to challenge management prerogatives, Whyte called for the salaried employee to resist the corporate organization.

Finally, Walker Evans pictorial portfolios used the past to pose a stinging rebuke to the present. Familiar with the magazine's long-standing embrace of the Margaret Bourke-White aesthetic that glamorized and celebrated business in all its modernist power, Evans's work repudiated such triumphalism. Evans mined the discarded relics of the industrial world, the old furniture, abandoned railroad depots, rusting signs, and discarded crates, to create a counternarrative of economic development. Renouncing nostalgia as "that blurred vision which destroys the actuality of the past" and "a cliché for an infirm mind," Evans focused on the "extraordinarily unbeautiful" artifacts of American industrial life. Combining the dilapidated remnants of industrial expansion, the "beautiful mess" of the old American city, and the faces of working-class Americans, Evans formulated a strenuous critique of American liberal business pieties.[6] Produced after his celebrated Depression-era heyday, using color film derided by contemporaries, and appearing in jarring fashion in a liberal business magazine, Evans's *Fortune* photographs have yet to receive the attention they deserve. Like Joseph Cornell's collages and boxes, Evans's pictures captured what Jackson Lears describes as "emblems of the sorcery of the marketplace before it was stabilized by managerial reality."[7]

Taken together, the work of Whyte, Bell, and Evans revealed a perceptive strain of criticism emerging from within the mass culture edifice. Their writings and photographs demonstrated the critical possibilities still available at Time Inc. More important, their work was enriched by their close engagement with mass culture. They offered a criticism of the 1950s ideology of liberal consensus from the inside, revealing possibilities within postwar corporate liberalism often discounted or invisible.

All three struggled with the role of intellectuals in a society corrosive of their values. Each formulated a different response to his experience at *Fortune*, responses that cannot easily be contained by prevailing understandings of the 1950s as an era of comfortable complacency. William Whyte advocated resistance to the organization, but insisted such resistance come from inside corporate institutions, not from a place of privileged independence. Daniel Bell sought to articulate a double identity of simultaneous detachment from and involvement with contemporary society. Walker Evans offered a complicated rejection of the contemporary world involving pictures that simultaneously documented decline and aestheticized decay. Each took advantage of his position at *Fortune*, both as a platform for his work and as a goad to his thinking. Yet each remained ambivalent about their jobs, viewing themselves as in, but not of, the magazine, just as each conceived the proper role of the intellectual as in, but not of, contemporary society. Working as interstitial intellectuals, they discovered possibilities for intellectual integrity within the organization that escaped the *Time* novelists and the critics of mass culture. Their experience presents a challenge to the homogenized worldview implied in the oft-used term liberal consensus.[8]

William H. Whyte, Jr.: The Businessman Critic

William H. Whyte, Jr., should have been the *Fortune* journalist Henry Luce had always wanted. Luce hired poets for his business magazine because poets could write and young businessmen could not. Unfortunately for Luce, poets rarely knew much about business, resisted his attempts to educate them, and frequently drew conclusions disturbingly different from those Luce expected. When Whyte graduated from Princeton in 1939 he went to work as a salesman for Vick's Vapo-Rub. The war interrupted his business career, but he arrived at *Fortune* after the war with more business than writing experience. Ironically, Whyte developed into a penetrating critic of America's business culture and the values it encouraged, suggesting that maybe it was not just poets whom Luce found untrustworthy. Whyte's criticism, his indictment of the "organization man," was first developed and published in *Fortune*.

Though he rarely made reference to the work of other intellectuals (with the exception of George Orwell's *1984*, a strong influence), Whyte's concerns mirrored the era's anxiety about the erosion of individual agency.

He traced the threat directly to the imperatives of bureaucratic organizations. Organizational America had presided over a disturbing shift in values. The Protestant ethic, with its outmoded emphasis on individualism, hard work, and initiative, had been eroded. Replacing it was a "social ethic" that "rationalized the organizational demands of fealty." Like Dwight Macdonald, the intellectuals of the Frankfurt School, and others, Whyte was concerned with the effects of the increasing bureaucratization of modern life. Seeing this new social ethic as a dire threat to both democratic decision making and the individual's essential humanity, Whyte advocated individual resistance. Speaking about the organization man, Whyte concluded, "he must *fight* The Organization." In this he joined a growing chorus of critics deploring the conformity of the consensus 1950s. Significantly, however, Whyte advocated that this resistance be launched from within the organization.[9]

William Hollingsworth Whyte III was born in West Chester, Pennsylvania, in 1917. He grew up exploring the small, walkable city twenty-five miles from Philadelphia and the neighboring Brandywine valley. Summers were spent at his grandmother's big house on Cape Cod. Whyte's father was a railroad executive, well ensconced in the upper reaches of the professional middle class. Little is known of Whyte's attitude toward his parents. His one memoir, published posthumously, neglects to mention them, concentrating instead on his summers on the cape and the activities of a roguish uncle.[10]

In eighth grade Whyte began attending the newly opened St. Andrew's boarding school, an Episcopal Church academy in Middleton, Delaware. The school based itself on the English and New England boarding school traditions, training students in the same muscular Christianity dispensed at schools like Hotchkiss. The living quarters were primitive and schoolwork included scrubbing floors and helping in the kitchen. "But we learned things," Whyte remembered, "especially how to write, thanks largely to a brilliant English teacher."[11] Whyte took writing seriously, and served as editor of the school newspaper by the time he graduated. School life was not all serious work, however, and by twelfth grade (sixth form), he spent more time thinking about debutante balls in the grand hotels of Philadelphia than about writing.

After St. Andrews, Whyte attended Princeton. Little is known of his college career. For reasons that remain unclear, he rarely spoke of his Princeton years. In a memoir of his days as a Marine on Guadalcanal, he spent pages recalling his youth in West Chester, his prep school days, and his years peddling Vicks to rural Kentucky storeowners, but devoted only one sentence to an acknowledgment that he attended Princeton. In another paragraph describing his road to *Fortune*, he mentioned St. Andrews but left Princeton out entirely.[12] While there, he majored in English and continued to write. He edited the *Nassau Lit* and wrote a prize-winning play. Despite his modest successes, Whyte seems not to have considered a literary career. Speaking of himself and his friends, he wrote, "we worried about our careers. We talked about individualism a lot, but we didn't practice it much. My friends were joining big corporations, early examples of *The Organization Man* at work." There is reason to treat this description with skepticism. Whyte later began the research that culminated in *The Organization Man* when he discovered college graduates of 1949 to be far less individualistic and far more committed to corporate employment than his own college class. Nevertheless, after graduation Whyte joined the management-training program of the Vick Chemical Company.

In *The Organization Man*, Whyte used his experience in the Vick School of Applied Merchandising as an illustration of the Protestant work ethic, in contrast with the social ethic inculcated by a new breed of management training programs.[13] This comparison, while useful for his book, was too facile, as Vick's training better resembled a social Darwinian struggle for survival than a program designed to develop the Protestant virtues.

Whyte's training involved one month of instruction in the history of Vick's Vapo-Rub, introduction to the full line of Vick's products, and immersion in the nefarious practices of "chiseling" competitors (there were no other kinds of competitors). As for management philosophy, "there was no talk about the social responsibilities of business," Whyte wrote, only a quick lesson in how to survive in a world of ruthless competition in the form of a hypothetical question requiring you to ruin a longtime supplier in order to get a better price. The Vick's school practiced what it preached. Of the twenty-eight members of Whyte's class, only six or seven would be offered jobs at the end of the program. The rest "graduated" to unemployment.

After a one-month "education," the students were dispatched to the field to sell Vick's products to rural general stores. Whyte grew depressed working long days driving the terrible roads of the hill country of eastern Kentucky. (In a letter to his father he described a day spent driving forty miles over hills and through stream beds, resulting in an evening breakdown: "the mechanic found that the carburetor had shaken loose from the feed lines, the ignition wires had been disconnected, the choke had become stuck, the fan belt loosened, the generator jogged out of place. I was amazed the whole car hadn't fallen apart.")[14] The country was desperately poor, and Whyte felt too sorry for the storeowners to push for sales.

Eventually Vicks dispatched a senior salesman to rescue Whyte. After a day observing Whyte's technique, the salesman told him, "you will never sell anybody anything unless you learn one simple thing. The man on the other side of the counter is the *enemy*." This was the beginning of Whyte's education as a salesman, when "innocence was lost." He soon began convincing struggling storeowners to order a year's worth of Vick's products and taking pleasure in screwing ugly metal flange signs into druggist's oak cabinets before he could be stopped ("if the druggist had been particularly mean, we could break the thread").[15]

Whyte survived the course and worked for Vicks for another year. He described the training as "a cram course in reality," and remembered it fondly. Part of this affection might have been retrospective, an appreciation for the toughness Vicks developed in him.[16] This strength served him well when he volunteered for the Marines in 1941, believing the country would (and should) soon be at war. If there was going to be a fight, Whyte decided, he wanted to be in an elite unit. Whyte served as a second lieutenant, in the Third Battalion, First Marine Regiment, First Marine Division. He landed on Gualalcanal on the first day of the American military's first counteroffensive of the war. He remained on Guadalcanal for four months, a time he remembered as the most exciting of his life. After this period of brutal fighting, captured in his battle memoir, *A Time of War*, he returned home to "civilization—to clean sheets, new uniforms, big steaks, beer, and women."[17]

Whyte could not shake the malaria he contracted on Guadalcanal, and in July 1943 he was sent home on sick leave. He soon became an instructor at the Marine Corps School at Quantico, Virginia, teaching officers about the Guadalcanal campaign and the fighting characteristics of the Japanese. While teaching he wrote a series of articles for *The Marine Corps Gazette*, drawing lessons from the Guadalcanal campaign and assessing America's intelligence gathering. Curiously for the future author of *The Organization Man*, his prescriptions emphasized a strict adherence to "correct" procedure and the necessity of subordinating the individual to the group.[18]

Whyte left the Marine Corps in January 1945. He had no interest in returning to Vicks and had gotten a great deal of satisfaction out of writing for the Marines. Armed with his clippings, he applied for a job at *Fortune*. He was made a writing apprentice at seventy-five dollars a week. Whyte realized within a few days that he was the worst writer on the staff. It took the rest of the editors and writers only a little while longer to agree. Though one editor tried to get rid of him, he managed to hang on. He later observed,

"I was so bad that I was not fired, but kept on as a kind of exhibit." He had a weakness for cliché and an inability to tie his writing around a theme or idea, yielding a rather baroque surface that failed to disguise the hollow scaffolding underneath. Detesting Whyte's metaphors and ornamentation, Herb Solow used Whyte's leads to teach new *Fortune* writers how not to write. If this was not bad enough, despite his Vicks experience, Whyte had a surprising lack of business sophistication. "The market interest," assistant managing editor Bill Harris repeatedly yelled at him, "What's the market interest? Can't you get that through your head?"[19] And this on a staff never known for its great attention to marketability.

In Whyte's defense, he spent his early years working on Shorts and Faces, the gulag of *Fortune* assignments. With subject material too thin to justify a real article, and space too short to develop an idea, Shorts and Faces was the bane of every *Fortune* writer. Writing these and the occasional story for the "bank," which rarely appeared in the magazine, Whyte had little opportunity to develop. It took him three years to win a listing on the masthead, and longer to back into a good assignment.

Whyte finally received his break in 1949. Managing editor Del Paine wanted a story on the graduating college class of 1949. The president of Yale had told him it was the best class ever, but no other *Fortune* writer would agree to take the assignment. In desperation, Paine turned to Whyte.[20] The story turned out quite different from Paine's expectations. When Whyte began interviewing students, guidance officials, and corporate recruiters, he was surprised to learn how cautious students were. What the Yale president had seen as greatness, Whyte concluded was merely a class "eager to make itself useful to business."[21] This might be seen as a conclusion a business magazine would welcome, but it disturbed Whyte.

In the wake of the Depression and world war, with many attending school after leaving the military, Whyte found the class of '49 had been "conditioned to organization," and to them "big business means security." The fear of risk and worship of safety shocked Whyte, who wondered if the new generation of graduates would "be so intent on achieving."[22] Implicitly assuming achievement stemmed from individual initiative, Whyte perceived a draining of vitality where others saw well-adjusted future leaders. In his first close look at the values underpinning business, he began to discern the pressures for group conformity he would dissect over the next seven years.

Whyte's article (published anonymously, of course) garnered *Fortune* a lot of shocked attention. It also displayed Whyte's gift for listening closely to the language businessmen used to describe themselves and their values. Identifying the assumptions underscoring their words, Whyte could move directly from language to values. His next project for *Fortune* launched an inquiry into business communication that yielded nine articles over almost two years. The project resulted in his 1952 book *Is Anybody Listening?* The title, ostensible questioning whether business communication was effective, held a double meaning for him. "Does anybody else hear what I hear when business speaks?" Whyte seemed to be asking his audience.

Whyte began with the free enterprise campaigns of the late 1940s, the efforts of businessmen to educate Americans about the virtues of the free enterprise system (either explicitly or implicitly, depending on the sophistication of the campaign) and the dangers posed by government and unions. Despite shaping up as one of the most intensive and expensive "sales" jobs in history, Whyte concluded, "it is not worth a damn." "The free enterprise campaign," he declared, "is psychologically unsound, it is abstract, it is defensive, and it is negative. Most important . . . it represents a shocking lack of faith in the American people, and in some cases downright contempt."[23]

To illustrate this contempt, Whyte penned an imaginary public-service announcement parodying the free enterprise campaign. Exploiting folksy, small-town American ways, the advertisement told the story of a young man checked by wise old "Doc Hubbard" for spouting off about the unjustifiable profits of big business. Motioning to a boy hawking newspapers on the corner, Doc said, "When you talk about monopolies and more taxes on big business, that's the fellow you're attacking." After a few more paragraphs of such "explanation," the young radical "began to see things differently." Let other people ("snake-oil peddlers") yell about their –isms, "Me . . . I'll take Vanilla." Only making Whyte's point further, a company missed the joke and requested a thousand reprints of the piece because it was such "a magnificent expression of real Americanism."[24]

Despite this example, Whyte was intrigued by why most businessmen he talked with agreed the campaign was useless, but continued to support it anyway. Where were the critics within business willing to stand up and say the program was a waste of time and money? Whyte's attempt to answer this question involved looking at the different ways business communicated and the values this communication conveyed. Looking at the office grapevine, the bosses "Open Door," and courses in business writing, he found a disturbing faith in expertise and technical engineering as the key to solving business problems. Communication was being transformed into a science, a species of social engineering (where, for example, "prose engineers" could mass produce effective business writing). "If we get the technical hang of it," managers believed, "all will be well." Technical expertise necessitated the suppression of "individual intuition, inspiration and hunch." "Hand in hand with this expertise," Whyte concluded, "has gone a comparable emphasis on group values."[25]

Whyte found the most surprising and disturbing expansion of group values taking place. In a pioneering article examining the corporate wife, Whyte discovered the search for reliable and loyal employees had extended into the employee's home. Firms were interviewing the wives of prospective hires (as potential new members of the "corporate family") and wives were expected to relish subordinating their interests to the needs of the organization. Especially shocking to Whyte, corporate wives seemed to not only accept this situation, but also actively welcomed it. "For the fact is that group-life is precisely what she seems to like, and she joins the corporation already equipped with the philosophy."[26] Foreshadowing his advice in *The Organization Man*, Whyte wrote a *Fortune* editorial "In Praise of the Ornery Housewife," applauding those women willing to defy this corporate expansion into private life.[27]

Asking "how conformity has been rationalized and made respectable," Whyte blamed the corporate social engineers who had been, in fact, engineering mediocrity in a "profoundly authoritarian" manner. Whyte linked social engineers with the larger culture in a discussion of the popularity of Herman Wouk's novel *The Caine Mutiny* (1951), a novel that made blind submission to the rules look like heroism and principled dissent resemble cowardice. At last linking social engineering with the free enterprise campaign, Whyte concluded corporate managers "promise us freedom from moral choice."[28]

Ironies abound. First, Whyte's book exposed the uselessness and perniciousness of the free enterprise campaign but Henry Luce believed in the campaign and directed his magazines to participate. *Fortune*'s declaration of fealty to the free enterprise system, published in the first issue that carries Whyte's name on the masthead, was part of the campaign. Second, Whyte published his attack on group values anonymously for *Fortune*, the magazine that practiced what Luce had dubbed "group journalism." Whyte hated that term, and led the fight to get bylines for *Fortune* writers in the early 1950s. *Is Anybody Listening?* was the first book published from *Fortune* work that was identified as the work of an individual author (Whyte and the Editors of *Fortune*, rather than just the Editors of *Fortune*). In the preface Whyte acknowledged the irony (and his own position) by thanking "my colleagues on *Fortune*—a collection of individuals whose contributions I would never describe as "group journalism.""[29]

Searching for a way to fight this growing authoritarian pressure to conform, with its resulting mediocrity and oppression, Whyte could only conclude that "a new respect for the individual must be kindled." "A revival of the humanities, perhaps . . . " was all he could come up with, suggesting a belief that the reassertion of human over technical values could turn the tide.[30] Four years later, he moved beyond this vague hope that organizations could recognize the problem and reform to an insistence that they needed to be actively resisted.

William Whyte's *The Organization Man* became one of the most influential books of the 1950s. Part of its fame (though only a small part) derived from its appendix, where Whyte taught readers how to cheat on the personality tests that were increasingly used by personnel managers ("Repeat to yourself," Whyte's advice began, "I loved my father and my mother, but my father a little bit more").[31] Cheating was one of the concrete ways he advocated for resisting the organization in an attempt to safeguard the individual's humanity.

Many of the same themes Whyte explored in the communication articles reappeared in *The Organization Man*. This time he set up his collected *Fortune* articles with an interpretive introduction. He laid bare the "social ethic," which he defined as "that contemporary body of thought which makes morally legitimate the pressures of society against the individual." The foundation of the ethic consisted of three beliefs: that creativity flowed from the group, that the individual's ultimate need was "belongingness," and that science could bring about this belongingness. The application of human relations science could yield a utopian outcome, where "society's needs and the individual's needs are one and the same."[32]

Whyte carefully separated his analysis from an attack on conformity or a rejection of the organization. He feared his attempt to recover individualism would be misread as a nostalgic yearning for an eighteenth-century idyll that never was. "I speak of individualism *within* organizational life," he insisted, making it clear that organizations were inevitable and necessary. This necessity made their character crucial, and put the struggle to reform them front and center.

Whyte linked this organizational inevitability directly to the intellectual's proper role in society. He directly addressed intellectuals who preached a rejection of institutional attachments. "Intellectual scoldings based on an impossible lofty ideal may be of some service in upbraiding organization man with his failures, but they can give him no guidance." Rather than join critics who would wish the organization away, he detailed how the individual "should fight the organization."[33] He expected intellectuals to enlist in the struggle.

Whyte held no illusions that he offered any utopian promise to counteract the organizational dystopia. The prime weapon the resister had was the awareness of the conflict between the imperatives of the organization and the interests of the individual. The role of the intellectual was to aid the individual in developing such an understanding. This consciousness could inoculate the individual against the subtly coercive ways group values corroded autonomy. Whyte also emphasized the one concrete weapon the organizational employee had: the power to quit. Even if quitting only involved movement from one organization to another, the availability of leaving opened up freedom of action. "To be able to dissent, to champion the unpopular view," Whyte maintained, "he must be able to move." The knowledge that he was "psychologically capable of it, is the guarantee of his independence."[34]

There is more in this argument than the tepid accommodation inferred by critics like Richard Pells. Arguing that the consciousness Whyte suggested would ultimately aid the institution, not the individual, Pells criticizes Whyte for his timidity. The "best one could do," Pells depicts Whyte as arguing, "was bend ... to the demands of managerial society, hoping to preserve some small areas of privacy and self-respect."[35] Whyte, however, was holding out the hope that the organization could be transformed by the actions of individuals aware of the need to fight the underlying assumptions of organizational life. Pells's belief that intellectuals must necessarily remain autonomous, untainted by institutional commitments, leads him to miss the crux of Whyte's argument. Naïve Whyte may have been, but tepid he was not.

Whyte had little patience for the arguments that intellectuals must separate themselves from organizational entanglements. Directly addressing the Luce novels (what he calls, more broadly, the "New York" novels), Whyte repudiated their contention that the intellectual hero could only find redemption by swapping the organization for country living and independence. These intellectual heroes have "left the battlefield where his real fight must be fought." "By puttering at a country newspaper and patronizing himself into a native, he evades any conflict," Whyte concluded, "All this may be very sensible, but it's mighty comfortable for a hairshirt."[36] Rather than offering a principled rejection of organizational life, Whyte called for intellectuals to engage it, aiding organizational men in developing a conscious sense of working "*in an organization rather than for it.*"[37] That consciousness was what allowed Whyte to pen his withering critique of American organizational life from the pages of America's preeminent business magazine. It was the consciousness that drove the work of all Time Inc.'s interstitial intellectuals.

Daniel Bell: Doubt over Certainty

Historians have yet to effectively come to terms with Daniel Bell. Viewed primarily as a case study in deradicalization, Bell's work is generally interpreted as part and parcel of the political reconciliation of radical intellectuals with America. The story of Daniel Bell has been the story of how the radicals of the 1930s turned their backs on the utopian aspirations of the left and, in its most simplistic versions, became apologists for the status quo. Unsurprisingly, such "slouching toward conservatism" narratives are invariably written as laments.[38]

Daniel Bell makes an odd choice as poster boy for a lost radicalism. First, he was much younger than most of the New York intellectuals, which affected the tenor of his politics. His 1930s radicalism was a boyhood radicalism, nurtured by the Jewish socialism of the Lower East Side and the radical sectarianism of City College. Second, he was never all that radical. He grew up as a right-wing socialist, always hostile to Stalin and Trotsky and dedicated to an evolutionary socialism. The absurdity of the radical lament interpretation is best revealed by Job Dittberner's interview with Bell for *The End of Ideology and American Social Thought*, where Dittberner takes him to task for abandoning his criticism of big business while he wrote for *Fortune*. Dittberner suggests that Bell's formulaic and mechanical Marxism, with its simple assumption that business leaders were united by a clear class consciousness and that the state functioned as the tool of capital, is preferable to his later nuanced and insightful analyses of the labor movement or the nature of work.[39] Reversing the politics, it would be like a critic of Dwight Macdonald lamenting all the work he did after he left *Fortune* because he had lost sight of the power and potency of businessmen like Henry Ford. Politics aside, there is no question Bell's later work is more penetrating and profound than his earlier political and polemical journalism. Yet most studies either salute his early work or view his later works only through the lens of lost radicalism. Even when such work yields important insights into recent American intellectual history, as in Howard Brick's *Daniel Bell and the Decline of Intellectual Radicalism*, it distorts Bell's career and his importance.

Following from the lost radicalism thesis, Bell's work is taken as emblematic of the suspension of criticism of America by so-called consensus intellectuals in the 1950s. Here critics have identified Bell's 1960 book *The End of Ideology* as a complacent and self-satisfied endorsement of the status quo. Bell's book, a loosely organized collection of essays written mainly during his *Fortune* years, emphasized the failure of ideologies of the left (Marxism) and the right (laissez-faire capitalism) to deal with America's social complexity. *The End of Ideology* was a work of criticism that attacked the American left but also contained a number of penetrating analyses of American society, and discerning criticism of the organization of work. Bell's key insights were lost, however, when C. Wright Mills, in his influential "Letter to a New Left," interpreted the book as a craven assent to an exploitative status quo. *The End of Ideology* was read as a goodbye to all that leftist ideology, and therefore a hearty endorsement of the anti-ideological status quo.[40] Mills's view has influenced interpretations of Bell's work ever since. Godfrey Hodgson's influential "Ideology of the Liberal Consensus" claims Bell's "career epitomized, in fact, the intellectual consensus that underpinned its political equivalent during the 1950s."[41] Richard Pells's survey of American intellectual life in the 1940s and 1950s heads his discussion of Bell "The Celebration of America."[42]

Bell was many things, and the tensions and inconsistencies that riddled *The End of Ideology* open him to many different criticisms, but a celebrant of capitalism he never was. Instead, in his postwar writings he wrestled with the relationship between politics and ethics in both political movements and intellectual life. Bell ultimately sketched out an unsettling standard of ambivalence as a positive and creative intellectual position. He advocated a simultaneous engagement and detachment, a stance of critical alienation tied inextricably to political involvement. This life lived in paradox posed difficult challenges for political movements offering absolutist visions and intellectuals advocating autonomous independence.

Born Daniel Bolotsky in 1919, Bell grew up in New York City's Lower East Side, absorbing the neighborhood's Jewish culture, orthodox religion, and radical politics. The son of Jewish immigrants, he spent most of his youth in a day orphanage after this father died when he was less than a year old and his mother was forced to take factory work. A garment worker like thousands of other young Jewish women, Bell's mother belonged to the International Ladies Garment Workers Union, which was still formally allied to the Socialist Party.

This connection probably influenced Bell's early radicalism, as did the 1932 presidential campaign of Norman Thomas and his reading of Upton Sinclair's *The Jungle*. In any case, he grew up very poor and "aware of the fact that something was wrong with the entire system."[43] In 1932, at age thirteen, Bell joined the Young People's Socialist League, the youth wing of the Socialist Party. At the same time, he turned his back on his religious upbringing, telling his rabbi he no longer believed in God. Despite his precocious trading of religious faith for political involvement, the competing gods of politics and religion would continue to define his intellectual life.

Like many young Socialists in 1934, Bell began to move toward Communism, driven by the growing threat of fascism and the Communist's presentation of themselves as the only force on the left capable of fighting the forces of reaction. His leftward drift was arrested, however, when anarchist cousins gave him pamphlets documenting the brutal nature of the Bolsheviks. The story of Trotsky's suppression of the sailors at Kronstadt served to destroy the appeal of Communism to Bell, but also kept him from joining the Trotskyists, as so many leftists who abhorred the Communists did.

In 1935 Bell enrolled at the City College of New York, a hothouse of leftist politics during the late 1930s. City College's young radicals of various complexions segregated themselves into different alcoves in the student union. The documentary film *Arguing the World* places Bell as a member of the anti-Communists and therefore includes him with the Trotskyists of Alcove One. This binary separation of the left into Stalinists and Trotskyists ignores the diversity on the left, and makes Bell seem more radical than he was. At City College, he remained active in socialist political organizations, though again remaining on the right wing of the Socialist Party. When the party split in 1936 he stuck with the "Old Guard," which continued to stress parliamentary democracy and anti-Communism. While opposed to the Stalinists at City College, Bell did not join the Trotskyists. In fact, his college politics might better be considered a species of left liberalism. While at City College, he and his friends formed a John Dewey Society, also called the Hopefully Confused Liberals. Opposed to the dogmatism of the Communists, they were armed with what Bell called the "courage of our confusion." These strains of pragmatism and skepticism remained with Bell.[44]

After a brief stint at Columbia's Law School, Bell began graduate work in sociology at Columbia in 1939, where he acquired a foundation in European sociology. After earning a masters degree, he joined the *New Leader*, a socialist weekly published by Sol Levitas.[45] When the managing editor's job became available, Levitas appointed Bell. Still in his early twenties, Bell took over the *New Leader* in late 1941. He was paid twenty dollars a week ("An old tradition," Bell remarked, "you pay half in money, half in ideology"[46]). The whole magazine was written by a couple of men, with Bell writing under his own name and four or five pseudonyms (including John Donne and Andrew Marvell). By his own estimate, he was writing 5,000 words a week for the paper. Despite the meager pay and immense workload, he considered himself lucky. "In those days," he remembered, "no one had any idea that you could have 'intellectual' jobs."[47] His college friends were desperately seeking work, taking and retaking the civil service exams.

In 1944 Bell left the *New Leader*, joining the editorial board of *Common Sense* and working on a book titled "The Monopoly State." The project became a defining moment in his intellectual development. Bell had written "about 300 or 400 pages" of a mechanical Marxist analysis of corporate influence on the state, when he decided, "all this was silly."[48] He recognized that he had no direct knowledge of the relations between corporate America and the government. Instead he had a theory, and he was busily pushing all the evidence into the pattern he expected to find. Bell abandoned the project, frustrated by what he perceived to be his own lack of education. He began reading Franz Kafka, Søren Kierkegaard, Simone Weil, and Reinhold Niebuhr, writers who emphasized the impact of bureaucratization on individual agency and the tragic nature of life. He also began rediscovering his Jewish roots, participating in the series of conversations conducted by Eliott Cohen that culminated in the founding of *Commentary* magazine. Looking to further his education along these lines, Bell soon left New York City for the University of Chicago.

During his years teaching at Chicago (1945–1948), Bell developed the intellectual perspectives that would enliven his later work. Much of his intellectual development at the time occurred in the long shadow cast by the Holocaust. Though hired to teach Marx, he spent most of his time reading Weber and Niebuhr and participating in a study group on Jewish intellectual identity. He wrote little during this period, especially compared to the torrentially prolific years on the *New Leader*. What he did publish marked his transition, in Job Dittberner's phrase, from "bitter political criticism to critical social analysis."[49]

Bell rethought his Marxism, never fully abandoning it, but regarding it as one of a number of useful conceptual tools. Where he found Marxism provocative, as in its analysis of alienation, he still drew on it, but where he found it unhelpful or even obfuscating, as in the analysis of a ruling class (which he had previously relied on and come to find unsatisfactory), he discarded it. His rediscovered Judaism likewise pushed him toward a deep appreciation of the value of alienation. These thoughts came together in an essay he published in *Jewish Frontier* in late 1946. In "A Parable of Alienation," Bell wondered about how to deal with the "quality of being lost [that] is the most pervasive symptom of the alienation of our times." "People move about," he observed, "in the huge caverns that modern technology has constructed, with little sense of relationship to meaningful events." Drawing on Weber, Bell argued that the growing rationalization of society, marked by the increasing separation of men from the results (and therefore the rationale) of their work, led to a deepening depersonalization. The result is a life of "otherhood" where the individual is divided from any sense of community or social identity. At this point, he traced this not only to the bureaucratization of society, but also to "the divorce in our contemporary world between moral and secular conceptions."[50] The Jew, Bell felt, was particularly attuned to this sense of displacement, and the Jewish intellectual particularly well situated to transform this negative alienation into a positive asset.

What Bell had in mind was a particular identity for the Jewish intellectual. Facing a bleak future in a bureaucratic age, he advocated permanent dissent.

> We reject the basic values of American society as they stand. The increasing centralization of decision, the narrowing of ideas of free moral choice, the extension into all domains, particularly the cultural, of the rationalized, stilted forms of mass organization and bureaucracy, the rising sense of nationalism as a product of the war, all of these heighten the awareness that the way of life resulting from these pressures—the rawness, vulgarity, mass sadism and senseless sybaritism, the money lust and barbaric extravagances—can only stifle creativity and free living.[51]

Drawing strength, however, from the "hardness of alienation, the sense of otherness," Bell advocated developing "a special critical faculty, an unwillingness to submit our values completely into any 'cause.'"[52] Bell's "assumption of alienation as a positive value" has traditionally been read as an invocation of Mannheim's "free-floating intellectual," standing apart from society in order to judge it.[53] Yet Bell's ideal here was not wholesale detachment, but rather a delicate balance of engagement and separation.

"The plight—and glory—of the alienated Jewish intellectual is that his role is to point to the need of brotherhood, but as he has been bred, he cannot today accept any embodiment of community as final," he concluded, "He can live only in permanent tension and as a permanent critic."[54]

Though in 1946 Bell viewed this position as essentially Jewish, the strenuous ideal he invoked did not necessarily require a Jewish identity. Bell acknowledged this in later years. In a 1949 review of Orwell's *1984*, he restated his view of the intellectual's identity. Facing the threat of the totalitarian organization of society, he concluded,

> One has to live in the world and accept it in all its frightening implications. One has to live consciously and self-consciously, in the involvement and in the alienation, in the loyalty and in the questioning, in the love and in the critical appraisal. Without that persistent double image, we are lost. At least we can live in paradox.[55]

Howard Brick takes this as the summation of Bell's views on the role of the critic, but perceives it as completely negative, concluding such a stance was "very meager consolation" for the Socialist.[56] Bell's view of the intellectual simultaneously engaged and distant, however, has more to offer than Brick and others acknowledge. Bell was not advocating (or styling himself as) the free-floating intellectual, a step Brick sees as a necessary component to deradicalization. Instead, Bell claimed, the critic must be at once involved and alienated. What Bell warned against was either the intellectual's complete submission to a political ideology, or a completely detached stance of criticism. As he later put it, "alienation had the sense of a double consciousness," it involved "a degree of detachment and involvement, yet never a complete involvement."[57]

The best evidence of Bell's intended meaning might be his own actions. During his Chicago years he remained politically active, continuing to pursue his social democratic politics through the labor movement. During his time in Chicago he served as the acting chair of the Commonwealth Federation, an attempt to combine nascent commonwealth movements in the Midwest into a socialist labor party. The effort involved A. Philip Randolph, members of the United Auto Workers, and Socialists throughout the region, and lasted for about eighteen months before falling apart. Bell's "alienation" did not prevent him from taking an active role in political organization, or to continue to work for his social democratic ideals.

In 1948, Bell accepted the job as labor editor of *Fortune*. The job came about through his friend Herb Solow, an ex-Trotskyist from the 1930s who had helped organize the Dewey Commission's investigation into the charges against Trotsky. Solow had been writing for *Fortune* since 1942. In early 1948 he called Bell to ask him to write up a memo for a new labor department in *Fortune*. Luce liked Bell's memo, and asked him to lunch to discuss the department. During their meeting, Luce wanted to know who Bell imagined the target audience should be. Would the department be written for business leaders dealing with unions or for union men themselves? Bell argued the column should be written for labor professionals in the field, the labor lawyers, personnel department managers, and union officials who dealt with labor issues every day. Bell claimed that if they read and respected *Fortune*'s coverage, it would become must reading. Luce agreed and offered him the position.

Bell's was immediately enthusiastic. Writing Lewis Corey, he enthused, "I am quite excited about the idea. I think it is a top journalistic job yet one that will give me time—and research help—to dig deep into the guts of the labor movement and the economy."[58] Making the job even more attractive, Luce planned to pay him $12,000 a year. This was triple his salary at the University of Chicago. It would allow him to support his daughter and ex-wife, and would get him back to New York City. Despite the money, Bell still hesitated to accept. He talked with his friends on the staff, Solow and John McDonald (another ex-Trotskyist) and others who he knew had worked for Luce (including Dwight Macdonald). Finding that the magazine valued writers and offered them "independence of a sort," Bell accepted.[59]

Bell soon found the job to his liking. He was allowed to do much of the work at home, coming to the office only a few days a month to work out his assignments and close each issue. After a few months, he found he could complete his month's work in roughly two weeks time, which left him plenty of time for his other writing (allowing the enormous productivity of these years). Still, working for *Fortune* exacted costs. Bell found that some of his old friends in New York cut him socially because he was working for Luce. When working at *Time* Irving Howe had been able to overcome this by presenting his job as a necessary compromise, and by letting people outside *Time* know he believed he had made a bargain with the devil. Bell seems not to have used this excuse. He appreciated the money and valued the inside connection with labor his post provided. More than that, he respected the magazine.[60]

"More than any other magazine I know," Bell declared, "*Fortune* has had a sharp sense of dedication to craftsmanship and journalism." He found an environment where writers were encouraged to write stories as they saw them. He recalled people who came to *Fortune* with the idea that they would just write what the magazine wanted. These were the writers, Bell observed, who "never lasted because they were quickly understood and resented."[61] At *Fortune*, he found editors who respected his independence and trusted his ability to decide how to shape labor's story. He also never found himself pressured to submit to editor's views of how labor should be reported. Overcoming an initial wariness toward the magazine, Bell made increasing use of his platform as his career at *Fortune* developed.

When Bell arrived at *Fortune*, his thoughts were already working in the two directions that would characterize his work through the 1950s. First, the failure of socialism to emerge in the wake of the Depression and war led him to attempt an explanation for its failure. Throughout 1949 and 1950 he worked on this project, which culminated in his first book, *Marxian Socialism in the United States* (1952). Tracing the history of socialism in America, he concluded it had failed because, adopting Martin Luther's old description of his church, it was "in the world, but not of it." For Bell, socialism in America had "lived in society, but transcended it by making a judgment outside of it."[62] Though this closely resembled what he had advocated for the intellectual in 1946, for a political movement Bell believed it was suicidal. Drawing on Weber's famous essay on politics as a vocation, he contrasted an ethic of conscience to an ethic of responsibility. Discerning an inevitable tension between politics and ethics, Bell decided socialists had consistently chosen a stance of moral repudiation rather than the risk the compromises the ethic of responsibility required. Whereas detached engagement was desirable for the individual intellectual, Bell believed it was fatal for a political organization.[63]

The failure of socialism to develop a practical political program led Bell back to the labor movement. If socialism had been too concerned with its moral purity, labor seemed a better candidate to adopt Weber's ethic of responsibility. Bell's years at *Fortune* were spent exploring labor's ability to live up to these hopes.

The labor department was introduced in October 1948, part of *Fortune*'s first major reconfiguration of itself. The editorial introducing the issue declared, "Briefly, *Fortune* ceases to be merely a magazine about American business and becomes as well a magazine in behalf of American business enterprise." *Fortune*'s transition was placed in the context of the new-found responsibility and legitimacy of business, signaled by the transition from

Babbitt to *Dodsworth* to Studebaker industrialist Paul Hoffman (a Luce and *Fortune* favorite) as the embodiment of the businessman in the popular imagination. Anticipating Thomas Dewey's defeat of Truman, *Fortune* claimed a businessman in the White House would give business the chance to reclaim its role at the center of American identity. *Fortune* was confident the new breed of American businessman was up to the task.[64]

As part of the new *Fortune*, a labor column would appear in each issue, written from the point of view of labor. Bell's first column introduced the major questions concerning organized labor, including labor's political role, its internal affairs (especially its fight to isolate the Communists in the movement), and the relationship between labor leadership and the shopfloor. Bell framed these issues around the question of competing loyalties. At a time when *Fortune* was busily articulating a key component of what would become the postwar liberal consensus—that cooperation could reign between workers and managers—Bell chose to focus on the competition between firm and union for worker loyalty. Crucial to assessing this contest, he believed, was determining whether workers defined themselves in individual or collective terms.

Bell's position on labor-business relations became clearer in early 1949. Commenting on the Twentieth Century Fund's *Partners in Production: A Basis for Labor-Management Understanding*, he noted the increasing efforts to make workers not just more productive, but more willing. The desire to see workers and managers engaged in a mutually beneficial partnership was a core tenet of *Fortune*'s developing corporate liberalism. Bell focused, however, on the key danger in such thinking for workers: efforts to provide workers with a sense of common purpose ignored the uncomfortable fact that firm's did not operate for their benefit and made decisions without their input. Cooperation would have to be on a more equal basis or it was chimerical. And Bell's focus on speed-ups at Ford emphasized the persistence of management's desire to maximize demands on labor without the corresponding benefits. To him, the so-called "new capitalism" still looked a lot like the old capitalism.[65]

Bell's skepticism toward *Fortune*'s more expansive views of the possibilities of business leadership became clearer over time. It demonstrated his own version of detached engagement. Pleased with the magazine and his work environment, he nevertheless held himself aloof from the magazine's prevailing optimism. In September 1949 *Fortune* published Russell Davenport's "The Greatest Opportunity on Earth," in which Davenport argued that business leadership provided the only bulwark against state socialism and the only protection for American liberties. The key, Davenport believed, was cooperative relations between business and labor, providing workers with security through collective bargaining and private welfare schemes. "The recognition by the employer," Davenport concluded, "that his employee is possessed of certain rights, the implementation of which is the joint concern of the boss and the worker," was a necessary precondition to "the humanizing of the shop," and the maintenance of American values. Denying the existence of real conflict between management and workers, Davenport believed that if business and labor leaders could act more "responsibly" industrial democracy would prevail. These beliefs remained the heart of *Fortune*'s liberalism, rearticulated in Davenport's *U.S.A. The Permanent Revolution*.[66]

The month after Davenport's "Greatest Opportunity" article, Bell titled his labor column "American Jitters," an allusion to Edmund Wilson's great book of Depression reporting. In his article, Bell documented the deep (and often violent) conflict that still prevailed between labor and management in some areas. He noted pockets of high unemployment, where class relations better resembled warfare than cooperation. In the same issue Davenport highlighted firms offering pensions. Bell soon unfavorably compared the benefits of such plans with those achieved through collective bargaining. Davenport highlighted ways in which cooperative efforts like the Scanlon plan had boosted productivity, profits, and pay, and called for real, meaningful participation for workers. Bell responded with a focus on how, despite gains in the acceptance of collective bargaining, in most instances "workers are treated as outsiders."[67]

Read together, Davenport's optimistic refashioning of capitalism and Bell's persistently pessimistic insistence on looking at workplace relations as they do exist, not as they should exist, revealed a serious difference. Bell never let Davenport's invocation of how business should treat workers be confused with the realities of how business did treat workers. Bell remained pessimistic about the possibility or the desirability of such cooperation. Davenport viewed responsible business administration of the economy as vital to the prevention of expanded government involvement in the economy, a prospect he saw as an inevitable outcome of the New Deal. Bell, of course, was looking for exactly the type of mixed economy Davenport feared.[68]

Bell's labor column quickly acquired the reputation in the labor field he had hoped to secure. Its success, and the support of his *Fortune* editors, encouraged him to expand his work for the magazine. In 1951 he wrote his first by-lined story (by-lines were beginning to emerge, due to the advocacy of writers like Whyte, and the increasing variety of perspectives among the writers, which made it difficult to speak of articles produced by a single *Fortune*). Titled "Do Unions Raise Wages?" it analyzed the so-called wage-price spiral. Bell's article argued that the inflationary pressure of union wage increases was an illusion. The major impact of unions, he argued, was sociological, as unionism "articulated a security-consciousness felt by the American worker." "In the largest sense," Bell concluded, "unionism had helped to create a political environment whereby the measures it demands become part of a wider program for the governmental undertaking of social-welfare polices."[69] Social welfare, Bell was in effect contending, came not from the initiative of newly responsible corporations, but from union pressure from below. From this point on, his most important writing in *Fortune* came in major articles, not in the separate labor department.

Following Bell's commentary in *Fortune*, it was possible to glean his growing frustration with organized labor. In "The Language of Labor," he tried to explain the paradox of labor's rhetoric—why it portrayed itself as an embattled minority oppressed by business at home but sang the virtues of free enterprise when presenting itself abroad—as a case of its vocabulary failing to keep pace with its institutional power. Labor's anti-business sloganeering was a holdover from its violent and difficult past. Radical language had helped galvanize labor during the titanic struggles of the 1930s. Now it was a relic, disguising the moderation of labor's stance, and making it difficult to realize that labor as a social movement was being replaced by labor as an institution. Labor's actions were what mattered, Bell again insisted, not its still radical rhetoric.[70]

In the October 1951 issue of *Fortune* devoted to "The New Capitalism," Bell announced "Labor's Coming of Middle Age." Bell believed that labor was shedding its left orientation and returning to traditional "market unionism" (his term for business unionism, or the containment of labor's demands within the context of collective bargaining for wages and benefits). Facing a new climate of government hostility toward labor, Bell expected labor to distance itself from its bolder social planning programs and return to old-fashioned bargaining for "more." Contrasting market unionism to political unionism, or labor as an institution versus labor as a social movement, Bell saw labor increasingly becoming a pressure group rather than a political movement with a social agenda. Even labor's fiercest denunciations of business, he concluded, were "a language of protest against exclusion. It challenged the right to rule, but not the nature of the rule."[71]

Bell's surgical analysis of this development should not be confused with advocacy (a persistent problem in evaluating his work). He subtitled his article "Exhaustion of the Left," his first use of a term that would reappear as the subtitle to *The End of Ideology: On the Exhaustion of Political Ideas in the 1950s*. It marked his first suggestion that Walter Reuther was failing in his campaign to keep labor on the offensive. Reuther had tried to move beyond bargaining over wages and supporting the Democratic Party to challenge the management prerogatives of business and create a wider social welfare system. Bell's many sympathetic *Fortune* columns had presented Reuther as the best hope for a revitalized labor movement.[72] By 1955, however, Bell reported in an article on the annual wage plan, "Reuther, the one-time Socialist, is seeking to make the American worker genuinely a middle class individual."[73] "Ideological unionism"—Bell's term for labor's historical solidarity built on industrial labor—had given way to market unionism. With the most radical figure in American labor turning his back on the old industrial movement culture, the incorporation of organized labor was perilously near completion.

Bell explored the consequences of labor's becoming part of "the control system of management" in his most important work of the 1950s, "Work and its Discontents." He traced the history of the ever-increasing rationalization of industrial work. He focused especially on the industrial engineers and sociologists who had, in their acceptance of efficiency as the preeminent goal, created a "cow sociology."[74] They concerned themselves entirely with the technical problems of increasing rates of production and levels of efficiency. The result was a relentless stripping of meaning from the work men did. Bell noted that, as "scientists," these efficiency experts were unconcerned with the moral questions raised by their alteration of the work environment. Some, however, insisted that survey data proved that workers were not unhappy with their jobs. Bell argued that answers to such questions could only be meaningful if workers had an understanding of alternative possibilities of organizing work. This they lacked, partially because intellectuals had failed to offer it. In the past machine civilization had given rise to literary and artistic protests, "but the poets have fled." The factory had been abandoned to the sociologist and the psychologist.[75]

"Short of pressure from the workers themselves," Bell concluded, "there is no action which would force modern enterprise to reorder the flow of work." Pressure from the workers was not forthcoming. First, the unions, embodiments of worker power, were uninterested in the problem. Indeed, collective bargaining agreements left the union responsible for disciplining the workforce and increasing production and efficiency. Second, intellectuals had abandoned concerns over the impact of industrial labor on the worker. They failed to offer workers a compelling criticism of their existing work lives, or a moving and viable alternative. In other words, labor's adoption of market unionism coincided with the defection of the intellectuals from labor's cause. Bell cited Freud's notion that work was the chief means of binding an individual to reality, and wondered what sort of reality this left workers with.[76]

Labor's gradual adoption of market unionism, which Bell lamented, suggested that the ethic of responsibility he had extolled presented serious risks. A politics of responsible compromise could quickly devolve into one of accommodation and stasis. When putting together *End of Ideology*, he purposely left out most of his *Fortune* work, planning, he claimed, "to rework these materials into a more unified book on the labor movement."[77] That book was never written, possibly because its conclusion would have posed a challenge to his dismissal of socialism.

Bell's position by the end of the *Fortune* years, then, was a complex one. Frustrated by labor's lack of real militancy, wary of the need of intellectuals for political potency, turned off by the appalling results of Communism and laissez-faire capitalism, Bell was left without a clear port in which to moor. He looked for pragmatic reform, not utopian liberation (because it was both desirable and possible). Yet the problems that concerned him most— especially the degradation of work, the stripping of the meaning of labor away from workers and into the hands of technocratic efficiency experts— were not really susceptible to ameliorative reform. Bell's great achievements were his warning against the perniciousness done in the name of ideological commitment, his assessment of the dangers of either the free-floating or the entirely committed intellectual, and his criticism of the stripped humanity of work. His great failing was his inability to recognize the need for a different, more modest and chastened, but still potent ideology to make the problems of contemporary capitalism clear and a course of action feasible.

Unfortunately, his achievements were largely unrecognized. The early positive views of *End of Ideology* were soon eclipsed by Mills's devastating criticism. Painting Bell as a complacent and comfortable defender of existing reality, Mills positioned himself as a proponent of the still possible. His letter established a view of Bell that has prevailed ever since, as the many invocations of Bell as a consensus intellectual attest. Yet the dilemma Bell posed—the tension between politics and ethics, or practical politics and a transcendental vision—continued to bedevil intellectuals. The new left could repudiate Bell, but they could not resolve their own attempt to be in, but not of, the world. Bell's grappling with the proper balance between politics and ethics, and his attempt to articulate a stance for the intellectual as simultaneously engaged and detached, are worth reconsidering.

Walker Evans: "A Leisured and Untethered Eye"

In his early work, Walker Evans would sometimes use a right angle lens to photograph a person unawares. Pointing his camera at a friend, he could instead photograph a person to his immediate right. He caught subjects in a more natural manner this way, their faces marked by their own concerns and thoughts. It was a way of capturing the inviolable significance of each individual, finding a moment when, as Evans wrote, "the guard is down and the mask is off."[78] The right-angle lens is also a useful metaphor for understanding Evans's relationship to the world framed by his camera lens. Walker Evans looked askance at the world other people inhabited. Yet, like the photographer standing on a crowded street or sitting on a subway car, his observations came from inside the milieu to which he watched others respond.

The life of Walker Evans reaches back through the whole history of intellectuals at Time Inc. Yet Evans's relation to the experiences of intellectuals of his generation was always detached and slightly askew. Older than Whyte or Bell, Evans was of the same generation as MacLeish, Matthews, Macdonald, and Davenport. His life followed a similar path: upper-middle class background, prep school, youthful determination to be a writer, eastern college, followed by the almost obligatory years in Paris, and the late 1920s return to New York City. There the similarities end, as Evans spent the 1930s learning photography and existing hand-to-mouth in the remains of New York's bohemian environs. Unlike the intellectuals who ended the 1920s writing for Henry Luce, Evans seems never to have felt the complicated pull of influence and class responsibility exerted by Time Inc., or the push of intellectual ambivalence. His worldly ambitions were more modest, his artistic commitment more steadfast.

Like T. S. Matthews, Walker Evans III, was born is St. Louis, though two years later, in 1903.[79] His mother's family was affluent and socially well connected. His father's family was more modest, but Walker Evans Jr. was an ambitious young advertising executive, described as "clearly a man on the move."⁸⁰ Their marriage was a major event on the St. Louis social calendar, indicating their place among the city's elite.

The Evans family moved from St. Louis to Chicago and finally to Toledo, each time because his father had found a more important advertising position. In Chicago they had lived in a quiet and exclusive suburb, but the move to Toledo in 1914 thrust him into the center of a thriving industrial city. In Toledo Evans's father began an affair with a married neighbor, and eventually abandoned his family to be with her. From that point on, Belinda Rathbone observes, "Walker lived under the shadow of his estranged parents' silent hostilities."⁸¹ That same year he was sent to boarding school.

Evans, bright but an inattentive and indifferent student, attended a series of eastern prep schools. He disliked school, intuitively rejecting the class pride and Christian service they inculcated. Unlike other aspiring intellectuals, Evans did not succeed in the classroom despite this hostility, nor did he discover an outlet in writing. He struggled academically and transferred schools twice before finding a measure of happiness at Phillips Academy in Andover. There he discovered a serious love for literature, though his marks remained mediocre. Despite his poor grades, he set his sights on Yale. It was not until he turned up on the New Haven campus in the fall of 1922 that he discovered he had not been accepted. Evans immediately traveled to Williams College, where he was able to enroll on the spot.

In conventional terms, Evans's single year at Williams was not a success. He flunked Latin twice and performed poorly in all his classes. But in more important terms, his year of college marked an important period of self-discovery. While at Williams he became, in his words, "a pathological bibliophile," who skipped most of his classes to pursue his own reading.⁸² With a small group of friends, Evans read the *Little Review*, the *Dial*, and *Criterion* almost as they rolled off the presses. He devoured the works of early modernists like Eliot, Joyce, Woolf, and Lawrence. The modernist's rejection of the bourgeois world he inhabited struck Evans like a slap across the face. For the first time he found help formulating his own instinctive rejection of the hypocritical sham of his parents' marriage and the mendacious manipulations of his father's profession. Evans left Williams after one year, convinced the education in literature he needed could not be found in the classroom. He also began to entertain the idea of becoming a writer.⁸³

If literature was his new love, he found the perfect job from which to court her. In 1924 he began work at the New York Public Library, after telling a librarian he would work for free if it meant access to the stacks. That led to a job, and Evans spent three years working at the library, reading voraciously, and experimenting with his own short stories. In 1926, he traveled to Paris, hoping as so many had that the city of lights would foster an artistic breakthrough. It was now his firm ambition to be a writer.

Unlike most aspiring writers, however, Evans initially traveled in the company of his mother. The fringe location he had inhabited at prep school and college—rejecting the ethos of success and service, yet not finding an outlet in intellectual achievement as other aspiring intellectuals did—continued in Paris. Evans observed the Paris literary set up close, visiting the same cafes, summering at the same beaches, and hanging out at Sylvia Beach's Shakespeare and Company. Though he often observed James Joyce in the bookstore, he never met him or any of the expatriate writers that gave literary Paris its attraction. His time in Paris left him "wide-eyed, tongue-tied, and lonely."[84] Despite "following in the migratory paths of the gregarious Parisian set," in James Mellow's description, Evans remained on the outside looking in. He also struggled to write. The youthful optimism of his initial days, when he could confidently boast of the masterpieces that he would write, gradually evolved into a severe case of depression and writer's block. As Evans later described his dilemma, "You see, I'd done a lot of reading and I knew what writing was. And if I tried to do it, what I did was ludicrous and I threw it away and blushed."[85] He destroyed most of what he wrote before returning to the States.

While in Paris, Evans began to take pictures. Most of them were typical tourist snapshots taken with a pocket camera, though he did experiment with a series of self-portraits, including a sequence of shadow profiles. Though he received high praise for these from friends, he did not take his photography seriously. He lived in Paris on the same street with Eugene Atget and Berenice Abbott, both later influences, but never met them. At the time, he remembered, he considered photography a "left hand hobby." Despite that dismissive attitude, he kept making pictures.[86] As Rathbone notes, Evans's emotionally guarded sensibility better suited him to photography than to the psychological dissections of fiction. "The deceptions and secrecies of his family life," Rathbone observes, "made him more inclined to be a spy than a confessor."[87]

Like other returning expatriates, he arrived back in New York in the late 1920s looking for a job. James Mellow endorses Evans's own retrospective view, that the return to New York marked the beginning of his career as an artist, as he "made the break with his family and its past."[88] At the time, however, Evans was just beginning to experiment with photography and was adrift. Frustrated and depressed by his failure to write in Paris, he let his brother-in-law find him a Wall Street job at the stock brokerage firm Henry R. Doherty and Company. He worked nights, checking stocks from six to eleven p.m., and soon found an identical job for his new friend, the poet Hart Crane. Little is known of Evans's attitude toward his work. Mellow accepts Crane's ambivalence as evidence of Evans's own. What is known is that Evans worked on Wall Street from 1928 through the spring of 1929. Meanwhile, he continued to write short stories and experiment with photographs.[89]

Increasingly, he defined himself as a photographer. Living in sight of the Brooklyn Bridge, he shot a series of pictures of the bridge. Some of the images were included in Hart Crane's epic poem, *The Bridge*. His collaboration with Crane went a long way toward reconciling him to the pursuit of photography instead of literature. In Rathbone's words, Evans's "collaboration with a poet who was determined to exercise the connection between words and images confirmed what he hardly dared to believe—that his photography could be the equal companion of poetry."[90] Evans began to believe he could realize with a camera what escaped him with a pen.

He increasingly devoted himself to his new vocation. "His early professional career," notes Mellow, "was a matter of . . . unexpected windfalls and second-hand accommodations."[91] He moved frequently between cheap apartments and friend's couches, and picked up paying work when he had to. Gradually, his photography of the city began to attract notice. In 1930 it came to the attention of Lincoln Kirstein, the young publisher of *Hound and Horn*. Immediately drawn to his artistic sensibility, the men became friends. Kirstein lined up work for Evans, including a study of America's neglected architecture. Both men were fascinated with the variety of American building styles, though a superficial similarity disguised their quite different temperaments. Kirstein was a preservationist, hoping to save and restore the American architectural heritage. Evans, on the other hand, already relished the poetic lyricism of decay. Despite this difference, and Evans's evident discomfort in being instructed, Kirstein continued to champion his career.[92]

He even tried to get Evans a position at *Fortune*, after interesting MacLeish in the photographer's work.[93] No job materialized. So Evans continued to develop his photography while avoiding work in such "bastard trades" as advertising and public relations as much as possible. He survived on various commissioned works, including a couple of assignments for *Fortune* in 1934. It was through one of these that he probably first met James Agee.

Lincoln Kirstein once described the relationship between Agee and Evans, writing, "Walker Evans' eye is a poet's eye. It finds corroboration in a poet's voice."[94] Agee and Evans discovered similar intellectual interests, disguised by vastly different temperaments. Both tried to look clearly and steadily at the world, interested in using their art to reveal the naked truth. Both distrusted politics and resented the attempts by others to claim their work for political purposes. They were both protest artists of a sort, criticizing the world as it was (especially those with power) but ultimately committed to protecting their work from the influence of outsiders. Paradoxically, both spent much of their careers working for others, and were able to use this dependence to fuel some of their finest work. Both were fascinated by the inscrutability of individuals, insisting that people could not be reduced to sociological generalizations or journalistic stereotypes. Finally, both were drawn to anonymous and found art. Evans spent his life collecting picture postcards. Agee once proposed to publish collections of found letters as art. Their conversation and collaboration deepened the work of both. Agee was one of the proximate influences that helped Evans create his most important work.

The second was the Resettlement Administration. Established in 1935 as a division of the Department of Agriculture, and headed by Rexford Tugwell, the RA's mission included documenting both rural poverty and the effects of New Deal programs in alleviating suffering. Evans was hired in June 1935. His first assignment was photographing the coal mining towns and farm communities of West Virginia. But before he accepted, he made it clear that there would be limits to his participation in a government program. In a handwritten memo, he wrote, "Mean never [to] make photographic statements for the government or do photographic chores for anyone in gov . . . this is pure record not propaganda . . . NO POLITICS whatever."[95]

Thus began the most productive and fruitful year of his life, the period between the summers of 1935 and 1936. Despite distrusting his RA (later renamed the Farm Security Administration) supervisor Roy Stryker as a sentimental and romantic man with little pure taste, Evans worked in a frenzy of excitement, producing many of the pictures for which he became famous. Despite being constantly hounded by Stryker to report in regularly, photograph specific scenes, and be more cognizant of the political pressures the FSA faced, Evans followed his own instincts and interests. He enjoyed what James Mellow calls a "subsidized freedom," managing to further his own interests while supplying some of the archive's most important and striking photographs, and influencing the approach of the entire department. As he would later at *Fortune*, "Evans made a point of working against the grain of the agency and its political intentions."[96]

In the summer of 1936 he was asked by Agee to join in the *Fortune* assignment to document the lives of southern tenant farmers. Evans received a leave from the FSA to undertake the trip. Again he faced the pressure of working for an organization, this time a magazine. Additionally, Evans and Agee felt pressure from their leftist friends to make their work matter politically. Both resisted, Evans reflecting that, "the problem is one of staying out of left politics and still avoiding Establishment patterns. I would not politicize my mind or work . . . The apostles can't have me. I don't think an artist is directly able to alleviate the human condition. He's very interested in revealing it."[97] Or, in Agee's words, describing Evans's pictures, the artist tried to reveal "the cruel radiance of what is."[98] What he successfully revealed appeared (eventually) in *Let Us Now Praise Famous Men*.

Despite *Fortune*'s refusal to use their material and Agee's struggles to finish his manuscript (it would not finally be published until 1941), Evans and Agee continued to work together. In 1937 they proposed to Time Inc. that they be collectively named editorial advisors to *Life*, with the intention of creating a new kind of visual journalism. Nothing came of their proposal, but both continued to search for creative possibilities within Time Inc.[99]

Evans's successful year led directly to his 1938 exhibition at the Museum of Modern Art, the first one-man show for a photographer in the museum's brief history. In the introductory essay to *American Photographs*, the book that accompanied the MoMA show, Lincoln Kirstein provided an insightful analysis of Evans's intentions and accomplishments. Noting that Evans was "an artist of the unrelieved, bare-faced, revelatory fact," he praised the photographer for the "rigorous directness" of his vision. "Even the inanimate things, bureau drawers, pots, tires, bricks, signs," Kirstein observed, "seem waiting in their own patient dignity, posing for their picture." "Looked at in sequence they are overwhelming in their exhaustiveness of detail, their poetry of contrast, and, for those who wish to see it, their moral implication."[100]

The MoMA show and *American Photographs* marked the high-water mark for critical acclaim for Evans's work. Following these triumphs, he made plans for future projects, organized his collections and prints, and conducted experiments. One included taking pictures of subway riders from a camera hidden in his coat, pictures that were much appreciated when they appeared in 1961. Continually pressed for money, in 1943 he managed to get a job writing for *Time*'s back-of-the-book, through the efforts of Wilder Hobson.

Despite his success as a photographer, the urge to write had never gone away. A job as a writer, even for *Time*, was worth taking.

Evans joined *Time*'s staff during the height of Matthews's influence on the cultural departments. Matthews had recently been promoted to managing editor, but he left the back-of-the-book in the hands of Whittaker Chambers, Wilder Hobson, James Agee, Louis Kronenberger, and Winthrop Sargeant. These were the writers Evans joined. He split the movie column with Agee, before expanding into book reviews and the occasional column for other departments. Eventually he settled in the art department, giving him a chance to treat subject matters close to his heart. The platform it offered was small, of course, but Evans valued the clarity and brevity it forced upon him, and took advantage of the opportunity to air his opinions. Reviewing a book of photographs documenting the bombing of London, Evans concluded, "Ruin sometimes adds beauty as well as pathos."[101]

Evans moved from *Time* to *Fortune* as staff photographer in 1945, a position he continued to hold for twenty years. The photographs he took for the magazine mark the largest single body of work of his career. With the exception of a handful of portraits of corporate executives, his *Fortune* work continued to mine the richest veins of his artistic conscience. His portfolios met his own standard for what he labeled lyric documentary: "the real thing that I'm talking about has purity and a certain severity, rigor, simplicity, directness, clarity, and it is without artistic pretension in a self-conscious sense of the word."[102] In the pages of *Fortune* he further refined his studies of architectural vernacular, continued his experiments in capturing human individuality unawares, and pushed further his examination of industrial aging and decay. Viewed in the pages of the business magazine, Evans altered the visual context of *Fortune* in dramatic ways. Always convinced that text and picture should exert equal demands on the viewer's attention, his portfolios presented a compelling counter-narrative to *Fortune*'s celebration of industry. For twenty years Evans used *Fortune* as his platform, in furtherance of his own artistic interests, and in constant querulous dialogue with America's industrial civilization.

More than twenty-five years ago, Lesley Baier complained that Evans's *Fortune* work had been neglected by critics. The situation has not improved greatly since.[103] Partially this is due to the centrality of his work to the iconography of the 1930s. For many, the pictures in *American Photographs* (1938) and *Let Us Now Praise Famous Men* (1941) remain the images that define what Depression era America looked like.[104] Evans's persistent aesthetic interest in American vernacular architecture, and his desire to consistently contrast simplicity with frippery, is more easily reconcilable with the 1930s than the 1950s. The work Evans produced between 1945 and 1965 looked more like his pictures of the 1930s than it looked like popular understandings of the postwar era. The obvious connections with his earlier work, made more jarring by its incongruity in the triumphalist 1950s, made it easier to assume Evans failed to develop artistically.

The difficulty in viewing the *Fortune* work compounds the problem. Rarely are portfolios of Evans's *Fortune* work included in larger exhibits (the massive show at the Metropolitan Museum of Art in 2000, for instance, included images from just two of his portfolios). The difficult-to-find Baier book, *Walker Evans at Fortune*, contains a small fraction of his work, and abstracts the pictures he took from the layouts he created for them. For many of his pictures no print exists, and the negatives have deteriorated too much to make new prints. As Baier concludes, "the best record of much of Evans' *Fortune* work is, therefore, in the pages of *Fortune* itself."[105] This situation makes it difficult to give his work the attention it demands.

One further factor has contributed to the neglect of this work. As the years passed, Evans's attitude toward his work at *Fortune* changed. Frustrated by the lack of attention his pictures received, and influenced by the hardening hostility to mass culture, he lost confidence in the importance of the work he produced. His own distancing of himself from his photography has made it easier for critics to accept his judgment. Biographical works on Evans repeatedly cite his professions of hostility toward business from the 1930s and his retrospective belittling of his work from the 1960s and 1970s, but rarely focus on the contemporary evidence suggesting the seriousness with which he took his *Fortune* photography. James Mellow's formulation is typical: "At the end of World War II, then, having elected to put his talents to work as a photographer in the service of American journalism, Evans made a choice that had consequences he may or may not have thought through."[106] But Mellow's own work demonstrates that Evans's photography never really served anyone's interests but his own.

After a few perfunctory assignments in 1945, Evans began to assert himself in the magazine in 1946. In what was otherwise a typical corporation story on the "Collins Co. Collins Conn.," Evans's photography departed from *Fortune* conventions. Rather than an imposing shot of the factory, a *Fortune* staple, he featured "an architectural detail" of the plant, a decidedly unindustrial red-planked shack, shot straight on, amid small piles of rocks and rusting scrap metal. He also executed a perfectly proportioned shot of the firm's offices situated in the town, set among passing train cars, parked automobiles, shops, and the street. In addition, the article contained a series of shots of isolated edge tools, prefiguring Evans's later study of hand tools. Though still a conventional *Fortune* article (what was more conventional than the corporation story), the pictures hinted at his intention to look at industry through his own eyes.[107]

Further photographs made the same point. An article on Kaiser-Frazer included a large picture of the factory floor. Such a shot was almost de rigueur in *Fortune*, either in the artfully stylized vision of Bourke-White, emphasizing found patterns among the machinery and the grandeur of the operation, or in later conventional pictures dissecting the machinery's operations. Evans's photograph, however, foregrounded a huge expanse of factory floor, empty except for small piles of electric motors, conveyor chains, and mechanical odds and ends.[108] Evans further declared his determination to look away from the action in a series of pictures of the New York Yankees Baseball team. An article subtitled "The Player's the Thing" included no pictures of the games. Instead he caught fans in small, perfectly framed clumps, ballplayers sitting isolated in the dugouts, and two large pictures featuring the row of billboards looming over the stands.[109]

By summer, his work had impressed managing editor Ralph Del Paine. Evans pushed for more autonomy, and Paine agreed. No longer assigned stories, he spent the summer traveling to the Midwest, as Time Inc.'s in-house publication *FYI* described it, on "a felicitous mission . . . to follow, on behalf of *Fortune*, where his sharp eye led him."[110] The trip yielded two important portfolios, both exploring signature Evans themes. The first, titled "Labor Anonymous," was a series of eleven shots of workers walking along a street in Detroit, shot against a blank background wall. The series built on Evans's series of subway rider pictures, close-up shots of people involved in their own thoughts, unaware of the camera. This time the subjects were in motion, but again the effect was to stress inscrutable human individuality. Positioned against the title "Labor Anonymous," the photographs forcefully proclaim the inadequacy of reducing individuals to a collective term (especially one so easily used and seldom interrogated as "labor"). The pictures built on the work Evans did with Agee, stressing each person's autonomy and mystery, his or her essential dignity and possible defiance. Evans's point was made explicit in the accompanying text, describing the subjects as "decidedly various" men who "appear to have preserved a sense of themselves as individuals. When editorialists lump them as 'labor,' these laborers can no doubt laugh them off."[111] Ten years before, *Fortune* had refused to publish Agee and Evans's insistence on the insufficiency of reducing human individuals to journalistic or sociological cliché. In 1946, Evans at last made their point.

Evans's second effort produced a tour de force, a major portfolio of images in which Evans, describing himself as "a leisured and untethered eye," explored midcentury Chicago. Beginning with a Michigan Avenue office building ("the skin-deep, perforated screen of the city," in his caption), Evans set the pattern for the portfolio by following it with a half-wrecked brownstone. Juxtaposition was his strategy, whether in individual pictures or through the layout of contrasting images. Two pictures contained a built in contrast. The first focused on statuary from the 1933 Century of Progress International Exhibition, sitting abandoned in a weed-strewn field. (In the accompanying text, Evans described "huddles of serio-comic sculpture that seems to have spent thirteen embarrassing years imploring someone to hack them to pieces.") The second picture featured a huge Pabst Blue-Ribbon Beer billboard dwarfing a series of Greek pillars. Evans also placed a shot of a theater crowd in the streets above a picture of a shoeshine booth and peanut vendor cart sitting in an empty alley. And he closed the portfolio with a close-up of a statue of a bare-chested rider pointing skyward. Due to his placement the straining rider pointed to a Dad's Root Beer billboard in the picture above.[112]

Evans had frequently utilized this sort of juxtaposition to striking effect. In an earlier *Fortune* series on American houses, he had set a shaker doorway immediately above a heavily decorated Victorian doorway in Mrs. Cornelius Vanderbilt's home.[113] In a famous picture from the 1930s, he had composed a beautiful shot of Phillipsburg, New Jersey, including the bridge across the river, a Pennsylvania Railroad warehouse, and a hillside containing houses. As Evans described it, "Look at the quite handsome, charming building down front. While to the left is a ridiculous house with a crenellated castle on it. The first is honest, the second is not honest; both are American."[114] In his Chicago portfolio Evans contrasted the boosterism so integral to Chicago's past (with the Century of Progress as an updated version of the ersatz White City) to the very American tendency to abandon past concerns completely. The boosterism of hollow culture dwarfed by the hucksterism of advertising gigantism. Both were essentially American.

There are some striking photographs in the Chicago series, some of which have been widely reproduced. Unfortunately, the cumulative effect of the portfolio can be felt only by viewing it in its entirety. Throughout his career, Evans fastidiously controlled how his pictures would be exhibited. He insisted on keeping photographs free of captions and identifying text. He hung his major museum installations himself, and he undertook the layout of *American Photographs*. The *Fortune* portfolios demonstrated the same attention to detail, where the final effect was greater than any single photograph.

The Chicago series prompted Evans's second major museum retrospective at the Art Institute of Chicago in 1947. It contained approximately seventy-five prints, as many as a third of which were from his Time Inc. work. The installation also earned him a major article in *Time*, titled "Puritan Explorer." The piece praised "the quiet clarity of each print [which] gave their commonplace subject matter the impact and beauty of things seen for the first time."[115]

The reaction to his portfolios pleased Evans enough that he sought to expand his responsibilities at *Fortune*. In the summer of 1948, in preparation for the magazine's makeover, he penned a long memo to Paine, criticizing *Fortune*'s "visual mind." He began by acknowledging the early success of the "*Fortune* style" (he clearly had Bourke-White in mind). Though Evans argued this "romanticization" had prevented the magazine from really looking at industry, he agreed it had gained the reader's attention. Unfortunately, it had now become "a weak and expected *Fortune* style which when used over and over slackens your reader's minds." Evans advocated applying the same high standards employed for the magazine's writing to its visual presentation. The magazine should dispense with the idea that it had to run certain pictures for each story (especially head shots of executives), and instead print only pictures that "take a long look at a subject, get into it, and without shouting, tell a lot about it." Countering the magazine's past insistence on size and grandeur, Evans called for pictures that were "quiet and true." He concluded, "Taste, let us admit, is a rather arrogant thing. If you have it, you have to use it rather arrogantly. But your arrogance may be so quiet and assured as to be unnoticeable: then, strange to say, people like it and fall in with you."[116] Evans hoped to guide the visual presentation of the magazine, shifting it toward his own direct, uncompromising aesthetic.

Paine approved. He wrote a memo to the staff naming Evans special photographic editor, noting "the real assignment is to develop a distinctive photography for the new *Fortune*." The new position meant Evans could now assign and direct photographers, choose pictures, and compose layouts for as many stories as he saw fit. He could also write his own copy for the portfolios he put together, increasing the control he had over the presentation of his own material. Most important, the managing editor would protect his independence. "I bespeak the complete cooperation of both editorial and art department staffs," Paine concluded, "in the important creative task that Walker has undertaken."[117] Twelve years after Evans's and Agee's failed attempt to guide the visual production of *Life*, Evans achieved their goal for *Fortune*.

For a while, he took the job quite seriously. He sought out photographs that were "literate, authoritative, and transcendent."[118] He hired photographers he admired, including Robert Frank, Tod Webb, and Ralph Steiner (who took over the monthly corporate executive portrait, known around the office as "super face").[119] He conceived ideas for portfolios (his own and others), though not all of these made it into the magazine. They were all, however, very much in line with his long-standing interests. Among those that never appeared (though the photography was completed for some), were outdoor signs, unhappy motoring, the awkward age of advertising, business Americana, and "street furniture" (a term referring to fire hydrants, mailboxes, streetlights, park benches and manhole covers).[120]

He also presented a portfolio drawn from his collection of postcards. Evans was an ardent fan of old postcards, appreciating their straightforward look at the urban landscape, their depiction of a slice of the American past, and, in their melding of picture with brief text, their window into the personal lives of the senders. He reproduced eighteen color cards, noting "on their tinted surfaces were some of the truest visual records ever made of any period." He provided a brief chronicle of the industry, observing how current productions had lost "all feeling for actual appearance of street, of lived architecture, or of human mien." He analyzed some of the examples, highlighting architectural details, and deciphering a scene between lovers in a wood: "How, with his masculine logic, did that pitiable male come up against the maddening cross-purposes met beneath that intractable sailor straw?"[121] To Evans, the picture postcards conveyed an authentic angle into a previous world, precisely because they were unselfconscious representations of that world.

Evans's enthusiasm for his new job waned as he found it keeping him from taking the pictures he wanted to take. He had a certain level of commitment to the magazine, but his own agenda took priority. As Belinda Rathbone notes, "*Fortune* gave Evans a platform from which to express his values and exercise his eye, and the freedom to travel where his instincts bade him go."[122] He was most successful in using the magazine to pursue his own photographic interests.

In a 1934 letter, Evans had listed some of the topics on which he hoped to focus his camera. He included:

> people, all classes, surrounded by the new down-and-out, automobiles and the automobile landscape, architecture, American urban taste, commerce, small scale, large scale, the city street atmosphere, the street smell, the hateful stuff, women's clubs, fake culture, bad education, religion in decay. The movies. Evidence of what people of the city read, eat, see for amusement, do for relaxation and not get it. Sex. Advertising.[123]

The list was an amazingly consistent chronicle of the subjects that drove his work. With few exceptions, these were precisely the themes he pursued in *Fortune*.

They were not, however, themes likely to have been chosen for an American business magazine by anyone else. "The more out of step with postwar America a subject was," Belinda Rathbone concludes, "the more Evans treasured it."[124] The postwar was a period of tempered steel, glass, and chemicals; Evans produced photographic essays on clay, fieldstones, and masonry.[125] The postwar period brought the explosion of suburban housing and shopping malls; Evans photographed sidewalk markets piled high with cheap goods and repeatedly sought out the neglected corners of the urban environment.[126] The 1950s were the age of the automobile and the superhighway; Evans ran four portfolios centered on railroads. His only work on automobiles was a collection of pictures of auto graveyards, featuring piles of rusting cars. The economic boom of the 1950s was driven by America's highly skilled and productive heavy industry; Evans produced a spectacular series of pictures of simple hand tools. Giving a full page to each tool, including a bricklayer's trowel, a crate opener, tin snips, pliers, and a crescent wrench, he wrote, "all the basic small tools stand, aesthetically speaking, for elegance, candor, and purity."[127] Those three words might stand for half of Evans's divided aesthetic. For a photographer who had, in Jed Perl's opinion, "a sense of proportion as fine as any American artist has ever had," the simple purity of hand tools perfectly embodied his insistence on simple, direct truths.[128]

Set against this was Evans's persistent appreciation for vulgarity. In 1949 he produced a portfolio of the enormous resort hotels of New Hampshire and

Maine, reveling in their architectural immodesty. His description captured some of the amusement he found and his pictures conveyed: "Catch one of these gay land arks in the late-day sunlight, under a fleeced sky: this is the nation's uttermost dream of secular grandeur, this clapboard castle, turreted, porticoed, balustraded, oriflammed."[129] His pleasure was not condescension. He enjoyed the inauthentic hollow grandiosity that suggested American insecurity as much as the simple modesty and presumed authenticity of a pair of pliers.

But the theme that dominated Evans's work for *Fortune*, that tied it together and gave it coherent meaning, was decay. Almost a third of his close to forty portfolios dealt with the altering of American physical spaces, through gradual decline or active destruction. Railroads were an obvious choice, and he subjected them to four separate treatments. First he shot pictures from a moving train, catching the country in "semi-undress." The landscapes covered typical Evans ground: empty factories on a Sunday morning, freight cars, isolated farm buildings, and run-down shacks festooned with large advertising posters.[130] In 1953 he published a series on small-town railroad depots, writing, "they are a chapter called the economic consequences of the automobile." Seeking to capture their attraction, he wrote, "A well-sooted depot today is what railroad stations have always been—focus and embodiment of heartbreak; citadel of boredom; and withal, portal of renewal."[131] There would be no renewal for railroads, however, and in 1957 and 1958 he ran two portfolios documenting the decline of painted freight cars and the eclipse of the steam engine. Charting the tendency to redesign the deeply familiar logos of venerable railroad lines, he concluded, "impiety could go no further."[132]

In addition to railroads, Evans focused on the New York City waterfront. There he photographed quiet stone streets and brick warehouses in early evening light. This was his most self-conscious attempt to make obsolescence and decay beautiful. His text nodded to his intent: "Late day sunlight repaints the most prosaic buildings in the town with unearned beauty, dressing up all plain things beyond their station." The pictures, however, owed their stark beauty less to the light than to the eye and temperament of their photographer. This portfolio contains two of his best *Fortune* photographs, both working familiar themes. The first, "North from Brooklyn Bridge," was shot along trolley tracks heading for the bridge in the background (it was in keeping with his fascination with reflection that the title worked from the perspective of the bridge, not from the viewer's stance). Running along the left side was a solid wall of brick warehouses in the fading light. The intersecting train lines, bridge cables, and wall shadows combined to produce an emotional effect quite at odds with the seemingly mundane material. The same could be said for a straight-on shot of a single warehouse, faded brick broken up by arched windows, the glass long ago replaced with now rusting metal. Still visible was the faded word "Coffee," once painted on the side of the building.[133]

Evans's evocation of the past—and especially the place of the past in the present—effaced, discredited, abandoned, hidden, but still there for the careful eye to discover—ran through his other portfolios as well. He produced a series on vintage office furniture, not yet colonized by contemporary designers ("the most triumphant group of professionals operating in the land today").[134] He depicted New York's financial district, as the buildings that had dominated it for thirty years were knocked down.[135] And he highlighted the surprising pleasure to be found in destruction. An early portfolio, "The Wreckers" documented the "complex spell of destruction caught mid act," as old buildings and homes met the wrecking ball. "Destruction answers a deep human need," claimed Evans, but one that must be met quickly, because of the frenetic pace of destruction in America.[136] He returned to the theme in "The Auto Junkyard," where it was possible to see the beauty of rusting, crushed machinery and enjoy "the fall of man from his high ride."[137]

Evans recognized that his work ran the risk of being misinterpreted as nostalgia. In the text for another collection of postcards, this time depicting the old urban downtowns, he explicitly renounced sentimentality and nostalgia. Instead he intended to document the "extraordinarily unbeautiful buildings" of the past, to take an honest look at the world as it had been, and as it was now represented to us.[138] Evans never confused honesty—his goal—with nostalgia—his anathema. "I hate that word," he later complained, "that's not the intent at all. To be nostalgic is to be sentimental. To be interested in what you see that is passing out of history, even if it's a trolley car you've found, that's not an act of nostalgia. You could read Proust as 'nostalgia' but that's not what Proust had in mind at all." The invocation of Proust was self-conscious. Evans reread *In Search of Lost Time* endlessly, and the effects he sought were heavily indebted to Proust.[139] The distinction might be suggested by considering what a romantic portfolio of antique office furniture might have looked like and compare it with his stark depiction of the corner of a Cincinnati office. Evans's picture focused on an old wooden desk and file cabinet, set against a dark wall, discolored with age. The overall effect was one of dust and distance, a terse evocation of a business culture far different from the streamlined, efficient modernism of the contemporary office. The picture juxtaposed the functional simplicity of earlier design with the chaos of an unorganized, unmanageable world.[140]

Stress on Evans's achievements in *Fortune* risks presenting a one-sided view of his work. The quality of his work during the *Fortune* years varied considerably. His use of color photography was not always successful, especially in the early years, when he struggled with the proper tinting. He later labeled color photography as inescapably vulgar, but that may not have been the insult critics perceived.[141] As he aged, he grew fascinated with the accouterments of wealth. The resulting photo essays on Rolls Royce, summer resorts, and golf were less able than the rest of his work. Finally, people lost their centrality to his work. His best work set the studies of the structures that housed people, usually presented without people, against representations of the people themselves.[142] Evans found less and less room for people in his work as time went on, throwing it off balance. Worse, when he did return to people as the focus, in a 1961 photoessay called "People and Places in Trouble," his work had lost its moral rigor. Most of the pictures presented the unemployed subjects as brutalized victims. His dramatization of "sheer personal distress," complete with captions calculated to wring emotion out of the reader, and a culminating image of a judging child's eyes, seemed disturbingly similar to the documentary style he deplored in the 1930s. For the first time in his career, Evans used the suffering of individuals to evoke pity, rather than to connect people's surroundings and circumstances inextricably with their humanity.[143]

By the mid1960s, Evans's involvement with the magazine was minimal. He would meet with the editor once a year, pitch a couple of portfolio ideas, then disappear. The magazine found it difficult to justify his salary, and the friends that had made the place human to Evans were mostly gone. Interest in his work was reviving, however, and when Yale offered him a faculty position in 1965, he left Time Inc. for good.

Walker Evans's twenty-year career at *Fortune* emphasized the strengths and weaknesses of work as an interstitial intellectual. Scholarship on him demonstrates the critical stigma such work too often carried. Evans managed to support himself economically and technically (a writer may only need paper, pen, and books, but a photographer needed equipment). He influenced the visual presentation of America's major business magazine. Most important, he found himself in creative argument with *Fortune*'s vision of America. Evans always worked best when he worked in collaboration with friends (especially poets like Crane and Agee) or against an organization. The best work of his career came when he was encouraged and stimulated by Agee while resisting the bureaucratic strictures of Roy Stryker and the Resettlement Administration. His work for *Fortune* lacked the guiding presence of an Agee or a Kirstein. Nevertheless, he found his rejection of *Fortune*'s American triumphalism, and the necessity to articulate an alternative aesthetic stance, to be artistically fruitful. Some of his portfolios for *Fortune*, including the essays on Chicago, hand tools, the New York waterfront, and the auto junkyard, rank just below the pinnacle he reached in 1935–36.

This view runs counter to most of the existing Evans criticism. Scholars blame *Fortune* for making Evans lazy and complacent. Belinda Rathbone notes that Evans had done little photography between his stints with the FSA and *Fortune*. Rather than concluding that Evans needed an employing organization against which he could define himself, she claims, "he had lost track of the pulse of his talent; the driving force had deserted him under the pressure of making a living and the surrender of unrealized ideas."[144] Such an assessment accepts too readily the assumption that making a living is selling out, that employment by an organization is inherently fatal to art. Evans found friends at *Fortune*, but he also discovered "a certain Satanic naiveté in the top editorial directions of Time Incorporated."[145] His position there allowed him to pursue his own deepest interests, goaded on by their absence from American culture, especially as embodied by *Fortune*'s business liberalism. Counterpoised against *Fortune*'s optimistic embrace of managerial efficiency, Evans presented the past as a constant presence, a pressing reminder of human impermanence and limitation. "His photography shows all the urgency of cultural and political witness," conclude Gilles Mora and John T. Hill, writing of this period, "rather than celebrating the inwardness of an America turning back to its traditions." Religious language might have come more easily to Agee than Evans, and seemed more apt, but in his *Fortune* portfolios, "in the face of the uncontrolled movement that was sweeping away the America he had loved, all Evans could do was to resist it by an act of faith."[146]

Describing his photography, Evans once claimed that his pictures were "a semi-conscious reaction against right-thinking and optimism."[147] The 1950s were a decade of such right thinking and optimism, terms that capture much of what Godfrey Hodgson describes as the ideology of liberal consensus. Time Inc., lead by Henry Luce, publishers of the most popular magazine in America (*Life*), the most widely read news source in the country (*Time*), and the most influential journalistic voice of American business (*Fortune*), were chief purveyors of this optimism. Luce's organization sought to include intellectuals in its embrace, but wanted them to be optimistic. They looked for the intellectual as "Man of Affirmation," not "Man of Protest."[148] Or, as Henry Luce once posed it to Edward Albee, why were all the major playwrights so negative? Why not write a musical comedy about Studebaker industrialist and Marshall Plan administrator Paul Hoffman?[149] Walker Evans's father once posed a similar question to him: "Why do you want to look at these scenes, they're depressing. Why don't you look at the nice things in life?"[150] The 1950s might be thought of as a decade long attempt to look at the nice things in life. This is a big part of why it has itself become the object of a nostalgia that would sicken Walker Evans.

In the center of right-thinking liberal optimism, Walker Evans focused his camera on images of decay and destruction. His photographs were an attack on optimism, and as such they were a quiet repudiation of Henry Luce's "American century." Together with William H. Whyte and Daniel Bell, Walker Evans challenged the liberal consensus on its home turf. The repudiation of the consensus in the 1960s owed something to Whyte's warnings against the threat to individual freedom posed by the corporation (the old boss merely wanted your sweat, Whyte claimed, "the new man wants your soul")[151] and his call for resistance. The new left's attack on liberalism substituted active political involvement for intellectual autonomy, but it suffered from its unwillingness to adhere to Bell's stance of simultaneous engagement and alienation. It too often chose certainty over doubt. Whyte's insistence on struggling against the impingement of managerial values remains pertinent in a time when economic logic so often trumps political or civic concerns. Bell's articulation of creative alienation as a viable intellectual position has much to offer in a society where intellectuals so often end up self-segregated behind academic walls. Walker Evans posed the most difficult questions, however, both for the readers of *Fortune* and for readers today. The most penetrating critics of capitalist society have often looked to the past more than to the future. Walker Evans looked directly and clearly at the presence of the past in the present. He looked against the American grain, without much hope of altering things, yet with the certainty of purpose that accompanies an act of faith. Sometimes looking honestly is all that we can ask of an artist.

EPILOGUE

Intellectuals in Their American Century and in Ours

William H. Whyte, Daniel Bell, and Walker Evans were the last major intellectuals to spend significant time on the staff of a Time Inc. magazine. Intellectuals wanting to write regularly for *Time*, *Fortune*, or *Life* faced growing obstacles in the late 1950s. The magazines were increasingly governed by what the official Time Inc. history approvingly called "a highly professional and businesslike administration."[1] The managerial culture at Time Inc. left little room and less desire for the amateur experimentalism cultivated and valued in the past.

By the late 1950s *Life* magazine was facing stagnating circulation and a significant threat from competitor *Look*. The more plebeian *Look* began to turn its down-market status to advantage, coloring *Life* as "standing above and apart from man." In a promotional campaign, *Look* characterized *Life* as "the lofty pundit, superior, condescending, jesting, ponderous with moral instruction for the lesser masses." *Look*'s message worried Luce, who recognized both its plausibility and its likely appeal. He emphasized the need to focus on "the simple, striking, wonderful human things," rather than pursue more ambitious avenues. Luce advised a return to basics, which meant a reemphasis of "picture-magic" instead of more intellectually challenging content.[2]

Rather than a return to earlier formulas, *Fortune* went in the opposite direction. Also facing more formidable competition, it gradually shed the features that had made it so original. In 1959 its leadership fell to Duncan Norton-Taylor, a self-professed proud Taft Republican whom Luce once called "one of the most professional pros in our business."[3] Pruned of its literary experimentation and its political iconoclasm, by the mid-1960s *Fortune* was well on its way to being virtually indistinguishable from other business magazines.

During the same period *Time* faced increasing criticism. Impertinent and mischievous in the Hadden years, sober and serious during the Matthews years, *Time* had since become arrogant and dogmatic. This was the conclusion of a 1958 internal report on *Time*'s correspondence from readers. James Linen, who ran the study, pointed to the large numbers of readers who resented the implication that they were "soft in the head or inclined towards Communism," if they viewed international events in a different light than *Time*. [4] External criticism also escalated, fueled by an expose of *Time*'s methods by a former stringer for the magazine, Ben Bagdikian. Summarizing the magazine, Bagdikian concluded, "each week the world is created absolute and dogmatic, the good guys on one side, the bad guys on the other, with *Time* holding the only scorecard."[5] A survey of *Time*'s university readers found the same complaints concerning the magazine's slanting of news to fit preconceived views. In response, internal memos exhibited a defensive insistence that its critics were "intellectuals," or "eggheads" whom *Time* was unlikely to ever please.[6] The banishment of the "men with pipes" had been so successful that they now existed only as enemies outside the walls of Time Inc. Though worried about *Time*'s reputation, the designation of their critics as intellectuals absolved the editors of the need to change the magazine.

A more professional, conservative, and static organization combined with growing competition meant room for experimentation was drastically curtailed. Even with a more welcoming climate for intellectuals at Time Inc., however, it is unlikely many would have appeared on the masthead of Luce's magazines. By the end of the 1950s there was general agreement in intellectual circles that the mass-circulation magazines were inimical to serious writers. Taking a freelance assignment on occasion was acceptable, but, in general, intellectuals were better off keeping their distance. Arthur Schlesinger, Jr., published an article in 1956 making clear that Time Inc. had no interest in critical writers, and intellectuals no longer had any interest in working for Time Inc.[7] Schlesinger treated the problem as essentially one of attitude. The editors of Time Inc., presumably following the lead of Luce himself, were uninterested in entertaining the criticisms intellectuals were likely to pursue. Radical intellectuals such as C. Wright Mills, on the other hand, traced the problem to its roots in the structure of the capitalist economy. Mills argued, "between the intellectual and his potential public stand technical, economic, and social structures which are owned and operated by others."[8] This passage accurately suggested how Mills perceived the problem: independent intellectuals had to find ways to circumvent the structures that stood between them and the public. William H. Whyte might insist that much of the public Mills and others sought was embedded in these technical, economic, and social structures, and that people retained the capacity to act independently from such locations. For Mills and others, however, such freedom as remained existed only outside such controlling institutions.[9] With such a pessimistic view taking hold, the hopes driving intellectuals at Time Inc. since the thirties, that they could speak through mass-circulation magazines, that as intellectuals they had an important voice in the cultural life of the nation, was abandoned.

Intellectuals still needed a perch from which to engage the public, however, and for many the university became this location. "By the early fifties," Irving Howe remembered, "word began to reach New York that it might be possible to find a job... teaching in a university."[10] Howe took the first of a steady series of academic jobs in 1952. Mills worked as a sociology professor at Columbia. Macdonald accepted a number of temporary university appointments. At roughly the same time the intellectuals of the old left began to find homes in the universities, a new left was forming (with Mills bridging the two). This new generation of radicals, though it based itself on an attack on institutions that frequently began in rebellion against the university, ended with many prominent members retreating to the academy.

Ironically, intellectuals have increasingly found obstacles in the academy similar to those they thought they were escaping. The university is both too separate from the outside world and at the same time becoming too much like the rest of the world. Professionalization and specialization *have* cut academics off from a broader engagement with the public. As Russell Jacoby observed, far too often academic freedom has merely meant the freedom to be academic. Intellectuals need engagement with the broader society, both to link their concerns with the experiences of their audiences and to stimulate their own thinking. Literature, poetry, criticism, and protest are all enriched when tested against Agee's "cruel radiance of what is." Detachment provides a certain necessary perspective, but engagement is equally vital.

The university is also, with the increasing penetration of business values into university management, too much like the rest of the world. Students as consumers, schools marketing themselves as brands, corporate sponsored research encouraging professors to act as entrepreneurs, all these developments have undermined the intellectual autonomy universities were supposed to sustain. The same sort of attitudes interstitial intellectuals at Time Inc. maintained—commitment to the goals of the organization, skepticism of the means of their implementation, hostility toward the forces tending to corrupt the process, and a final commitment to their own ideas instead of the goals of the organization—are now the attitudes necessary for academics committed to reaching outside the university. The interstitial intellectuals of midcentury Time Inc. may have been the precursors for countless interstitial intellectuals in current academic halls.

Recent scholarship on intellectuals in the academy stresses the limits to what intellectual endeavor can achieve.[11] This chastened sense of intellectual possibility, while salutary in some respects, risks downplaying the importance of the things at which intellectuals excel. Ironically, it is of a piece with the typical evaluation of the work of intellectuals who were employed by Time Inc. Shaking their heads at the thought of James Agee writing for *Time*, or the picture of Alfred Kazin trying to argue Henry Luce around to appreciating Emerson's vision of democracy, or the image of Walker Evans spending all those years taking pictures for a business magazine, critics have treated the involvement of intellectuals with Luce's magazines with bemusement, scorn, ridicule, or contempt.

Cultural life is enriched when men and women of talent, with commitments to values arising before and existing beyond their workplace, seek to express these values through their work. This is true of intellectuals, but it also has broader resonance. Life is enriched when people refuse to passively accept the values and assumptions that propel institutions, be they corporate workplaces, university offices, or government agencies. The sell-out charge is leveled at more than intellectuals. It is a charge familiar to many who profess to strive for political or social change yet work in corporate environments. The counterpart to the selling out charge is the familiar rationalization of moral agnosticism: "if I don't do it, someone else will." Acceptance of that rationalization legitimates the evasion of personal responsibility, it sacrifices individual autonomy to corporate values. Both need to be combated by individuals—intellectuals or not—willing to stand up for their views.

When he published *The Last Intellectuals*, Jacoby believed he was calling for the return of Dwight Macdonald. Actually, he was calling for the return of Archibald MacLeish. Or, at least, the MacLeish of "the Irresponsibles" who defined the responsibility of the intellectual in the broadest of strokes. MacLeish believed in the power of ideas and in the responsibility of the people who wielded those ideas to take their ideas into the corridors of power. MacLeish's conception of the role of the public intellectual is broader and more compelling than Jacoby's. Jacoby views the intellectual as central to the culture but an outsider when it comes to power. The world of political and economic power is to be observed, considered, and judged. For MacLeish, the engagement of the intellectual needs to be more direct. The values of the intellectual need to penetrate to the heart of political and economic power.

Seeking to raise awareness for the Spanish Republican cause in 1937, Archibald MacLeish found himself delivering an address promoting the film *The Spanish Earth* before an audience of Communists who sought to adopt him as their own. MacLeish knew his association with this group, the League of American Writers, would be used to paint him as a communist sympathizer, as it was. Resisting this, he argued from the stage, "the man who refuses to defend his convictions for fear that he may defend them in the wrong company, has no convictions."[12] Intellectuals at Time Inc. lived MacLeish's insistence, as do intellectuals and others today when they refuse to subordinate their values to the political, educational, or corporate institutions, the "technical, economic, and social structures which are owned and operated by others," that structure but do not determine our lives.

Richard Hofstadter once offered a definition of the intellectual that now seems refreshingly old fashioned. "The whole business of the intellectual is to enter," he argued, as completely as possible "within the limits of things human, into the disinterested pursuit of truth."[13] In ways that are real even though they are immeasurable, Archibald MacLeish, Dwight Macdonald, James Agee, John Hersey, Walker Evans, and William H. Whyte pursued truth, humanized and deepened journalism, and placed their efforts in service of a worthy goal. They sought to deepen the experience, to challenge the expectations, and to upset the assumptions of their audience. Their efforts enriched the lives of their readers. It also deepened their art and their thinking.

The world has changed since the 1950s. The locations intellectuals created for themselves at Time Inc. cannot be recreated. Yet the values that drove their work—an insistence on engaging a wide public, an awareness that we are all enmeshed inside the culture mass circulation magazines speak to (and seek to speak for), a dedication to speaking in their own voice despite the obstacles, a commitment to the goals of journalism united with a stern dissent from their present pursuit—are worth rehabilitating. As John McGowan has recently written of intellectuals, "you do the work you can where you are, without knowing how or if it will make any difference in the short or long run."[14] It is the responsibility of the intellectual to live in the world as it is, while never accepting any iteration of that world as final. That was how interstitial intellectuals at Time Inc. worked, and it remains a model worth emulating.

ARCHIVAL SOURCES AND ABBREVIATIONS

James Agee Papers, Harry Ransom Humanities Research Center, The University of Texas at Austin (JA Collection)
Robert Cantwell Papers, Special Collections, University of Oregon (RC Papers)
Columbia University Oral History Research Office Collection (CUOHROC)
Russell W. Davenport Collection, Library of Congress Manuscript Division (RD Collection)
John Hersey Papers, Yale Collection of American Literature, Beinecke Rare Book and Manuscript Library (JH Papers)
Ralph Ingersoll Collection, Howard Gotlieb Archival Research Center, Boston University (RI Collection)
A. J. Liebling Collection, Cornell University Rare and Manuscript Collections (AJL Collection)
Henry R. Luce Collection, Manuscript Division, Library of Congress (HRL Collection)
Dwight Macdonald Papers, Sterling Library, Yale University (DM Collection)
Archibald MacLeish Collection, Manuscript Division, Library of Congress (AM Collection)
W. A. Swanberg Collection, Rare Book and Manuscript Library, Columbia University (WAS Collection)
Theodore H. White Papers, Harvard University Archives (THW Papers)

AJL   A. J. Liebling
AM   Archibald MacLeish
DM   Dwight Macdonald

HRL   Henry R. Luce
JA   James Agee
JH   John Hersey
RC   Robert Cantwell
RD   Russell Davenport
RI   Ralph Ingersoll
THW   Theodore H. White
TSM   T.S. Matthews
WAS   W. A. Swanberg

NOTES

Introduction: Intellectuals in Mass Culture America

1 Kenneth Fearing, *The Big Clock* (New York: Harcourt, Brace, 1946); William Brinkley, *The Fun House* (New York: Random House, 1961); John Brooks, *The Big Wheel* (New York: Harper & Brothers, 1949); Ralph Ingersoll, *The Great Ones: The Love Story of Two Very Important People* (New York: Harcourt, Brace, 1948); Merle Miller, *That Winter* (New York: William Sloane, 1948); Charles Wertenbaker, *The Death of Kings* (New York: Random House, 1954).

2 Fearing, *The Big Clock*, 45, 85, 10, 174.

3 Dwight Macdonald, *Against the American Grain: Essays on the Effects of Mass Culture* (New York: Random House, 1962), 4, 5, 37.

4 This is the argument of Andreas Huyssen, "Mass Culture as a Woman: Modernism's Other," in Huyssen, *After the Great Divide: Modernism, Mass Culture, Postmodernism* (Bloomington: Indiana University Press, 1987), 47.

5 "Our Country and Our Culture," *Partisan Review* 19, 3–5 (1952): 282.

6 Irving Howe, "This Age of Conformity," *Partisan Review* 21, 1 (1954): 13; emphasis in original.

7 This line of criticism overlaps a great deal with the contemporary Frankfurt school. See Max Horkheimer and Theodor W. Adorno, "The Culture Industry: Enlightenment as Mass Deception," in Horkheimer and Adorno, *Dialectic of Enlightenment* (New York: Herder and Herder, 1972). The major proponents of this argument were only vaguely aware of Adorno and Horkheimer. Instead, the confluence suggests the ubiquity of these sentiments among intellectuals in the 1940s. See Neil Jumonville, *Critical Crossings: The New York Intellectuals in Postwar America* (Berkeley: University of California Press, 1991), 155; Michael Wreszin, *A Rebel in Defense of Tradition: The Life and Politics of Dwight Macdonald* (New York: Basic Books, 1994), 289.

8 Norman Mailer, "Our Country and Our Culture," *Partisan Review* 19, 3 (May–June 1952): 298.

9 Gertrude Himmelfarb, "Anonymity, 'Time,' and Success," *Commentary* (July 1960): 83–86.

10   Dwight Macdonald, "On Selling Out," in Macdonald, *Discriminations: Essays and Afterthoughts, 1938-1974* (New York: Grossman, 1974), 173.

11   Wallace Makefield, "Children of the Fattening '50s: Our Non-Generation Revisited" *New Leader* (18 March 1957): 21-22; Murray Kempton, "Ralph Ginzburg: Panderer," *New York World Telegram* (16 March 1966). Kempton is often left out of accounts of 1950s intellectuals, especially the "New York intellectuals," but he was a major influence on many young writers living in the city. See Dan Wakefield, *New York in the 1950s* (Boston: Houghton Mifflin, 1992), 60-64. For evidence of Time Inc. as stand-in for mass culture, see C. Wright Mills, *White Collar* (London: Oxford University Press, 1951), 149.

12   Steven Biel, *Independent Intellectuals in the United States, 1910-1945* (New York: New York University Press, 1992).

13   Macdonald, *Against the American Grain*, 20.

14   Howe, "This Age of Conformity," 11.

15   Mills, *White Collar*, 142-60.

16   C. Wright Mills, "The Social Role of the Intellectual," in *Power, Politics and People: The Collected Essays of C. Wright Mills*, ed. Irving Louis Horowitz (New York: Oxford University Press, 1963), 299.

17   Huyssen, "Mass Culture as a Woman," 52-53.

18   Macdonald, "On Selling Out," 173.

19   Archibald MacLeish, *Archibald MacLeish: Reflections*, ed. Bernard A. Drabeck and Helen E. Ellis (Amherst: University of Massachusetts Press, 1986), 78-79.

20   Alfred Kazin, *New York Jew* (New York: Knopf, 1978), 59.

21   Mills, *White Collar*, 142.

22   Ibid., 143; emphasis in original.

23   Lewis Coser, *Men of Ideas: A Sociologist's View* (New York: Free Press, 1965), viii. What did Mills and Coser live off, if not ideas?

24   Quoted in Biel, *Independent Intellectuals*, 53.

25   Irving Howe, *A Margin of Hope: An Intellectual Autobiography* (New York: Harcourt Brace, 1982), 126.

26   My approach has been influenced by the work of both Clifford Geertz and Pierre Bourdieu, though, as should become clear, my borrowing from both is eclectic, not systematic. Clifford Geertz, *The Interpretation of Cultures* (New York: Basic Books, 1973); Pierre Bourdieu, *The Field of Cultural Production: Essays on Art and Literature* (New York: Columbia University Press, 1993).

27   Howe, *A Margin of Hope*, 124.

28   MacLeish, *Archibald MacLeish: Reflections*, 78-79. MacLeish began work at *Fortune* in early October 1929.

29   Macdonald, *Against the American Grain*, 13.

30   James L. Baughman, *Henry R. Luce and the Rise of the American News Media* (Boston: Twayne, 1987), 169-71; Robert T. Elson, *The World of Time Inc.: The Intimate History of a Publishing Enterprise, 1941-1960* (New York: Atheneum, 1973), 182-83.

31 Baughman, *Henry R. Luce*, 34.
32 Kazin, *New York Jew*, 55.
33 Howe, *A Margin of Hope*, 125.
34 Daniel Aaron, *Writers on the Left: Episodes in American Literary Communism* (1961; New York: Columbia University Press, 1992); Michael Denning, *The Cultural Front: The Laboring of American Culture in the Twentieth Century* (London: Verso, 1996).
35 Denning, *The Cultural Front*, 389.
36 The term "interstitial intellectual" was inspired by Jackson Lears's description of Sherwood Anderson as having written "in the interstices of a life still dedicated to marketing paint." T. J. Jackson Lears, "Sherwood Anderson, Looking for the White Spot," in *The Power of Culture: Critical Essays in American History*, ed. Richard Wightman Fox and T. J. Jackson Lears (Chicago: University of Chicago Press, 1993).
37 William L. Bird, Jr., *"Better Living": Advertising, Media, and the New Vocabulary of Business Leadership, 1935–1955* (Evanston, Ill.: Northwestern University Press, 1999); Alfred D. Chandler, Jr., *The Visible Hand: The Managerial Revolution in American Business* (Cambridge, Mass.: Harvard University Press, 1977); Richard Wightman Fox and T. J. Jackson Lears, ed., *The Culture of Consumption: Critical Essays in American History 1880–1980* (New York: Pantheon, 1983); William Leach, *Land of Desire: Merchants, Power, and the Rise of a New American Culture* (New York: Random House, 1993); Jackson Lears, *Fables of Abundance: A Cultural History of Advertising in America* (New York: Basic Books, 1994); Roland Marchand, *Advertising the American Dream: Making Way for Modernity, 1920–1940* (Berkeley: University of California Press, 1985); Roland Marchand, *Creating the Corporate Soul: The Rise of Public Relations and Corporate Imagery in American Big Business* (Berkeley: University of California Press, 1998); Richard Ohmann, "Where Did Mass Culture Come From? The Case of Magazines," *Berkshire Review* 16 (1981): 85–101; Martin J. Sklar, *The Corporate Reconstruction of American Capitalism, 1890–1916* (Cambridge: Cambridge University Press, 1988); Warren I. Susman, *Culture as History: The Transformation of American Society in the Twentieth Century* (New York: Pantheon, 1984); Olivier Zunz, *Making America Corporate: 1870–1920* (Chicago: University of Chicago Press, 1990).
38 Michael Augspurger, *An Economy of Abundant Beauty: Fortune Magazine and Depression America* (Ithaca, N.Y.: Cornell University Press, 2004); Terry Smith, *Making the Modern: Industry, Art, and Design in America* (Chicago: University of Chicago Press, 1993).
39 Erika Doss, ed., *Looking at Life Magazine* (Washington, D.C.: Smithsonian Institution Press, 2001).
40 This is a gloss of Augspurger's argument in *Economy of Abundant Beauty*.
41 It should also be noted that this was a highly gendered world. Time Inc. functioned on a rather strict sexual division of labor: men were the editors and writers, women were the researchers. Women rarely broke into print in these years, the major exceptions being photographer Margaret Bourke-White and journalist and novelist

Laura Z. Hobson. See Margaret Bourke-White, *Portrait of Myself* (New York: Simon and Schuster, 1963); Vicki Goldberg, *Margaret Bourke-White: A Biography* (Cambridge, Mass.: Harper and Row, 1986); Laura Z. Hobson, *Laura Z: A Life* (New York: Arbor House, 1983); Laura Z. Hobson, *Laura Z: A Life: Years of Fulfillment* (New York: Donald Fine, 1986).

42   Jean Chalaby's influential recent work on journalism heavily emphasizes the discipline imposed by the market. "Indubitably," he claims, "journalists writing for a popular audience, and any audience for that matter, are highly consumer-conscious and continually adjust this discourse to the demands of the market." Chalaby leans heavily on Habermas's depiction of the public sphere weakening under commercial pressures, but what begins as a salutary introduction of social theory ends in a determinist trap, as the motivations of journalists and their press lords ushered out the front door (as Chalaby seeks to escape the emphasis on personalities that dominates journalism history) are scuttled in the back as simplistic assumptions of intent. Jean K. Chalaby, *The Invention of Journalism* (New York: St. Martin's, 1998), 87 passim; see also Michael Schudson, "News, Public, Nation," *American Historical Review* 107, 2 (April 2002): 481-92.

43   T. S. Matthews, CUOHROC.

44   Laurence Bergreen, *James Agee: A Life* (New York: E.P. Dutton, 1984).

45   Dwight Macdonald, *A Moral Temper: The Letters of Dwight Macdonald*, ed. Michael Wreszin (Chicago: Ivan R. Dee, 2001).

46   In addition to those works discussed in the text, see Raymond Aron, *The Opium of the Intellectuals*, trans. Terence Kilmartin (Garden City, N.Y.: Doubleday, 1957); Loren Baritz, "The Lonely Intellectual," *The Nation* (21 January 1961): 50-52; Loren Baritz, *The Servants of Power: A History of the Use of Social Science in American Industry* (New York: John Wiley, 1960); Jacques Barzun, *The House of Intellect* (New York: Harper & Brothers, 1959); Richard Hofstadter, *Anti-Intellectualism in American Life* (New York: Knopf, 1966); Richard Hofstadter, "A Note on Intellect and Power," *American Scholar* 30, 4 (1961); H. Stuart Hughes, "Is the Intellectual Obsolete?," in *An Approach to Peace and Other Essays* (New York: Atheneum, 1962), 157-75; George B. de Huszar, ed., *The Intellectuals: A Controversial Portrait* (Glencoe, Ill.: Free Press, 1960); Alfred Kazin, "Writing for Magazines," *Commentary* (July 1960): 57-59; Andrew Kopkind, "Serving Time," *New York Review of Books* (12 September 1968): 23-28; Christopher Lasch, *The New Radicalism in America 1889-1963* (New York: Norton, 1965); Seymour Martin Lipset, "American Intellectuals: Their Politics and Status," *Daedalus* 88, 3 (Summer 1959): 460-86; F. O. Matthiessen, *The Responsibilities of the Critic: Essays and Reviews* (New York: Oxford University Press, 1952); Philip Rieff, ed., *On Intellectuals: Theoretical Studies, Case Studies* (Garden City, N.Y.: Doubleday, 1969); Rosenberg, "The Intellectual and His Future," in Rosenberg, *Discovering the Present*; Rosenberg, "Twilight of the Intellectuals," in Rosenberg, *Discovering the Present*; Arthur M. Schlesinger, Jr., "*Time* and the Intellectuals," in Schlesinger, *The Politics of Hope* (Boston: Houghton Mifflin, 1963); Edward Shils, "The Intellectuals and the

Powers: Some Perspectives for Comparative Analysis," *Comparative Studies in Society and History* 1 (1958–1959): 5–22; Garry Wills, "*Time*style," *National Review* (3 August 1957): 129–30.

47 Russell Jacoby, *The Last Intellectuals: American Culture in the Age of Academe* (New York: Basic Books, 1987). James Atlas set the stage for Jacoby with his "The Changing World of New York Intellectuals," *New York Times Magazine* (25 August 1985) 22. In addition to the works discussed in the text, see Morris Dickstein, *Double Agent: The Critic and Society* (New York: Oxford University Press, 1992); Ron Eyerman, *Between Culture and Politics: Intellectuals in Modern Society* (Cambridge: Polity Press, 1994); Leon Fink, *Progressive Intellectuals and the Dilemmas of Democratic Commitment* (Cambridge, Mass.: Harvard University Press, 1997); Jeffrey C. Goldfarb, *Civility and Subversion: The Intellectual in Democratic Society* (Cambridge: Cambridge University Press, 1998); Paul R. Gorman, *Left Intellectuals and Popular Culture* (Chapel Hill: University of North Carolina Press, 1996); Christopher Hitchens, *Unacknowledged Legislation: Writers in the Public Sphere* (London: Verso, 2000); Jeremy Jennings and Anthony Kemp-Welch, eds., *Intellectuals in Politics: From the Dreyfus Affair to Salman Rushdie* (London: Routledge, 1997); György Konrád and Iván Szelényi, *The Intellectuals on the Road to Class Power*, trans. Andrew Arato and Richard E. Allen (New York: Harcourt Brace Jovanovich, 1979); Charles C. Lemert, ed., *Intellectuals and Politics: Social Theory in a Changing World*, Key Issues in Sociological Theory 5 (London: Sage, 1991); Ian MacLean, Alan Montefiore, and Peter Winch, eds., *The Political Responsibility of Intellectuals* (Cambridge: Cambridge University Press, 1990); Jack Miles, "Three Differences Between an Academic and an Intellectual: What Happens to the Liberal Arts When They Are Kicked Off Campus?" *Crosscurrents* 49, 3 (Fall 1999); accessed at http://www.crosscurrents.org/miles.htm, 31 January 2010.; Thomas Molnar, *The Decline of the Intellectual* (New Brunswick, N.J.: Transaction, 1994); Editors, "The Future of the Public Intellectual: A Forum," *The Nation* (12 February 2001): 25–36. Richard Rorty, "Intellectuals in Politics," *Dissent* 38 (Fall 1991): 483–90; Michael Walzer, *The Company of Critics: Social Criticism and Political Commentary in the Twentieth Century* (London: Peter Halban, 1989); Tom Wolfe, "In the Land of the Rococo Marxists," *Harper's Magazine* (June 2000): 73–82.

48 Jacoby, *The Last Intellectuals*, 13–14, x, 235.

49 Jacoby revives a line of argument that dates back to Julien Benda's 1927 jeremiad *The Betrayal of the Intellectuals*, trans. Richard Aldington (Boston: Beacon Press, 1955), 43. Edward Said works similar ground, though to different effect, in his 1993 Reith lectures.

50 Michel Foucault, *Power/Knowledge: Selected Interviews and Other Writings 1972–1977* (New York: Pantheon, 1980), 126–33.

51 John Michael, *Anxious Intellects: Academic Professionals, Public Intellectuals, and Enlightenment Values* (Durham, N.C.: Duke University Press, 2000); Bruce Robbins, *Secular Vocations: Intellectuals, Professionalism, Culture* (London: Verso, 1993); Andrew Ross, *No Respect: Intellectuals and Popular Culture* (New York: Routledge, 1989);

Hugh Wilford, *The New York Intellectuals: From Vanguard to Institution* (Manchester: Manchester University Press, 1995). The public intellectual has also been attacked from the opposite direction by Richard Posner. He argues public intellectuals are sloppy thinkers whenever they leave their field of expertise. In effect, Posner is arguing for the superiority of the intellectual in academia, if only such intellectuals would learn to be happy with their incorporation. Posner's market analysis has all the problems typical of economic reasoning, where assumptions are made and quickly forgotten. Here Posner simplifies the appeal of the public intellectual to a simple equation of whether the writer in question was right or wrong. How odd that a practitioner of market analysis should be deaf to the appeal of a marketplace of ideas. Richard A. Posner, *Public Intellectuals: A Study of Decline* (Cambridge, Mass.: Harvard University Press, 2001).

52   Robbins, *Secular Vocations*, 13.

53   Wilford, *New York Intellectuals*, 244–45.

54   Andrew Ross, "On Intellectuals in Politics," *Dissent* (Spring 1992): 263–65.

55   Note the alchemy by which Coser's anecdotal evidence becomes "systematic alienation and frustration" as sociological jargon seeks to turn opinion into fact. Coser, *Men of Ideas*, 334.

56   Joseph Epstein, "Intellectuals—Public and Otherwise," *Commentary* 109, 5 (2000): 48. See Douglas Tallack, "Seeing Out the Century," *Journal of American Studies* 35, 1 (2001): 128.

57   Walzer, *The Company of Critics*, ix, x, 22.

58   Cynthia Ozick, *Quarrel and Quandary: Essays* (New York: Vintage, 2001), 125.

59   Russell Jacoby, *The End of Utopia: Politics and Culture in an Age of Apathy* (New York: Basic Books, 1999).

60   John Updike, "No Use Talking," *New Republic* (13 August 1962): 12.

Chapter 1. On the Road to Time Inc.

Epigraph: John Brooks, *The Big Wheel* (New York: Harper and Brothers, 1949), 148.

1   Archibald MacLeish, *Archibald MacLeish: Reflections*, ed. Bernard A. Drabeck and Helen E. Ellis (Amherst: University of Massachusetts Press, 1986), 20.

2   Scott Donaldson, *Archibald MacLeish: An American Life* (Boston: Houghton Mifflin, 1992), 116–17; MacLeish, *MacLeish: Reflections*, 17–21; Archibald MacLeish, *Letters of Archibald MacLeish, 1907 to 1982*, ed. R. H. Winnick (Boston: Houghton Mifflin, 1983), 103.

3   Archibald MacLeish, *The Happy Marriage and Other Poems* (Boston: Houghton Mifflin, 1924); Archibald MacLeish, *The Pot of Earth* (Boston: Houghton Mifflin, 1925); Archibald MacLeish, *Streets in the Moon* (Boston: Houghton Mifflin, 1926); Archibald MacLeish, *Nobodaddy* (Boston: Houghton Mifflin, 1926); Archibald MacLeish, *The Hamlet of A. MacLeish* (Boston: Houghton Mifflin, 1928); Edmund Wilson, "The Muses Out of Work," in Wilson, *The Shores of Light: A Literary Chronicle of the 1920s and 1930s*

(Boston: Northeastern University Press, 1985) 197–211; Yvors Winters, "Streets in the Moon," *Poetry* 29 (February 1927): 278–81; Louis Untermeyer, "MacLeish Emerges," *Saturday Review of Literature* (12 February 1927): 578; Conrad Aiken, "Another Murex," *New Republic* (9 February 1927): 337.

4   Malcolm Cowley, *Exile's Return: A Literary Odyssey of the 1920s* (New York: Viking, 1951), 206.

5   The best account of this process remains Christopher Lasch, *The New Radicalism in America 1889–1963: The Intellectual as a Social Type* (New York: Norton, 1965).

6   Cowley, *Exile's Return*, 144; emphasis in original.

7   Donaldson, *Archibald MacLeish*, 71.

8   T. S. Matthews, *Name and Address, an Autobiography* (New York: Simon and Schuster, 1960), 176.

9   Steven Biel, *Independent Intellectuals in the United States, 1910–1945* (New York: New York University Press, 1992), 40.

10   Matthews, *Name and Address*, 155.

11   Quoted in Robert James Cummings, "The Education of Dwight Macdonald, 1906–1928: A Biographical Study" (Ph.D. dissertation, Stanford University, 1988), 237.

12   Cowley, *Exile's Return*, 4–5.

13   This characterization appears regularly. See discussion in Biel, *Independent Intellectuals*, 38–44.

14   Matthews, *Name and Address*, 204.

15   Dwight Macdonald, "On Selling Out," in Macdonald, *Discriminations: Essays and Afterthoughts, 1938–1974* (New York: Grossman, 1974), 171.

16   Quoted in Cummings, "The Education of Dwight Macdonald," 232.

17   Edmund Wilson, "The Literary Consequences of the Crash," in *The Shores of Light*, 493.

18   Edmund Wilson, *I Thought of Daisy* (1929; Baltimore: Penguin, 1963).

19   See, for example, Biel, *Independent Intellectuals*; Russell Jacoby, *The Last Intellectuals: American Culture in the Age of Academe* (New York: Basic Books, 1987).

20   T. J. Jackson Lears, *No Place of Grace: Antimodernism and the Transformation of American Culture, 1880–1920* (Chicago: University of Chicago Press, 1981), xvi.

21   Lasch, *The New Radicalism*, 256; emphasis in original

22   MacLeish, *Letters of Archibald MacLeish*, 103, 45–46, 51.

23   Matthews, *Name and Address*, 3.

24   Cummings, "The Education of Dwight Macdonald," 213–14.

25   György Konrád and Iván Szelényi, *The Intellectuals on the Road to Class Power*, trans. Andrew Arato and Richard E. Allen (New York: Harcourt Brace Jovanovich, 1979).

26   Donaldson, *Archibald MacLeish*, 40.

27   Owen Johnson, *Stover at Yale* (New York: Grosset & Dunlap, 1912).

28 Brooks Mather Kelley, *Yale: A History* (New Haven, Conn.: Yale University Press, 1974), 298.

29 On the decline of religion at Yale (and campuses elsewhere), see George M. Marsden, *The Soul of the American University: From Protestant Establishment to Established Nonbelief* (New York: Oxford University Press, 1994), esp. 123–33.

30 Quoted in Kelley, *Yale: A History*, 298–99.

31 Ibid., 311–24. At the same time Kelley argues intellectual values were gaining the upper hand at Yale, he writes, "Very few at Yale rejected the hustling world of the early twentieth century. Yale liked competition; it admired success; and even in a ruthless business culture it thought the curriculum should promote these values" (298).

32 MacLeish, *Archibald MacLeish: Reflections*, 16–17.

33 Donaldson, *Archibald MacLeish*, 60.

34 Matthew Arnold, *Essays in Criticism: Second Series* (London: Macmillan, 1913), 203–4.

35 Donaldson, *Archibald MacLeish*, 61.

36 Ibid., 71.

37 Ibid., 109.

38 AM to Martha Hillard, Andrew, and Ishbel MacLeish, 23 November 1924, in *Letters of Archibald MacLeish*, 151.

39 Archibald MacLeish, *Collected Poems, 1917–1952* (Boston: Houghton Mifflin, 1952), 41.

40 Quoted in Donaldson, *Archibald MacLeish*, 176.

41 Wilson, "The Muses Out of Work," 204, emphasis in original.

42 Donaldson, *Archibald MacLeish*, 171.

43 AM to Martha Hillard MacLeish, 21 September 1924, in *Letters of Archibald MacLeish*, 148.

44 William H. MacLeish, *Uphill with Archie: A Son's Journey* (New York: Simon and Schuster, 2001), 69.

45 AM to Ranald H. Macdonald, Jr., 8 June 1928, in *Letters of Archibald MacLeish*, 213.

46 AM to John Peale Bishop, 8 August 1925, in ibid., 169.

47 Archibald MacLeish, *Poems: 1924–1933* (Boston: Houghton Mifflin, 1933), 19–20.

48 AM to Ernest Hemingway, 14 December 1928, in *Letters of Archibald MacLeish*, 220.

49 R. P. Blackmur, "Am Not Prince Hamlet Nor Was Meant to Be," *Hound and Horn* 2, 2 (January–March 1929): 167–69.

50 Conrad Aiken, "Unpacking Hearts with Words," *Bookman* 68, 5 (January 1929): 576–77.; AM to Robert N. Linscott, c. 24 January 1929, in *Letters of Archibald MacLeish*, 222.

51 Theodore Spencer, "Two Poets," *New Republic* 57 (1929) 226–27.

52 Louis Untermeyer, "Everyman's Soliloquy," *Saturday Review of Literature* 5

(1928) 463; AM to Louis Untermeyer, 24 June 1929, in *Letters of Archibald MacLeish*, 229.

53 Brooks Atkinson, "He Speaks for America," *Pembroke* 7 (1976): 9; MacLeish, *MacLeish: Reflections*, 79.

54 The prevailing explanation for why MacLeish agreed to work at *Fortune* is that he needed the money. In his biography, Scott Donaldson writes, "with the crash of October 1929, the dividends on the Carson Pirie Scott stock he had inherited started slowing down, and it became clear that he would have to find employment to support his family." In the Donaldson account, a fortuitous call from Henry Luce arrived to make the decision easy. Luce agreed to let MacLeish work half time, working six straight months then devoting the rest of the year to poetry, for $5,000 a year. With this generous arrangement guaranteeing both income and time to write, MacLeish accepted. The difficulty with this account is the timing. MacLeish began work for *Fortune* on 10 October 1929, at a time when Carson Pirie Scott remained economically healthy and the stock market crash was still two weeks away. If he began work on 10 October, he certainly accepted the job some time before. Donaldson, *Archibald MacLeish*, 192. This account is echoed in William MacLeish's memoir, with the same confusion over dates. MacLeish, *Uphill with Archie*, 89–90.

55 This account draws heavily on Matthews's own memoir and his interview with the Columbia Oral History project. See the T. S. Matthews, CUOHROC, and Matthews, *Name and Address*, 161.

56 Ibid. 104, 17, 30.

57 Ibid. 157, 58, 52.

58 F. Scott Fitzgerald, *This Side of Paradise* (New York: Scribner's, 1920), 36.

59 Quoted in Don Oberdorfer, *Princeton University: The First 250 Years* (Princeton, N.J.: Trustees of Princeton University, 1995), 122. During the 1920s college enrollments swelled dramatically, from just over 500,000 in 1920 to more than a million by 1930. In 1922, trying to counteract the pressures from increasing enrollment, Princeton initiated selective admission, which Don Oberdorfer concludes, "led to a notable narrowing of the student body and contributed to Princeton's reputation as a country club for the social elite." Wesley C. Mitchell, *Recent Social Trends in the United States: Report of the President's Research Committee on Social Trends* (New York: McGraw-Hill, 1933), 1: 388; Matthews, *Name and Address*, 116.

60 Matthews, *Name and Address*, 177, 63.

61 T. S. Matthews, CUOHROC, 50; Matthews, *Name and Address*, 163–64.

62 *The Book of the Tuesday Evening Club* (Princeton, N.J.: Princeton University Press, 1922).

63 Matthews, *Name and Address*, 177, 60.

64 Ibid., 162.

65 Noel F. Busch, *Briton Hadden: A Biography of the Co-Founder of Time* (New York: Farrar, Strauss, 1949), 74–75.

66 Matthews, *Name and Address*, 176.

67   Ibid., 191.
68   Ibid., 215.
69   Matthews, CUOHROC, 21.
70   David W. Levy, *Herbert Croly of the New Republic: The Life and Thought of an American Progressive* (Princeton, N.J.: Princeton University Press, 1985), 276–98. For a history of the *New Republic* before Matthews's arrived, see Charles Forcey, *The Crossroads of Liberalism: Croly, Weyl, Lippmann, and the Progressive Era: 1900–1925* (New York: Oxford University Press, 1961).
71   Matthews, CUOHROC, 5, 6.
72   Matthews, *Name and Address*, 188.
73   Ibid., 189.
74   Matthews, CUOHROC, 3.
75   The best account is in James Webb, *The Harmonious Circle: The Lives and Work of G. I. Gurdjieff, P. D. Ouspensky, and Their Followers* (New York: Putnam, 1980); esp. 288–336. Other versions are by admirers of Orage who see his years with Gurdjieff as a sad anomaly: Philip Mairet, *A. R. Orage* (London: J.M. Dent, 1936); Wallace Martin, *The New Age Under Orage: Chapters in English Cultural History* (Manchester: Manchester University Press, 1967); or by followers of Gurdjieff: Louise Welch, *Orage with Gurdjieff in America* (Boston: Routledge and Kegan Paul, 1982). Matthews's own account is in *Name and Address*, 204–7.
76   Quoted in Levy, *Herbert Croly*, 298.
77   Welch, *Orage with Gurdjieff in America*.
78   His involvement received greater attention in a later memoir, T. S. Matthews, *Under the Influence: Recollections of Robert Graves, Laura Riding, and Friends* (London: Cassell, 1977).
79   Martin, *The New Age Under Orage*, 289; Matthews, *Name and Address*, 207.
80   Ibid., 216.
81   Ibid., 211.
82   Ibid., 238.
83   T. S. Matthews, *Angels Unawares: Twentieth-Century Portraits* (New York: Ticknor and Fields, 1985).
84   *Book of the Tuesday Evening Club*, 32.
85   Matthews, *Name and Address*, 222; Matthews, CUOHROC, 20.
86   Quoted in Michael Wreszin, *A Rebel in Defense of Tradition: The Life and Politics of Dwight Macdonald* (New York: Basic Books, 1994), 4. Most of the details of Macdonald's life are drawn from Wreszin and from Cummings, "The Education of Dwight Macdonald."
87   Quoted in Wreszin, *A Rebel in Defense of Tradition*, 4.
88   Quoted in Cummings, "The Education of Dwight Macdonald," 8–9.
89   Quoted in Wreszin, *A Rebel in Defense of Tradition*, 6.
90   Ibid., 7–9.
91   Mitchell, *Recent Social Trends*, 388.

92 David Levine's study of American colleges concludes, "After World War I, institutions of higher learning were no longer content to educate; they now set out to train, accredit, and impart social status to their students." David O. Levine, *The American College and the Culture of Aspiration, 1915–1940* (Ithaca, N.Y.: Cornell University Press, 1986), 19.

93 Quoted in Paula S. Fass, *The Damned and the Beautiful: American Youth in the 1920s* (Oxford: Oxford University Press, 1977), 255.

94 George Wilson Pierson, *Yale: The University College, 1921–1937* (New Haven, Conn.: Yale University Press, 1955), 258.

95 Quoted in Wreszin, *A Rebel in Defense of Tradition*, 12.

96 Ibid.

97 Quoted in Cummings, "The Education of Dwight Macdonald," 210–11.

98 Ibid., 211.

99 Johnson, *Stover at Yale*.

100 Wreszin, *A Rebel in Defense of Tradition*, 15–17.

101 Quoted in ibid., 13.

102 Cummings, "The Education of Dwight Macdonald," 224–25.

103 Fass, *The Damned and the Beautiful*, 366.

104 Quoted in Cummings, "The Education of Dwight Macdonald," 228.

105 Ibid., 235–36; emphasis in original.

106 Ibid., 238.

107 Quoted in Wreszin, *A Rebel in Defense of Tradition*, 22.

108 Van Wyck Brooks, *The Ordeal of Mark Twain* (New York: E.P. Dutton, 1920).

109 Quoted in Robert T. Elson, *Time Inc.: The Intimate History of a Publishing Enterprise, 1923–1941* (New York: Atheneum, 1968), 104.

110 Manfred Gottfried, *Prelude to Battle* (New York: John Day, 1928).

111 Quoted in Biel, *Independent Intellectuals*, 35; see 31–53 for general discussion.

112 Michael Kammen, *The Lively Arts: Gilbert Seldes and the Transformation of Cultural Criticism in the United States* (New York: Oxford University Press, 1996); Gilbert Seldes, "Debunking the Debunkers," *New York Herald Tribune* (21 October 1928) Section XII, 1-3; (28 October 1928) Section XII, 12–13, 16.

113 Harold Stearns, ed., *Civilization in the United States, an Inquiry by Thirty Americans* (New York: Harcourt, Brace, 1922).

114 Cowley, *Exile's Return*, 210. MacLeish always denied he was part of Cowley's cast of exiles, even calling Cowley crazy, but his life reads like a blueprint for the structure of Cowley's narrative. See MacLeish, *Archibald MacLeish: Reflections*, 23–24.

115 Ann Douglas, *Terrible Honesty: Mongrel Manhattan in the 1920s* (New York: Farrar, Strauss and Giroux, 1995), 13.

116 Cited in Ben Yagoda, *About Town: The New Yorker and the World It Made* (New York: Scribner, 2000), 27.

117 Cowley, *Exile's Return*, 208.

118 John Kenneth Galbraith, *The Great Crash: 1929* (Boston: Houghton Mifflin, 1954), 78.

Chapter 2. Giving the People the Truth the Time Inc. Way

Epigraph: John Hersey, *Life Sketches* (New York: Knopf, 1989), 29.

1 *Time* prospectus, quoted in Robert T. Elson, *Time Inc.: The Intimate History of a Publishing Enterprise, 1923–1941* (New York: Atheneum, 1968), 7–9.

2 Quoted in Eric Hodgins, *The Span of Time: A Primer History of Time Incorporated* (New York: Time Inc., 1944), 3.

3 Noel F. Busch, *Briton Hadden: A Biography of the Co-Founder of Time* (New York: Farrar, Strauss, 1949), 87.

4 James L. Baughman, *Henry R. Luce and the Rise of the American News Media* (Boston: Twayne, 1987), 3.

5 John K. Jessup, ed., *The Ideas of Henry Luce* (New York: Atheneum, 1969), 7.

6 John Kobler, *Luce: His Time, Life and Fortune* (New York: Doubleday, 1968), 2.

7 Joseph Epstein, "Henry Luce and His Time," *Commentary* 44, 5 (1967): 35.

8 Gertrude Himmelfarb, "Anonymity, 'Time,' and Success," *Commentary* (1960): 83–86; Murray Kempton, "Ralph Ginzburg: Panderer," *New York World Telegram* (16 March 1966); Garry Wills, "*Time*style," *National Review* (3 August 1957): 129–30, 143. See also "*Time*: The Weekly Fiction Magazine" *Fact* 1 (January–February 1964): 3–23.

9 W. A. Swanberg, *Luce and His Empire* (New York: Scribner's, 1972).

10 David M. Kennedy, *Over Here: The First World War and American Society* (Oxford: Oxford University Press, 1980), 45–92.

11 See, for example, Harold D. Lasswell, "The Psychology of Hitlerism," *Political Quarterly* 4, 3 (July–September1933): 373–84

12 Paul R. Gorman, *Left Intellectuals and Popular Culture* (Chapel Hill: University of North Carolina Press, 1996), 60–83 and passim.

13 It was not until the late 1980s that scholarship began to see Luce and his media power more clearly, beginning with Baughman's excellent *Henry R. Luce*. He replaced Swanberg's imputation of nefarious intent to Luce's every action with a more evenhanded analysis of Luce's role in American media and political history.

14 Quoted in Baughman, *Henry R. Luce*, 34.

15 Michael Augspurger, *An Economy of Abundant Beauty: Fortune Magazine and Depression America* (Ithaca, N.Y.: Cornell University Press, 2004).

16 This account of Luce's early life is drawn primarily from Baughman, *Henry R. Luce*; Robert E. Herzstein, *Henry R. Luce: A Political Portrait of the Man Who Created the American Century* (New York: Scribner's, 1994); Swanberg, *Luce and His Empire*; Elson, *Time Inc.* Swanberg is the most detailed, Baughman the most insightful.

17 Jessup, ed., *Ideas*, 89–90.

18 David Halberstam, *The Powers That Be* (New York: Knopf, 1979), 47–58.

19 Henry R. Luce, "Let It Die," in Jessup, ed., *Ideas*, 91–94. Henry R. Luce, "Indispensable Men," HRL Collection; Jessup, ed., *Ideas*, 224. For full text of this speech,

see Luce speech delivered 19 April 1934, Scranton, Pennsylvania, WAS Collection), Box 20.

20 T. S. Matthews, CUOHROC, 70. The division between curiosity and ideology is explored in Halberstam, *The Powers That Be*, 49.

21 Luce, "Indispensable Men."

22 Quoted in Swanberg, *Luce and His Empire*, 52. Swanberg reproduces this quote and concludes that service "could perhaps be translated as gaining and exercising power. The urge to power was a driving force, the greatest in his life." This passage demonstrates a recurring problem in Swanberg's account: while he pays careful attention to any and all evidence of Luce's evident attraction to power, he is deaf to Luce's idealism, his serious belief that members of his class had a responsibility to serve society. That this service was best rendered as leadership, in Luce's view, further muddied the waters.

23 Details on Hadden's life are drawn from Busch, *Briton Hadden* and the more recent Isaiah Wilner, *The Man Time Forgot: A Tale of Genius, Betrayal, and the Creation of Time Magazine* (New York: HarperCollins, 2006). Wilner's book begins as a salutary attempt to restore credit to Hadden for *Time*, but suffers from a tendentious overestimation of Hadden (he seems to have "invented" everything), and a persistent underrating of Luce (Hadden was Luce's "last, best chance," at age 23! [75]).

24 This quote, possibly apocryphal, appears in virtually every account on Hadden and Luce. Swanberg, *Luce and His Empire*, 43.

25 Elson, *Time Inc.* 42.

26 WAS Collection, Box 2, Sudler Correspondence.

27 Swanberg, *Luce and His Empire* 40; Elson, *Time Inc.*, 44.

28 Swanberg, *Luce and His Empire*, 45–46.

29 Busch, *Briton Hadden*, 45; Wilner, *The Man Time Forgot*, 63.

30 Swanberg, *Luce and His Empire*, 32.

31 Edwin Emery and Henry Ladd Smith, *The Press and America* (New York: Prentice-Hall, 1954), 621–45. This is still the best account of newspapers in the early 1920s.

32 Richard Ohmann, "Where Did Mass Culture Come From? The Case of Magazines," *Berkshire Review* 16 (1981): 85–101.

33 On the history of advertising, see Roland Marchand, *Advertising the American Dream: Making Way for Modernity, 1920–1940* (Berkeley: University of California Press, 1985); Jackson Lears, *Fables of Abundance: A Cultural History of Advertising in America* (New York: Basic Books, 1994).

34 On the history of magazines, in the "golden age" and after, see Frank Luther Mott, *A History of American Magazines*, 5 vols. (Cambridge, Mass.: Harvard University Press, 1938–1968); Theodore Preston, *Magazines in the Twentieth Century* (Urbana: University of Illinois Press, 1964); Matthew Schneirov, *The Dream of a New Social Order: Popular Magazines in America, 1893–1914* (New York: Columbia University Press, 1994); John Tebbel and Mary Ellen Zuckerman, *The Magazine in America, 1741–1990* (New

York: Oxford University Press, 1991); James Playsted Wood, *Magazines in the United States*, 3rd ed. (New York: Ronald Press, 1971).

35   Thomas Kunkel, *Genius in Disguise: Harold Ross of the New Yorker* (New York: Random House, 1995), 87–94; Ben Yagoda, *About Town: The New Yorker and the World It Made* (New York: Scribner, 2000), 33–40.

36   Tebbel and Zuckerman, *The Magazine in America*, 182–84.

37   Elson, *Time Inc.*, 3.

38   *Time* prospectus, reproduced in ibid., 7–9; emphasis in original.

39   Emil J. Emig, quoted in Baughman, *Henry R. Luce*, 25.

40   On the *World's Work* as pioneer for the newsmagazine, see Christopher P. Wilson, "The Rhetoric of Consumption: Mass-Market Magazines and the Demise of the Gentle Reader, 1880–1920," in *The Culture of Consumption: Critical Essays in American History 1880–1980*, ed. Richard Wightman Fox and T. J. Jackson Lears (New York: Pantheon, 1983), 39–64.

41   Baughman, *Henry R. Luce*, 50; Busch, *Briton Hadden*, 194; Wilner, *The Man Time Forgot*, 161–62.

42   Busch, *Briton Hadden*, 65–80; Elson, *Time Inc.*, 53–66; Swanberg, *Luce and His Empire*, 49–56.

43   Elson, *Time Inc.*, 59.

44   Ibid., 69.

45   Luce and Hadden's implementation of their journalistic assembly line hardly represented an unprecedented threat to previously autonomous journalists. S. S. McClure, whose magazine did so much to create the mass market magazine and the model of muckraking journalism (long taken as a high water mark for journalism), regularly assigned topics to writers, both of journalism and fiction. Nelson Lichtenstein, "Authorial Professionalism and the Literary Marketplace, 1885–1900," *American Studies* 19, 1 (1978): 44. On the commercialization of the writer's craft, see also Daniel H. Borus, *Writing Realism: Howells, James, and Norris in the Mass Market* (Chapel Hill: University of North Carolina Press, 1989).

46   On planning and staffing for *Time*, see Busch, *Briton Hadden*, 65–88; Elson, *Time Inc.*, 58–73; Wilner, *The Man Time Forgot*, 76–113.

47   Matthews, CUOHROC.

48   *Time* (3 March 1923): 12.

49   Joan Shelley Rubin, *The Making of Middlebrow Culture* (Chapel Hill: University of North Carolina Press, 1992).

50   Neal Gabler, *Winchell: Gossip, Power and the Culture of Celebrity* (New York: Knopf, 1994), xiii; Michael Kirkhorn, "This Curious Existence: Journalistic Identity in the Interwar Period," in *Mass Media Between the Wars: Perceptions of Cultural Tension, 1918–1941*, ed. Catherine L. Covert and John D. Stevens (Syracuse, N.Y.: Syracuse University Press, 1984). See also Miguel Covarrubias's caricature of Lippmann and Winchell on Broadway in *Publisher's Weekly* 115 (9 February 1929): 740. It was Alexander Woollcott who labeled the 1920s "the era of the Two Walters," Alexander

Woollcott, "The Little Man with the Big Voice," *Hearst's International Cosmopolitan* 94, 5 (May 1933): 48–49.

51   Walter Lippmann, *Liberty and the News* (New York: Harcourt, Brace and Howe, 1920). See also Walter Lippmann, *Public Opinion* (New York: Simon and Schuster, 1922); Marion Tuttle Marzolf, *Civilizing Voices: American Press Criticism, 1880–1950* (New York: Longman, 1991), 110–25.

52   Wilner, *The Man Time Forgot*, 130.

53   See Kobler, *Luce*, 43–67 and Busch, *Briton Hadden*, 109–27 for *Time*'s early style. Wilner, *The Man Time Forgot*, 126–43.

54   Charles A. Beard and Mary R. Beard, *America at Midpassage* (New York: Macmillan, 1939), 360–61.

55   Wolcott Gibbs, "Profiles: Time...Fortune...Life...Luce," *New Yorker* (28 November 1936): 20–25.

56   Martin, "Proceedings"(paper presented at the American Society of Newspaper Editors, Washington D.C., 16 April 1937): 68-80. Quote from p. 71. Martin himself provided a good example of *Time* technique when he wrote a widely praised and reproduced account of the Coolidge funeral. Martin wove telling details of the funeral procession through a summary of Coolidge's career. Typical of *Time* in these years, Martin wrote the entire piece from his desk, as the magazine still did not cover events. Adopting storytelling technique to the news proved easier with a liberal use of the imagination. As Michael Schudson points out, the narrative form of journalism helps structure both content and meaning. In its ideal state news would be all information, no form. Michael Schudson, "The Politics of Narrative Form," *Daedalus* (Fall 1982): 110. Or, borrowing from Kenneth Burke, news would carry semantic meaning, not poetic meaning. Kenneth Burke, "Semantic Meaning and Poetic Meaning," in *The Philosophy of Literary Form: Studies in Symbolic Action* (Berkeley: University of California Press, 1973), 140.

57   Elson, *Time Inc.*, 88–89; Kunkel, *Genius in Disguise*, 100–101; Yagoda, *About Town*, 25–40.

58   Busch, *Briton Hadden*, 192–94. For other examples of Hadden's efforts to sabotage *Time*'s circulation drives, see Wilner, *The Man Time Forgot*, 197–98.

59   Busch, *Briton Hadden*, 172–73; Wilner, *The Man Time Forgot*, 167.

60   Kobler, *Luce*, 66.

61   Baughman, *Henry R. Luce*, 49.

62   Jessup, ed., *Ideas*, 56–57.

63   Baughman, *Henry R. Luce*, 48. Michael Schudson argues that objectivity became the dominant journalistic value in the early decades of the century largely as a reaction to the decreasing faith in the ability of facts to speak for themselves and a larger skepticism about the claims of rationality. If he is right, and decreasing certainty fueled a defensive objectivity, *Time* stood this trend on its head. Schudson, *Discovering the News: A Social History of American Newspapers* (New York: Basic Books, 1978), 121–59.

64   Hodgins, *The Span of Time*, 12.

65 Ibid., 5, 6. Unsurprisingly, Hadden objected, but his opposition no longer counted for much once he became ill.

66 Ibid., 129.

67 Luce quoted in "Picturing Business: The Photography of FORTUNE, 1930–1965" (New York: International Center of Photography, 2000), 1.

68 Jessup, ed., *Ideas*, 223.

69 *Time* (28 October 1929): 38–40.

70 The *New Yorker*, in the early days of a serious feud with Time Inc., claimed it weighed as much as a "good size flounder." Gibbs, "Profiles," 23.

71 On the allegorical female and cornucopia see Lears, *Fables of Abundance*, 26–39.

72 The archaic imagery might seem an odd beginning for an avowedly modern magazine. But as Terry Smith had observed, corporate liberal modernism has frequently tried to project its future by cannibalizing its own prehistory. Terry Smith, *Making the Modern: Industry, Art, and Design in America* (Chicago: University of Chicago Press, 1993), 138.

73 For a stimulating but overly speculative analysis of *Fortune*'s aesthetics, see ibid., 159–98. Also John Robert Stomberg, "Art and "Fortune": Machine-Age Discourse and the Visual Culture of Industrial Modernity" (Ph.D. dissertation, Boston University, 1999).

74 On Bourke-White at *Fortune*, see Margaret Bourke-White, *Portrait of Myself* (New York: Simon and Schuster, 1963); Elson, *Time Inc.*, 135–36; Vicki Goldberg, *Margaret Bourke-White: A Biography* (New York: Harper and Row, 1986), 101–24.

75 Smith, *Making the Modern,* 182.

76 For these examples and more see *Fortune* (February–December 1930).

77 Jessup, ed., *Ideas*, 94–101; emphasis in original.

78 Henry R. Luce, "Education and Aristocracy," Speech at University of Chattanooga, 1936, HRL Collection, Box 74.

79 Jessup, ed., *Ideas*, 100.

80 Luce, "Education and Aristocracy."

81 Jessup, ed., *Ideas*, 99.

82 Ibid., 221–22.

83 Luce, "Education and Aristocracy."

84 Jessup, ed., *Ideas*, 221–23.

85 Luce, "Indispensable Men." For New Era thought, see William J. Barber, *From New Era to New Deal: Herbert Hoover, the Economists, and American Economic Policy, 1921–1933* (Cambridge: Cambridge University Press, 1985).

86 Luce, "Indispensable Men."

87 Elson, *Time Inc.*; Luce, Speech, April 1933, Des Moines, Iowa, WAS Collection.

88 Jessup, ed., *Ideas*, 222–23.

89 Time Inc., *Fortune's Wheel* (New York: Time Inc., 1936), 6.

90   Elson, *Time Inc.*, 128; Kobler, *Luce*, 70.

91   Dwight Macdonald, "Luce and His Empire: A Radical Critique of a Liberalistic Biography of a Reactionary Tycoon," in Macdonald, *Discriminations: Essays and Afterthoughts 1938–1974* (New York: Grossman, 1974), 275.

92   *Fortune's Wheel*, 1.

93   Baughman, *Henry R. Luce*, 73.

94   "New York in Third Winter," *Fortune* (January 1932): 41–48, 109, 121. "Housing" ran in six installments from February through July 1932. "Unemployment: No One Has Starved," *Fortune* (September 1932): 18–29, 80–88. For critical corporation stories see "Mr. Ford Doesn't Care," *Fortune* (December 1933): 63–69, 121–34. For positive reaction to New Deal see "U.S. Supreme Council," *Fortune* (September 1933): 44–48, 100–102; "Tennessee Valley Authority: The Project Is Important," *Fortune* (October 1933): 81–97; "U.S. Communist Party," *Fortune* (September 1934): 69–74, 154–62.

95   "Cockfighting: Not to Eat, Not for Love" *Fortune* (March 1934): 90–95, 146; "The Business of Burlesque, A.D. 1935," *Fortune* (February 1935): 66–73, 140–53; "Reno: Passion in the Desert," *Fortune* (April 1934): 100–107, 124–32.

96   Roy Hoopes, *Ralph Ingersoll: A Biography* (New York: Atheneum, 1985), 103; Elson, *Time Inc.*, 222.

Chapter 3. The Search for a "Radical Capitalism" at *Fortune* Magazine

Epigraph: Archibald MacLeish, "Poetry and Journalism: A Lecture Delivered at Northrop Memorial Auditorium, Minneapolis, on October 12, 1958," Gideon D. Seymour Lecture Series 8 (Minneapolis: University of Minnesota Press, 1958), 17.

1   *Time* (28 October 1929): 43–46.

2   Ibid., 39–41.

3   *Fortune* (May 1933): 51–57, 78–84; (June 1933): 59–63, 78–95; (July 1933): 68–76.

4   "Ivar Kreuger I," *Fortune* (May 1933): 51, 52.

5   Quoted in Robert T. Elson, *Time Inc.: The Intimate History of a Publishing Enterprise, 1923–1941* (New York: Atheneum, 1968), 137.

6   All Lloyd-Smith's surviving writing is housed in the RD Collection, Box 102, Folder 8.

7   Ralph Ingersoll, "High Time" typescript, RI Collection, Box 14, Folder 16, vol. 2, chap. 4, 6.

8   In September 1931, for no apparent reason, Lloyd-Smith leaped to his death from the roof of his apartment building. He left friend and *Fortune* colleague Russell Davenport a long poem by way of explanation. It ended:

"Fool!
I had been looking at eternity!
Madly, I flung myself into the dazzling,
Scintillating beauty.

And fell...
Fall..."

(RD Collection, Box 17, Folder 2)

9   "High Time," RI Collection, vol. 2, chap. 4, 5–6.

10 RI, "My Years with Luce," RI Collection, Box 15, Folder 6, 65.

11 Dwight Macdonald, *A Moral Temper: The Letters of Dwight Macdonald*, ed. Michael Wreszin (Chicago: Ivan R. Dee, 2001), 37.

12 See Eric Hodgins, *Trolley to the Moon* (New York: Simon and Schuster, 1973), 455–57.

13 Macdonald, *A Moral Temper*, 40.

14 Scott Donaldson, *Archibald MacLeish: An American Life* (Boston: Houghton Mifflin, 1992), 194.

15 Hodgins, *Trolley*, 448.

16 RD Collection, Box 17, Folder 2.

17 Roy Hoopes, *Ralph Ingersoll: A Biography* (New York: Atheneum, 1985), 61, 80.

18 AM Collection, Library of Congress, Box 11, RI Folder.

19 Hoopes, *Ingersoll*, 52.

20 James Agee, *Agee: His Life Remembered*, ed. Ross Spears and Jude Cassidy (New York: Holt, Rinehart and Winston, 1985), 29–31.

21 James Agee, *The Collected Short Prose of James Agee*, ed. Robert Fitzgerald (Boston: Houghton Mifflin, 1968), 15.

22 Agee, *Agee: His Life Remembered*, 36.

23 Agee, *Short Prose of Agee*, 50–51.

24 Hodgins, *Trolley*, 431–32.

25 Letter to DW, 3 July 1929, DM Collection, Box 57, Folder 1375, 5.

26 Archibald MacLeish, *Letters of Archibald MacLeish, 1907 to 1982*, ed. R. H. Winnick (Boston: Houghton Mifflin, 1983), 243.

27 Agee, *Agee: His Life Remembered*, 48. In this particular case, the fear may have been specific: Agee's writing so impressed Luce that he wanted to send the writer to business school. Instead he assigned Agee a highly technical piece on railroad finances and tried to personally teach Agee the necessary financial background. The experiment failed, and Agee returned to stories better attuned to his gifts.

28 DM to DW, 16 June 1929, DM Collection, Box 57, Folder 1375.

29 DM to DW, 16 October 1929, DM Collection, Box 57, Folder 1376.

30 DM to DW, 23 April 1930, DM Collection, Box 58, Folder 1377.

31 DM to DW, 13 June 1930, DM Collection, Box 58, Folder 1377. This letter appears in Macdonald, *A Moral Temper*, 42–45, but the quotation above is edited out, as are most positive references to his work at *Fortune*.

32 Almost all his bitter reflections on *Fortune* are accompanied by laments about his failed love life. See DM to DW, 12 December 1929, DM Collection, Box 58, Folder

1377; DM to DW, 2 February 1932, DM Collection, Box 58, Folder 1380; DM to DW, unmailed 1932, DM Collection, Box 58, Folder 1381.

33 DM to DW, 15 July 1929, DM Collection, Box 57, Folder 1375.

34 DM to DW, 13 June 1930, DM Collection, Box 58, Folder 1377 and DM to DW, 21 September 1931, DM Collection, Box 58, Folder 1380.

35 Dwight Macdonald, *Against the American Grain: Essays on the Effects of Mass Culture* (New York: Random House, 1962), 33.

36 T. S. Matthews at *Time* did not take the organization seriously until he got to know Luce in the late 1930s. After meeting Luce he, too, got caught up in the publisher's enthusiasm and began in earnest the career in Time Inc. that is examined in Chapter 5.

37 "High Time," Folder 16, vol. 2, chap. 10, 8.

38 Donaldson, *Archibald MacLeish*, 199.

39 Hemingway to Maxwell Perkins, 15 December 1929, in Hemingway, *Ernest Hemingway Selected Letters, 1917–1961*, ed. Carlos Baker (New York: Scribner's, 1981), 317.

40 From October 1929 until 1934 he took only one extended vacation, that for four months. The only evidence of Luce's agreement to let MacLeish come to work only as long as he needed to each year appears to be MacLeish's memory. In November 1933 Luce did agree to allow MacLeish six months off every two years, at full pay. It is possible MacLeish confused this offer with Luce's initial offer of employment. See Henry Luce to AM, 6 November 1933, AM Collection, Box 8, *Fortune* Folder.

41 Editors of *Fortune*, *Writing for Fortune: Nineteen Authors Remember Life on the Staff of a Remarkable Magazine* (New York: Time Inc., 1980), 8, 12.

42 "Anthracite: Labor," *Fortune* (February 1931): 75–77.

43 "Unions: A Burlesque Tyrant," *Fortune* (November 1930): 59, 118.

44 Kim McQuaid, *A Response to Industrialism: Liberal Businessmen and the Evolving Spectrum of Capitalist Reform, 1886–1960* (New York: Garland, 1986), 165. See also *The Nation* (25 February 1931): 207; *Literary Digest* (7 March 1931): 12; *Harper's* (August 1931): 275–83.

45 "Life of Owen D. Young I," *Fortune* (January 1931): 31–40, 90–101.

46 "Life of Owen D. Young III," *Fortune* (March 1931): 89–98.

47 McQuaid, *Response to Industrialism*, 98–157.

48 "Gallery of Calamity," *Fortune* (April 1931): 89–93, 134.

49 "American Workingman," *Fortune* (August 1931): 54–69, 131.

50 The Bourke-White picture, taken for earlier *Fortune* articles, had not previously made it into the magazine. Those that did, interestingly, were of craft workers, like her famous glassblower picture, not of industrial workers. Ibid., 56.

51 Ibid., 131.

52 Ibid. 66, 131; Archibald MacLeish, "To the Young Men of Wall Street," *Saturday Review of Literature* 8, 26 (16 January 1932): 454.

53 "American Workingman," 65, 66.

54 "Who Killed Cock Robin?" *Fortune* (August 1931): 125.

55 "Government's Biggest Business Venture" and "To Symbolize Solidity," *Fortune* (November 1931): 36–41, 123–30, 140; 54–55.

56 "Eyes on Washington," *Fortune* (February 1932): 53–60; "Seven Against the Depression," *Fortune* (April 1932): 42–45; Also, Archibald MacLeish, "Fourteenth Amendment," *Fortune* (June 1932): 53–55, 104–12; "Housing," *Fortune* (February 1932): 61–69, 86–94; (March 1932): 44–47, 113–18; (April 1932) 34–39, 108–10; (May 1932): 67–73, 135–51; (June 1932): 67–71, 114–15; (July 1932): 60–69, 104–10; "Russia, Russia, Russia," *Fortune* (March 1932): 57–96, 120–35.

57 Dwight Macdonald, "'Fortune' Magazine," *The Nation* (8 May 1937): 528.

58 *Fortune* editors, *Writing for Fortune*, 7.

59 "High Time," vol. 2, chap. 8, 7.

60 Donaldson, *Archibald MacLeish*, 210. The example comes from *Fortune* articles on silver and currency published in the preceding months. "From Currency to Commodity," *Fortune* (October 1930): 70–72; "Great Gold Argument," *Fortune* (February 1931): 69–71, 116.

61 Archibald MacLeish, "Nevertheless One Debt," *Poetry* 38, 4 (July 1931): 214–15.

62 Donaldson, *Archibald MacLeish*, 188; MacLeish, "Nevertheless One Debt," 216.

63 Archibald MacLeish, *Collected Poems, 1917–1952* (Boston: Houghton Mifflin, 1952), 93–95.

64 Richard H. Pells, *Radical Visions and American Dreams: Culture and Social Thought in the Depression Years* (New York: Harper and Row, 1973), 183.

65 Note the repeated shift in terms of address in the poem, from Senora to Fraulein, Lady, Tovarishch, and finally Barinya.

66 MacLeish, "Young Men," 453.

67 AM to Harriet Monroe, 4 June 1931, in MacLeish, *Letters of Archibald MacLeish*, 240.

68 MacLeish, "Young Men," 454, 453.

69 "My Years with Luce," 32, RI Collection, Box 15, Folder 6; "High Times," vol. 2, chap. 8, 7, Box 14, Folder 16. Quoted in Hoopes, *Ingersoll*, 96.

70 Quoted in William Stott, *Documentary Expression and 1930s America* (Chicago: University of Chicago Press, 1973), 14.

71 "No One Has Starved," *Fortune* (September 1932): 18–29, 80–88. William Leuchtenburg claimed this article was central to the country acknowledging it was in Depression. Leuchtenburg, ed., *The New Deal: A Documentary History* (Columbia: University of South Carolina Press, 1968), xiv.

72 "Housing I," *Fortune* (February 1932): 61.

73 "Arms and the Men," *Fortune* (May 1934): 52–57, 113–26.

74 "Passion in the Desert," *Fortune* (April 1934) 100–107, 124–32; "Not to Eat, Not for Love," *Fortune* (March 1934): 90–95, 146; "The $3,000,000 Machine," *Fortune*

(December 1930): 96–98; "The Accident of Birth," *Fortune* (February 1938): 83–86, 108–14; "Burlesque," *Fortune* (February 1935): 66–73, 140–53.

75 This characterization runs directly counter to the interpretation offered by Terry Smith. He contrasts emotionally "cool photographs," deploying a new visual vocabulary of modernity, with "hot texts" straining to fabulize corporate America. His account, however, rests on a narrow consideration of the visual content of the magazine, excluding photo reproductions purchased from news agencies, art reproductions, maps, and visual diagrams to concentrate exclusively on the visual style of Margaret Bourke-White. As important as her style was to *Fortune*, it never constituted more than a small percentage of the visual imagery of any issue. Further, Smith's characterization of her pictures as cold and mechanical denies the emotional impact they do carry—the awesome size and scale, the beauty created from her modernist deployment of size, repetition, shape, light, and shadow. As for the text, Smith leans far too heavily on the corporation story, which may have been, as he claims, *Fortune*'s great formal innovation, but which rarely held pride of place in the magazine. Smith ignores the majority of the content. When he was faced with emotionally "hot" writing he dismisses it as "spectacularly inept." Terry Smith, *Making the Modern: Industry, Art, and Design in America* (Chicago: University of Chicago Press, 1993), 190–93.

76 MacLeish, "Poetry and Journalism," 15, 17.
77 "My Years with Luce," 33, RI Collection, Box 15, Folder 6.
78 "The Project Is Important," *Fortune* (October 1933): 81–97.
79 "The Great American Roadside," *Fortune* (September 1934): 53–63, 172–77. Details of the fate of Agee's extra writing are in Hodgins, *Trolley*, 414–15.
80 Quoted in Donaldson, *Archibald MacLeish*, 213.
81 "My Years with Luce" 34-35, RI Collection, Box 15, Folder 6.
82 "The Case Against Roosevelt," *Fortune* (December 1935): 102–7, 140. Henry R. Luce, *The Ideas of Henry Luce*, ed. John K. Jessup (New York: Atheneum, 1969), 224.
83 "High Time," vol. 2, chap. 8, 10.
84 Ibid.
85 The words are from Luce's summation of fascism in the preface to *Fortune*'s special issue on Italy, *Fortune* (July 1934): 45.
86 Luce, *Ideas*, 225, 28.
87 "Berkshire Knitting Mills," *Fortune* (January 1932): 54–49, 110.
88 DM to DW, 15 November 1931, DM Collection.
89 DM to DW, 8 January 1934, in Macdonald, *A Moral Temper*, 46.
90 "U.S. Communist Party," *Fortune* (September 1934): 69–74, 154–62.
91 DM to Nancy Rodman, 16 July 1934, in Macdonald, *A Moral Temper*, 49.
92 DM to Rodman, 20 July 1934, ibid.
93 DM to DW, 18 September 1935, DM Collection, Box 59, Folder 1386.
94 DM to DW, 20 December 1935, DM Collection, Box 59, Folder 1386.
95 Ibid.
96 "Republic Steel," *Fortune* (December 1935): 76–84, 142–52.

97 DM to DW, 6 November 1935, in Macdonald, *A Moral Temper*, 64. See also DM to Esther Dette Hamill, 2 November 1935, in ibid., 63.

98 DM to Luce with supporting materials, c. 1936, DM Collection, Box 29, Folder 757.

99 DM to DW, 20 December 1935, DM Collection.

100 "The Corporation," *Fortune* (March 1936): 59–67, 152–205.

101 "U.S. Steel II: Prices," *Fortune* (April 1936): 126–36.

102 DM to DW, 16 March 1936, in Macdonald, *A Moral Temper*, 71–72.

103 DM to James Baughman, 29 September 1978, DM Collection, Box 191, Folder 20.

104 "U.S. Steel III: Labor," *Fortune* (May 1936): 92–97, 134–47.

105 "U.S. Steel IV—Macdonald Manuscript," DM Collection, Box 130, Folder 714.

106 Elson, *Time Inc.*, 254.

107 RI to Hodgins Memo, 21 April 1936, DM Collection, Box 130, Folder 711.

108 DM to "Ned"[?], DM Collection, Box 84, Folder 253; "U.S. Steel: IV," *Fortune* (June 1936): 113–16, 164–72; "Myron Taylor," ibid., 117–20, 172–74.

109 Elson, *Time Inc.*, 254–56.

110 "My Years with Luce," 323, RI Collection, Box 15, Folder 8.

111 DM to DW, 10 June 1936, in Macdonald, *A Moral Temper*, 76; DM to DW, 13 May 1936, DM Collection Box 59, Folder 1387.

112 Macdonald later claimed he was trying to get fired in writing his pieces on U.S. Steel, a conclusion supported by biographer Michael Wreszin. The evidence, however, suggests otherwise. Michael Wreszin, *A Rebel in Defense of Tradition: The Life and Politics of Dwight Macdonald* (New York: Basic Books, 1994), 52.

113 Macdonald, "Fortune," 527.

114 AM to Hodgins and RD, 26 April 1938, RD Collection Box 54, Folder 41; emphasis added.

115 Elson, *Time Inc.*, 314–16.

116 See Robert S. McElvaine, *The Great Depression, America 1929–1941* (New York: Times Books, 1993) for a popular synthetic account echoing this interpretation.

117 Smith, *Making the Modern*; Michael Augspurger, *An Economy of Abundant Beauty: Fortune Magazine and Depression America* (Ithaca, N.Y.: Cornell University Press, 2004); Thomas Ferguson, "Industrial Conflict and the Coming of the New Deal: The Triumph of Multinational Liberalism in America," in *The Rise and Fall of the New Deal Order, 1930–1980*, ed. Steve Fraser and Gary Gerstle (Princeton, N.J.: Princeton University Press, 1989), 3–31.

Chapter 4. Intellectuals Visible and Invisible

Epigraph: James Agee and Walker Evans, *Let Us Now Praise Famous Men* (Boston: Houghton Mifflin, 1941; reprint 1960), 100–101.

1 Most recently see Michael Lofaro, ed., *Agee Agonistes: Essays on the Life,*

Legend, and Works of James Agee (Knoxville: University of Tennessee Press, 2007). For book-length studies, see Alfred T. Barson, *A Way of Seeing: A Critical Study of James Agee* (Amherst: University of Massachusetts Press, 1972); Hugh Davis, *The Making of James Agee* (Knoxville: University of Tennessee Press, 2008); Mark A. Doty, *Tell Me Who I Am: James Agee's Search for Selfhood* (Baton Rouge: Louisiana State University Press, 1981); Richard H. King, *A Southern Renaissance: The Cultural Awakening of the American South, 1930–1955* (New York: Oxford University Press, 1980); Victor A. Kramer, *James Agee* (Boston: Twayne, 1975); Victor A. Kramer, *Agee and Actuality: Artistic Vision in His Work* (Troy, N.Y.: Whitston, 1991); James Lowe, *The Creative Process of James Agee* (Baton Rouge: Louisiana State University Press, 1994); David Madden and Jeffrey J. Folks, eds., *Remembering James Agee*, 2nd ed. (Athens: University of Georgia Press, 1997); Peter H. Ohlin, *Agee* (New York: Ivan Oblensky, 1966); Kenneth Seib, *James Agee: Promise and Fulfillment* (Pittsburgh: University of Pittsburgh Press, 1968); Ross Spears and Jude Cassidy, eds., *Agee: His Life Remembered* (New York: Holt, Rinehart and Winston, 1985); Alan Spiegel, *James Agee and the Legend of Himself: A Critical Study* (Columbia: University of Missouri Press, 1998); William Stott, *Documentary Expression and Thirties America* (New York: Oxford University Press, 1973).

2   James Agee, *Let Us Now Praise Famous Men, A Death in the Family, Shorter Fiction* (New York: Library of America, 2005); James Agee, *Film Writing and Selected Journalism* (New York: Library of America, 2005).

3   Gregory D. Sumner, *Dwight Macdonald and the Politics Circle: The Challenge of Cosmopolitan Democracy* (Ithaca, N.Y.: Cornell University Press, 1996); Michael Wreszin, *A Rebel in Defense of Tradition: The Life and Politics of Dwight Macdonald* (New York: Basic Books, 1995); Stephen J. Whitfield, *A Critical American: The Politics of Dwight Macdonald* (Guilford, Conn.: Archon, 1984); Paul R. Gorman, *Left Intellectuals and Popular Culture in Twentieth Century America* (Chapel Hill: University of North Carolina Press, 1996); Dwight MacDonald, *A Moral Temper: The Letters of Dwight Macdonald*, ed. Michael Wreszin (Chicago: Ivan R. Dee, 2001); Dwight Macdonald, *Interviews with Dwight Macdonald*, ed. Michael Wreszin (Jackson: University of Mississippi Press, 2003).

4   Scott Donaldson, *Archibald MacLeish: An American Life* (Boston: Houghton Mifflin, 1992); Archibald MacLeish, *Letters of Archibald MacLeish, 1907–1982*, ed. R. H. Winnick (Boston: Houghton Mifflin, 1983); Archibald MacLeish, *Archibald MacLeish: Reflections*, ed. Bernard A. Drabeck and Helen E. Ellis (Amherst: University of Massachusetts Press, 1986); David Barber, "In Search of an 'Image of Mankind': The Public Poetry of Archibald MacLeish," *American Studies* 29, 2 (1988): 31–56. It is significant that the only book about MacLeish to appear recently is a memoir by his son. William H. MacLeish, *Uphill with Archie: A Son's Journey* (New York: Simon and Schuster, 2001).

5   Richard H. Pells, *Radical Visions and American Dreams: Culture and Social Thought During the Depression Years* (New York: Harper and Row, 1973); Richard H.

Pells, *The Liberal Mind in a Conservative Age: American Intellectuals in the 1940s and 1950s* (New York: Harper and Row, 1985).

6 Quoted in Donaldson, *Archibald MacLeish*, 268.

7 Archibald MacLeish, "The Affirmation," in MacLeish, *A Time to Speak: The Selected Prose of Archibald MacLeish* (Boston: Houghton Mifflin, 1940), 9.

8 MacLeish, "Public Speech and Private Speech in Poetry," *A Time to Speak*, 65.

9 Poll quoted in David M. Kennedy, *Freedom from Fear: The American People in Depression and War, 1929-1945* (Oxford: Oxford University Press, 1999), 400-403.

10 Archibald MacLeish, "Post-War Writers and Pre-War Readers," *New Republic* (10 June 1940): 789-90.

11 Ernest Hemingway quoted in "Writer's Influence," *Time* (24 June 1940): 92.

12 Edmund Wilson, "Archibald MacLeish and 'the Word,'" *New Republic* (1 July 1940): 30-32.

13 Ibid.

14 Morton Zabel, "The Poet on Capitol Hill," *Partisan Review* 8, 1 (January-February 1941): 3.

15 Van Wyck Brooks, *Opinions of Oliver Allston* (New York: E.P. Dutton, 1941), 239, 231.

16 Dwight Macdonald, "*Kulterbolshewismus* Is Here" *Partisan Review* (hereafter *PR*) 8, 6 (November-December 1941): 442-51, reproduced as "*Kulterbolshewismus* and Mr. Van Wyck Brooks," in *Memoirs of a Revolutionist: Essays in Political Criticism* (New York: Farrar, Strauss and Cudahy, 1957), 205, 213; emphasis in original. See also "On the Brooks-MacLeish Thesis," *PR* 9, 1 (January-February 1942): 38-47; T. S. Eliot, "A Letter to the Editors," *PR* 9, 2 (March-April 1942): 115-16; Harold Rosenberg, "Taste and Ego," *PR* 9, 3 (May-June 1942): 269.

17 MacLeish, "The Irresponsibles," *A Time to Speak*, 103, 104-5.

18 Ibid., 105-6.

19 Ibid., 107.

20 Ibid., 109.

21 Ibid., 112, 113, 114.

22 Ibid., 116. See MacLeish's letter to Brooks on this score: AM to Van Wyck Brooks, 20 August 1941, in *Letters of Archibald MacLeish*, 305-6.

23 Ibid., 118.

24 Ibid., 119.

25 MacLeish, "Public Speech," *A Time to Speak*, 59.

26 William Butler Yeats, *The Collected Poems of W. B. Yeats* (New York: Collier, 1989), 348.

27 MacLeish, "In Challenge, Not Defense," *A Time to Speak*, 6.

28 Charles A. Goodrum and Helen W. Dalrymple, *The Library of Congress* (Boulder, Colo.: Westview Press, 1982), 42-47; John Y. Cole, ed., *The Library of Congress in Perspective* (New York: Bowker, 1978), 25-32. See also William McGuire, *Poetry's*

Catbird Seat: The Consultantship in Poetry in the English Language at the Library of Congress, 1937–1987 (Washington, D.C.: Library of Congress, 1988).

29 Quoted in Donaldson, *Archibald MacLeish*, 350; see 349–63 for MacLeish's involvement with OFF.

30 Brett Gary makes the argument that MacLeish himself became a "nervous liberal," but his analysis does not support this conclusion. Gary demonstrates that MacLeish consistently advocated for his own beliefs. That he did not always succeed, and that he was willing to accept partial victory rather than resign, does not mean he backed away from his commitments. Had he resigned, any replacement would have been far less likely to act as MacLeish acted. Brett Gary, *Nervous Liberals: Propaganda Anxieties from World War I to the Cold War* (New York: Columbia University Press, 1999).

31 Selden Rodman, "Twixt Pundit and Poet," *Saturday Review of Literature* (11 August 1948): 29; H. C. [Hayden Carruth], "MacLeish's Actfive," *Poetry* 73 (February 1949): 287–89; Robert Fitzgerald, "Oracles and Things," *New Republic* (22 November 1948): 23; Peter Viereck, "Indignant Sing-Song," *New York Times Book Review* (21 November 1948): 35.

32 Quoted in Donaldson, *Archibald MacLeish*, 398.

33 Archibald MacLeish, "The Conquest of America," *Atlantic Monthly* 184 (August 1949): 17–22; reprinted in Archibald MacLeish, *Freedom Is the Right to Choose: An Inquiry into the Battle for the American Future* (Boston: Beacon Press, 1951), 79, 81, 92.

34 Cleanth Brooks, *Modern Poetry and the Tradition* (Chapel Hill: University of North Carolina Press, 1939).

35 Compare, for example, Richard Eberhart, "The Pattern of MacLeish's Poetry," *New York Times Book Review* (23 November 1952): 5, 48 with Frederick Morgan, "Six Poets," *Hudson Review* 6 (1953): 131.

36 Archibald MacLeish, *J.B.: A Play in Verse* (Boston: Houghton Mifflin, 1958), 153.

37 Brooks Atkinson, "From 'Job' to 'J. B.'" *New York Times*, 4 May 1958, sec 2, 1.

38 MacLeish, *J.B.*, 11.

39 Quoted in Donaldson, *Archibald MacLeish*, 458.

40 Dwight Macdonald, "Masscult and Midcult," in *Against the American Grain* (New York: Random House, 1962) 40, 44–46.

41 Ibid., 48.

42 Christopher Lasch, "The Anti-Intellectualism of the Intellectuals," in *The New Radicalism in America: The Intellectual as a Social Type* (New York: W.W. Norton, 1965), 286–348.

43 Ibid., 485.

44 Archibald MacLeish, *A Continuing Journey* (Boston: Houghton Mifflin, 1968), v.

45 Cited in Donaldson, *Archibald MacLeish*, 332.

46 See Whitfield, *A Critical American*, 90–91.

47 Dwight MacDonald, "The Responsibility of Intellectuals," *Politics* (April 1945); reproduced in *Memoirs of a Revolutionist*, 104.

48 Dwight Macdonald, "Politics Past," *Memoirs of a Revolutionist*, 9.

49 Ibid., 11.

50 Wreszin, *Rebel in Defense of Tradition*, 75–76; Dwight Macdonald, "Kronstadt Revisited," in *Discriminations: Essays and Afterthoughts, 1938–1974* (New York: Grossman, 1974), 355–60.

51 Wreszin, *Rebel in Defense of Tradition*, 83. The story, which Macdonald told frequently, is probably apocryphal.

52 Randolph S. Bourne, *War and the Intellectuals: Collected Essays, 1915–1919* (New York: Harper and Row, 1964), 3–14. See Macdonald, "Politics Past," 3 for Macdonald quoting Bourne.

53 Macdonald, "Politics Past," 7, 9; Dwight Macdonald, "War and the Intellectuals: Act Two," *PR* 6, 3 (Spring 1939): 3–20.

54 Clement Greenberg and Dwight Macdonald, "10 Propositions on the War," *PR* 8, 4 (July–August 1941), 10; Prop, 271.

55 Macdonald, "Politics Past," 10.

56 Greenberg and Macdonald, "10 Propositions." See also Dwight Macdonald, "National Defense: The Case for Socialism" *PR* 7, 4 (1940): 250–66. Dwight Macdonald, "Reading from Left to Right," *PR* 8, 1 (January–February 1941): 24–32; Dwight Macdonald, "The Future of Democratic Values," *PR* 10, 4 (July–August 1943): 321–44.

57 Macdonald, *Interviews with Dwight Macdonald*, 160.

58 A similar argument is made in Robert Westbrook, "The Responsibility of Peoples: Dwight Macdonald and the Holocaust" in *America and the Holocaust*, ed. Sanford Pinsker and Jack Fischel (Greenwood: Penkcvill, 1984), 35–68.

59 Wallace's distinction is made in many of his wartime speeches. For example, see Henry Wallace, "The Price of Free World Victory," in *The Century of the Common Man* (New York: Reynal & Hitchcock, 1943), 14–22; and Macdonald's response in Dwight Macdonald, "The (American) People Century," *PR* 9, 4 (July–August 1942): 294–310.

60 Sumner, *Dwight Macdonald and the Politics Circle*.

61 Dwight Macdonald, "Why *Politics*," *Politics* 1 (February 1944): 6.

62 Ibid.

63 See the description in Wreszin, *Rebel in Defense of Tradition*, 131–59.

64 Daniel Bell, "Politics in the 1940s," in Bell, *The End of Ideology: On the Exhaustion of Political Ideas in the Fifties* (New York: Free Press, 1962), 305–7.

65 Wreszin, *Rebel in Defense of Tradition*, 142.

66 For a typical example see Martha Gellhorn, "Das Deutsches Volk: 'We Were Never Nazis': The Germans in Defeat, April 1945," *Colliers* (26 May 1945): 13, 36, reprinted in *Reporting World War II*, vol. 2: *American Journalism 1944–1946* (New York: Library of America, 1995), 671–78. Macdonald was a voracious consumer of news

and undoubtedly saw Gellhorn's piece and others framed with similar assumptions. Macdonald took the article's title from Chiramonte.

67 Dwight Macdonald, "The Responsibility of Peoples," *Politics* (March 1945): 82–92, reprinted in *Memoirs of a Revolutionist*, 37, 38, 42.

68 Ibid., 51; emphasis in original.

69 Ibid., 51 (emphasis in original), 52.

70 Ibid., 51.

71 Ibid., 56–57, 60 (emphasis in original), 71.

72 Ibid., 61.

73 Quoted in Michael Wreszin, *A Rebel in Defense of Tradition*, 163.

74 Ibid,. 164.

75 Dwight Macdonald, "The Root Is Man," *Politics* (April 1946): 97–115, quotes 99, 100; Dwight Macdonald, "The Root Is Man II," *Politics* (July 1946): 194–214.

76 Macdonald, *Against the Grain*: , ix.

77 Macdonald, "Masscult and Midcult," 37, 38.

78 Dwight Macdonald, "Theory of Popular Culture," *Politics* 1 (February 1944): 21.

79 Macdonald, "Masscult and Midcult," 71.

80 Dwight Macdonald, "On Selling Out," *Discriminations*, 171.

81 Spiegel, *James Agee and the Legend of Himself*, 6, 12.

82 See memoirs of Agee by Macdonald and Fitzgerald in Madden and Folks, eds., *Remembering James Agee* 163–85, 37–88.

83 James Agee, *Letters of James Agee to Father Flye*, 2nd ed. (Boston: Houghton Mifflin, 1971), 5. See also W. M. Fruhock, "James Agee: The Question of Unkept Promise," *Southwest Review* 42, 3 (1957): 221–29.

84 James Agee, *The Collected Short Prose of James Agee*, ed. Robert Fitzgerald (Boston: Houghton Mifflin, 1968), 17; emphasis in original.

85 Laurence Bergreen, *James Agee: A Life* (New York: E.P. Dutton, 1984). Bergreen's use of evidence is deceptive. He regularly presents quotations from works published much later as parts of contemporary conversations. This is problematic throughout, but especially misleading given his misguided characterization of Luce and Time Inc. See 108–9, 120, 179 for instances of Dwight Macdonald's later writings taken as contemporary expressions of his feelings. Compare Bergreen's account of Agee's fantasy of shooting Luce (150) with the account in Fitzgerald's memoir on which it is based, Madden and Folks, eds., *Remembering James Agee* 38–39.

86 Belinda Rathbone, *Walker Evans: A Biography* (Boston: Houghton Mifflin, 1995), 163.

87 James Agee and Walker Evans, *Let Us Now Praise Famous Men* (Boston: Houghton Mifflin, 1941; reprint, 1960), 13, 9.

88 This was part of his fascination with personal letters, combined with the unself-consciousness of their expression.

89 His half-serious desire to publish *Famous Men* on impermanent newsprint reflected his fear of his book becoming acceptable, which he equated with artistic failure.

90 "Saratoga," *Fortune* (August 1935), reproduced in James Agee, *James Agee: Selected Journalism*, ed. Paul Ashdown (Knoxville: University of Tennessee Press, 1985), 113.

91 JA to FF, 17 February 1936, reproduced in Agee, *Letters of James Agee to Father Flye*, 85.

92 JA to FF, 17 September 1935, reproduced in ibid., 81.

93 "The U.S. Commercial Orchid," *Fortune* (December 1935), reproduced in *James Agee: Selected Journalism*, 117.

94 JA to FF, 17 February 1936.

95 JA to AM, 25 February 1936, AM Collection, Box 1, James Agee Folder.

96 Stott, *Documentary*, 262. For evidence, Stott cites a caption of a Bourke-White photograph of a working family's library, containing a dictionary, *Saturday Evening Post*, and a labor newspaper. This picture is not characteristic of the article, even less of the series. "Success Story," *Fortune* (December 1935): 115–26.

97 "Family on Relief," *Fortune* (February 1936): 64–68, 98–102.

98 JA to FF, 18 June 1936, reproduced in Agee, *Letters of James Agee to Father Flye* 92.

99 Agee, *Famous Men*, xiv.

100 Bergreen, *Agee* 145, 59. One of the nastiest bits of *Famous Men* was its inclusion of a *New York Post* profile of Bourke-White. It underlined the stark contrast between her slumming-it-up with the poor and Agee's self-doubt. Including it was an example of what Agee called "Hung with Their Own Rope." See *Collected Short Prose of Agee*, 137.

101 See accounts in Bergreen, *Agee*, 158–261; John Hersey, *Life Sketches* (New York: Knopf, 1989), 55–62.; Stott, *Documentary* 261–66.

102 Ibid., 266.

103 Agee, *Collected Short Prose*, 34.

104 Stott, *Documentary*, 262–63. Bergreen's account is unreliable on this period. He mistook the order of succession at *Fortune* and mischaracterized Hodgins, Ingersoll, and Davenport.

105 Bergreen, *Agee*, 179–80.

106 Rathbone, *Walker Evans*, 144.

107 Agee, *Famous Men*, 11, 13.

108 Ibid., 11.

109 See, for example, Paula Rabinowitz, *They Must Be Represented: The Politics of Documentary* (London: Verso, 1994), 46.

110 Quoted in Stott, *Documentary*, 292.

111 Agee, *Famous Men*, 7.

112 See ibid., 230–42.

113 Stott, *Documentary*, 266.
114 Agee, *Famous Men*, 235.
115 "Plans for Work, October 1937," reproduced in Agee, *Collected Short Prose*, 131–48.
116 JA to AM, 18 November 1937, JA Collection, Box 11, Folder 16.
117 "Notes and Suggestions on the Magazine Under Discussion," undated, JA Papers; excerpts in James Agee, *Agee: Selected Literary Documents*, ed. Victor A. Kramer (Troy, N.Y.: Whitston, 1996), 288–90. See also Victor A. Kramer, "Agee and Plans for the Criticism of Popular Culture," *Journal of Popular Culture* 4, 4 (1972): 755–66. This document may have been for the intellectual magazine discussed in Chapter 5 of this book.
118 From a summary of American film Agee wrote to MacLeish, in his capacity as librarian of Congress. JA to AM, 6 August [1944], JA Papers, Box 11, Folder 17.
119 Hersey, *Life Sketches*, 64.

Chapter 5. The Intellectual as Insider at Time Inc.

Epigraph: Robert T. Elson, *Time Inc.: The Intimate History of a Publishing Enterprise, 1923–1941* (New York: Atheneum, 1968), 419.

1 T. S. Matthews, *Name and Address* (New York: Simon and Schuster, 1960), 232.
2 This quote comes from a letter written in 1952. It follows a pattern familiar from other writer's reminiscences of going to work for *Fortune*. Davenport implicitly denied taking the job for any but financial reasons, while claiming that only the need for money kept him from being an independent writer. Neither claim was true. Russell Davenport to Henry R. Luce, RD Collection, Box 56, Folder 4.
3 See Jack Jessup's biographical sketch in Russell W. Davenport, *The Dignity of Man* (New York: Harper & Brothers, 1955), 6–7; Marcia Davenport, *Too Strong for Fantasy* (New York: Scribner's, 1967), 240–41.
4 Paul R. Gorman, *Left Intellectuals and Popular Culture* (Chapel Hill: University of North Carolina Press, 1996), 142.
5 Andreas Huyssen, "Mass Culture as a Woman: Modernism's Other," in Huyssen, *After the Great Divide* (Bloomington: Indiana University Press, 1987).
6 The details of Matthews's career at *Time*, unless otherwise cited, are from Matthews, *Name and Address*, 216–70.
7 T. S. Matthews, *Under the Influence: Recollections of Robert Graves, Laura Riding, and Friends* (London: Cassell, 1977), 124.
8 T. S. Matthews, *The Moon's No Fool* (New York: Random House, 1936); Matthews, *Under the Influence*, 147. The remarkable and sordid tale of Matthews's involvement with Riding is best told in *Under the Influence*; and Deborah Baker, *In Extremis: The Life of Laura Riding* (New York: Grove Press, 1993).
9 TSM to RC Papers, 1 July 1935, Box 1, Folder 8.
10 Ibid.

11   Matthews, *Name and Address*, 228.
12   TSM to RC, 11 September 1935, Cantwell Papers, Box 1, Folder 8.
13   James L. Baughman, *Henry R. Luce and the Rise of the American News Media* (Boston: Twayne, 1987), 42–61.
14   Matthews, *Name and Address*, 232.
15   Ibid., 238.
16   Ibid., 237.
17   Ibid.
18   Ibid., 237–38.
19   Quoted in Morris Dickstein, *Double Agent: The Critic and Society* (New York: Oxford University Press, 1992), ix.
20   Matthews, *Name and Address*, 240.
21   Reminiscences of T. S. Matthews, CUOHROC, 64–65.
22   Charles Wertenbaker, *The Death of Kings* (New York: Random House, 1954), 3–13. Robert T. Elson claims the memo was drawn from internal documents written up the year before and excerpted in his account. Without the actual memo, however, it is impossible to judge exactly what Luce covered in the memo for Matthews and his friends. Robert T. Elson, *Time Inc.: The Intimate History of a Publishing Enterprise, 1923–1941* (New York: Atheneum, 1968), 380.
23   Matthews, *Name and Address*, 243.
24   Dwight Macdonald, "Liberal Soap Opera," in *Memoirs of a Revolutionist: Essays in Political Criticism* (New York: Farrar, Straus and Cudahy, 1957).
25   Elson, *Time Inc.*, 379.
26   Ibid., 419.
27   Ibid., 381.
28   Robert T. Elson, *The World of Time Inc.: The Intimate History of a Publishing Enterprise*, vol. 2, *1941–1960* (New York: Atheneum, 1973), 63.
29   TSM to RC, 16 January 1940, Cantwell Papers, Box 2, Folder 3.
30   Matthews, *Name and Address*, 260.
31   Ibid., 266.
32   Matthews, CUOHROC, 100.
33   Irving Howe, *A Margin of Hope: An Intellectual Autobiography* (New York: Harcourt Brace Jovanovich, 1982), 122–27.
34   Louis Kronenberger, *No Whippings, No Gold Watches: The Saga of a Writer and His Jobs* (Boston: Little, Brown, 1970), 42.
35   Matthews, *Name and Address*, 265.
36   Matthews, CUOHROC, 101. The same problem occurred at *Fortune*, where legends about unstable writers flourished. Wilder Hobson allegedly once sat at his desk for three weeks staring at the same blank piece of paper. Such behavior could be absorbed better at a monthly magazine.
37   Matthews, *Name and Address*, 260.
38   Elson, *The World of Time Inc.*, 207.

39   Ibid., 363.

40   In later years Matthews came to agree with Prentice, publishing a study of the British newspapers that concluded, "the Press is not our daily bread but our daily sugar pill." T. S. Matthews, *The Sugar Pill: An Essay on Newspapers* (London: Victor Gollancz, 1958), 9.

41   Elson, *The World of Time Inc.*, 68–69.

42   See Louis Kronenberger's memoir for evidence of this transition, *No Whippings*.

43   Elson, *The World of Time Inc.*, 66.

44   Quoted in James R. Mellow, *Walker Evans* (New York: Basic Books, 1999), 479.

45   Quoted in Matthews, *Name and Address*, 244. Matthews had shown the Wilson essay criticizing *Time* to Luce and the other editors.

46   "You Only Live Once," *Time* (11 January 1937): 36.

47   In its dismissive accounts of existentialism, interestingly, the verbal tics crept back in. *Time* described Sartre as "France's stubby (5 ft.), scholarly, Jean-Paul Sartre," *Time* (21 July 1947): 94–96.

48   Quoted in James Agee, *The Collected Short Prose of James Agee*, ed. Robert Fitzgerald (Boston: Houghton Mifflin, 1968), 41.

49   Ibid., 40.

50   James Agee, *Agee on Film: Criticism and Comment on the Movies*, ed. Martin Scorsese (New York: Modern Library, 2000), ix. W. H. Auden for example, rarely attended the movies, but read Agee's reviews religiously.

51   Kronenberger, *No Whippings*.

52   The best of these are collected in James Agee, *Selected Journalism* (Knoxville: University of Tennessee Press, 2005).

53   "Ghosts on the Roof," *Time* (5 March 1945); reprinted in Whittaker Chambers, *Ghosts on the Roof: Selected Journalism of Whittaker Chambers, 1931–1959*, ed. Terry Teachout (Washington, D.C.: Regnery Gateway, 1989), 111–15.

54   "Victory: The Peace," *Time* (20 August 1945): 19–21; reprinted in Elson, *The World of Time Inc.*, 134–35.

55   T. S. Matthews, *Angels Unawares: Twentieth-Century Portraits* (New York: Ticknor and Fields, 1985), 238.

56   Elson, *The World of Time Inc.*, 66.

57   Kronenberger, *No Whippings*, 122. For more evidence of the regard writers felt for Matthews, see Elson, *The World of Time Inc.*, 204–5.

58   His wife, Clare Booth Luce, resented it even more. One year she presented each Time Inc. writer who had published a book with a special leather-bound edition of the writer's work. On the cover she had each book stamped "Written on Harry's Time." Thomas Griffith, *Harry and Teddy: The Turbulent Friendship of Press Lord Henry R. Luce and His Favorite Reporter, Theodore H. White* (New York: Random House, 1995), 139.

59 Matthews, *Angels Unawares*, 236.
60 Whittaker Chambers, *Witness* (Chicago: Henry Regnery, 1952), 478.
61 Elson, *Time Inc.*, 8.
62 Elson, *The World of Time Inc.*, 65.
63 Details of Davenport's life are drawn from the biographical sketch by John Jessup in Davenport, *Dignity of Man*, 118–41; and Davenport, *Too Strong for Fantasy*, 65–243.
64 "Reply of the Young Men of Wall Street to Mr. A. MacLeish," RD Collection, Box 51, Folder 1, Economics, 1931. This essay was never published.
65 Writing to his college friend F. O. Matthiessen about Matthiessen's book on T. S. Eliot, Davenport delivered a closely argued indictment of his friend's evasion of the relationship between poetry and the living beliefs of an age, criticizing him for seeking a pure poetry rather than a poetry connected to the issues animating the poet's time. In his acknowledgments, Matthiessen noted that "many pages have benefited from the vigorous onslaught of Russell Davenport, who takes exception to much that I have said here and elsewhere, or am likely to say in the future." RD to F.O. Matthiessen, 26 October 1934, RD Collection, Box 12, Folder 16. F. O. Matthiessen, *The Achievement of T.S. Eliot: An Essay on the Nature of Poetry* (New York: Oxford University Press, 1958), xv.
66 Kronenberger, *No Whippings* 69.
67 RD Collection, Box 54, Folder 40; emphasis in original.
68 Staff Luncheon Minutes, 18 November 1937, RD Collection, Box 54, Folder 40.
69 AM to Eric Hodgins and RD, 26 April 1938, RD Collection, Box 54, Folder 41.
70 The Business and Government editorials have been studied in James David Isbister, "The Political Consciousness of *Fortune* Magazine" (M.A. thesis, George Washington University, 1966); James R. Jensen, "The 'New Conservatism' of *Fortune* Magazine (1930–1952)" (Ph.D. dissertation, University of Iowa, 1956); Joseph Jacobs Thorndike, "The Liberal and Salutary Path: *Fortune* Magazine and the Search for a Business Liberalism" (M.A. thesis, University of Virginia, 1993), 611–76. None of these works say much about how the "Business and Government" page came into being. Each incorrectly takes Davenport's editorials as indicative of a unified *Fortune* ideology, in place from 1930 to 1950.
71 RD to AM, 28 April 1938, RD Collection, Box 20, Folder 24.
72 "Business and Government," *Fortune* (February 1938): 58.
73 *Fortune* Researchers to RD, 7 April 1938, RD Collection, Box 54, Folder 41.
74 RD to staff, 11 April 1938, RD Collection, Box 54, Folder 4; emphasis in original.
75 "Policy for Business News," 7 March 1940, RD Collection, Box 54, Folder 40; emphasis in original.
76 RD to AM, 28 April 1938, RD Collection, Box 20 Folder 24.
77 Elson, *Time Inc.*, 417.

78   "Business and Government," *Fortune* (April 1940): 46–47; emphasis in original.

79   Wendell L. Willkie, "We, the People," *Fortune* (April 1940): 64–65, 162–64, 168–73.

80   Steve Neal, *Dark Horse: A Biography of Wendell Willkie* (Lawrence: University of Kansas Press, 1984), 49.

81   "War and Peace," *Fortune* (January 1940): 26-27.

82   Lewis Mumford to HRL, 4 February 1940, RD Collection, Box 54, Folder 14.

83   RD to LM, 5 February 1940, RD Collection, Box 54, Folder 14.

84   "The Case Against the Intellectuals," 19 February 1941, RD Collection, Box 98, Folder 15.

85   Archibald MacLeish, "The Irresponsibles," in *A Time to Speak: The Selected Prose of Archibald MacLeish* (Boston: Houghton Mifflin, 1940), 103–21.

86   Russell W. Davenport, "The Next President Must Be . . . Wendell L. Willkie," *Fortune* (October 1940): 68–71, 116–18; John Chamberlain, "The Next President Must Be . . . Franklin D. Roosevelt," *Fortune* (October 1940), quoted in Elson, *Time Inc.*, 442. Chamberlain, author of the popular book *Farewell to Reform* (1934), was another intellectual who spent years at *Fortune* and Time Inc. After MacLeish left *Fortune*, he marked the left flank at the magazine, but he moved steadily to the right throughout the 1940s. At one point Chamberlain requested "the works" (half work at full pay) from Luce, writing to RD, "I've got to get going on my own projects—life's too short to let the years go by as I have the past seven. A writer can't afford to be institutionalized or anonymized (if that's a word) unless he checks 100 percent with his organization." RD Collection, Box 56, Folder 1.

87   Dan Longwell to RD, 23 May 1941, RD Collection, Box 75, Folder 9.

88   In what may be read as a commentary on mixing literary style with political ideas, Davenport wrote to a friend about the phrase "you will lose us," "the goddamn hell of the whole thing is that I only put those words in for the rhythm," quoted in Elson, *The World of Time Inc.*, 23.

89   RD to HRL, 24 October 1942, RD Collection, Box 71, Folder 8.

90   Quoted in Elson, *The World of Time Inc.*, 28.

91   RD to HRL, 17 March 1943, RD Collection, Box 71, Folder 8.

92   For the text of Davenport's broadcast see RD Papers, Box 27, Folder 6.

93   RD to AM, AM Papers, Box 6, Russell Davenport Folder.

94   Russell W. Davenport, *My Country* (New York: Simon and Schuster, 1944).

95   FOM to RD, no date, RD Collection, Box 97, Folder 6.

96   Davenport, *Dignity of Man*, 26–27.

97   Ibid.,14.

98   *Time* (11 June 1956): 65–70. For a critical account of this development, see Arthur M. Schlesinger, Jr., "*Time* and the Intellectuals," in *The Politics of Hope* (New York: Houghton Mifflin, 1963) 230–36.

99   John Chamberlain memo to HRL, RD Papers, Box 70, Folder 24, p. 3. The

history of *Magazine X* is briefly considered in Robert J. Vanderlan, "Time Inc. and the Intellectuals" (Ph.D. dissertation, University of Rochester, 2004), 292–301.

100   Griffith, *Harry and Teddy*, 165.

101   Details of Schlamm's career are from Elson, *The World of Time Inc.*, 206; Alfred Kazin, *New York Jew* (New York: Knopf, 1978), 59–62; Dwight Macdonald, "Memo to Mr. Luce," in MacDonald, *Memoirs of a Revolutionist: Essays in Political Criticism* (New York: Farrar, Straus and Cudahy, 1957) 254–61.

102   Kazin, *New York Jew*, 62.

103   A proper name was never found. The magazine was known variously as *Magazine X*, *Truth*, *Measure*, *Quest*, and even *The Atomic Age and the New Statesman*. Elson refers to it as *Measure*, but that name was still not in use when subscription letters went out in November 1947. See HRL to Tomlinson, 18 November 1947, RD Collection, Box 70, Folder 4.

104   Willi Schlamm to HRL, "Notes on the New Magazine," RD Collection, Box 70, Folder 49.

105   Ibid.

106   Rosalind Constable, Untitled response to Magazine "X", RD Collection, Box 71, Folder 2.

107   Macdonald, "Memo to Mr. Luce." 255.

108   Schlamm, "Notes on the New Magazine."

109   Matthews, CUOHROC, 111.

110   TSM to HRL, 11 June 1947, RD Collection, Box 70, Folder 24.

111   Ibid. Schlamm, "Notes on the New Magazine."

112   TSM to HRL, 11 June 1947, RD Collection, Box 70, Folder 24.

113   Matthews, CUOHROC, 114.

114   Davenport was alluding to Arnold's description of Shelly as a "beautiful, ineffectual angel." Interestingly, Davenport substituted "mutilated" for Arnold's "luminous." The text reads "A beautiful and ineffectual angel, beating in the void his luminous wings in vain." Matthews Arnold, *Essays in Criticism: Second Series* (London: Macmillan and Company, 1913), 203–4.

115   RD to Eric Hodgins, 31 March 1947, RD Collection, Box 19, Folder 32; emphasis in original.

116   Schlamm, "Notes on the New Magazine," 20.

117   RD to HRL, "Preliminary Notes on Magazine X," 8 July 1947, RD Collection, Box 70, Folder 49.

118   Dwight Macdonald, "The Root Is Man," *Politics* (April 1946): 97–115.

119   Evidence of this antipathy, and of the equation of Time Inc. with mass culture generally, is ubiquitous. For examples, see Norman Mailer, "Our Country and Our Culture," *Partisan Review* 19, 3 (May–June 1952): 298; Gertrude Himmelfarb, "Anonymity, 'Time,' and Success," *Commentary* (July 1960): 83–86; Dwight Macdonald, "On Selling Out," in *Discriminations: Essays and Afterthoughts, 1938–1974* (New York: Grossman, 1974) 171–73; Wallace Makefield, "Children of the Fattening '50s: Our Non-

Generation Revisited," *New Leader* (18 March 1957): 21–22; Murray Kempton, "Ralph Ginzburg: Panderer," *New York World Telegram*, (16 March 1966); C. Wright Mills, *White Collar* (London: Oxford University Press, 1951), 149.

120   Untitled Meeting Notes on the "Dummy" Issue of Magazine "X," RD Collection, Box 70, Folder 39.

121   Matthews, CUOHROC, 113.

122   John Chamberlain to HRL, RD Collection, Box 70, Folder 48.

123   Elson, *The World of Time Inc.*, 207.

124   And for Schlamm too. Schlamm returned to Europe, where his views became increasingly alarming. He ended his career pushing for a preemptive nuclear strike against the Soviet Union, arguing that if it was right to resist evil, it did not matter how many people might be killed. Quoted in Kazin, *New York Jew*, 61–62.

125   Quoted in Griffith, *Harry and Teddy*, 200.

126   Matthews, *Name and Address*, 274.

127   Matthews, CUOHROC, 126–29.

128   See "About Life's Round Tables," RD Collection, Box 64, Folder 11.

129   RD to HRL, "Notes on Election," 5 November 1948, RD Collection, Box 25, Folder 2.

130   Quoted in Davenport, *Dignity of Man*, 20.

131   Editors of *Fortune* with Russell Davenport, *U.S.A.: The Permanent Revolution* (New York: Prentice-Hall, 1951), 67, 78–79.

132   RD to HRL, 20 February 1952, RD Collection, Box 56, Folder 4.

Chapter 6. Journalism and Politics at *Time* Magazine

Epigraph: Archibald MacLeish, *Conquistador*, in *Poems: 1924–1933* (Boston: Houghton Mifflin, 1933), 239–41.

1   Thomas Griffith, *Harry and Teddy: The Turbulent Friendship of Press Lord Henry R. Luce and His Favorite Reporter, Theodore H. White* (New York: Random House, 1995), 168.

2   John Hersey, "The Legend on the License," *Yale Review* (1980): 2.

3   THW to RW, 9 February 1945, THW Papers, Box 4, Folder 31; Theodore H. White, *In Search of History: A Personal Adventure* (New York: Harper & Row, 1978), 242.

4   Theodore H. White, "Eagles in Shansi," *Time* (18 December 1939): 22. The byline inaugurated a practice of running bylines for reporters who faced physical dangers to file their stories. W. A. Swanberg, *Luce and His Empire* (New York: Scribner's, 1972), 184; Robert T. Elson, *The World of Time Inc.: The Intimate History of a Publishing Enterprise*, vol. 2, *1941–1960* (New York: Atheneum, 1973), 470.

5   THW Diary entry, 1938, THW Papers, Box 193, Folder 1.

6   Quoted in Whittaker Chambers, *Ghosts on the Roof: Selected Journalism of Whittaker Chambers, 1931–1959*, ed. Terry Teachout (Washington, D.C.: Regnery Gateway, 1989), xx.

7   The focus on war production opened up arenas where the magazine explicitly criticized America's business leadership. With boosting production as the most important goal, the magazine published searching exposé social problems that threatened to slow or disrupt the war effort, including trenchant criticisms of racial conflict and discrimination.

8   Elson, *The World of Time Inc.* 148-49; Editors of *Fortune*, *Writing for Fortune* (New York: Time Inc., 1980), 37-50.

9   John Chamberlain, *The Enterprising Americans: A Business History of the West* (New York: Harper and Row, 1963); John Chamberlain, *Farewell to Reform: Being a History of the Rise, Life, and Decay of the Progressive Mind in America* (New York: Liveright, 1932); Editors of *Fortune*, *Writing for Fortune*, 23-36. *Fortune* did employ ex-Trotskyists such as Herbert Solow and John Mcdonald, but their political views were largely confined to an anti-communism that fit in well at Time Inc. Interview with Daniel Bell (16 February 2004).

10   John Kenneth Galbraith, *A Life in Our Times: Memoirs* (Boston: Houghton Mifflin, 1981), 256-69.

11   Quoted in Griffith, *Harry and Teddy*, 123.

12   Scott Donaldson, *Archibald MacLeish: An American Life* (Boston: Houghton Mifflin, 1992), 277-79; Michael Wreszin, *A Rebel in Defense of Tradition: The Life and Politics of Dwight Macdonald* (New York: Basic Books, 1994), 49.

13   See AM to Goldsborough, 22 February 1937, 23 February 1937; AM to Goldsborough, Luce, and Hodgins, 22 February 1937, AM Collection, Box 8, "Fortune."

14   Robert E. Herzstein, *Henry R. Luce: A Political Portrait of the Man Who Created the American Century* (New York: Scribner's, 1994), 97.

15   Ibid., 110.

16   JH to Mother and Father, 12 May 1935, JH Papers, Box 1, Letters to Grace Baird Hersey, Folder 8 (by my count). Before graduation, he presented his friends with a privately published volume of his poetry, and he appears to have written drafts of a couple of novels during these years. On the poetry, see Heckscher reminiscences in Carter Wiseman, "A Life in Writing: John Hersey, 1914-1993" *Yale Alumni Magazine* (October 1993) (accessed at http://www.yalealumnimagazine.com/issues/93_10?html on 4 march 2003). On the novels, see Brendan Gill to JH, undated, JH Papers, Box 2, corr. "G" 1937-1951. The reference to Hersey's showing novels to "Red" (Sinclair Lewis) is ambiguous. It is possible that the novels Gill refers to are his own.

17   Sanders, *John Hersey* (New York: Twayne, 1967), 21.

18   Gott to JH, various dates, JH Papers, Box 2, Corr "T" 1937-1951.

19   JH to M&F, 28 November 1938, JH Papers, Box 1, Letters to GBH.

20   JH to M&F, 13 January 1939, JH Papers, Box 1, Letters to GBH.

21   Swanberg, *Luce and His Empire*.

22   JH to THW, 29 January 1940, JH Papers, Box 2, Corr "W" 1937-1951.

23   Sanders, *John Hersey*, 23.

24   John Hersey, *Men on Bataan* (New York: Knopf, 1942) 7. The book's fulsome praise of MacArthur later embarrassed Hersey, who asked his publisher to take it out of print.

25   See discussion of reviews in Sanders, *Hersey Revisited* (Boston: Twayne, 1990) 4–5; Nancy Lyman Huse, *John Hersey and James Agee: A Reference Guide* (Boston: G.K. Hall, 1978), 7–8.

26   John Hersey, "The Battle of the River," *Life* (23 November 1942): 99–116, reproduced in *Reporting World War II*, vol. 1, *American Journalism 1938–1944* (New York: Library of America, 1995), 402–19.

27   Interview with John Hersey," *The Paris Review* 100 (August 1986) 210–49, quote 228.

28   Compare, for example, "a lone bullet would sing over our heads like a supercharged bee" in *Life* with "a lone bullet would sing over our heads, and hundreds of men would involuntarily duck" in the book (17). Hersey could not resist the word sing, using it to set up the observation that followed (one of the rare reaches for literary effect that remained): "The music in that valley made them almost elderly."

29   Hersey, "The Battle of the River," in *Reporting World War II*, vol. 1, 413

30   John Hersey, *Into the Valley* (New York: Knopf, 1943), 73–75.

31   John Hersey, "Dialogue on Gorki Street," *Fortune* (January 1945), 149–51; John Hersey, "Joe Is Home Now," *Life*, (3 July 1944): 68-80; John Hersey, "Nine Men on a Four Man Raft," *Life* (2 November 1942): 54–57; John Hersey, "Prisoner 339, Klooga," *Life*, (30 October 1944): 72–83; John Hersey, "Survival," *New Yorker* (17 July 1944): 31–34. The response to "Joe Is Home Now" was so positive that Time Inc. studied the possibility of making it into a feature film. Though they ultimately failed to pursue the project, the article did influence the Oscar-winning "Best Years of Our Lives." See JH Papers, Box 13, Folder "Joe Is Home" for analysis by Audience Research Inc.

32   Hersey, "Hersey," 223.

33   John Hersey, *A Bell for Adano* (New York: Knopf, 1944), v, 48.

34   John Hersey, *Hiroshima* (New York: Knopf, 1946); John Hersey, *The Wall* (New York: Knopf, 1950).

35   TSM to JH, 19 September 1943, JH Papers, Box 2, Corr "M" 1937–1951.

36   The best source on issues of anti-Semitism and Time Inc. is Herzstein, *Luce*.

37   Ibid., 51.

38   White, *In Search of History*, 51, 53.

39   "Conversation"/"observation" in THW Diary, 2; "Squirming" quoted in Hoffmann, *White*, 22.

40   White, *In Search of History*, 76, 65.

41   Ibid., 80, 72.

42   Ibid., 84.

43   THW to JH, 21 July 1939, THW Papers, Box 3, Folder 1; JH to THW, 29 January 1940, THW Papers, Box 3, Folder 3.

44   White, *In Search of History*, 101.

45 Ibid., 103.
46 Griffith, *Harry and Teddy*, 9.
47 THW to Mary and Gladys White, 4 June 1943, THW Papers, Box 4, Folder 11; THW to Mary and Gladys White, 5 August 1944, THW Papers, Box 4 Folder 26; THW to Mary and Gladys White, 3 May 1943, THW Papers, Box 4, Folder 10; Time Inc. cable, David Hurlburd to THW, reproduced in THW to Mary and Gladys White, 4 July 1943, THW Papers, Box 4, Folder 12.
48 Joyce Hoffmann, *Theodore H. and Journalism as Illusion* (Columbia: University of Missouri Press, 1995), 43.
49 White, *In Search of History*, 144.
50 Ibid., 144–56.
51 Ibid., 154.
52 Ibid., 155.
53 THW to JH and Wilma Hersey, 24 July 1944, THW Papers, Box 4, Folder 25.
54 THW to "Joe" [Liebling], n.d., THW papers, Box 8, Folder 25. Liebling was gathering material in 1949 for a *New Yorker* profile on Henry Luce. It was never written. See Abbott Joseph Liebling, "Notes on Henry R. Luce, Time and Related Materials," AJL Collection, Box 10.
55 THW to HRL, n.d., THW Papers, Box 3, Folder 21.
56 White later described these as a "remarkable intellectual volleying" as he invoked "Alfred North Whitehead and Science and Reason against [Luce's] Christ and Confucius." Thomas Griffith claims the exchanges read as if "the two men were dragging up half-remembered history and philosophy from their college courses, each trying to overwhelm the other." Griffith seems to have been influenced by the name-dropping (Whitehead in particular), and misses the seriousness of the exchange. It reveals two men thinking hard to make sense of China, grasping for a narrative of change that could explain current events.
57 HRL to THW (copies to Billings, Osborne, Jessup, and Schlamm), 3 April 1944, and THW to HRL, n.d., THW Papers Box 3, Folder 21.
58 Sam Tanenhaus, *Whittaker Chambers: A Biography* (New York: Random House, 1997), 3. Biographical details of Chambers's life come from Tanenhaus; Whittaker Chambers, *Witness* (Chicago: Henry Regnery, 1952); Allen Weinstein, *Perjury: The Hiss-Chambers Case* (New York: Random House, 1978); Terry Teachout, "Introduction to Chambers," in *Ghosts on the Roof*, xiii–xxix. I am also indebted to the characterizations of Chambers and his ideas in Irving Howe, "God, Man and Stalin," in Howe, *Celebrations and Attacks: Thirty Years of Literary and Cultural Commentary* (New York: Horizon Press, 1979) 80–86; Murray Kempton, *Part of Our Time: Some Ruins and Monuments of the 1930s* (New York: Modern Library, 1998), 17–45; Lionel Trilling, *The Middle of the Journey* (New York: Avon, 1975).
59 For treatments of all three, including their ongoing relations with Chambers, see Alan M. Wald, *The New York Intellectuals: The Rise and Decline of the Anti-Stalinist Left from the 1930s to the 1980s* (Chapel Hill: University of North Carolina Press, 1987).

60 Tanenhaus, *Chambers*, 22–23.
61 Chambers, *Cold Friday*, 107.
62 Ibid., 115.
63 Tanenhaus, *Chambers*, 26–28.
64 Chambers, *Cold Friday*, 229.
65 Trilling, *The Middle of the Journey*, xiii.
66 Chambers, *Cold Friday*, 115.
67 Tanenhaus, *Chambers*, 30–32.
68 Chambers, *Witness*, 195.
69 At the time, it was called the Worker's Party of America.
70 Tanenhaus, *Chambers*, 55.
71 Whittaker Chambers, "Can You Make Out Their Voices," *New Masses* (March 1931), reprinted in *Ghosts on the Roof*, 3–21.
72 Tanenhaus, *Chambers*, 71–72.
73 Robert Cantwell, "The Chambers Story," *Newsweek* (26 May 1952): 101–2.
74 The Editors, "To All Intellectuals," *New Masses* (May 1932): 1. In 1952 Chambers affirmed authorship, adding "I would not change a word of what, having written it in 1932, I have so richly proved in 1948." Quoted in Tanenhaus, *Chambers*, 540n39.
75 Chambers, *Witness*, 276.
76 Trilling, *The Middle of the Journey*, ix.
77 T. S. Matthews, *Angels Unawares: Twentieth-Century Portraits* (New York: Ticknor and Fields, 1985), 169–70.
78 Chambers, *Witness*, 86. Chambers misremembered the quote. It actually went: "One bomby Sunday afternoon. . . . " See "The Menacing Sun," *Time* (1 May 1939), reprinted in Chambers, *Ghosts on the Roof*, 49.
79 Matthews, *Angels Unawares*, 170.
80 Louis Kronenberger, *No Whippings, No Gold Watches: The Saga of a Writer and His Jobs* (Boston: Little, Brown, 1970), 132.
81 "Finnegans Wake," *Time* (8 May 1939): 78–84.
82 Tanenhaus, *Chambers*, 156; Elson, *The World of Time Inc.*, 103–4.
83 Chambers, *Witness*, 474–76.
84 Ibid., 477.
85 "The New Pictures: 'The Grapes of Wrath,'" *Time* (12 February 1940), reprinted in Chambers, *Ghosts on the Roof*, 58–59.
86 Tanenhaus, *Chambers*, 164.
87 Ibid., 166.
88 "The Revolt of the Intellectuals," *Time* (6 January 1941), reprinted in Chambers, *Ghosts on the Roof*, 60–62.
89 Matthews, *Angels Unawares*, 172.
90 By this time Chambers had tired of his Episcopalian faith, finding it too tepid, moving on to Quakerism. He found George Fox to be, in an oddly revealing

interpretation, a "man of force," as if the Quaker founder had been some sort of early day Lenin. Tanenhaus, *Chambers*, 171.

91 Editors of *Fortune*, "A Chambers Legacy," *Fortune* (September 1961): 90. William Ernest Hocking, "What Man Can Make of Man," *Fortune* (February 1942): 91–93, 136–47 (quote 91); William Pepperall Montague, "Philosophy in a World at War," *Fortune* (March 1942): 103–12; Jacques Maritain, "Christian Humanism," *Fortune* (April 1942): 106–7, 160–73 (quote 164); William A. Sperry, "Our Moral Chaos," *Fortune* (May 1942): 102–8.

92 Julian Huxley, "The Biologist Looks at Man," *Fortune* (December 1942): 139–41, 146–52 (quotes 146, 139).

93 Reinhold Niebuhr, "A Faith for History's Greatest Crisis," *Fortune* (July 1942): 99–100, 122–31. Other authors in the series included Alfred Noyes, Robert M. Hutchins, Charles Morris, Charles W. Hendel, Bertrand Russell, Susanne K. Langer, Ernst Cassirer, and John Dewey.

94 Tanenhaus, *Chambers*, 173–75; Elson, *The World of Time Inc.*, 101–24; Chambers, *Witness*, 493–96.

95 Quoted in Elson, *The World of Time Inc.*, 96.

96 Letter to Luce, quoted in ibid., 105.

97 Chambers, *Witness*, 497.

98 Elson, *The World of Time Inc.*, 105–7; Griffith, *Harry and Teddy*, 133–48.

99 Quoted in Tanenhaus, *Chambers*, 180.

100 Roy Larsen eventually donated the cables to Harvard, where they can be compared with what appeared in the magazine. Unfortunately, White's Stilwell story (see below), having been smuggled home, is not in the collection. See "Time Inc. Dispatches from *Time* Magazine Correspondents: First Series, 1942–1955," Houghton Library, Harvard College Library. Robert Herzstein makes excellent use of these, comparing the content of the cables with the finished magazine to demonstrate how Time Inc. editors (and Luce) rewrote the news to fit their ideology. Robert E. Herzstein, *Henry R. Luce, Time, and the American Crusade in Asia* (Cambridge: Cambridge University Press, 2005).

101 HRL to JH, 5 November 1944, JH Papers, Box 7, Folder 5.

102 JH to HRL, 14 November 1944, JH Papers, Box 7, Folder 5.

103 Dick Lauterbach to JH, 27 November 1944, JH Papers, Box 2, Corr "L" 1937–1951. Lauterbach was the correspondent Chambers trusted least. The recently released Venona transcripts contain two mentions of Lauterbach. According to John Earl Haynes and Harvey Klehr's account of the transcripts, Lauterbach was named twice, both times because he had been approached by Soviet agent Jack Soble. Haynes and Klehr write that Lauterbach told Soble he had been pressured to write an anti-Soviet piece and had refused and threatened to resign. Because of his positive views on the Soviet Union, Soble thought Lauterbach should be investigated with intent to draw him in to the KGB apparatus. Nothing seems to have come from this as Lauterbach is not mentioned again. Soble also claimed that Lauterbach was a secret member of the CPUSA, though no

confirming evidence for this charge is offered. Though Haynes and Klehr do not label a Lauterbach a Communist agent, the paragraphs that follow consider Stephen Laird, of whom they claim "Venona cables show that he, too, was a KGB agent." If this is meant to imply that they believe Lauterbach to be an agent, it seems a reach from the insufficient evidence they provide. Dick Lauterback was sympathetic to the Soviet Union. He may or may not have been a member of the CPUSA. There is no evidence to suggest he worked for the KGB. John Earl Haynes and Harvey Klehr, *Venona: Decoding Soviet Espionage in America* (New Haven, Conn.: Yale University Press, 1999), 237.

104   JH to "Patch," 13 December 1944, JH Papers, Box 7, Folder 1.

105   White, *In Search of History*, 247.

106   Michael Schaller, *The United States and China: Into the Twenty-First Century*, 3rd ed. (Oxford: Oxford University Press, 2002), 67–86.

107   White, *In Search of History*, 208–10.

108   Tanenhaus, *Chambers*, 180.

109   Chambers, *Witness*, 498.

110   Griffith, *Harry and Teddy*, 227.

111   For examples, see Theodore H. White, "*Life* Looks at China," *Life* (1 May 1944): 98–110. Even White's favorable report on the Communists in Yenan, which followed the Stilwell article, was careful to distinguish the Communists from the agrarian liberal myth. Theodore H. White, "*Life* Looks at China: Inside Red China," *Life* (18 December 1944): 39–46.

112   In February 1944 White wrote to a friend, warning her not to see the Soviets as acting altruistically. Sure, they were winning the war, White admitted, but not for us. He believed the Soviets had a shared interest in peace, but were "not averse to putting something over on us if she can, willing to drive a hard bargain, willing to break the bargain if she thinks it's to her best interest, but willing to stick to a bargain if the other party deals with her on the same basis of ruggedness." THW to "Butsy," 15 February 1944, THW Papers, Box 4, Folder 24.

113   "Crisis," *Time* (13 November 1944), reprinted in *Ghosts on the Roof*, 104–10.

114   White, *In Search of History*, 209. White guessed, probably correctly, that Luce would not have let such an important China story pass without his knowledge.

115   THW to Mama and Gladys White, 3 December 1944, THW Papers, Box 4, Folder 26.

116   White, "*Life* Looks at China." Almost without exception, American journalists and foreign-service officers returned from Yenan with similar positive impressions. Evaluating the reliability of these reports has been difficult. Chambers and like-minded critics concluded they were all fellow travelers (or worse) deliberately distributing Communist propaganda. This conclusion is insupportable. Their reports were influenced by a combination of factors. First, the stark contrast between Communist and Nationalist treatment of the press. Second, the effectively disguised Communist management of the visitor's experience. Finally, a more open Communist Party at the time (a hidden repressive apparatus existed within the party, but tolerance was far greater

during the campaigns to win control than it would be once political power was seized). See Carolle J. Carter, *Mission to Yenan: American Liaison with the Chinese Communists, 1944–1947* (Lexington: University Press of Kentucky, 1997); Schaller, *United States and China*, 87–104; Michael Schaller, *The U.S. Crusade in China, 1939–1945* (New York: Columbia University Press, 1979), 177–231; Kenneth E. Shewmaker, *Americans and Chinese Communists, 1927–1945* (Ithaca, N.Y.: Cornell University Press, 1971).

117   Quoted in Griffith, *Harry and Teddy*, 123.

118   THW to "Bobby," 9 February 1945, THW Papers, Box 4, Folder 31.

119   "Historic Force," *Time* (5 February 1945), quoted in Tanenhaus, *Chambers*, 189.

120   "The Ghosts on the Roof," *Time* (5 March 1945), reprinted in *Ghosts on the Roof*, 111–15.

121   Elson, *The World of Time Inc.*, 114–15; Tanenhaus, *Chambers*, 190.

122   Chambers, *Witness*, 500–501.

123   Swanberg, *Luce and His Empire*, 223–25.

124   Herzstein, *Luce*, 416.

125   John Earl Haynes, "The Haunted Wood: Soviet Espionage in America—The Stalin Era (Book Review)" *Journal of Cold War Studies* 1, 2 (1999): 121–23.

126   So-called traditionalists have long stressed distinctions between different brands of anti-communism. Unfortunately, such nuance is often missing from more popular works, which have seized on the revelations to justify all variants of the war on communism. John Earl Haynes, *Red Scare or Red Menace? American Communism and Anticommunism in the Cold War Era* (Chicago: Ivan R. Dee, 1996).

127   Arthur Herman, *Joseph McCarthy: Reexamining the Life of America's Most Hated Senator* (New York: Free Press, 2000); Ann H. Coulter, *Treason: Liberal Treachery from the Cold War to the War on Terrorism* (New York: Crown, 2003). Herman provides a scholarly assessment and partial defense, Coulter a screed. The slipperiness by which verification of Communist infiltration slides into defense of the persecution of suspected Communists can be seen in Michael Warner's claim that there is widespread agreement "that Senator McCarthy was indeed loathsome—but was so only because of his virulence, not because of his aims." Michael Warner, *Many are the Crimes* (Book Review) *Journal of Cold War Studies* 3, 2 (Spring 2001): 101–3. In similar fashion, Patricia Neils has written a blow-by-blow exoneration of Luce. The best that can be said of Neils's work is that it is tendentious and unsophisticated. At its worse, it is incompetent and misleading. Her book can be easily dismissed: any historian who believes the opinion of Madame Chiang is sufficient to rebut historical scholarship is not to be trusted. Neils begins her book by quoting Madame Chiang's attack on critics of Luce, and seems to believe this discredits such critics. One further example of the caliber of Neils's work: she acknowledges White's reaction to the Honan famine, then undercut its importance by noting that famines have always occurred in China and would be worse under the Communists (how famines years in the future could be relevant to White's thinking in 1943 is left unexplained). She then speculates, in her inimitably awkward prose, that

"chagrin, frustration and ego upset all seem to be plausible factors" for White's turn against Chiang. Neils's questions—what's the big deal about famine? and whose famine killed more?—were irrelevant. White's question—was the government alleviating or exacerbating famine?—was the proper one. Patricia Neils, *China Images in the Life and Times of Henry Luce* (Savage, Md.: Rowman & Littlefield, 1990), 1, 103–4.

128 Chambers would likely have smiled at this characterization. The descriptions "not above" (suggesting Chambers's refusal to hold himself to a higher standard) and "crimping" (suggesting a gentle molding and shaping) were worthy of the man who reduced Chiang's brutal authoritarianism to ruling "high-handedly."

129 Tanenhaus, *Chambers*, 181.

130 Chambers wrote a profile of Marx for *Time* on the anniversary of the publication of *The Communist Manifesto* calling him the man of the century. "In the historic sense," he declared, "Karl Marx has only just begun to live." "Dr. Crankley's Children," *Time* (23 February 1948), reprinted in *Ghosts on the Roof*, 175–83.

131 Chambers, *Witness*, 541, 25.

132 James A. Linen, "A Letter from the Publisher," *Time* (10 February 1947): 17.

133 "In Egypt Land," *Time* (30 December 1946), reprinted in *Ghosts on the Roof* 134–40; emphasis in original.

134 Linen, "A Letter from the Publisher."

135 "The Challenge," *Time* (17 March 1947); "The Tragic Sense of Life," *Time* (28 April 1947); "Faith for a Lenten Age," *Time* (8 March 1948); "The Devil," *Life* (2 February 1948); all reprinted in *Ghosts on the Roof* 141–55, 84–93, 66–74.

136 Luce backed Chambers, but was shocked to discover he had spied. They agreed it would be better for *Time* if Chambers resigned. Later attempts to bring Chambers back to *Time* never worked out. See Tanenhaus, *Chambers*, 318–20, 444–46.

137 WC to Willi [Schlamm], September 1954, quoted in Chambers, *Cold Friday*, 232.

138 Ibid., 67, 87.

139 JH to HRL (cable), 14 November 1944, JH Papers, Box 7, Folder 5.

140 "Patch" to JH, 8 March 1946, JH Papers, Box 7, Folder 4.

141 John Hersey, "Marine in China," *Life* (27 May 1946): 17–24; John Hersey, "Ricksha No. 34" *Life* (3 June 1946): 63–70; John Hersey, "Red Pepper Village," *Life* (26 August 1946): 92–105; John Hersey, "A Reporter in China: Two Weeks' Water Away," *New Yorker* (18 May 1946): 59–69 and (25 May 1946): 54–69.

142 This article, written beyond the reach of Luce's editors, still had Hersey declaring "though it might be comforting to think of the Chinese Communists as simply agrarian reformers, I think it is a mistake. They are Communists all right." John Hersey, "Reporter at Large: Communization of Red Crow Village," *New Yorker* (27 July 1946): 38–47.

143 John Hersey, "A Reporter at Large: Hiroshima," *New Yorker* (31 August 1946): 15–68.

144 Griffith, *Harry and Teddy*, 155.

145   Hersey, "Hersey," 228.
146   George Santayana, *The Last Puritan* (New York: Scribner's, 1936), 602.
147   John Hersey, "The Novel of Contemporary History," *Atlantic* (November 1949): 80–84.
148   Hersey, "The Legend on the License." For Hersey's relationship to "new journalism," see John Hollowell, *Fact & Fiction: The New Journalism and the Nonfiction Novel* (Chapel Hill: University of North Carolina Press, 1977), 36; John C. Hartsock, *A History of American Literary Journalism: The Emergence of a Modern Narrative Form* (Amherst: University of Massachussetts Press, 2000).
149   White, *In Search of History*, 210.
150   Jacoby also worked for *Time* out of Chungking. Her husband, *Time* correspondent Melville Jacoby, had provided vivid coverage of the Philippine disaster before being killed in a plane accident in early 1942. When New York recalled her, she asked for an "eighteen-hour-a-day job—right in the middle of the war." She eventually made it to Chungking, where she teamed up with White. Elson, *The World of Time Inc.* 4, 5; Theodore H. White and Annalee Jacoby, *Thunder Out of China* (New York: William Sloane, 1946).
151   THW to HRL, 26 June 1946, THW Papers, Box 3, Folder 21.
152   White, *In Search of History*, 247. White enlisted *Hiroshima* as evidence here, but Hersey's book appeared in August, more than a month after White's break with Luce. Still, Luce's anger at Hersey was well known by June 1946.
153   Ibid., 248–49; Griffith, *Harry and Teddy*, 154–60. THW to HRL, 26 June 1946, and HRL to THW, 29 June 1946, THW Papers, Box 3, Folder 21. White's account makes it look like he quit in early July, the date his book was chosen by the Book of the Month Club. In fact, Luce's letter firing him was dated 29 June.
154   White, *In Search of History*, 255–57.
155   Elson, *The World of Time Inc.* 148; White, *In Search of History*, 261, 355.
156   Hoffmann, *White*, 74; David Halberstam, *The Powers That Be* (New York: Knopf, 1979), 85.
157   THW to Wertenbaker, 18 April 1952, THW Papers, Box 9, Folder 22.
158   Theodore H. White, *Fire in the Ashes* (New York: William Sloane, 1953).
159   See Joyce Hoffmann's thoughtful analysis of White. Hoffmann, *White*, 109.
160   White, *In Search of History*, 229.
161   Theodore H. White, *The View from the Fortieth Floor* (New York: William Sloane, 1960), 374.
162   Quoted in Griffith, *Harry and Teddy*, 26–27.
163   White, *In Search of History*, 450.
164   Theodore White, "Action-Intellectuals," *Life* (9 June 1967): 43–76; (16 June 1967): 44–74B; (23 June 1967): 76–87.
165   THW to David Maress, 5 April 1967, THW Papers, Box 28, Folder 4.

Chapter 7. Interstitial Intellectuals and the Liberal Consensus

Epigraph: Daniel Bell, *New Leader* (25 June 1949): 8.

1   Macdonald first used the phrase to describe his own politics in a 1952 debate with Norman Mailer. It gained widespread currency. Dwight Macdonald, *Memoirs of a Revolutionist: Essays in Political Criticism* (New York: Farrar, Straus and Cudahy, 1957), 197–200.

2   "Our Country and Our Culture," *Partisan Review* 19, 3–5 (1952): 444.

3   Accusations of partisanship against *Time* are not based solely on the memoirs of disgruntled *Time* employees like Matthews, or even on a reading of the magazine, though both sources support such a conclusion. That *Time* was biased in favor of the Republicans in 1952 is also the conclusion of Time Inc.'s official history. Robert T. Elson, *The World of Time Inc.: The Intimate History of a Publishing Enterprise*, vol. 2, *1941–1960* (New York: Atheneum, 1973), 316.

4   The novels that best explored these dilemmas were Kenneth Fearing, *The Big Clock* (New York: Harcourt Brace, 1946); Merle Miller, *That Winter* (New York: William Sloane, 1948); John Brooks, *The Big Wheel* (New York: Harper and Brothers, 1949); Charles Wertenbaker, *The Death of Kings* (New York: Random House, 1954). Others include Ralph Ingersoll, *The Great Ones: The Love Story of Two Very Important People* (New York: Harcourt, Brace, 1948); William Brinkley, *The Fun House* (New York: Random House, 1961); John S. Martin, *General Manpower* (New York: Simon and Schuster, 1938). Finally, Sloan Wilson's best-selling *The Man in the Gray Flannel Suit* (New York: Simon and Schuster, 1955) was based on his experiences at Time Inc.

5   Max Horkheimer and Theodor W. Adorno, "The Culture Industry: Enlightenment as Mass Deception," in *Dialectic of Enlightenment* (New York: Herder and Herder, 1972); Dwight Macdonald, *Against the American Grain: Essays on the Effects of Mass Culture* (New York: Random House, 1962); Dwight Macdonald, "The Responsibility of Peoples," *Politics* (March 1945): 82–93; Dwight Macdonald, "The Root Is Man," *Politics* (April 1946): 97–115; (July 1946): 194–214. See also W. H. Auden, *The Age of Anxiety: A Baroque Eclogue* (New York: Random House, 1947); William Graebner, *The Age of Doubt: American Thought and Culture in the 1940s* (Boston: Twayne, 1991); Arthur M. Schlesinger, Jr., *The Vital Center: The Politics of Freedom* (Boston: Houghton Mifflin, 1949).

6   Walker Evans, "When 'Downtown' Was a Beautiful Mess," *Fortune* (January 1962): 100–106.

7   Jackson Lears, *Fables of Abundance: A Cultural History of Advertising in America* (New York: Basic Books, 1994), 412.

8   The perceived dominance of the managerial culture of the 1950s has driven historians to celebrate opposing perspectives. Locating opposition in the form of competing ideologies, including working-class communalism, carnivalesque release, or artistic spontaneity, historians inadvertently exaggerate the repressive ideological coherence of the managerial perspective. Jack Metzgar, *Striking Steel: Solidarity Remembered* (Philadelphia: Temple University Press, 2000); Lears, *Fables of Abundance*;

Daniel Belgrad, *The Culture of Spontaneity: Improvisation and the Arts in Postwar America* (Chicago: University of Chicago Press, 1998).

9   William H. Whyte, *The Organization Man* (New York: Simon and Schuster, 1956; reprint Philadelphia: University of Pennsylvania Press, 2002), 6, 404; emphasis in original. The Orwell influence on Whyte's thinking is obvious. For direct examples, see William H. Whyte, *Is Anybody Listening? How and Why U.S. Business Fumbles When It Talks with Human Beings* (New York: Simon and Schuster, 1952), 212, 224–39.

10   Details of Whyte's life are taken largely from William H. Whyte, *A Time of War: Remembering Guadalcanal, a Battle Without Maps* (New York: Fordham University Press, 2000) and Editors of *Fortune*, *Writing for Fortune: Nineteen Authors Remember Life on the Staff of a Remarkable Magazine* (New York: Time Inc., 1980).

11   Whyte, *A Time of War*, 8.
12   Ibid.
13   Whyte, *The Organization Man*, 112–19.
14   Whyte, *A Time of War*, 9.
15   Whyte, *The Organization Man*, 117–19, emphasis in original.
16   Certainly the letters home he quotes reveal him to have been miserable most of the time. See Whyte, *A Time of War*, 1–14.
17   Ibid., 87.
18   Ibid., xxii–xxiv.
19   Editors, *Writing for Fortune*, 189.
20   Ibid., 191.
21   "The Class of '49," *Fortune* (June 1949): 84–87, 163–70.
22   Ibid.
23   Whyte, *Is Anybody Listening?* 7–8. Elizabeth Fones-Wolf has studied the free enterprise campaigns in depth, and claims they played a key role in limiting the New Deal, undercutting organized labor, and creating a more conservative political culture. She provides very little evidence of reception, however, and is left to claim it cannot be proven that the campaign was not effective. In short, she assumes it played a role in the 1950s relegitimation of business. Elizabeth A. Fones-Wolf, *Selling Free Enterprise: The Business Assault on Labor and Liberalism, 1945–1960* (Urbana: University of Illinois Press, 1994), 4–10. Her evidence of reception is on 84–85. For far more subtle and persuasive accounts of this process, see William L. Bird, Jr., *"Better Living": Advertising, Media, and the New Vocabulary of Business Leadership, 1935–1955* (Evanston, Ill.: Northwestern University Press, 1999) and Roland Marchand, *Creating the Corporate Soul: The Rise of Public Relations and Corporate Imagery in American Big Business* (Berkeley: University of California Press, 1998).

24   Whyte, *Is Anybody Listening?* 30–31.
25   Ibid., vii–xii.
26   Ibid., 203.
27   "In Praise of the Ornery Housewife," *Fortune* (November 1951): 11.
28   Whyte, *Is Anybody Listening?* 203, 209, 229–31.

29 Ibid., xii. Author interview with Daniel Bell, 16 February 2004.
30 Ibid., 239.
31 Whyte, *The Organization Man*, 405–10.
32 Ibid., 7.
33 Ibid., 11, 12; emphasis in original.
34 Ibid., 165.
35 Pells's observation of a persistent tension in Whyte's approach between constructive and destructive criticism is more properly directed at his first book. There, Whyte appears to be offering both an indictment of American business, and a helpful corrective of some disturbing characteristics of an otherwise sound proposition. He offered a self-help manual for business (how to understand and manage office gossip) and a careful criticism of business's more manipulative and undemocratic aspects. The tension is still present in *The Organization Man*, but Whyte clearly comes down on the side of the resisting individual. Richard H. Pells, *The Liberal Mind in a Conservative Age: American Intellectuals in the 1940s and 1950s* (New York: Harper & Row, 1985), 232–38.
36 Whyte, *The Organization Man*, 250.
37 Ibid., 212; emphasis in original.
38 The best book on Bell is Howard Brick, *Daniel Bell and the Decline of Intellectual Radicalism: Social Theory and Political Reconciliation in the 1940s* (Madison: University of Wisconsin Press, 1986). Though Brick presents a sophisticated and convincing explanation of the erosion of radicalism in certain intellectual circles, his emphasis on Bell's early years does distort Bell's career. For less nuanced depictions of Bell, see Job L. Dittberner, *The End of Ideology and American Social Thought: 1930–1960* (Ann Arbor, Mich.: UMI Research Press, 1979); Godfrey Hodgson, "The Ideology of the Liberal Consensus," in *America in Our Time: From World War II to Nixon, What Happened and Why* (New York: Vintage, 1976); Pells, *The Liberal Mind in a Conservative Age*, 130–47. Nathan Liebowitz dissents from this perspective, along lines similar to those developed here. Liebowitz's account has not altered the tenor of work on Bell. It also suffers from its own tendency to see all of Bell's work as a prelude to his later work on the public household, and is marred by an attempt to force Bell's work into an overly schematic divide between Hellenism and Hebraism. Nathan Liebowitz, *Daniel Bell and the Agony of Modern Liberalism* (Westport, Conn.: Greenwood Press, 1985).
39 Dittberner, *The End of Ideology and American Social Thought*, esp. 321–24.
40 C. Wright Mills, "Letter to the New Left," *New Left Review* (September/October 1960): 18–23.
41 Hodgson, "Ideology of Liberal Consensus," 74.
42 Pells, *The Liberal Mind in a Conservative Age*, 130.
43 Brick, *Daniel Bell*, 54.
44 Liebowitz, *Daniel Bell*, 49.
45 Technically, the editor was James Oneal, but Levitas gradually assumed more control while Bell was there.

46 Bell interview in Dittberner, *The End of Ideology and American Social Thought*, 311.
47 Ibid.
48 Ibid., 319.
49 Ibid., 169.
50 Daniel Bell, "A Parable of Alienation," *Jewish Frontier* (1946): 12, 13.
51 Ibid., 18.
52 Ibid., 19.
53 Ibid.; Brick, *Daniel Bell*, 10–14.
54 Bell, "A Parable of Alienation," 19.
55 Bell, "Utopian Nightmare," *New Leader* (25 June 1949): 8.
56 Brick, *Daniel Bell*, 192.
57 Dittberner, *The End of Ideology and American Social Thought*, 315.
58 DB to Lewis Corey, 10 June 1948, quoted in Brick, *Daniel Bell*, 252n13.
59 Author interview with Daniel Bell, 16 February 2004.
60 Ibid.
61 Dittberner, *The End of Ideology and American Social Thought*, 324.
62 Daniel Bell, *Marxian Socialism in the United States* (Princeton, N.J.: Princeton University Press, 1952; reprint 1967), ix.
63 For an apt evaluation of Bell's book, see Michael Kazin, "The Agony and Romance of the American Left," *American Historical Review* 100, 5 (December 1995): 1488–1512.
64 *Fortune* (October 1948): 35.
65 *Fortune* (February 1949): 172; "Management's Prerogatives," *Fortune* (September 1949): 173–76. Passages from this article were reprinted in "Work and Its Discontents." Daniel Bell, *The End of Ideology: On the Exhaustion of Political Ideas in the 1950s* (Glencoe, Ill.: Free Press, 1960), 233–36.
66 Russell Davenport, "The Greatest Opportunity on Earth," *Fortune* (September 1949): 65–69, 200–208; Editors of *Fortune* with Russell Davenport, *U.S.A.: The Permanent Revolution* (New York: Prentice Hall, 1951).
67 "American Jitters," *Fortune* (November 1949); Russell Davenport, "Enterprise for Everyman," *Fortune* (January 1950): 55–59, 152–59; "The New Kind of Collective Bargaining," *Fortune* (January 1950): 61–62.
68 For the best view of what Bell hoped for at the time, see Daniel Bell, ""America's Un-Marxist Revolution: Mr. Truman Embarks on a Politically Managed Economy," *Commentary* (March 1949): 207–15. Interestingly, he made the same mistake here that Davenport had made in *Fortune*, exaggerating small pieces of evidence that the changes he desired were happening while ignoring evidence to the contrary.
69 Daniel Bell, "Do Unions Raise Wages?" *Fortune* (January 1951): 65, 138–40.
70 Daniel Bell, "The Language of Labor," *Fortune* (September 1951): 86–88, 202–11. This was part of series on "Business Communication," the only one not written by Whyte and not included in *Is Anybody Listening?*

71 Daniel Bell, "Labor's Coming of Middle Age," *Fortune* (October 1951): 114–15, 137–50.

72 "Labor Notes," *Fortune* (July 1951): 41–48; "Labor Notes," *Fortune* (August 1951): 43–50; Daniel Bell, "Labor's New Men of Power," *Fortune* (June 1953): 148–62.

73 Daniel Bell, "Beyond the 'Annual Wage,'" *Fortune* (May 1955): 92–95, 205–10.

74 Bell, *The End of Ideology*, 242. Bell had previously dissected this "cow sociology" in Daniel Bell, "Adjusting Men to Machines: Social Scientists Explore the World of the Factory," *Commentary* (January 1947): 79–88; and Daniel Bell, "Screening Leaders in a Democracy: How Scientific Is Personnel Testing?," *Commentary* (April 1948): 368–75.

75 Bell, *The End of Ideology*, 241, 37.

76 Ibid., 255, 62.

77 Ibid., 17.

78 Walker Evans, *Walker Evans at Work* (New York: Harper & Row, 1982), 152.

79 Biographical material comes from Evans's own writings and interviews, and the biographies by Belinda Rathbone and James Mellow. Both are strong works. Mellow's is more detailed and tentative, but ends in 1957 (Mellow died before completing the manuscript).

80 Belinda Rathbone, *Walker Evans: A Biography* (Boston: Houghton Mifflin, 1995), 3.

81 Ibid., 11.

82 Ibid., 20.

83 James R. Mellow, *Walker Evans* (New York: Basic Books, 1999), 34; Rathbone, *Walker Evans*, 20–21.

84 Mellow, *Walker Evans*, 27.

85 Mellow, *Walker Evans*, 49–50.

86 Ibid., 44.

87 Rathbone, *Walker Evans*, 28.

88 Mellow, *Walker Evans*, 60, 73–74.

89 Ibid., 77, 80–81; Rathbone, *Walker Evans*, 40, 45.

90 Ibid., 52.

91 Mellow, *Walker Evans*, 116.

92 Rathbone, *Walker Evans*, 65–67.

93 Ibid., 68.

94 Quoted in Mellow, *Walker Evans*, 252.

95 Reproduced in Evans, *Walker Evans at Work*, 112.

96 Mellow, *Walker Evans*, 272, 381.

97 Quoted in ibid., 308.

98 James Agee and Walker Evans, *Let Us Now Praise Famous Men* (Boston: Houghton Mifflin, 1941; reprint 1960), 11.

99 Rathbone, *Walker Evans*, 153.

100 Walker Evans, *American Photographs* (New York: Museum of Modern Art, 1938).

101   Quoted in Rathbone, *Walker Evans*, 194.

102   Evans, *Walker Evans at Work*, 238.

103   Gilles Mora and John T. Hill are exceptions, tracing Evans's artistic development during his *Fortune* years, rather than interpreting these years as futile. Gilles Mora and John T. Hill, *Walker Evans: The Hungry Eye*, trans. Jacqueline Taylor (New York: Harry Abrams, 1993).

104   Hilton Kramer: "For how many of us, I wonder, has our imagination of what the United States looked like in the nineteen 1930s been determined . . . by the work of . . . Walker Evans," quoted in William Stott, *Documentary Expression and 1930s America* (Chicago: University of Chicago Press, 1973), 267.

105   Lesley K. Baier, *Walker Evans at Fortune 1945–1965* (Wellesley, Mass.: Wellesley College Museum, 1977), 57.

106   Mellow, *Walker Evans*, 489.

107   "Collins Co., Collinsville Conn.," *Fortune* (January 1946): 110–15, 193–94.

108   "Adventures of Henry and Joe in Autoland" *Fortune* (March 1946): 96–103, 228.

109   "The Yankees," *Fortune* (July 1946): 130–39, 169.

110   From Time Inc.'s house journal, *FYI*, quoted in Rathbone, *Walker Evans*, 200.

111   Walker Evans, "Labor Anonymous," *Fortune* (November 1946): 152–53.

112   Walker Evans, "Chicago: A Camera Exploration," *Fortune* (February 1947): 112–21.

113   "Homes of Americans," *Fortune* (April 1946): 148–57.

114   Quoted in Mellow, *Walker Evans*, 274.

115   Ibid., 507–14.

116   WE to Ralph Delahaye Paine Jr., 23 July 1948, reproduced in Evans, *Walker Evans at Work*, 180–81.

117   R. D. Paine, Jr., to Staff, reproduced in ibid., 182.

118   Rathbone, *Walker Evans*, 206–7.

119   Evans himself took a number of these portraits, twenty-four of which were featured in the magazine between 1951 and 1954. See the listing in Baier, *Walker Evans at Fortune*, 62–63.

120   Rathbone, *Walker Evans*, 208.

121   "Main Street Looking North From Courthouse Square," *Fortune* (May 1948): 102–6. Examples from Evans's collection appeared in "When 'Downtown' Was a Beautiful Mess" and "Come on Down," *Architectural Forum* (July 1962): 96–100. *Architectural Forum*, also a Time Inc. publication, featured Evans's work many times. Baier, *Walker Evans at Fortune*, 63.

122   Rathbone, *Walker Evans*, 209.

123   WE to Ernestine Evans, February 1934, reproduced in Evans, *Walker Evans at Work*, 98.

124   Rathbone, *Walker Evans*, 210.

125 "Clay: the Commonest Industrial Raw Material," *Fortune* (January 1951): 80–88; "The Stones of duPont," *Fortune* (May 1957): 167–70; "American Masonry," *Fortune* (April 1965): 150–53.

126 "The Pitch Direct," *Fortune* (October 1958): 139–43; "Downtown: A Last Look Backward," *Fortune* (October 1956): 157–62.

127 "Beauties of the Common Tool," *Fortune* (July 1955): 103–7.

128 Jed Perl, "In the American Grain," *New Republic* (14 February 2000): 31–37. I am indebted to Perl's incisive reading of Evans's career.

129 "Summer North of Boston," *Fortune* (August 1949): 74–79.

130 "Along the Right-of-Way," *Fortune* (September 1950): 106–13.

131 "The U.S. Depot," *Fortune* (February 1953): 138–43.

132 "Before They Disappear," *Fortune* (March 1957): 141–45; "The Last of Railroad Steam," *Fortune* (September 1958): 137–41.

133 "On the Waterfront," *Fortune* (November 1960): 144–50.

134 "Vintage Office Furniture," *Fortune* (August 1953): 123–27.

135 "Downtown," *Fortune* (October 1956): 157–62.

136 "The Wreckers," *Fortune* (May 1951): 102–5.

137 "The Auto Junkyard," *Fortune* (April 1962): 132–37.

138 "When 'Downtown' Was a Beautiful Mess," *Fortune* (January 1962): 100–106.

139 Quoted in Mellow, *Walker Evans*, 214. I use the title *In Search of Lost Time* both as a better translation of *A la rechercche du temps perdu* than *Remembrance of Things Past* and as more suggestive of Evans's aesthetic. Evans read Proust in French.

140 "Vintage Office Furniture."

141 Evans in 1973, while experimenting with Polaroid color shots: "Color is vulgar and should never be tried under any circumstances." This was one of the numerous times he called color vulgar. Quoted in Evans, *Walker Evans at Work*, 234. See also Mora, *The Hungry Eye*, 336. Evans ran a study of photographers working in color in *Fortune*, praising Edward Weston's mastery of muted colors. Evans himself attained such mastery by the early 1960s. "Test Exposures," *Fortune* (July 1954): 77–80.

142 This distinction was the organizing principle of Evans, *American Photographs*.

143 "People and Places in Trouble," *Fortune* (March 1961): 110–17.

144 Rathbone, *Walker Evans*, 216.

145 Mellow, *Walker Evans*, 486.

146 Mora, *The Hungry Eye*, 259.

147 Mellow, *Walker Evans*, 76.

148 "Parnassus, Coast to Coast," *Time* (11 June 1956): 65–70.

149 David Halberstam, *The Powers That Be* (New York: Knopf, 1979), 51.

150 Mellow, *Walker Evans*, 76.

151 Whyte, *The Organization Man*, 397.

Epilogue: Intellectuals in Their American Century and in Ours

1 Robert T. Elson, *The World of Time Inc.: The Intimate History of a Publishing Enterprise*, vol. 2, *1941–1960* (New York: Atheneum, 1973), 438.

2 Ibid., 426–28.

3 Ibid., 454.

4 Ibid., 443.

5 Ben Bagdikian, "Time Study," *New Republic* (23 February 1959): 9–15. This piece was based on the series Bagdikian wrote for the *Providence Journal-Bulletin* in October 1958.

6 Elson, *The World of Time Inc.*, 447–48.

7 Arthur M. Schlesinger, Jr., "*Time* and the Intellectuals," in Schlesinger, *The Politics of Hope* (Boston: Houghton Mifflin, 1963).

8 C. Wright Mills, "The Social Role of the Intellectual," in Mills, *Power, Politics and People* (New York: Oxford University Press, 1963), 296.

9 Contrast William H. Whyte, *The Organization Man* (New York: Simon and Schuster, 1956; reprint Philadelphia: University of Pennsylvania Press, 2002) with C. Wright Mills, *White Collar* (London: Oxford University Press, 1951).

10 Irving Howe, *A Margin of Hope: An Intellectual Autobiography* (New York: Harcourt Brace Jovanovich, 1982), 181.

11 John Michael, *Anxious Intellects: Academic Professionals, Public Intellectuals, and Enlightenment Values* (Durham, N.C.: Duke University Press, 2000), 14–15.

12 Archibald MacLeish, "The Communists, the Writers, and the Spanish War," in MacLeish, *A Time to Speak* (Boston: Houghton Mifflin, 1940), 99.

13 Richard Hofstadter, "A Note on Intellect and Power," *American Scholar* 30, 4 (1961): 594.

14 John McGowan, *Democracy's Children: Intellectuals and the Rise of Cultural Politics* (Ithaca, N.Y.: Cornell University Press, 2002), 90.

INDEX

Adorno, Theodor, 260, 309n.7
Agee, James, 9, 12, 18, 28, 124–26, 155–66, Fig. 10, 173, 210, 304–6, 335n.85, 337n.118; biographical sketch, 96–97; and Walker Evans, 12, 13, 14, 160–63, 165, 287–89, 292, 293, 295, 299, 300; at *Fortune*, 8, 96–97, 98, 111–12, 117, 121, 158–65, 168, 289–90, 326n.27, 329n.79; on journalism, 98, 124, 163–66; *Let Us Now Praise Famous Men*, 12–14, 124, 159–64, 289–90, 336n.100; at *Time*, 8, 13, 165–66, 170, 179, 182–84, 206, 249, 290, 339n.50
Aiken, Conrad, 37
Aikins, Russell, 82, 117, Fig. 7
Albee, Edward, 301
"The American Century" (Luce), 13, 62, 65, 196, 215
Anderson, Margaret, 45
Anderson, Marian, 249–50
Anderson, Sherwood, 311n.36
anti-communism, 136, 212–14, 248, 273, 344n.9, 250nn.126, 127
anti-Stalinism, 125, 144–45
Arendt, Hannah, 150
Atkinson, Brooks, 38, 138, 243
Atlantic Monthly 199, 200, 253
Auden, W. H., 137, 339n.50

Bagdikian, Ben, 303
Baker, E. H., 83
Barzun, Jacques, 250

Baughman, James, 62, 79, 320n.13
Beard, Charles and Mary, 76
Bell, Daniel, 8, 9, 13–14, 147, 148, 258, 260–62, 271–84, 301–2, 355n.38, 45, 356n.68, 357n.74; biographical sketch, 272–76; *End of Ideology*, 13–14, 272; on involvement and alienation, 258, 272, 274–76, 283–84; labor department of *Fortune*, 260–61, 277–83; and *Politics*, 147, 148
Benda, Julien, 19, 151
Beneker, Gerrit A., 102
Benét, Stephen Vincent, 33, 68, 73, 100, 134, 139
Benton, Thomas Hart, 102
Bergreen, Laurence, 18, 157, 335n.85, 336n.104
Berle, Adolph and Gardiner Means, 116
bias: *Fortune*'s bias against business, 119; *Fortune*'s bias for free enterprise, 120–21, 189; *Time*'s political bias, 117, 216, 259, 303, 353n.3
Biel, Steven, 27
Billings, John Shaw, 174, 181, 196, 204–5
Bingham, Alfred, 114
Bishop, John Peale, 100
Blackmur, R. P., 37
Bogan, Louise, 140
Bourke-White, Margaret, 160, Figs. 4, 5, 6, 11, 311n.41, 327n.50, 336n.96; distinctive style, 117, 160, 261, 292, 329n.75; foil for Walker Evans, 261, 292,

Bourke-White, Margaret, (cont'd) 294, 336n.100; at *Fortune*, 82, 83, 101, 102; *You Have Seen Their Faces*, 160
Bourne, Randolph, 10, 21, 145–46
Brandeis, Louis, 118
Brick, Howard, 271, 276, 371n.38
Brooks, Cleanth, 137
Brooks, John, 25
Brooks, Van Wyck, 57, 130–31, 133, 146
Broom, 58
Buell, Leslie, 200, 214
Burke, Kenneth, 45, 323n.56
Bundy, McGeorge, 140
Busch, Niven, 77
Business Week, 81

Caldwell, Erskine, 160
Calhoun, Filmore, 240
Cambridge University, 217
Camus, Albert, 21
Canby, Henry Seidel, 68, 72, 73, 172
Cannon, James P., 145
Cantwell, Robert, 96, 118, 202, 234, 235; at *Time*, 8, 12, 13, 28, 172–75, 178–79; *Land of Plenty*, 13, 118, 172
capitalism, 13, 15, 89, 115, 118, 119, 141, 144, 146, 154, 168, 187, 190, 195, 210, 272, 283; *Fortune*'s "popular capitalism," 208, 260, 279–81; *Fortune*'s "radical capitalism," 100–107
Capra, Frank, 112
Carson Pirie & Scott, 98, 317n.54
Chamberlain, John, 96, 195, 199, 204, 214, 341n.86
Chambers, Whittaker, 13, 14, 17, 200, 202, 212–14, 221, 230, 347n.90; and anti-communism, 236–49, 259, 348n.103, 349n.116; biographical sketch, 230–35, 351n.128; and communism, 233–36, 248, 250, 347nn.74, 78, 351n.130; at *Fortune*, 238–39; at *Life*, 250–51; at *Time*, 8, 179, 183, 184, 212–13, 235–51, 259, 290, 348n.103, 349n.116, 351nn.128, 136
Chambers War, 212, 239–49

Chiang K'ai-shek, 223–29, 242–45, 248, 254–56, 350n.127, 351n.128
Chennault, Claire, 242, 243
Chiaromonte, Nicola, 147
China, 64, 67, 211, 214, 217, 218, 221–29, 240, 242–46, 254–55, 346n.56, 349nn.115, 116, 350n.127, 352n.150
Citizen Kane, 62
Cleland, Thomas Maitland, 82, Fig. 1
Coffi, Andrea, 147
Cohen, Eliott, 274
Cold War, 13, 21, 22, 63, 136, 140, 182, 212, 213, 239, 247, 257, 258, 260
cold war consensus, 13, 21, 182, 257, 258
Colliers, 101
Commentary, 274
commercialization, 18, 154, 322n.45
Committee for Public Information (Creel Commission), 63, 135
Common Sense, 115, 274
communism, 17, 115, 119, 122, 159, 200, 201, 212, 230, 234–38, 244, 246–48, 250, 251, 255, 258–60, 273, 279, 283, 303, 306, 349n.103, 350nn.126, 127, 351n.142; and China, 211, 223, 225, 228–29, 240–45, 248, 252, 349n.111, 116; and fascism, 103, 106, 124, 128, 130
Communist Party of the U.S.A., 88, 115, 134, 144, 153, 212, 230, 233–36, 244, 247, 248, 255, 258, 273, 279, 306, 330n.127
Congress of Industrial Organizations (CIO), 122
Congress for Cultural Freedom, 258
Connelly, Cyril, 8
Constable, Rosalind, 201
Cornell, Joseph, 261
corporate liberalism, 3, 13, 14, 15–16, 62, 260, 262, 279, 324n.72
corporations and American life, 3, 4, 9, 15–18, 20, 116, 122, 142, 151, 154–55, 259, 264, 266–71, 301; *Fortune* and corporate leadership, 85, 86, 101, 113, 114, 117–20. *See also* market
Coser, Lewis, 10, 20, 147, 314n.55
Coughlin, Charles Edward, 122

Index

Cowley, Malcolm, 26, 27, 37, 58, 59, 237, 319n.114
Crane, Hart, 35, 45, 287, 299
Croly, Herbert, 44–46
cultural front, 3, 128
Cummings, Robert, 53

Daily Princetonian, 43, 50
Davenport, Marcia (Gluck Clarke), 95, 186
Davenport, Russell W., 8, 284, 340n.65; biographical sketch, 95, 185–86; at *Fortune*, 28, 57, 95, 121, 162, 168, 185–95, 207–8, 214, 260–61, 279–81, 337n.2, 340n.70, 356n68; and intellectuals, 169, 185, 187, 193–95, 198–99, 204, 208; at *Life*, 195–96, 207, 341n.88; and Luce, 17, 167–68, 188, 189–91, 195–96, 197, 200, 203, 342n.114; and *Magazine X*, 199, 200, 203–5; and Wendell Willkie, 192–93
Davies, Joseph E., 240
De Beauvoir, Simone, 21, 202
democracy, 9, 84, 124, 134, 145, 186, 192, 197, 198, 219, 220, 241, 261, 305; and communism, 115, 149, 229, 243–45, 273; and fascism, 127, 128, 135, 141, 148; industrial, 118, 280; and journalism, 12, 18, 63–64, 178; and mass culture, 20, 66, 75, 84, 207; and New Deal, 3, 121
Democratic Party, 101, 122, 205, 207, 282
Denby, David, 182
Denning, Michael, 13
Dennison, Edward, 102
Depression, Great, 12, 13, 44; and *Fortune*, 38, 83, 87–89, 92, 97, 98, 102–8, 113, 122, 160; and writers, 7, 13, 26, 29, 38, 59, 98, 100, 113, 190, 210, 215, 261, 266, 278, 280, 290
Dewey Commission, 277
Dewey, John, 145, 273, 348n.93
Dewey, Thomas, 193, 207, 259, 279
The Dial, 58, 285
Disraeli, Benjamin, 68, 84
Dittberner, Job, 271, 274, 355n.38
Divver, Patricia, 195
Dos Passos, John, 42, 100, 129, 210, 234

Douglas, Ann, 58
Drucker, Peter, 8, 200
Duncan, Robert, 148
Dupee, Fred, 51, 99

Eisenhower, Dwight D., 198, 205, 241
Eliot, T. S., 75, 130, 137, 206, 210, 274, 285, 340n.65
Elson, Robert, 67, 338n.22, 342n.103
Epstein, Joseph, 20, 62
Esquire, 125
Evans, Walker, 8, 9, Figs. 9, 10, 11, 12, 13, 14, 302, 305, 359n.139, 141; and James Agee, 12, 13, 157, 161–62, 165, 288–89, 293, 299–300; biographical sketch; 284–87; at *Fortune*, 12, 115, 161–62, 165, 261–62, 289, 290–301, 358nn.103, 119; *Let Us Now Praise Famous Men*, 12, 13, 14, 161–62, 289; at *Time*, 289

Fairbank, John King, 223
Farm Security Administration (FSA), 161, 288–300
Farrar, John, 68, 73, 74,
Fass, Paula, 54
Fearing, Kenneth, 1–4, 259; *The Big Clock*, 1–4
Filene, Edward, 102
Fitzgerald, F. Scott, 26, 41
Fitzgerald, Robert, 8, 156, 162, 170, 174–76, 179, 182, 184, 335n.85
Fixx, Calvin, 174, 239
Flye, Father James, 97, 98, 156, 159, 160
Forbes, 81
Ford, Henry, 54, 57, 102, 103, 104, 271, 279
Ford, John, 236
Foucault, Michel, 20
Frank, Robert, 295
Frank, Waldo, 45
Frankfurt School, 263, 309n.7
Frankfurter, Felix, 126
Fromm, Erich, 202
Frost, Robert, 134, 137

Gabler, Neil, 76
Galbraith, John Kenneth, 8, 215
Gibbs, Wolcott, 77

Gide, Andre, 202
Girdler, Tom, 116
Gold, Mike, 234
Goldsborough, Laird, 97, 216
Goodman, Paul, 147
Goodwin, Richard, 257
Gorman, Paul, 168,
Gottfried, Manfred, 57, 72
Graebner, Walter, 211, 241
Graves, Robert, 171, 172, 175
Greenberg, Clement, 146
Griffith, Thomas, 243, 346n.56
Grover, Allen, 181, 240
Gruin, Fred, 243, 244
Guadalcanal, 218, 263, 265
Gurdjieff, G. I., 45–46, 171, 318n.75

Hadden, Briton, 43, 48, 61, 67–73, 76–78, 80, 87, 175–76, 303, 321n.23, 322n.45, 323nn.58, 65
Harper and Brothers, 161
Harper's magazine, 199, 200
Harvard University, 51, 96, 97, 222, 223, 256, 348n.100
Hemingway, Ernest, 26, 38, 100, 129, 139
Hersey, John, 9, 13, 14, 17, 166, 222, 251–54; 344n.16, 345nn.24, 28, 352n.148; biographical sketch 216–17; and Chambers War, 241–43, 246; at *Life*, 218–20, 241–42, 251–52; at *New Yorker*, 252–53, 351n.142; at *Time*, 8, 170, 179, 206, 210–13, 216–21, 224, 228, 241–43, 246, 259, 352n.152
Herzstein, Robert, 216, 247, 348n.100
Himmelfarb, Gertrude, 5, 62
Hiss, Alger, 212, 213, 235, 251
Hitler, Adolph, 130, 146, 150, 173, 210
Hobson, Wilder, 51, 53, 56, 57, 95, 98, 101, 113, 117, 239, 289–90, 338n.36
Hocking, William Ernest, 238
Hodgins, Eric, 96, 97, 117, 119, 120, 160, 203, 216, 336n.104
Hodgson, Godfrey, 238, 300
Hoffman, Paul, 279, 301
Hoffmann, Joyce, 256
Hofstadter, Richard, 306

Hoover, Herbert, 88, 101, 104, 108, 113
Horkheimer, Max, 260, 309n.7
Hotchkiss School, 32, 65, 67, 96, 134, 200, 217, 263
Houghton Mifflin, 39, 161
Hound and Horn, 37, 287
Howe, Irving, 5, 6, 8–13, 20, 23, 304; at *Time*, 8, 10–13, 179, 277
House Committee on Un-American Activities (HUAC), 251, 259
Hughes, Langston, 234
Hugo, Victor, 231
Hurley, Patrick, 243
Hutchins, Robert, 62, 348n.93
Huxley, Aldous, 239
Huxley, Julius, 239

Ingersoll, Ralph McAllister: biographical sketch, 96; at *Fortune*, 57, 96–97, 99, 105, 107–8, 111–14, 115, 117, 119, 189, 336n.104; at *New Yorker*, 57, 96; *PM*, 175; at *Time*, 120, 175, 216; and U.S. Steel article, 119–20
intellectuals: independent, 6, 11, 14, 19–20, 22, 26, 27, 30, 39, 47, 126, 132, 155–56, 168, 170, 171, 172, 184, 188, 303–4; interstitial, 4, 14, 21, 22, 166, 169, 170, 184, 206, 230–31, 262, 271, 299, 304–5, 311n.36

Jackson, C. D., 94, 241
Jackson, Schuyler, 42–44
Jacoby, Annalee, 254, 352n.150
Jacoby, Russell, 19, 20, 22, 304, 305, 313n.49
Jeffers, Robinson, 134
Jessup, John K., 188, 214
Jewish Forward, 150
Johnson, Owen; *Stover at Yale*, 32–33, 52
journalism, *Fortune*'s innovations, 80–88, 92–93; literary, 3, 92–94, 110–13, 158–66, 167, 174–75, 183–84, 211, 217, 219–21, 246–47, 249–50, 252–54; "new journalism," 110, 253, 352n.148; and poetry, 8, 12, 91, 94, 97–98, 105–7, 110–12, 127, 166, 169, 173, 178–79, 183–14; *Time*'s innovations, 69–80
Joyce, James, 75, 130, 182, 210, 236, 285, 286

Kazan, Elia, 138
Kazin, Alfred, 8, 12, 200, 230, 305
Kempton, Murray, 6, 62, 310n.11
Kennan, George, 249
Kennedy, Ed, 95
Kennedy, John F., 256
Kirstein, Lincoln, 287–89, 300
Kobler, John, 62
Koestler, Arthur, 202
Konrád, György and Iván Szelényi, 31
Kronenberger, Louis, 8, 96, 170, 179, 182, 184, 188, 206, 258, 290
Kreuger, Ivar, 91–93, 111, 112

labor movement, 79, 117, 151, 214, 216, 258; and *Fortune*, 14, 102–5, 113, 116, 118–22, 190, 192, 260–61, 271, 276–83, 287, 292–93, 354n.23
Larsen, Roy, 177, 348n.100
Lasch, Christopher, 31, 139
Lauterbach, Richard, 211, 240–42, 348–49n.103
Lenin, V. I., 118, 119, 144, 233, 235, 237, 248
Levitas, Sol, 273–74, 355n.45
Library of Congress, 134–35
liberal consensus, 15, 260, 262, 272, 279, 300–301
Liebling, A. J., 228, 346n.54
Life magazine, 1, 3, 4, 11, 13, 14, 15, 62, 63, 165, 177, 181, 195–96, 199, 207, 211, 214–16, 217, 219, 220, 222, 226, 228, 229, 240–42, 245, 250–52, 257, 259, 289, 295, 300, 302, 345n.28
Life Roundtable, 207
Linscott, Robert, 39, 98
Lewis, Sinclair, 30, 33, 58, 78, 109, 217, 344n.16
Literary Digest, 69, 70, 71, 73
Little Review, 45, 58, 285
Lippmann, Walter, 30, 44, 72, 75–76, 89, 107, 128
Lloyd-Smith, Parker, 57, 94–97, 216, 325n.8
Long, Huey, 122
Longwell, Dan, 195–96, 204
Luce, Clare Booth, 221, 226, 339n.58
Luhan, Mabel Dodge, 45

MacArthur, Douglas, 218, 256, 345n.24
Macdonald, Dwight, 11, 26–31, 56–60, 87–89, 124–26, 130, 141–56, 157, Fig. 9, 168, 177, 186, 232, 257, 258, 271, 277, 284, 304, 305, 334n.51, 353n.1; biographical sketch, 48–56; on "Brooks-MacLeish thesis," 130–31; at *Fortune*, 7, 8,13, 18, 94–99, 105, 114–21, 158, 190, 216, 330n.112; and intellectual independence, 5–6, 126, 143, 145, 154–56; on masscult and midcult, 4–5, 7, 19, 139–40, 154, 260, 263; and *Partisan Review*, 144–47; and *Politics*, 147–53; and "The Responsibility of Peoples," 149–51; and U.S. Steel article, 117–20, Fig. 7, 189
Macdonald, Nancy, 114, 115, 147
MacLeish, Andrew, 35
MacLeish, Archibald, 7–9, 11–14, 17, 25–31, 49, 56–60, 63, 65, 68, 73, 88–89, 91, 124, 142, 143, 159, Fig. 8, 168, 197, 200, 209, 217, 232, 237, 284, 319n.114, 333n.30; biographical sketch, 32–38; and fascism, 127–36, 146, 168, 187, 216; at *Fortune*, 38–39, 92–114, 116, 117, 121, 158, 162, 173, 179, 186–91, 210, 287, 310n.28, 317n.54, 327n.40; "Invocation of the Social Muse," 106–7; "The Irresponsibles," 129–34, 195, 305; as public intellectual, 14, 124–27, 131–41, 155, 156, 305–6
Macy's, 55–56, 86, 236
Magazine X, 199–207, 259, 342n.99, 103
Mailer, Norman, 5, 6, 353n.1
Makefield, Wallace, 6
Malraux, André, 210
Mannheim, Karl, 275
Mansfield, Katherine, 171
Mao Zedong, 255
Maritain, Jacques, 238
The March of Time, 1, 61, 62
market, 6–7, 17–18, 22, 58, 66, 84, 93, 102, 105, 107, 119, 121–22, 154, 255, 261, 312n.42, 313n.51; mass market, 1–3, 8, 14, 15, 19, 21, 69–71, 322n.45; stock market, 54, 59, 87, 95; stock market crash (1929), 30, 87, 88, 91, Fig. 1. *See also* corporation

Marsh, Reginald, 102, 108
Martin, John, 43–47, 50, 57, 72, 77, 171, 174, 175, 178, 323n.56
Marx, Karl, 144, 147, 152, 230, 248, 274, 351n.130
Marxism, 120, 137, 144, 147, 148, 149, 151, 152, 230, 234, 248, 271, 272, 274, 278, 351n.130
Mason, Larry, 33–35
mass culture, 2–7, 14, 15, 19–21, 58, 63, 88, 148, 153–54, 157, Fig. 9, 170, 206, 254, 259–62, 291, 342n.119
Matthews, T. S., 8, 12, 26–31, 49–51, 56–57, 59–60, 63, 72, 88, 94, 167–70, 208, 232, 284, 337n.8, 339n.40; biographical sketch 39–48; and interstitial intellectuals, 17, 179–80, 184, 199, 206; at *Magazine X*, 199, 202–5; relations with Luce 172, 175–78, 180, 185, 205–6, 327n.36, 338n.22; at *Time* as "back of the book" editor, 174–75, 290; at *Time* as book reviewer, 171–74; at *Time* as managing editor, 175–85, 205, 221, 235, 236, 238, 240, 245–47, 249, 303, 339n.45
Matthiessen, F. O., 198, 340n.65
McCarthy, Joseph, 141, 248, 255, 256, 259, 350n.127
McDonald, John, 277, 344n.9
McGowan, John, 306
Mellow, James, 286–88, 291, 357n.79
Mencken, H. L., 29, 50, 71, 202, 210
Michael, John, 20
middlebrow culture, 4, 5, 7, 16, 139, 140, 153, 154, 172. *See also* mass culture
Miller, Henry, 182
Mills, C. Wright, 5, 6, 9, 10, 19, 20, 147, 272, 283, 303–4, 310n.23
Milton, John, 32, 35, 68, 132, 133, 140
Miscellany, 28, 99
Mission to Moscow, 148, 240
Montague, William Pepperell, 238
Mora, Gilles and John T. Hill, 300, 358n.103
Morris, G. L. K., 51, 99
Mumford, Lewis, 193–94, 237
Mussolini, Benito, 114

The Nation, 58, 78, 120, 129, 142, 144, 146, 165, 179, 182, 191
Nation's Business, 81
New Deal, 3, 12, 14, 15, 17, 88, 93, 105, 114, 115, 116, 122, 152, 173, 189–92, 210, 214, 226, 237, 260, 280, 288, 354n.23
New Era, 15, 66, 85, 86, 107, 114
New International, 142, 144
New Leader, 200, 273, 274
New Masses, 100, 121, 234, 235, 347n.74
New Republic, 28, 29, 37, 43–48, 56, 57, 78, 106, 129, 144–46, 168, 171, 175, 179, 255
New York Times, 69, 71, 73, 101, 138, 211, 243
New Yorker, 96, 125, 142, 143, 252, 254, 324n.70, 346n.54
Newspaper Guild, 113, 190, 214
Niebuhr, Reinhold, 239, 250, 274, 290
Norris, Frank, 176, 211
Norton-Taylor, Duncan, 302
Nye Hearings, 109

Oakes, Walter, 148
objectivity, 17, 79, 110, 112, 121, 133, 163, 185, 191, 249, 323n.63
Office of Facts and Figures (OFF), 124, 135
Office of Price Administration (OPA), 215
Orage, A. R., 45, 46, 318n.75
organization, 1–5, 9–10, 14, 15–18, 20, 28–29, 33, 73–75, 101–2, 104, 109, 114, 149–51, 153–55, 169, 188, 254–55, 261–72, 275–76, 299–300, 303–6
Orpen, Sir William, 83
Ortega y Gasset, José, 84
Orwell, George, 21, 143, 202, 262, 276, 354n.9
Osborne, John, 176, 211, 240
Oxford University, 28, 43, 68
Ozick, Cynthia, 22

Paine, Ralph Delahaye, 266, 292, 294, 295
Partisan Review, 4, 5, 51, 125, 130, 142, 144–46, 168, 199, 200, 258; "Our Country and Our Culture," 5, 258

Patton, George, 220
Pells, Richard, 106, 126, 270, 272, 355n.35
Perl, Jed, 296, 359n.128
Peyton, Green, 96
Phelps, Robert, 156
Phillips Exeter Academy, 26, 49–51, 143
Phillips, William, 144, 145
PM, 150, 175,
Politics, 4, 125, 142, 147, 148, 152, 153, 199, 201, 204
Porter, Katherine Anne, 234
Potsdam Conference, 183
Pound, Ezra, 35, 187
Prentice, Pierre, 180, 339n.40
Princeton University, 26, 41–44, 46–48, 50, 57, 72, 94, 222, 256, 262–64, 317n.59
Proust, Marcel, 298, 259n.139
Pulitzer Prize, 13, 39, 124, 125, 138, 211, 220

Randolph, A. Philip, 276
Rahv, Philip, 125, 144, 145
Ransom, John Crowe, 35
Rathbone, Belinda, 285–87, 295, 296, 300
Reader's Digest, 69, 70, 76, 193
Republican Party, 30, 47, 62, 65, 113, 152, 181, 190, 192, 194, 196, 197, 203, 205, 207, 208, 230–32, 258, 259, 302, 353n.3
Resettlement Administration (RA), 288, 300
Reuther, Walter, 282
Riding, Laura, 172, 173, 175, 337n.8
Riis, Jacob, 109
Rittase, William, 82
Rivera, Diego, 105, 106
Robbins, Bruce, 20
Rodman, Selden, 114
Roosevelt, Franklin D., 63, 68, 73, 105, 113, 114, 121, 122, 124, 134–36, 141, 173, 190, 192, 195–97, 210, 223, 226, 240, 242, 243
Roscoe, Burton, 130
Ross, Andrew, 20, 21
Ross, Harold, 57, 69–70, 96, 252

Said, Edward, 19, 143, 313
Sandburg, Carl, 134

Sanders, David, 218
Sargeant, Winthrop, 290
Saturday Evening Post, 11, 58, 62, 255
Saturday Review of Literature, 66, 137
Schachtman, Max, 145
Schlamm, William, 17, 200–205, 214, 343n.124
Schlesinger, Arthur, Jr., 303
Seldes, Gilbert, 58
selling out, 3, 5, 7, 18, 20, 155, 300, 305
Serge, Victor, 147
Seven Arts, 45
Shawn, Wallace, 252–53
Silone, Ignazio, 210
Sinclair, Upton, 273
Skull and Bones, 52, 65, 72, 95, 186, 217
socialism, 26, 42, 44, 46, 47, 114–16, 119, 122, 145, 146, 148, 151–52, 181, 271–73, 276, 278, 279, 282, 283
Socialist Party, 42, 47, 272, 273
Socialist Workers Party, 145
Solow, Herb, 231, 266, 277, 344n.9
Spanish Civil War, 129, 173, 210, 214, 216
Sperry, William A., 238
Spiegel, Alan, 156
Stalin, Joseph, 210, 235, 237, 238, 240, 246, 247, 271; Stalinism, 103, 144, 246, 258, 273
St. Paul's School, 41
Stearns, Harold, 58
Steinbeck, John, 236
Steiner, Ralph, 295
Stevenson, Adlai, 205
Stillman, Charles, 97, 117, 180
Stillwell, Joseph, 226, 242–46, 256, 348n.100, 349n.111
Stott, William, 160, 161, 164, 336n.96
Stryker, Roy, 108, 161, 288, 300
Sturges, Preston, 165
Sumner, Gregory, 147
Swanberg, W. A., 62–63, 247, 320n.13, 321n.22
Swope, Herbert Bayard, 68, 72

Tanenhaus, Sam, 232, 233, 248, 249
Tate, Alan, 37, 134

Taylor, Myron, 118
Tennessee Valley Authority, 98, 111
Thomas, J. Parnell, 124, 134
Thomas, Norman, 42, 273
Toomer, Jean, 45
Townsend, Francis, 122
Toynbee, Arnold, 250
Trilling, Lionel, 175, 231, 235
Trotsky, Leon, 39, 144, 145, 271, 273, 277; Trotskyists, 115, 125, 142–45, 273, 277, 344n.9
Truman, Harry S, 136, 258, 259, 279
Tucci, Niccolo, 147
Tuesday Evening Club, 28, 42,
Tugwell, Rexford, 288

United Auto Workers, 276
Untermeyer, Louis, 37
Updike, John, 22
U.S. Steel, 7, 117–20, 143, Fig. 7, 189, 330n.112

Van Doren, Mark, 73, 74, 231, 233

Wall Street, 58, 93, 107, 187, 208, 287
Wallace, Dewitt and Lila, 70
Wallace, Henry, 147, 255, 334n.59
Walzer, Michael, 21
Webb, Tod, 295
Weber, Max, 10, 64, 274, 275, 278
Weil, Simone, 147, 274
Welles, Orson, 127
Wertenbaker, Charles, 96, 176, 177, 211, 241
Wheeler, Dinsmore, 51, 53, 55, 98, 117
White, Theodore, 255–57, 259; biographical sketch, 221–24; and Chambers War, 212, 242–47, 348n.100; on intellectuals, 223, 256–57; relationship with Luce, 222, 225–26, 228–29, 246–47, 254–55, 346n.56; at *Time*, 8, 17, 179, 210, 218, 221–22, 224–30, 241–55, 350n.127, 352n.152, 153

Whyte, William H., 8, 13, 284, 301, 302, 304, 306, 354n.9, 355n.35; biographical sketch, 262–65; at *Fortune*, 9, 14, 261–62, 266–71, 281; and intellectuals, 262–63, 269–71, 302–3; *Is Anybody Listening?*, 261, 267–69; *Organization Man*, 14, 261, 264, 269–71
Wilder, Thorton, 33, 51, 68, 139, 252
Wilford, Hugh, 20
Willkie, Wendell, 62, 181, 186, 192–96, 214
Wills, Garry, 62
Wilson, Edmund, 8, 13, 30, 35, 37, 41, 44, 57, 129, 130, 181, 202, 234, 280, 339n.45
Wilson, Woodrow, 54, 65, 145, 146,
Winchell, Walter, 75–77, 176
World War I, 63, 109, 121, 129, 135, 145, 146, 186, 201, 318n.92
World War II, 1, 4, 7, 13, 125, 141–43, 146, 154, 183, 212, 213, 258, 266, 291
World's Work, 71, 322n.40
Wouk, Herman, 268
Wreszin, Michael, 18, 50, 149, 151, 330n.112, 334n.51

Yale Daily News, 51, 52, 67, 217
Yale Literary Review, 51, 57, 97, 186
Yale University, 35, 41, 43, 48, 138, 256, 266, 285, 299, 316n.29, 31, Hadden at, 61, 67; Luce at, 61, 65–67; Time Inc. writers at, 31–34, 49–54, 57, 72, 94–97, 134, 186, 190, 200, 217, 222. *See also* Russell Davenport; Manfred Gottfried; Briton Hadden, John Hersey; Ralph Ingersol; Dwight Macdonald; Archibald MacLeish
Yalta, 183, 246
Yeats, William Butler, 133, 137
Young, Owen D., 101–4, 107
Young People's Socialist League, 273

Zabel, Morton, 130

ACKNOWLEDGMENTS

A book is a peculiarly solitary endeavor that nevertheless depends on the aid and assistance of many other people. I would like to acknowledge those who have helped me throughout this project. I apologize to anyone who I have neglected to single out.

Many fine research librarians and archivists provided valuable assistance throughout this process. Linda Long at the University of Oregon was very helpful in guiding me through the Robert Cantwell collection, despite being separated by 3,000 miles. Tara Wenger provided valuable information about James Agee's papers at the Harry Ransom Humanities Research Center, the University of Texas at Austin. Paul Sprecher, the Trustee of the James Agee Trust, was encouraging and supportive. The reference departments at Cornell's Olin and Kroch Libraries, where I did most of my reading and writing, were invariably helpful. I apologize for all the hundreds of times I hauled down the heavy volumes of *Fortune* and *Life*. The librarians at the University of Rochester, especially Karl Kabelac, who taught me valuable research skills in my first year at Rochester, were also cooperative. I also thank Karl for entrusting me with an almost complete run of *Fortune*'s first two decades, volumes that were otherwise headed for the pulper. I also made extensive use of the collections in the Manuscript Department at the Library of Congress, a place that remains my favorite place to conduct research.

I also benefited from assistance at the Department of Special Collections at Boston University, the Oral History Collection and the Rare Books and Manuscript Library at Columbia University, the Hamilton College Library, The Houghton Library and Harvard University Archives, Syracuse University's George Argents Research Library, and both the Beinecke and Sterling Libraries at Yale University. Unfortunately, the Time Inc. corporate archives, with rare exceptions, were closed to outside scholars while I conducted my research. I never received permission to examine their materials. Luckily, much of the relevant material appeared in other collections.

A number of scholars shared their expertise with me. Alan Brinkley met with me and offered advice on the first incarnation of this project. He regularly and consistently answered many questions concerning Henry Luce, allowing me to benefit from his knowledge of the Time Inc. archives. Robert Hertzstein also shared information on Luce sources. David Halberstam promptly granted me permission to examine his papers on Time Inc. at Boston University. Robert Cummings graciously shared his exhaustive research on Dwight Macdonald. Interviews were obviously impossible for most of the writers I consider, but Daniel Bell generously granted me a long interview at his home in Cambridge.

I was lucky enough to be able to stay with friends and family on most of my research trips. Many thanks to Christine Vanderlan, Gretchen Hollmer, Eric DeSilva, Eric Wakin, Eliot DeSilva, and Mary Bachman for sharing their homes. With all I shared good food, good conversation, and the thrill of exploring some of my favorite cities.

Robert Westbrook at the University of Rochester has long served as a model to me of what a scholar and an intellectual should be. I have been indelibly marked by his piercing intelligence, scrupulous scholarship, moral sensibility, and democratic commitments. I also benefited from the encouragement and conversation of Dan Borus, Joan Shelley Rubin, Lynn Gordon, Mary Young, Stewart Weaver, and Celia Applegate. I would also like to thank Dan Moses, John Summers, Karen McCally, Jeff Jackson, Chuck Brotman, Drew Maciag, and Mike Easterly for reading some of my early work on this project and for enlivening many seminars. I am especially grateful for the friendship and encouragement of Chris Martin and Laura Beveridge. Chris read most of the early chapters, and improved the quality of my prose and the presentation of the material remarkably. For curing me of my ill-advised infatuation with the semi-colon, I will always be grateful.

While living and writing in Ithaca I was invited to join a remarkable group of young historians. The members of the Chapter House Beer and History Group—Jeff Cowie, Michael Trotti, Derek Chang, Michael Smith, Aaron Sachs, and for brief periods Finis Dunaway, Joel Dinnerstein, and Adriane Smith—afforded me much needed fellowship and the most detailed and contentious readings my work received. It will be many years before I stop hearing each of their voices echoing in my ears as I persist in making the same mistakes.

I am especially grateful to Jeff Cowie, who provided me with a great deal of support and encouragement, but also consistently urged me to push my ideas as far as I could. I appreciate his strong belief in this project, and the many ways in which he has served as a mentor.

I have taught in a number of history departments while working my way through this project. I thank my colleagues in the history department at Cornell, in the School of Industrial and Labor Relations at Cornell, and in the history departments at Hamilton College, Ithaca College, and SUNY Cortland. It is always inspiring to meet smart, dedicated, and engaging historians at each new stop.

Bob Lockhart has proved to be a great editor and a friend. I appreciate his consistent belief in my project and all the ways he has helped to make this a better book. He, and all the people at Penn, including Alison Anderson and Julia Rose Roberts, have been a pleasure to work with. Parts of this book appeared in different form in *Raritan* and in *Reconstruction*. I appreciate the permission to reprint those materials here. I also appreciate receiving permission from Houghton Mifflin to reprint excerpts from Archibald MacLeish's poetry.

In the tradition of James Agee, I would like to thank a small number of unpaid agitators, including Jackson Lears, George Orwell, Bill Watterson, and my bookselling comrades at Borders (1990–1995).

Thank you to friends and family who helped make this possible, through child care and other assistance: my parents, Robert and Claudia Vanderlan, my wife's parents, Alan and Mochiko DeSilva, and friends Janis Whitlock, Christine Lux, and Joe and Elizabeth Ellis.

Audrey DeSilva was the person that showed me an institution (marriage, in fact) could be made your own. She is an extraordinary woman, and I needed all her support, encouragement, forbearance, and love to complete this book. My sons, Benjamin and William, both grew up with this book. They have never been very impressed with it. To them my writing just sucked up time we could be doing more important things like playing with trains and having pillow fights in the early years, playing soccer and going camping more recently. Early on I would point proudly to the stack of pages I'd written, but I could never convince them of their importance. But Ben did provide me with one of those early moments that I drew sustenance from as the months turned into years. I wrote much of this at Cornell University. One day, as I was explaining why I had to go to work for the afternoon, I pointed to the clock tower atop the hill and said, "that is where

Daddy works." Ben looked for a moment, took a deep breath, and said, "you work in a castle."

For bringing to my work a heroism and grandeur it rarely warranted, and for all those fun distractions, I thank Ben and Will. They are old enough now to realize that I didn't write this in a castle, and that writers don't live in castles. When they are a little older still maybe they will reflect on that fact, and begin to appreciate why I wrote it.

Stafford Library
Columbia College
1001 Rogers Street
Columbia, Missouri 65216